The Founders of Indus Valley Civilisation and their Later History

The History of the Indigenous People of India
Vol. 1

Dr. Naval Viyogi

Originals
(an imprint of Low Price Publications)
Delhi-110052

Distributed by
D.K. Publishers Distributors (P) Ltd.
4834/24, Ansari Road, Darya Ganj,
New Delhi-110002
Phones: 23278584, 23278368, 23261465,
e-mail: dkpd@del3.vsnl.net.in
visit us at: www.dkpd.com

Ist Hindi Edition 1984
2nd Hindi Edition 1995
Ist English Edition 1995
2nd English Edition 2003

ISBN 81-88629-09-X

Published by
Originals
(an imprint of Low Price Publications)
A-6, Nimri Commercial Centre,
Near Ashok Vihar Phase-IV, Delhi-110052
Phones: 27401672, 27452453
e-mail: lpp@nde.vsnl.net.in
visit us at: www.lppindia.com

Printed at
D K Fine Art Press P Ltd.
Delhi-110052

PRINTED IN INDIA

Dedicated

To

The Sacred memory of

My beloved Wife

Late Shrimati SANTOSH KUMARI

Who always stood by me

Through Thick and Thin

and

devoted her entire life

with

deep affection& service to the cause

without which I would have not

been able to Complete This

Tough and Arduous Job

PRELUDE

I take pleasure in expressing my views about the classical work brought out by Mr. Naval Viyogi, a National Awardee and a Veteran ancient history scholar who has dug out truths on the basis of anthropology, genetics, sociology and archaeology which were never unveiled by any other scholar so far. He had gone very deep in describing the basic reasons which had led India to slavery for a number of centuries. How the aboriginals were put down, oppressed and depressed by Aryans and other foreign invaders, what were their sinister designs and what kind of politics they played to establish their Kingdom on the sacred Indian soil. No human values were kept in view, but the hunger for power and pelf.

It is a matter of surprise that Mr. Viyogi is the officer of Railways, but have taken keen & deep interest in such a problematic thesis as remained unlocked upto centuries together. He used full energy, mind and soul for this noble cause. He has brought new historical data for the consumption of human beings in order to know what reality is.

Although this book had already published in Hindi language & brought high reputation and reward for his sincere labour, yet the English version, I am sure, will definitely bring popularity and real honour to him. This work does not relate to only one discipline, it pertains to many other aspects of life as well.

Many hidden truths will see the light of the day and become and attract controversies which would apparently be of only superficial state. Mr. Naval Viyogi has solved many social, ethnical, racial, historical and psychological problems through this venture.

It is now for the modern readers to decide whether this research work would enrich their knowledge and beautify their information. It is a sacred thesis for down-troddens but a pointer to the high-ups.

I congratulate Mr. Naval Viyogi for this formidable and prolific research work which he is able to present before the readers after spending many precious decades of his life. It may be expected that the modern reader would reap suitable benefit out of this work

30th August, 1995

Harlal Singh
Director,
Punjab School Education Board
S.A.S. Nagar (Mohali) Chandigarh.

FOREWORD

Ever since the discovery of the Indus Valley Civilization in 1922, countless research articles and books have been written and published, taking the issue of Pre-Aryan and Non-Aryan origin of this great civilization. Politics and religion had their lion's share in deciding the fate of the Indus people. All these years the Harappans have remained silent and never bothered for the drastic, selfish and subjective conclusions or remarks passed on them . Histories have been written and are being written with an ulterior purpose or in order to satisfy a sect or view of a section, region or country.

Sri Naval Viyogi who combines in himself the lucidity of a poet and objectivity of a fearless researcher, brought to light very many hitherto unknown facets of the interpretation of the relics of the Indus valley people and their stock.

In this great endeavour Sri Viyogi had to travel through a jungle of untrodden paths. His Journey through these untrodden paths ultimately made him to see the light at the other end of the cave.

The author has made a thorough and indepth analysis of all the available and latest sources covering very wide and diverse subjects to provide new insight to ascertain socio-economic and religious shades of the life and times of the founders of Indus Valley Civilization and thereafter.

The work of Sri Viyogi is highly commendable for it opens many avenues of new thought on the hitherto unsolved history of the original inhabitants of Bharatavarsha in general and those of the founders of the Indus Valley Civilization in particular.

'The founders of Indus Valley Civilization and their Later History' is certainly the magnum opus of Sri Naval Viyogi.

(Y.KUMARSWAMY.)

M.A.,(Hist),M.A., (Arch.),M.A.(Phil)
M.A.,(Eco), M.A., (Soc), Ph.D.,
Reader, Department of
History & Archaeology,
Nagarjuna University,
Nagarjunanagar-522 510, A.P.

29.1.93

Foreword to the second Edition

While, writing foreword to the second edition of my research work entitled "The Founders of Indus Valley Civilization and their Later History" I feel great pleasure, since scholars have taken a great interest in its subject matter and readers have shown their great desire in reading it to the extent that we have been pressed to reprint its second edition in such a short term. This, also gives me immense joy that this edition, is being published, through the most capable hands of M/s Originals (*an imprint of Low Price Publications*), having a network to put the work into the hands of each and every able reader, not only in India but also abroad. I hope my venerable readers, will maintain a likewise trend in future also to encourage me to write a better book than the book in their hand.

Dr. Naval Viyogi
25th May, 2003

PREFACE

In 1882, the world famous historian Sir Max Muller[1] had remarked during his speech at the Cambridge University "Why do we read history? Only to know as to who were our ancestors? How were they in physical form? What did they think? What were their professions? What were their religious thoughts and beliefs?"

In the light of above definition of history given by Prof. Max Muller, we can say that the Indian history of 'Ancient Period' is the history of Aryan Kshattriyas and Brahmans, thereafter comes the history of the Rajputs. Later has been written the history of Muslim emperors and now in the end the history of British lords. But the history of Sudras which comprises 85 percent of the total population of the country,[2] was never written. If ever written, that was coloured as Kshattriya or Brahman. In this way this book can be said to be the first genuine publication on 'Origin and History of Sudras or Indigenous people of this country.'

In 1856, James William Burtel of a British Construction Company, who constructed the 100 Miles long railway line from Multan to Lahore, acquired the earth and rubble for the construction of the line from the ruins of Harappa. The British officers who were working there found that the seals unearthed from the ruins were never seen anywhere else before. At last, the excavation work was started there in 1920-21 by Daya Ram Sahni under the direction of John Marshall, the Director-General of the Department of Archaeology, Govt. of India. By that time there had remained no trace of the fortress[3] referred to by Mason in 1826 and Colonel Burns in 1831 and there was no sign of the buildings referred to by General Cunningham[4] in 1857 as all bricks had been looted. In 1920, the Govt. of India made a law banning this type of loot.

---

1. Bhadarkar D.R., 'Some aspects of Ancient Indian Culture'. P.1

2. (a) Sarkar S. S. ' The aboriginal races of India'. P19.

   (b) Bose, Nirmal Kumar, 'The Cultural Society in India'. P187.

3. Shastri, Kedar Nath, 'Sindhu Sabhyata Ka Adi Kendra, Harappa'. P6.

4. 'The ancient Geography of India'. P178

The pre-historic antiquity of Harappa came to notice when Rakhal Dass Banarjee found out goods of the same pattern in the exploration of Mohenjo-daro in 1922. A comparative study of those goods proved that the civilizations of Harappa and Mohenjo-daro were not only one and the same but they had a deeper relation with the Mesopotamia also. Madho Sarup Vatsa and Kashi Nath Dikshit got the excavation work done with effect from 1926 to 1933. Sir E. Makay also added hands to this great work.

The archaeological excavation carried out so far have proved the Indus Valley Civilization to be very vast. It had extended in the east up to Bahadurabad in district Saharanpur, upto Bhatpur and Manpur in Bulandshahar and Kosambi near Allahabad.

In south-east it had extended up to Saurashtra, upto Surat in Gujarat where remains of Lothal have been found from the Sabarmati Valley. Its boundaries had touched Mehgaon, Resod, Rojadi on the banks of Narbada river and Adkat on the banks of Yadar river, on the sea shore Rangpur and Somnath patan have been found. In the west up to the Makran Valakot near Sonmiani Sonkakoh near Pasni and up to Satkanjendor on the shore of the Arabian sea and in the north it had extended from Ropar to the entire Sapta-Sindhu region.

According to Dr H.P.Frankfurt[5]*, an archaeologist, he has found remains of the Indus Valley Civilization in the north-western region of Afghanistan. These remains are located in the Shartgai town of Tarbar province which is about 800 Km away from the Pakistan border. From the excavations carried out there, remains of a town belonging to the Harappa period have been found. The articles found from that site date back to the 1500 to 2500 B.C. Dr Frankfurt has also said that the present day Pakistan was the centre of this civilization and from the geographical point of view this civilization was four times larger than the Egyptian civilization. In this way, this great civilization had extended in the north from the Russian border to Bombay in the South-east. The main*[6] *sites from where excavations have been carried out include Ali Murad, Amri,*

5. (a) The daily Hindustan, dated 8th December, 1980. P5.
   (b) This civilization has developed over years and has not come up abruptly as some scholars are of the view .... hundreds of sites have been got excavated during the past 10 years, its period and geographical expansion has been increasing constantly. Science-Today, January, 1982. PP 22-26.

6. Wheeler, M. 'The Indus Civilization'. PP 2-3.

Valakot, Chanhudaro, Davarkot, Deravar, Kot-Dijjian, Gajishah, Harappa, Kalibanga, Kotla Nihang, Lothal, Lohri, Mohenjo-daro, Ropar, Sikhri, Sonkahkoh, Satkanjendor, Thana Bulikhan, Trikhan -Bala -Dera, Alamgir and Kosambi etc. According to Shri J.P.Joshi, Director General of Archaeological Survey of India, about 500 sites have been excavated so far in India and a similar number or less have been found in Pakistan (exact figures have not been received from Pakistan). The main special feature of this civilization was that most of the towns were located on huge platforms having 56-60 feet height, having fortification, town planning, pucca houses, straight roads and streets, intersecting each other at right angles, covered sewerage system[7], latrines having English bond seats and bath rooms and wells in every house. One stands amazed on seeing the glamour of tiles[8] fitted in the bathrooms and drawing rooms in Kalibanga and the water locking system in the Lothal harbour.

In India, the work relating to the town planning, sewerage system, and latrines with the provision of flush system has started after independence except some big cities. Still not to speak of smaller towns, even some big cities are deprived of such fine scientific facilities. It is very astonishing to note that almost similar types of facilities were available to the commom man of the Indus valley about 4-5 thousand years ago. According to Rigveda[9], the citizens of that country led a very Luxurious life, their ladies used to take bath with milk.

D.D. Kosambi[10] throwing light on the subject writes, "Nowhere else was civic organisation of such complexity and excellence to be found so carefully planned at so early a date. The Egyptian cities were architecturally insignificant compared to the mountainous tombs of their rulers and to the great temples. Sumeria, Akkad, Babylon had brick-built cities nearer to the Indus type, but they just grew. The streets in all these cases, as in Rome, London, Paris and for that matter in later Indian towns followed irregular country paths. The Indus cities show town planning of a truly amazing nature. Besides the straight streets meeting at right-angles, there was a superb drainage system for carrying away rain-water and cesspools for clearing the sewage. No Indian city possessed anything of the sort till modern times, far too many still lack these amenities."

---

7. Mackay, E. 'Early Indus Civilization'. P35.

8. Rao, S.R.' Lothal and the Indus Civilization'. P35 and Marshall. P207.

9. Rigveda I-104-3.

10. 'The culture and civilazation of Ancient India'. P54

It clearly indicates that in the Indus Valley, the central power was very much aware of the interest of the common lot. Most probably that might have been a welfare Govt. or governments. If this work had been entrusted to the local bodies, only such facilities would have remained confined to limited cities and not to all the cities of this culture.

The historians[11] are of the view that the Mesopotamia civilization was the greatest among the three oldest civilizations of the world. Mesopotamians had constructed huge palace-like temples, (jagurat) developed the irrigation system and constructed big canals. Thereafter comes the Egyptian civilization. The great pyramids, which are known to be one of the seven wonders of the world were constructed during this very period. At the third place comes the Indus Valley civilization. But in my opinion the scholars have done a great injustice to the great people of the Indus Valley by placing the greatness of the civilizations in the above mentioned order. Construction of huge pyramids and temples (Jagurat) by the means of the exploited money of the common man and the army of poor slaves by using force, cannot be a correct measurement of greatness of a civilization. I think the base of such measurement should be the standard of living of common man, the availability of facilities of life and the prosperity of the people, which were certainly available to the common folk of the Indus Valley. To corroborate this, S.R.Rao[12] writes. "A potter of Mohenjo-daro lived in a multi-storyed house consisting of many rooms, his house had a well, a bath room, a beautiful verandah and a vast compound. Contrary to this, the potters in Mesopotamia lived in single room houses. In Egypt the army of slaves lived in barracks."

It has been already stated that the basis of the glory of Egypt and Mesopotamia was a large army of slaves who lived like animals. The above two civilizations cannot be considered to be great in the same way as the Republican system in ancient Rome as republic[13]. The reason being that in Rome this system was confined to the rich class of people only called patricians while the common man (plebeian commoner)[14] was a slave. He neither had the right to vote nor the right to contest elections.

---

11. Hawkes Jacquetta "The First Great Civilization".
12. Rao S.R. 'Lothal and the Indus Civilization'. P21.
13. Arjun Dev. 'Manav Samaj Ka Itihas'. Delhi (1980)

Some scholars regard the engineering technique used in the sewerage system of Indus Valley to be Higher than the technique used in the construction of pyramids of Egypt and the temples (Jagurat) in Mesopotamia. Similarly, the huge statues made of stone in Egypt are 80-90 feet high but the gestures and fineness of art of the statue of a dancing girl cast in bronze, which has been found from Mohenjo-daro, was unique during that period. The larger size of the statues of Egypt is nothing as compared to the high technical skill used in casting this statue. It can, therefore, be said that the Indus Valley civilization was the greatest among the three ancient civilizations of the world and the founders of this civilization were really great.

Now we take up the standard of the civilization of Nordic Aryans who are held responsible for the destruction of this civilization (see Chapter IV). According to Rapson and Isaac Tailor[15], the Nordic Aryans were semi civilized savage shepherds. They lived in villages, in huts made of grass etc. They were not aware of the pucca brick pieces[16]. They were semi-nude and wore animal hides. They used the skulls of their enemies for drinking water.

According to Piggot the Victory of Aryans over the great Indus Valley civilization can be termed as the victory of the uncivilized people over the civilized ones. As Changez Khan, a militant leader of uncivilized Mongols, did so in Asia during Historic age. Thus, the nordic Aryans, after the massacre of the menfolk of the Indus Valley, enslaved the women and children who were left behind and assigned them the domestic chores which are entrusted to the slaves. Till today, many of them are doing the same jobs such as cleaning of utensils, brooming etc. for their Aryan masters. The only difference being that they were given a new name Sudra after inclusion in the Aryan Varna system and their origin was declared to be divine. Even today, the scholars who support colonialism are trying to veil their great historical origin and creating hinderances in the way of this truth. Mr

---

14. Ghurye G.S. 'Caste and the Races in India'. p. 170.

15. (a) Tailor Isaac. 'The origin of the Aryan'. p 77.

    (b) Rapson, E.J. "The Cambridge History of India". Vol. I, p 99

16. Hawks Jacquetta and Woolly Leonard "History of Mankind". p 458.

B.K. Thapar, stressed the view that the Aryans did not come from outside and that they were Indian aboriginals. But I have refuted his theory in chapter IV of this book. Some scholars say that it has not been mentioned clearly in the Vedas that the Aryans had come from outside, whereas the Rigveda was first of all got edited and written by the Maharaja Vijayanagarama Hare Krishna Rai under the supervision of his learned Brahman minister Sayan towards the end of the 14th century A.D.[17], and nobody knows how many changes must have been affected therein by that time.

Recently S.R.Rao[18] has expressed the view that the Indus script was Brahmi and vedic, whereas, Asko parpola of Scandanavia and Iravatham Mahadevan of South India have declared it to be Dravidian and world famous Russian Linguist Yuria-Knorozov has deciphered the Indus script and given his verdict clearly in my favour- As the mother of north Indian Aryan languages, i.e. Punjabi, Hindi, Bengali etc. was Sanskrit, similarly, the south Indian Dravidian languages i.e. Malayalam, Kanari, Tamil etc. were related to the language which was written in the Indus script[19]. Dr. H.D. Sankalia has expressed his views during the correspondence made by me- 'It is yet to be decided as to who were the founders of the Indus Valley civilization?' whereas I have put forth irrefutable evidences at every step to prove this fact, that is why Bhartiya Dalit Sahitya Academy has honoured me with Dr Ambedkar National Award in 1986 on the Hindi Version of this book.

First of all the great leader of Sudras, Dr Ambedkar wrote on the subject regarding the origin of sudras. He wrote his book "Who were the sudras?" in 1947, in which he[20] has proved that the sudras originated from that Suryavanshi clan of Aryan Kshattriyas who were prevented by the Brahmans to perform the investiture ceremony of the sacred thread out of hostility. As has been said above, I am of the view that the sudras originated from amongst the Kshattriyas but

---

17. Macdonell A.A., "The India's Past". p22.

18. 'Lothal and the Indus civilization', pp 127-134.

19. (a) 'Sunday Standard', London, 14th April, 1980

    (b) Knorozov Y., "Proto Indica", p 15 Moscow (1981)

20. Dr Ambedkar B.R. "Who were the Sudras?" pp 171-190.

those Kshattriyas were not Aryans but non-Aryans. They were the offspring of the brave rulers and the professional soldiers of the Indus Valley killed in combat with Aryans (see chaper10).

In 1958, Prof. R.S. Sharma of Delhi University wrote a book entitled, "Sudra in Ancient India" in a purely historical method in which a detailed study was conducted on the historical origin of sudras. He has, while refuting the above view of Dr B.R.Ambedkar, proved that the sudras originated from that class of Aryans who were meek, weak and backward. I have refuted his views in chapter 15 of this book.

When,a copy of above book was presented to Shri J.P.Joshi, the then Director General of Archaeological Survey of India, in his office, he, with a divine smile on his face, could not help to say that' "he is also of the view that it was a reality that the sudras are related to the founders of Indus Valley civilization. Only the scholars having colonial views oppose this concept and create obstacles in the powerful flow of history otherwise the fact is crystal clear. There is no doubt about it."

Similarly, I came into contact with the famous revolutionary poet and writer Shri Manmathanath Gupta after some correspondence and I discussed this topic with him and I felt that as if there was suddenly a dazzle in his eyes and while going deep into his thoughts he spoke: "As the theory of communism of Karl Marx gave birth to thousands of revolutions in this world, similarly, this will also give birth to hundreds of revolutions in this country, I think so".

Dr. K.L. Nanda, ex-professor of the Department of Foreign Languages of Guru Nanak Dev University (Amritsar) and a renowned scholar is my close friend. He has extended heartiest cooperation in preparing the present English edition. Dr K.N. Sharma, former principal of Arya College, Dhuri , presently Chief Editor, MBD Competition Books and author of numerous books on political science and public administration has helped me in improving the language of this edition. He once remarked about the present book that he had never seen any such complicated book in his life which is supported with so many concrete evidences from history and so many other subjects.

Mr. B.K.Kapoor has put in hard labour in typing the manuscript of this book.

Shri D.L. Baitha Ex-Deputy Minister in Central Govt. has been kind enough in giving me his blessings and cooperation at every step. Similarly, I have no words for-appreciating most honourable S. Har Lal Singh, Director School Education Board Punjab, Dr. Satish Menan and Dr. Lekhraj Parwana who have extended all sort of help in printing and publication of this book. I may not have attained success without the help and cooperation for which I am indebted to all of them.

Ludhiana (Punjab) **NAVAL VIYOGI**

25 September 1994

ACKNOWLEDGEMENT

I am sincerely thankful to the authors and publishers of the following works from which I have frequently quoted matter in my humble venture;

Asthana Shashi, History and archaeology of India's contract with other countries, 1947 (B.R. Pub Corp, Delhi). Buddha Prakash, Rigveda and the Indus Valley Civilization, 1966 (Visveshvaranand Institute, Hoshiarpur); Bridget and Allchin Raymond, The Rise of Civilization in India and Pakistan, 1983 (Select Book Service Syndicate, New Delhi); Chanda R.P., The Indo-Aryan races, 1969 (Indian studies past and present, Calcutta); Chattopadhyaya s; Racial affinities of early North Indian Tribes, 1973 (Munshi Ram Manohar Lal, Delhi); Ghurye G.S., Caste and races in India, 1969 (Popular Prakashan,Bombay); Gokhley B.G; Samudra Gupta,1962 (Asia Pub. house, Delhi); Goyal S.R., A History of the Imperial Gupta, 1967 (Central Book Depot, Allahabad); Hutton J.H., Caste In India, 1961 (Oxford University Press); Kosambi D.D., The culture and civilization of Ancient India in historical out line, 1975 (Vikas Pub House, Delhi); Mackay E., Early Indus civilization, 1976 (Indological book corp.,Delhi); Mahajan Vidyadhar, Prachin Bharat Ka Itihas, 1973 (S. Chand, Delhi); Majumdar D.N., Races and culture of India, 1961 (Asia Pub. house, Delhi); Mookerji R.K., Chandra Gupta Maurya and his time, 1966 & Gupta Empire, 1968 (Moti Lal Banarsi Dass, Delhi); Muir J., original Sanskrit Text, 1972 (Orient Pub., Delhi); Possehl L. Gregory, Ancient cities of the Indus, (1979) and Harappan civilization, (Vikas Pub.& Oxford & IBH pub Delhi); Taylor Isaac, The origin of the Aryans, 1980 (Bahari Pub., Delhi); Tripathi Vibha, painted grey ware; an Iron age culture of N. India, 1979 (Concept Pub., Delhi); Vishva-Nathan S.V., Racial synthesis in Hindu culture, 1978 (Orient book corp.,Delhi) and articles of R.L. Raikes, Dales George F, J.P. Joshi & Madhubala.

I feel highly indebted to all the authorities on the subject, mentioned above, upon whom I have heavily drawn. I shall fail in my duty if I don't place on record my gratitude to them.

Ludhiana **NAVAL VIYOGI**

29.10.1994

CONTENTS

Abbreviations

'A'

AA	American Anthropology
ACI	Ancient Cities of Indus
AI	Ancient India
Ait Bra	Aitreya Brahman
AOMM	Anthropology on the March, Madras
AP	Ancient Pakistan
Apt D.S.	Apastamba Dharma Suttra
ASIAR	Archaeological Survey of India, Annual Report
ASIC	Anthropological Survey of India, Calcutta
AV (A-Veda)	Atharvaveda

'B'

BASI	Bulletin of Archaeological Survey of India
BDCRI	Bulletin of the Deccan College Research Institute
BNISI	Bulletin of the National Institute of Science in India

'C'

CHI	Cambridge History of India

'D, E, G'

EAI	Ethnography of Ancient India
EI	Epigraphia Indica
Gaup .Bra	Gaupath Brahman
Gaut DS	Gautam Dharam Sutra

'H, I, J'

IA	Indian Antiquary
IAB	Indian Antiquary, Bombay
IAR	Indian Archaeological Review
ICWTC	India's Contribution to World Thoughts and Culture (Vivekanand Rock Memorial Committee)
IHQ	Indian Historical Quarterly
JAOS	Journal of the American Oriental Society
JBBRASB	Journal of the Bombay Branch of the Royal Asiatic Society. Bombay
JBORS	Journal of Bihar and Orissa Research Society
Jem Bra	Jemini Brahman
JOI	Journal of Oriental Institute
JRAS	Journal of the Royal Asiatic Society
JRASB	Journal of the Royal Asiatic Society of Bengal
JRASGBI	Journal of the Royal Asiatic Society of Great Britain and Ireland

K.L.M'

Kat ss	Katyayan Sraut Sutra
Kaum	Kaumudimahotsva
LSI	Linguistic Survey of India
Mait Samh	Maittrayani Samhita
MASI	Memoirs of the Archaeological Survey of india
MB &MBH	Mahabharata
MR	Modern Review

`N O P'

Panch Bra	Panchavimsa Brahman

`R, S'

Rig (R.V.)	Rigveda
Satp.Bra	Satpath Brahman
SBE	Sacred Books of East
Taitt Bra	Taittreya Brahman
Taitt Samh	Taittreya Samhita

'U V '

VP	Vishnu Purana

'WXYZ'

ILLUSTRATIONS

CHAPTER I

A brief History of Indus Valley Civilization

How great were the Harappans?

About 10,000 B.C. and at the end of the palaeolithic age a strange development occurred in the brain of man and he stepped in the neolithic age. The weapons and tools of this age were good well chiselled and bright as compared to those of the earlier age. From this period onward man after stepping on to the highway of civilization began to make rapid progress. In the midst of 6th millennium B.C. man learnt the art of agriculture and adopted a permanent and settled rural life relinquishing the impermanent and unstable hunting life. Besides agriculture he also learnt cattle rearing and making clay-pottery. As a result of the progress in agriculture,the human population began to increase[1]. This was all due to man's change from a 'food gatherer' to 'food producer' onward,rapid progress was all due to the same reason.

The places where copper mines were situated, the extraction of copper after melting ore was started Thus,the copper age marked its beginning in about 5th millennium B.C. Although the weapons of copper were better than the stone weapons,yet man did not leave the use of stone weapons immediately. The initial period of the copper age has been known as chalcolithic age, among the archaeologists. 'Chalco' is a greek word meaning copper.It was during this age that three most ancient great civilization came into existence.The Indus Valley Civilization is one of the above family of this age.

Among the three most ancient civilizations of this age, the Mesopotamia civilization and the Egyptian civilization flourished on the banks of the rivers Euphratis, Tigris and the Nile, respectively, whereas the Indus Civilization flourished on the bank of the river Indus .

The Indus valley civilization had spread in almost the entire north-west of India which included the existing Pakistan, Punjab, Haryana, some parts of Rajasthan and the major parts of Gujarat and Uttar Pardesh . The area was four times than that of the area of Egypt and more than twice the area of Mesopotamia and Egypt both . Besides several other cities, the main cities i.e. Mohenjo-daro and Harappa were situated on the banks of the river Indus and its tributaries, so it has been named "The Indus Valley Civilization" because it was first traced out at the site of Harappa, hence archaeologist have given it an another name "The Harappan Civilization". Harappa was situated on the bank of the river Ravi to the south-west of Lahore and Mohenjo-daro was situated on the bank of the Indus to the north of Karachi.

Important Cities

Mohenjo-daro : Mohenjo-daro, which literally means the 'Mound of the

Dead' is situated on the Karachi Dadu railway line at a distance of seven miles from Dokri in Larkana district. There are several mounds in the remains. The highest mound has been indicated by the name 'Stupa Mound' which being 70 feet in height attracts the attention of the on-lookers from a great distance. The other mounds are situated to its east and they are raised above 40-50 feet to the nearby fields. The area surrounded by the mounds measures about 240 acres but undoubtedly the city itself was extended far beyond the present boundaries of the these mounds in the past. The stupa mound was the royal fort of the city surrounded by the fortress where the topmost ruler of the city used to reside. Here are situated a Great Bath and the Assembly Hall resting on pillars[2]. The remaining mound in the east constituted the part of the main habitation of the city which had a network of main roads and streets from east to west and north to south. Banerji and Marshall have discovered six to seven strata. In other words this city got destroyed six to seven times and was rebuilt on its remains; its main cause can be the floods in the river Indus. The Indus river flowed to its east which is at present at a distance of three miles to the east.

Harappa : The remains of Harappa are extended 15 miles in the south-west to the district montgomery of Pakistan. Even today a big village with the same name exists there. The entire mound spreads in a circumference of three miles. The mound 'A B' situated in the west was the fort of the city where its ruler used to reside. It extended in a region measuring 460 yards in length from north to south and 215 yards in east-west. The main inhabitation of the city was confined to mound 'F' in the east on whose northern part the Ravi used to flow some time, which flows at a distance of 6 miles in the north at present.

Kalibangan : Similarly Kalibangan, which was discovered by Mr Ghosh in 1953, is situated on the left bank of the dried up bed of the Ghaggar near Hanumangarh, has also two mounds. The western mound was a fort and the bigger mound of the east was the dwelling place of the people[3]. The main city was surrounded by a high wall. Similary, Kotdijji and Satkajendor had their own forts.

Lothal : Lothal is situated in the valley of the river Sabarmati at a distance of 80 kilometres south of Ahmadabad. Today it is very far-off the sea but in the Harappan age it was situated at a distance of about 3 miles from the Bay of Cambay and the rivers Sabarmati and Bhogwa flowed near it. While Harappa and Mohenjo-daro had two mounds each, Lothal had only one mound which made a big platform in the middle and it has a slope from south to north. Its south-east part which is higher than the other part appears like a high fort as compared to the lower town. Western deeper part was the bed of the river and northern deeper part was a canal through which the water flowed to the dock.

Chanhudaro : Its remains exist in district Nawabshah in Sind to the south-east at a distance of 80 miles from Mohenjo-daro. It is stretched in an area of nine acres and is constituted of three mounds. But in the beginning this city was extended beyond these boundaries. This site was discovered by Nanigopal Majumdar in February, 1931. The first mound is the largest one. Its circumference is 1060 feet and the height 28 feet approximately. In its north-west, there is another mound which is the smallest one having a circumference of 450 feet and height 13 feet. The third mound is situated in the south-west at a distance of 150 feet. It extends in a circumference of 950 feet and its height is 22 feet. The three mounds belong to the same period and existed in the form of a big mound in the beginning. Later on, due to the furious floods in the river Indus some crevices occurred in them and three mounds came in appearance in place of one mound. This was smaller than Mohenjo-daro and Harappa, but it was the centre of various arts and crafts. Many things such as stone beads, seals, weights and goods of bones, shell and ivory were made here. Now the river Indus flows at a distance of 28 miles which used to flow near it at some time.

Town Planning : Roads, streets and Drainage System

On reviewing the Indus Valley cities sewerage system and rows of beautiful houses of same type and size, one gets the impression that these were constructed under a pre-planned outline and almost all the cities were erected on the man-made high platforms. Here we take up the town planning of Mohenjo-daro. Leaving aside some exceptions, the streets are straight here and they intersect each other at right angles. Despite some shortcomings it is evident that the city was developed under some powerful authority so that no haphazard construction might take place there.

Roads : The streets of Mohenjo-daro were all aligned from east to west or from north to south, for the reason that the prevailing winds always come from the two latter quarters. A north or south wind, sweeping down a broad thoroughfare, would suck the stagnant air out of the smaller streets and lanes running at right angles, which in this way would be amply ventilated. It is uncertain whether the builders of the city realized that this would be the case from the first or whether it was an entirely fortuitous arrangement; in any case it has also been observed in some of the later Babylonian cities.

Some of the main streets of Mohenjo-daro are of considerable size. First street, whose course has been traced for over half a mile (Site Plan), runs in a straight line from north to south and divides the largest mound into two parts. It must have been a most important thoroughfare, for in places it is over thirty-three feet wide and could easlily have accommodated several lines of wheeled traffic, the cart and chariot being in those days the usual mode of transport.

East Street, which crosses it at right angles near its southern limit, is apparently wider, but as only a small part of it has been cleared, it is impossible to give its average width. Central Street also at right angles to First Street, averages eighteen feet in width at the higher levels, which alone have been excavated. The most important thoroughfare, in the Stupa mound is about thirteen and a half feet wide, and runs from north to south; while the smaller streets range from nine to twelve feet in width, and the lanes and alleys from four feet upwards. Not one of these streets or lanes is paved, and the people who used them were probably ankle-deep in dust or mud, according to the season of the year. An attempt was made at one period to protect the surface of First Street by using a mixture of broken bricks and potsherds, which were thrown down, probably on the wet earth, and trodden in; this method cannot have been a success, as, so far as is known, it was only tried on the one occasion in a single street.[4]

It is, of course, impossible to say whether a civic body or a single official supervised the building activities of the city, but they were evidently in very competent hands, and it is interesting to note that these ancient cities of the Indus plains are the earliest sites yet discovered where a scheme of town-planning existed. There is no evidence of such a scheme at Ur as late as 2000 B.C., though there are traces of one at Babylon at about that date, and also at the Twelfth Dynasty town of Kahun in Egypt[5].

The cities of Sumeria, Akkad, and Babylon were also pucca like those of the Indus valley but they were not planned at all. They had only developed. The outer walls were ugly. The streets were similar to those of Rome, London, Paris and Indian cities which had zig zag of paths. The excavated minor streets of Mohenjo-daro are much more impressive in appearance than the wider ones, as the buildings on them are so much better preserved. This is entirely due to the rains which through the centuries have poured down the wider streets and gradually reduced the height of the walls on either side. In spite of this the walls of the principal street now stand some eighteen feet high, and will stand much higher when further digging has been done, as they obviously go still deeper into the soil. Some of the walls in the narrower streets are now over twenty-five feet high though here also the lowest levels of the city have not yet been reached.

The corners of some of the smaller by-ways show evidence of having been rubbed by pack-animals or the clothing of passers-by, and in some cases the angles of a building were purposely rounded off so that pack-loads should not become dislodged, a device which has also been observed in ancient Ur. Unless porters were largely employed, it must be assumed that the humble donkey was used in the narrow as well as in the wider streets, although its remains have not yet been discovered anywhere in the city.

Drainage System (Network of underground drains)

There were pucca drains in each street and small drains were connected with the larger ones. The drains were covered with bricks which could be removed after removing the earth covering them for the purpose of inspection. Very big drains were also constructed which were covered with huge lime stones. Like today sumps or mainholes were constructed at various places which were made in such a beautiful manner after cutting the bricks that their joints are still invisible. There was the provision of stairs inside them so that one may enter into them for cleanliness or inspection. These were cleaned from time to time.[6]

Where one drain entered another from a higher level, a little brick-lined pit was provided so that the water might not escape into soil. These facilities were not available in any Indian city till some time back from now. Still several cities do not enjoy these hygienic facilities.

Architecture and Masonry

Both Harappa and Mohenjo-daro[7] were built entirely of burnt bricks, except in those few places where foundations have been found composed of burnt and unburnt bricks in alternate courses, or, more rarely still, of unburnt bricks alone. All the bricks, burnt and unburnt, are well proportioned, as a rule they are twice as long as they are wide and half as thick. They vary in size from 10.25 × 5 × 2.25 inches to 20.5 × 8.5 × 2.25 inches, but the very large bricks were intended only for special purposes-to cover drains, for example-and are not found in ordinary masonry, for which the most usual size of bricks 11 × 5.25 × 2.25 inches. Where unburnt brick was used the sizes most favoured vary from 13.9 × 7.35 × 3.5 inches to 15 × 7.15 × 3.1 inches, all larger sizes than the common kind of burnt bricks.

The bricks were shaped in an open frame-mould of exactly the same type as that in use in India and other parts of the East to-day, and were made from the alluvial soil of the neighbourhood with no binding material. Surplus clay was removed by passing a piece of wood across the top of the mould, and the faces of the bricks were always smooth and flat, no examples of recessing or frogging being known. On the whole, they were well baked to a pleasing light red colour, the comparatively few over-fired specimens having a slightly vitrified surface of an apple-green hue. The fuel used for firing was wood, of which there was a plentiful supply, and as no brick kilns have been found the probability is that the bricks were stacked for firing in large heaps with flues between. The outside of the pile would then have been plastered with mud to keep in the heat.

Bricks of other shapes were made for special purposes. Wedge-shaped bricks were used in the lining of wells, though, curiously enough, this kind of brick was never used for vaulting. Only the corbel-arch was in use, in spite of the fact that the true arch was known in Mesopotamia at the same period, or even earlier. For pavements and other special purposes, ordinary bricks were often cut down to a smaller size, such as 9.5 × 4.35 × 2 inches, and the edges and faces were then carefully rubbed smoothly, in this way a bath room pavement could be rendered practically water-tight. No patterns are ever found in these pavements, which are always severely plain, though care was taken to break the joints. L-shaped bricks were occasionally used for corners.

In building walls, what is known as "English bond" was usual-that is, a course of stretchers alternating with a course of headers. Here, too, care was taken to break the joints by using a half-brick where necessary. These bricks were plastered with gypsum or mortar of lime or clay. Gypsum mixed with mud mortar got affixed in the joints of the bricks and made the walls strong.

Nowhere the use of stone is made and the windows have been found nowhere. There were certainly ventilators high up near the ceiling. Only one door in the house opened towards the street. Outside some big houses or on the corners of the streets, there was a cabin made for the watchman. Each part was divided into a ward. The watchman kept watch on them throughout the night.

The construction of the houses was beautiful and uniform and were made of blocks measuring 200 × 400 Yards. The measurement of the floors of the houses was 27 × 30 feet. A big house was twice bigger in measurement. A space of two feet was kept in-between the two houses and those narrow lanes were closed on one side.

The thickness of the walls suggests that the buildings were multi-storeyed and in order to make the upper storey strong big empty spaces have been left in some walls to lay across thick beams. The signs of the wooden stair case still exist which led to the upper floors.

The roofs of the houses were square in shape and were made of wooden beams and mats as are made in India at present. The gutters made of pottery for the drainage of rain water can be seen even today. Perhaps wooden gutters were also used.

Examination of the doorways does not throw much light on how its doors were closed. Perhaps doors were set in a wooden frame. No trace of an arch and a round column has been found in the city. The use of square pillars, of course has been made whereas round columns have been used in Sumer at that period.

Every house had a kitchen where fuel was placed on a raised platform of bricks. In a big house a brick fire-place was constructed on a raised floor in which wood was burnt. An oven has been found at one place in which the chapatis were baked by burning fuel as is done in the Punjab today. According to Mr. Woolley, such ovens were also used in Mesopotamia at that period.

Practically every house had a bathroom. Their floors were pucca having slope and the water flowed through a pucca earthen pipe into the street drain. Some floors still bear the prints of the rubbing of feet or the lubricity of the oils used in bathing. It is really surprising that some examples have been found in Kalibangan in which the floors of the bathrooms and rooms have been studded with tiles as like those of today[8]. Generally latrines were made between the bathroom and the main street which had English bond seats. They were mostly on the ground floors which were connected by a sloped brick drain or pucca pipes made of clay with the underground pucca drains outside in the streets[9].

Almost every house had a well which had a door inside. But when the population increased their doors were made towards the main street.

Perhaps the rich, traders, government officials, big craftsmen, artisans and labourers lived in these houses. There were big stores in the north of the city. There were six huge palatial buildings in the city.

The Great Bath

The most important place in the fort of Mohenjo-daro is the Great Bath[10] which is built of burnt brick and measuring thirty-nine feet three inches in length and twenty three feet and two inches in width. This bath can be entered at either end by means of staircase. When the bath was emptied, the water flowed through a small square hole in the south west corner. There was a vertical manhole at the western end which was used to clean it. There was a large well in a room to the east of the bath which was perhaps used to fill the bath.

North to the Great Bath there are eight more bath rooms. Each room was carefully paved and had a stair way which led to an upper storey, now destroyed. Perhaps this Great Bath was used only on certain occasions of Ceremony by the Harappans.

Granary: Near the Great Bath, a granary was built in the fort part of Mohenjo-daro which measured 163×134 feet. Similarly, a granary of the same type has been found in Harappa built on a platform outside the fort in the north which was situated towards the bed of the river. Evidently, this place was selected for the transportation of foodgrains by boats. Such granaries have also been found in Lothal.

Mode of living and dress

The stone statue having a beard and no moustaches resembles a priest of the Sumerian type which is clad in an embroidered or dyed shawl from right to left shoulder. Similarly we come to know on seeing another statue that it is dressed in tunic[11]. It is really surprising that despite all the facilities available for a happy living such as wealth, cotton, invention of cloth, the Indus people remained naked except one cloth wrapped around the waist. Its possible reason can be the hot climate of the region, otherwise the rich and top ranking persons led a happy and prosperous life and put on beautiful clothes of the best quality. The women used to put on skirts like the modern women of south India.

Make Up: With regard to the methods of doing the hair, more is known of the styles favoured by the men than of those in vogue among the women, for the head-dresses worn by the female figurines prevent the hair from being seen. A piece of statuary exists, however, in which a woman's curly hair hangs down in a mass at the back of head, and a badly damaged head of a small steatite figure has exactly the same arrangement. The hair of the bronze dancing girl passes from over the left ear in a large coil across the nape.

The figures of goddesses on the amulets sometimes have a plait tied with a bow at the end, and as this is a favourite way of dressing the hair in modern India it is unlikely that plaits were reserved exclusively for divinities.

Men had varied styles of hair-dressing. The steatite, bust of a diety wears his hair parted in the middle, and the short locks at the back of the head are kept tidy by a woven fillet. Other statues show it closely gathered up in a bun, after the fashion of ancient Sumer, certain folds in the bun suggesting that the hair was first plaited. Several clay figures have the hair coiled in a ring on the top of the head and in similar rings concealing the ears; the latter arrangement is also found in Sumerian statuary. Yet another fashion is a plaited lock carried outwards from the back of the head in a large loop which turned in again and was secured by a fillet. A clay figure of a crawling infant with curly hair has been found at Mohenjo-daro, and it is quite probable that some of the people, at any rate, had curly or wavy hair[12].

Cosmetics : Combs were sometimes worn in the hair, a custom which still prevails among Indian of both sexes. A fine, double toothed comb of ivory, decorated on both faces with a series of incised, concentric circles, was found close by the skull of a young girl and another comb V-shaped in design seems to have been made for combing long hair, although its exceptionally fine and closely set teeth would imply that it also had other uses.

Round buttons of copper, bronze, steatite or faience are common, but it is uncertain whether they were merely decorative or utilitarian[13].

Three mirrors, one of small size for a child, are of bronze and severely plain in style, though the wooden handles, which have not survived, may have been ornamented; a raised edge round one face of these mirrors served to protect the polished side from scratches. Mirrors were probably quite common, for without them the various cosmetics discovered could not have been satisfactorily applied.

Kohl-pots and sticks prove that the women, and perhaps the men, used this, or some similar black substance, for the eyes; and an interesting find of rouge contained in cockle-shells provides a link with contemporary Sumer, for the same type of shell, used to hold face-paints, has been taken from graves at Kish and Ur. Carbonate of lead has also been discovered at Mohenjo-daro and Harappa, where it was possibly employed to whiten the face, a practice known in ancient Greece and also in China. On the other hand, it may have served as an eye-ointment or a hair-wash. Cinnabar, too, was used at Mohenjo-daro, probably as a cosmetic; and the finding of lumps of a green substance, identified as terre verte, tempt the writer to believe that this material was, like kohl, used for the eyes, as was malachite in ancient Egypt.

Both men and women decorated their bodies with costly and beautiful ornaments which will be described in detail in Chapter X, which includes ornaments of gold, silver, conch shell and different types of precious stones. On seeing these ornaments these words escaped from the lips of John Marshall : "These ornaments are so beautiful that it seems that they have not been discovered from the remains of ancient cities of 5000 years ago but have been recently got from a fashionable shop of New York."

Class Society and Religion

"It cannot be said that such a highly organised society as the Harappan was entirely classless, but there is no evidence to show that slavery was practised.

The mere fact that labour was employed for building houses, pounding grain in the public granaries and for haulage of cargo in the dock and warehouse need not imply that the labourers were slaves. On the other hand, it is observed at Lothal and elsewhere that both the rich and the poor lived together in the same locality. There was however a clear distinction between the ruler and the ruled, the former living with his relatives and friends in impressive mansions built in the Acropolis which enjoyed maximum civic amenities. All others including the rich merchants and the poor craftsmen lived in the Lower Town without any sort of isolation from one another. This is attested to by the location of the two-or three-roomed houses of shell-workers and copper-smiths by the side of the impressive dwellings of wealthy merchants in the bazar street during the most prosperous days of Lothal. There is no convincing evidence from any phase to show that the indigenous population, identified with the authors of the Micaceous Red ware, occupied a lower status in society than the Harappan technicians and merchants did.[14]

Classless secular society

As we shall presently see religion too did not dominate the public life of the people, nor was the ruler a priest-king as in Mesopotamia or a god-king as in Egypt. A secular authority ruled over each city or province and perhaps owed allegiance to a central authority. The Harappan society can be said to be neither caste-ridden nor class ridden. The existence of a military class is presumed by some on the ground that barracks were built for the soldiers within the citadel. It is however necessary to observe that the mere construction of houses in regular rows according to a blue print need not necessarily mean that a contingent of soldiers lived here. On the other hand, the quarters at Harappa seem to have been occupied by the copper-smiths as did the beadmakers of Lothal. Alternately the labourers employed by the ruler or the corporate body might have lived in these barrack-like structures, which are said to suggest a high degree of regimentaion which is inevitable in an overall planning of the city. But it is wondered if two rows of houses forming the so-called military barracks were sufficient for accommodating a regular army meant for defending so vast a city as Mohenjo-daro[15].

Religious Belief and Customs

The Indus Valley people worshipped the mother goddess, Pashupati Nath and a diety named Bal, whose detailed description will be given in Chapter X. The most important contribution to the data amassed at present is John Marshall's identification of the male figure on certain seal-amulets as Shiva, or his ancient prototype; for using this theory as a basis it has been possible to assume that many of the features of modern Indian cults are derived from very primitive sources; they perhaps date back even to a period anterior to that in which the people of Mohenjo-daro and Harappa built their great brick cities.

The worship of the Mother Goddess, for example, is a very early Indian cult, and probably existed in the country before the arrival of the Harappa people. This is possibly true also of tree worship, which later developed into the adoration of a tree-deity for this cult in both its forms is still world-wide today. Animal worship is also inherent in most primitive communities, and has existed in India and elsewhere for so long that its origin is untraceable. On the other hand, the horned human deity does not appear in the mythology of either historic or modern India, and it seems safe to say that it was introduced into that country by the Harappan people, and disappeared again with them. The same is true of the man-bull, who may have been a minor deity, a hero, or a demon. The horned deity and the man-bull, as before mentioned, occur in contemporary Ṣumerian mythology also, probably because the two civilizations derived these cults from some parent source.[16]

S.R.Rao[17] excavator of Lothal site, observes, "It is in the spiritual field that the Indian subcontinent has retained many of the Harappan concepts even to this day. The concentration of human faculties on a sense of contemplation by practising yoga, the veneration of the Mother Goddess as Universal Spirit or Sakti, the love for animals shown in the worship of Siva as Pasupati and the adoration of the Fire-God by offering sacrifices are some of the contributions made by the Indus Civilization to the philosophy and ritualism of Indian Culture."

Asko Parpola, a Scandinavian linguist, holds the opinion that Hinduism is a pre-Aryan religion which was related to the Dravidians[18]. Gilbert Slotter[19] has supported this view in these words: "when the Dravidians were coming under the influence of the Aryan language, the Aryans had come under the domination of the Dravidian civilization".

Although there was no state religion and the ruler of the city was not a priest-king, gradually more and more people took to ritualistic worship of fire so much so that fire-altars came to be built in public places in phase III, whereas in the preceding phase they were confined to private houses in the Lower Town. A section of the Lothal population practised animal-sacrifice also[20].

It will, therefore, be no exaggeration in saying that the edifice of Hinduism is resting on the foundation of the religion of the Indus Valley.

Agriculture

The big and populous cities of Mohenjo-daro and Harappa must have felt the necessity of an economic set up based on occupations, industries and agriculture for the middle class.

The Indus Valley and its vast plain has been fully covered by the silt brought by the rivers during four thousand years. So, it is difficult to estimate how fertile it was and what was produced there. Whatever information is possible to gather can be collected from the remains of habitation that has come to our hands and from what we can recognise. Both barley and wheat could be recognised. The grain was ground on a square stone slab with a pestle. We have come across the evidences of a rotating stone mill in the excavation at Lothal[21].

"All vestiges of small village settlements and irrigation canals lie buried under flood deposits. The gabarbands in Baluchistan and the traces of canals around Lothal are however indicative of the existence of dams and canals in the protohistoric period. The agrarian system must have been well organised as indicated by the role played by the granaries in the economy of the state.

No remnants of agricultural implements have been found in any Harappan settlement. But it is surmised that wooden ploughs and sickels, the latter set with chert blades, were known to them. A seed-drill of the type engraved on a terracotta seal from Lothal was another important tool used in agricultural operations"[22].

The seeds of pea and melon have been found in the remains of the cities. Date-stones have come to hand in Mohenjo-daro. The vessels unearthed during the excavation bear the pictures of date-palm and coconut. Among other trees, banana is considered to be the fruit of entire South Asia. The most interesting thing is the discovery of the traces of cotton cloth. One of its examples has been found in Lothal where it appears to exist quite early.

Animals and Birds

As stock farmers, the Harappans had domestic dogs, humped cattle, buffalo, and, more doubtfully,pigs, the bones of which occur in some quantity but may represent semi-wild scavengers. The probable use of the camel, the horse, the ass, and less certainly the elephant by the Harappans has already been noted.

That the cat, useful in all societies for preserving grain from rodents, was known in Harappan times is proved by a brick from Chanhu-daro bearing the footprint of a cat slightly overlapped by those of a dog. The two tracks on the brick must have been impressed when it was freshly laid out to dry in the sun. The one with the mark of the posterior lobe tripartite on the hind margin of the main lobe evenly outlined is that of a dog. The deep impress of the pads and their spread indicate the speed of both animals[23]. Other animals are represented only by terracotta figurines or life like representation on seals. From these we can infer that, in addition to the great humped cattle, there was a short-horned humpless species, and it may be added that in one form or another there is evidence also for monkeys, hares, doves, parrots and other birds and many major wild animals such as Indian bison, rhinoceros, tiger, bear, sambhar, spotted deer, and hog-deer, some of which have vanished from the Indus. As a whole, the fauna is a varied one and implies in part the proximity of jungle or tall grass[24]. Even today such type of domestic and pet animals are found in this region, while some of the wild animals have shifted to other parts due to change of weather.

Fine Arts and Craft:

In that age, the Indus Valley was unparalleled in sculpture even though statues had been built in Mesopotamia and in Egypt— the statues are so high (80-90 feet) that one gets struck with wonder. Most of these statues are made of stone but four and a half inch high brass statue of a dancing-girl discovered from H.R. area of Mohenjo-daro has no parallel in that age from the point of view of depiction of emotions and expression. It can be regarded as the best specimen of art.

The head and shoulders of a bearded man[25], the whole fragment 7" high, carved in steatite, was found at Mohenjo-daro in the D.K. area at a depth of only 4.5 feet and may therefore be of late Harappan date...The head is bearded with the upper lip shaved, the eyes are narrowed to an extent which has been thought to indicate a state of yogi. Across the left shoulder is a cloak carved in relief with trefoils which were originally filled with red paste. Human statues have been found which probably bears the sign of being wrapped in fine cloth.

In the same way pictures of different animals and birds have been engraved on the seals and they have been found in large quantity at almost all the places. Similarly, there is no dearth of pictures made on clay utensils. Heaps of clay and metal utensils have been found.

Trade and Industries

The main bases of economic set up of the Indus Valley civilization were their Trade and Industries. According to Rao and Mackay, on the basis of the evidences got from excavation, the people of Chanhu-daro and Lothal were mainly craftsmen. In other words, these were the two industrial cities of the Indus Valley where beadmakers, shell workers and makers of gold and silver ornaments and the makers of bronze and brass utensils used to live. We have found there the factories of the craftsmen, implements and furnaces along with heaps of semi-finished or finished goods. The work of bead-making was done mostly in Lothal and Chanhu-daro. The finished goods were sent to the western countries of Babylon, Mesopotamia, Akkad and Bahrein (probably called Dilman) from the harbours like Lothal[26].

Chanhu-daro : S.R. Rao[27] expresses his opinion about the residents of Chanhu-daro as follows;

"The residents of Chanhu-daro were essentially craftsmen and included bead makers, shell workers and coppersmiths. Of particular interest is a furnace with a brick-floor overlying a criss-cross of flues. It is entered from two door-ways and the enclosing walls are thick. The excavator is of the opinion that it was built for glazing minute steatite beads, a concrete mass of which was found nearby.............From the large number of copper tools and weapons beads and weights of stone and seals and ornaments of steatite recovered from the houses of the second Harappan phase at Chanhu-daro, it is evident that craftsmen lived in period Ib also."

Kedarnath Shastri[28] says about the residents of this town- "Although Chanhu-daro was a smaller town than Mohenjo-daro and Harappa, yet it was the centre of various arts and crafts. Stone beads, seals, weights etc., different types of articles of bones, shell and ivory and the buttons of faience, nose and ear tops, etc. were made here. Unfinished and semifinished articles of stone, shell and ivory which have been recoverd from these mounds reveal that Chanhu-daro was a centre of crafts and trade."[29] He has given an account of the following furnaces roundfrom there, "It is very essential to make a mention of those sixteen furnaces inside and outside the dwellings of the craftsmen which were unearthed during the excavation of mound'F'. One of the furnaces was of earthen pot, another was of the shape of a quadrilateral and still other fourteen were earthen lamp shaped. The pieces of vitrified material struck to the inner walls of many furnaces reveals that the goods of fience clay were baked in them and the seals impressions were glazed."

Lothal: Mr Rao participated in the excavation of Lothal. An account of the evidence of the crafts existing in Lothal is given in his[30] own words as under:

"Of particular interest are the workshops of shell-workers and a coppersmith noticed in the bazaar street. The Former consists of two rooms in one of which a dump of shells and shell-beads were encountered. The coppersmith's workshop is also a two-roomed structure with a rectangular furnace of vertically-laid bricks. A cubical stone anvil was also found **in situ**. The smith's kit consisted of copper tools and terracotta crucibles, the latter being used for melting the metal. At the northern end of the city another smithy was built to enable a number of coppersmiths to work under a single roof. Here five brick paved sink-like structures are encountered besides half a dozen pot-furnaces meant for heating and casting the metal. Not far from this structure is a furnace wherefrom an earthen bowl used for smelting copper ingots was recovered.

Bead factory: A mud-brick structure consisting of a central courtyard and eleven rooms of varying sizes was built in Block F on the western flank of the Acropolis. It served as a bead factory where several lapidaries worked together on a central platform and lived in the rooms built around it. A couple of store-rooms and a guard room were also provided within the factory premises. The entry to the working platform lay from the main street which was screened off by a wall. The main entrance to the stores and living quarters was guarded by a watchman. Two earthen jars containing more than 600 beads of gemstones in various stages of manufacture found embedded in the working platform confirm that lapidaries worked here. Two more jars containing the raw material were noticed in the store-rooms. The total area covered by the factory is 500 sq meters.

Similarly, several furnaces have been found where beads were glazed. One of them is round in shape which has four holes in the lower part connected with each other for blowing the air, another hole was for placing and taking out goods. These furnaces were used for baking precious stones before making beads as also for glazing the beads. In both the cases, clay pots were used for baking as is done in Cambay today.

Two different types of furnaces which are round-shaped were used by copper smiths. Here moulding of the tools and ornaments was done. Similarly, the furnace of another coppersmith is rectangular in shape which is made of burnt brick. It measures 75 × 60 × 30 centimetres in length, breadth and depth, respectively. In these furnaces copper bricks were melted."

Weights and Measures

A.S.Hemmy, who has examined the weights from Mohenjo-daro and also some from Harappa, states that the system used was binary in the case of the smaller weights and decimal in the case of the larger ones, the succession being in the ratios 1, 2,1/3, × 8, 4, 8, 16, 32, 64, 160, 200, 320, 640, 1600,3200,6400, 8000, 12,800 and that the unit weight had the calculated value of 0.8565 gram. The same authority is of the opinion that, with the possible exception of a very few weights, the system used by the Harappa people bears no relation to that of the Babylonians, and though one group of weights strongly resembles the ancient Egyptian beqa, he regards them, nevertheless, as quite independent. Very few of the weights from Mohenjo-daro, considering the great number found, were bad or fraudulent, a fact which shows that stringent trading regulations existed in the city.

Only one measure has been discovered and that also a fragment, consisting of a slip of shell marked with division of 0.264 inches of which nine remain. The mean error of graduation on this scale is only 0.003 inch and two different marks on it indicate that it was once part of a longer measure on the decimal system[31].

Foreign Trade and Navigation: The Indus country trade was carried on both by land and sea routes. Foreign trade was probably carried on by sea route. The Harappans had elaborate trade relations with Cheldia and Babylon. It continued even when they migrated to south India. Dr. Sayce has mentioned in his Hevart Lecture (1887 p 130-37) the fact of taking sandalwood, ivory, monkeys and peacocks from India in the boats by Jewish King Soleman. The Jewish word 'Tukian' a synonym of peacock resembles the Tamil word 'Tokai' which is also a synonym of peacock. The use of the word 'Indus' for muslin in their language reveals that this cloth was imported from the Indus land[32].

Mr Kosambi[33] expresses his opinion regarding the above subject as under:

"The great trade depot for exchange between the Indus region and Iraq was the Island of Bahrein in the Persian Gulf. This was the Tilmun of Mesopotamian legend. Here the deathless, legendary Sumerian Noah Ziusudda spent his days after surviving the deluge and was sought out by the hero Gilgamesh in search of the secret of immortality. The cuneiform clay tablets that speak of trade through Bahrein conducted by a special class of merchants, the Alik Tilmun, have been amply confirmed by modern excavation, though about 100,000 grave mounds still remain unopened. Certain round button seals found in the Indus cities and in Mesopotamia seem to have originated in Bahrein. Later, the merchants traded under the special protection and partnership of the Assyrian King, who took a major share of the profits, but must also have been their greatest customer. The Indus region seems to have been called Meluha[34] by the Mesopotamians. All mention of Meluha ceases by about 1750 B.C., which means that trade contacts were then interrupted, presumably by invaders. There was some other intermediate trade centre, Megan or Makkan, not properly identified, probably on the coast between Bahrein and India. Most of the trade was carried on in cosmetics and luxury goods. Wheat, barley and rice grew in abundance in the valley."

Now we talk of Lothal, a main trade centre situated on the sea coast. According to S.R. Rao,[35] "Owing to good environment for agriculture, soil, water and being situated in the middle of region infested with forests the growth of Industries was inevitable in Lothal- - - - - The growing prosperity of the city in Phase III is indicated by a rise in the number of spacious houses of merchants and craftsmen and the establishment of new factories and workshops, particularly of metalsmiths, bead makers and shell-workers. Foreign trade must have contributed in a large measure to the material wealth of the inhabitants as can be surmised from the artifacts of Mesopotamian origin found in Phase III. A few houses of merchants have yielded earthen wares decorated in what is known as the 'Reserved Slip Ware' technique which was very popular in the Diyala Valley. A hoard of gold jewellery recovered from a wealthy merchant's residence included nine circular beads with axial tubes simulating those from the Royal Cemetery at Ur. The occupant of the house exported beads of gemstones and inlays of ivory and shell to Mesopotamian ports wherefrom he obtained painted jars and jewellery. His house has yielded four Indus seals besides the goods he exported or imported. The industrial products of Lothal reached the Indus Valley, the Bahrein Islands, the Euphratis-Tigris valley, the north Syrian ports and the Island of Cyprus. The lapidaries imported semi-precious stones from the Narbada Valley for processing them into beautiful beads which were very much in demand by the Sumerian and Egyptian Kings. In return for cotton goods, stone beads, shell inlays and ivory objects, Lothal obtained copper, tin, gold and perhaps wool too."

It is quite evident from the above mentioned facts that the merchants of the Indus countries were more interested in foreign trade rather than internal trade. It is because of this fact that they had become so prosperous.

Navigation and Lothal Dock: On the discovery of the artificial Dock of Lothal in the excavation we easily reach the conclusion that the Indus merchants used sea route more than the land route for carrying on their foreign trade. SR Rao[36] gives an account of the Lothal dock as follows:

"The greatest contribution made by the Lothal engineers to the advancement of science and technology consists in building an artificial dock for berthing ships. It is the largest structure ever built by the Harappans or any Bronze Age community for handling cargo, and is also the most scientifically designed after taking into consideration the direction and force of the current, the water-thrust and other problems. The Lothal dock is noted for its unique water-locking device introduced in the spill-way which could be closed or kept open according to necessity. It regulated the flow of water at high tide and ensured floatation of ships at low tide without allowing the basin to be silted up. In design and execution the Lothal dock was far ahead of the Phoenician and Roman docks of later days. It was built not in the main stream, but away from it, to minimize the danger from silting and floods. The nullah connected the basin of the dock with the river which swelled at high tide as is even now the case in the Bhogawa near Lothal. Being the earliest of its kind built by the maritime nations of the world some structural details may be noted here.

A trapezoid basin measuring on an average 214 × 36 metres was excavated on the eastern flank of the city and closed by masonry walls of kiln-fired bricks with necessary gaps for the inlet and spillway in the shorter arms on the north and south respectively. The length of the embankment walls is 212.4 metres on the west, 209.3 metres on the east, 34.7 metres on the south and 36.4 metres on the north. The maximum depth was 4.15 metres. There was a dockyard in the North and the merchants ships from Babylon and Sumer used to come and go there. The vastness of the Lothal dock-yard can be estimated by comparing the measurements of the Lothal dockyard with those of the modern docks in India[37] given in the schedule."

Name of the port	Length (in metres)	Breadth (in metres)	Depth (in metres)
1. Lothal	209.3(E) 212.4 (W)	34.7 (S) 36.4 (N)	4.15
2. Bombay (Small)	152.40	19.96	6.71 (minimum depth over silt)
Bombay (Large)	304.80	30.48	10.6
3. Vishakhapatnam	111.56	18.29	4.27

(Table of the measurement of ports-extracted from S.R.Rao)

It is indeed a great achievement of the people of Lothal. It established that the Indus Valley people were more advanced in the technique of navigation as far, back as 4000 years and they carried on most of their trade through sea route. But it is noteworthy that some scholars[38] are not prepared to accept this view. In their opinion, it was simply a water-reservoir for the use of the inhabitants which was also used for irrigating the nearby fields.

Political Life

The scholars hold different opinions regarding the political set up of the Indus region. D.D.Kosambi[39] has put forth his views as under:-

"The two great cities have been regarded by some distinguished British archaeologists as the northern and southern capitals of an empire; not only on the analogy of Egypt but perhaps because of the feeling that anything so advanced in India could have resulted only from strong imperial rule (like the British). This opinion needs no further comment."

Dr Mackay[40] has pointed to the obvious importance of the great central building, or buildings, now capped by the ruined stupa, and itself set high upon an artificial platform of mud-brick some twenty feet thick. Dr Wheeler has recently investigated just such a central mass of buildings among the ruins of Harappa, which he regards as a citadel and the stronghold of a bureaucratic or priest-king regime. At Mohenjo-daro there is some evidence that the regime was a theocracy, very similar in type to the contemporary theocracies of Sumer.

But S.R.Rao[41] has refuted the opinion of Mr Mackay. Thus the opinion of Mr Kosambi appears to be more plausible.

Weapons and military life

The Indus valley people were ignorant of the use of iron. Most of the weapons of that period such as axes, spears, daggers, mace etc., are made of copper and brass. Two swords of brass, the longest one being 18 .5" having hilts, have been recovered, both of them are quite thick and in good condition. Such swords have been rarely discovered in such an ancient age. These swords compare favourably to the swords which have been discovered by Flinders petrie from the remains of Tel-al-Ajul in Palestine. The spearheads recovered from the Indus valley are of special type which are 15" in length and about 5" in breadth. Daggers are of such a type that it becomes difficult to differentiate them from the Knives. They are long having the shape of a thin piece of metal. Many knives have also been recovered which are of different shape and size. The arrow heads have also been found which are made of a sheet of metal.

A heap of weapons has been found piled up at one place in Mohenjo-daro. They are engraved. Such engraved implements have been found in abundance in Harrapa. But the script engraved on them has not been deciphered so far.Perhaps they might have belonged to some temple or government[42]. The Indus civilization inevitably derived its wealth both from agriculture and trade. How far these sources were supplemented and enlarged by military conquest is at present beyond conjecture, but it is to be supposed that the wide extent of the civilization was initially the product of something more forcible than peaceful penetration.......... As at present known fortifications at the two major cities are confined to the citadels, it is not apparent that the lower city was in either instance fenced. We can take ordinary blades as weapons which have been recovered from excavations in each of the Harappan city. They were made of brass and bronze. But neither the shields nor the armours and helmets have been found here[43]. It is thus evident that although the Indus people were familiar with military life and did not lag behind colliding with the enemies, yet they led a peaceful life. They had developed weapons of war but had not developed the means of defence and they relied on their strong forts and ramparts of the city.

Recreation

The Indus Valley people were quite prosperous. They spent their leisure in sports and other recreational activities[44]. They enjoyed singing and dancing. Drums covered with skin on both sides on two amulets can be seen. A drum is hanging in the neck of an earthen statue. The bronze statue of a dancing girl is an outstanding proof of the practice of dancing there. Hunting, cock-fighting, in-door games were their means of recreation.

Disposal of the Dead

The cemetery R-37 found in Harappa proves that the Indus people burried their dead in graves. They did not cremate them like the Aryans. Some burial-jars have been found in which besides the bones of the dead, some other things were kept for the peace of the souls of the dead. We shall give its detailed description in the next chapter.

Conclusion

The Indus region extended in double the combined area of its two contemporary civilizations of Egypt and Mesopotamia. In fact, the Harappans were the first people who established a vast empire by uniting people of different types where all were considered equal, respected one another and were economically prosperous. Their greatest achievement is that probably peaceful method was adopted for the establishment of such an extensive empire. It is really a remarkable thing to run the government for four or five centuries without any war and religious and political disorder. This lengthy peace resulted in happiness and prosperity and rapid progress. Most probably the Indus Valley people built dams on the rivers and used canals as artificial means of irrigation for agriculture, produced plenty of foodgrains and filled the big granaries of Mohenjo-daro and Harappa. Those granaries remind us of the vast granaries which have been constructed in modern India after the green revolution.

A network of crafts and industries was laid due to the peace that prevailed in the Indus region. Not only that, industrial centres were established in Chanhu-daro and Lothal whose products were consumed not only in the nook and corner of the vast Indus region but were also exported to other civilized countries of that age by land and sea routes. A network of industries has been laid in India after its independence in 1947, but the dream has not been realised which the Harappans transformed into reality about four to five thousand years ago. They had captured the market of civilized world of that age. The goods manufactured in their workshops and factories were demanded even by the Kings of Assyria and Egypt which may be called far-off inaccessible country considering the means of transportation of that period. This trade monopoly of the Indus people made the country float in wealth and riches. Even the ordinary people began to lead a happy and prosperous life. The state government lavishly spent money on town planning at a large scale and drainage system for the welfare of the masses. Common people began to live in multi-storeyed pucca houses and they enjoyed the best amenities of life there (such as latrines with English bond seats, wells, bathrooms, rooms and baths sometimes decorated with tiles, courtyards decorated with flowers and creepers) which are enjoyed only by a few rich persons of the country today. It clearly shows that their standard of living was quite high. They used wooden furniture in the houses. They took nutritious and tasty food in beautiful coloured and brightly shining utensils. The rich put on beautiful coloured and embroidered cotton clothes. Men and women dressed their hair in different styles. They perhaps also used scented oils. The maidens added to their physical beauty by wearing beautiful and precious ornaments. They enhanced their beauty by applying powder and lipstick. They decorated the corners of their eyes with collyrium.

S.R. Rao[45] expresses his views regarding the great progress made by the Indus people in these words: "The Harappans made a substantial contribution to the science of engineering as a whole. As pioneers in the construction of an artificial dock with water-locking arrangements, they laid the foundation of marine engineering in the world. It is they who introduced what now goes by the name of English bond in masonry. Their contribution to other branches of engineering can be guaged from the invention of the compass, the auger-drill and the circular saw. They are the authors of a linear system of measurement with a unit equal to the angula of the Arthsastra, which was used in India till recently. As the Harappans were the earliest growers of rice in the world, they may also be supposed to have domesticated the plant for the first time in the Indian subcontinent. Far more important is the idea of standardization of goods and services, which the Harappans meticulously implemented in every field of human activity without smothering initiative. The form and content of weights and measures, seals and sealings, earthen and metalwares, tools and weapons, toys and ornaments, houses and drains were fixed and rigorously enforced for half a millennium years all over the vast Empire. It is the Indus people who made the later civilizations realize the benefits of standardization which are of unquestionable value even to a highly industrialized society such as ours."

It is a surprise to learn how the Harappan managed to climb so many rungs of the ladder of progress of human civilization. But we are all the more surprised when we learn that the sun of civilization had set in India with the destruction of the Indus civilization in the Indian peninsula. Its actual dawn occurred when India got independence on 15th August 1947 after a slavery of thousands of years, when a constitution was made that all people should have equal rights, all should respect one another on the basis of equality, the state should spend its revenue for the welfare of the common people and agriculture, industries and trade should form the basis of the economy. But still it appears to be a dream and the common people simply hope the realisation of this dream.

After the above given accounts we can undoubtedly say that the Indus valley people founded a great civilization about four to five thousand years ago. They were indeed great. The whole nation can feel proud of them.

References

1. Shastri Kedar Nath "Sindh Sabhayata Ka Adikendra Harappa", page 23.
2. Marshall John,"Mohenjo-daro and the Indus Civilization" Vol I p-125
3. Rao, S.R. "Lothal and the Indus Civilization" PP 34-35.
4. Mackay, E., "Early Indus Civilization" PP 19-20.
5. After Mackay,E.P 18.
6. After Mackay E, PP 35-36.
7. After Mackay E.PP 21-29.
8. Rao, S.R. plate IV.
9. Marshall John, Vol. I,P 207.
10. Mackay, E.PP 42-43.
11. After Mackay, E.PP.77-78.
12. After Mackay, E.PP 80-81.
13. After Mackay, E,PP 90-91.
14. Rao, S.R. P P 110-111.
15. Rao, S.R .P 111.
16. Mackay, E. P 75.
17. Rao, S.R. P 190.
18. Parpola Asko, 'The Indus Script Decipherament", (Madras 1970).
19. "The Dravidian elements in Indian culture," P 63.
20. Rao, S.R. P 57.
21. Rao, S.R.Plate XXXI
22. Rao. S.R. P 79.
23. Mackay, E."Chanhudaro", P 222.
24. Wheeler Mortimer, "The Indus Civilization" PP 85-86.
25. After Wheeler, P 86.
26. After Rao, S.R. PP 86-108.
27. After Rao, S.R. P 24.
28. Sindhu Sabhyata Ka Adikendra "Harappa", P 18.
29. After Shastri Kedar Nath, P 203.
30. After Rao, S.R. P 68.
31. Mackay, E. P.103.
32. Reo Vishweshwar Nath, 'Rigved Par Ek Itihasik Drishti' P 236.
33. Kosambi D.D.'The culture and civilization of ancient India' P 59.
34. Parpola-Asko P 11.

    Melukha-is a Dravidian word (Mel-akom-pronounced as Ahom-means western country, P12). In Pali and Sanskrit Mlechchha-later on commonly used for barbarian-even today sudras are humiliated by calling them 'Mlechchha'.

35. Rao. S.R. P. 57.
36. Rao, S.R. P.70.
37. Rao, S.R. P. 72.
38. Lawrence, S.Leshnik, "The Harappan Port at Lothal' Ed.by Possehl L.Gregory ACI, PP 210-211.
39. After Kosambi D.D. P 69.
40. Mackay, E. P XII-XIII
41. Rao, S.R. P.6.
42. Mackay, E. P P 98-100.
43. Wheeler, M. P P 72-73.
44. Mackay E, P 141.
45. Rao, S.R. P P 189-190.

Chapter II

Who were the Harappans?

People of India

In order to discover as to who were the Harappans, it is first of all essential to determine as to which races and castes the people which live in India at present belong and what their past history was. A number of scholars such as H.H. Rislely, Dixan, Hutton, Hendon and Guha conducted research on the subject and put forth their own point of view. However, the view point of Risley, who was the first to conduct anthropological survey of India, received recognition from scholars all over the world. We shall, therefore, examine first of all the view point of H.H. Risley.

Risley's view

Risley[1] divides the Indian people into seven categories. 1. The Dravidians 2. The Indo-Aryans(Nordics) 3. The Turko Iranians 4. The Scytho-Dravidians 5. The Aryo Dravidians 6. The Mongoloids 7. The Mongolo-Dravidians

The Dravidians. They are mostly found in South India. Their stature is short or below mean; the complexion very dark, approaching black; hair plentiful with an occasional tendency to curl; eyes dark; head long; nose very broad, sometimes depressed at the root, but not so as to make the face appear flat.

The Indo-Aryans. They are mostly found in Kashmir. Punjab, Rajputana. Their stature is mostly tall; complexion fair; eyes dark; hair on face plentiful; head long; nose narrow and prominent, but not specially long.

The Turko Iranians. They occupy the western part of Pakistan and Baluchistan. They are generally found in the districts situated to the West of Sind. Their stature is above mean; complexion fair; eyes mostly dark, but occasionally grey; hair on face plentiful; head broad; nose moderately narrow, prominent, and very long.

The Scytho Dravidians.(Broad Headed Alpine). They are found in eastern Sind, Gujarat and Maharashtra. The people of this race are small in stature as compared to the Turko-Iranians. Their head is broad, complexion fair, hair on face rather scanty; nose moderately fine and not conspicuously long.

The Aryo-Dravidians. The people of this race are found in eastern Punjab, Bihar and Uttar Pradesh. Their head form is long with a tendency to medium; the complexion varies from lightish brown to black; the nose ranges from medium to broad, being always broader than among the Indo-Aryans; the stature is lower than in the latter group, and is usually below the average by the scale given above. The Aryan blood is more predominant in the West than in the east.

The Mongoloids. These people are found in Burma, Assam and different regions of the Himalayas. Their head is broad; complexion dark with a yellowish tinge; hair on face scanty; stature small or below average; nose fine to broad; face characteristically flat; eyelids often oblique.

The Mongolo-Dravidians: The Mongolo-Dravidians type of people are generally found in Bengal, Orissa and eastern parts of Bihar. Probably they represent a blend of Dravidian and Mongoloid elements with a strain of Indo-Aryan blood in the higher groups. The head is broad; complexion dark; hair on face usually plentiful; stature medium; nose medium with a tendency to broad.

View of J.H. Hutton.

Huttons' earlier view was based on Risley's view that the Dravidians were the original inhabitants of India. But later on he changed his opinion and agreed to the view of some other scholars that some Negrito type races lived in India prior to the Dravidians. In 1933, he made a mention of the entry of eight types of races. First of all the Negritos from Africa entered here. And a few signs of this race are in existence in the Indian Peninsula even at present. After this the Proto-Australoids (Caucacian) came here whose ancestors can be traced in Palestine even today. After this an early branch of mediterranean race came here. The people of this race spoke an undeveloped broken language which gave birth to modern Australian languages. They had imperfect knowledge of agriculture and their civilization was that of the palaeolithic age. Later on, another mediterranean race from East Europe made its advent in India. Their civilization was more developed than that of the earlier people. They had knowledge of metals. These people began the City State Government system and developed the civilization. These people were related to the Indus Valley civilization. They developed a high urban civilization in third and fourth millennium BC. These people spoke perhaps some Dravidian language and lived in Mesopotamia prior to this. At last, in 1500 B.C. long-headed Aryans entered the Punjab. He has mentioned other races also such as Armenoid, Alpinoid and the Mongoloids[2].

View of Dr. Guha

Dr. B.S. Guha, the late Director of Anthropological Survey of India, holds the latest view. He has expressed his view in his book entitled **"Racial Elements in the Population"**[3]. According to his opinion, six races made their entry in India-Negrito, Proto-Australoid, Mediterranean type, Western Brachy Cephalic Alpine, Nordic (Aryans) and Mongoloid The Mongoloid race is an admixture of long and broad headed palae-Mongoloids and Tibeto-Mongoloids races. They had a peculiar type of head which resembled those having long heads. It was an early form of human species in India. This race is found in Assam and frontier regions of Burma. Mediterranean type of people were long headed. They are found in Kannada, Tamil, Malyalam speaking regions, the Punjab, Uttar Pradesh, Sind and Rajputana. Small headed Western races have a mixture of Alpinoid-Dinaric and Armenoid races. He holds the view that the Negrito race has almost disappeared in India. This race came from Africa and is still found in

Andaman and Nicobar and Malaya. The proto-Australoid came from the Mediterranean coastal region. They were black-complexioned and long-headed. Dr. Guha further states that it should be properly understood that it is very difficult to separate these races. Now these races have become mixed by their assimilation.

From linguistic point of view, the racial division as mentioned by Dr. Guha is as follows: (1) Mundari, (2) Dravidian-mediterranean type, (3) Aryans-Western broad-headed Alpine and Nordic, (4) Sino-Tibetan.

A Brief Schedule of Races

Risley	**Hutton**	**Guha**
1. The Dravidians	1. The Negrito	1. The Negrito
2. The Nordic Aryans	2. The Proto-Australoid	2. The Proto Australoid (Mundari language)
3. The Turko-Iranians	3. The Mediterranean type	3.The Mediterranean type (Dravid language)
4. The Scytho-Dravidians	4. The later Mediterranean type	4. The Western broadheaded Alpinoid (Aryan language)
5. The Aryo-Dravidians	5. The Armenoid	5. The Nordic (Aryan language)
6. The Mongoloids	6. The Alpinoid (Scythian)	6. Mongoloids (Sino-Tibetan Language)
7. The Mongolo-Dravidians	7. The Nordic Aryan	
	8. The Mongoloid	

We shall now give evidences to prove that the founders of the Indus valley civilization were Australoids and Mediterranean type of people, who were joined by Alpinoid as invaders at a later stage. It will therefore be quite in the fitness of things to give here a detailed description about their origin and history.

The Proto-Australoid (caucacian): This race has made an original contribution to the inhabitants of India. This race made its entry several times in different parts of India. This race must have got mixed up with other Indian races particularly with the people of mediterraneans, Negritos and the Mongoloids. Some elements of the above races are found in Kols, Mundas and Assamis in India and in the people of Burma and Indo-China in the east. Munda languages are related to the Australian family of languages. It is prevalent in the east of Central India, in the southern boundary of the Himalayas and Kashmir and East Nepal. Dr. Stenkono holds the view that Kol races were widespread in the whole of northern and southern India at some time. S.C. Roy has also supported this view.[4]

Munda languages have contributed a lot to the Aryan languages. Their legacy includes the names of birds, trees and parts of bodies. The words SHALMALI (Silk-Cotton), BAL (hair), KAMBAL (Blankets), KADALI, KAPPAS (cotton), TAMBUL (betel leaves) etc. have been derived from the Munda languages.

Dr. S. K. Chatterjee has written in this context: "Whatever the original Australoid race contributed to the Indian culture is proved by the following things- potteries the knowledge of which was conspicuous by its absence to the Negritos, the development of the civilization of palaeolithic age in neolithic age, the development of the technique of boomerang, cultivation with the rods which were used for sowing rice."

J.H. Hutton[5] throws light on the racial type & original home of these people, "Whether or not we are to count the Negritos among the races which have contributed to India's population there is no doubt about the Australoid race which is often alluded to as pre-Dravidian or proto-Australoid. This is a racial element which may be ultimately allied to the so-called 'Brown Race' of south-east Europe, or which may have developed from a subhuman ancestry in south-east Asia itself. The type is allied to the aborigines of Australia and to primitive race spread over the Indian archipelago and it very widely spread all over India, particularly among the lower castes and humbler classes of society. It is found in the least adulterated form in some of the more primitive of the southern Indian hill and forest tribes, but generally appears mixed with other elements in all grades of society, though it is much less evident among the higher classes than the lower. It is characterized by very wavy, even curly, hair, a broad nose and rather coarse features generally, and by a darkish skin. There can be little doubt but that the ancestors of people of this type formed the bulk of the population of the Indian peninsula at some very early date, and probably before anyone else, except perhaps, Negritos has entered it."

The Dravidians. The Dravidians made their entry in India from the mediterranean region. They had three branches. All of them spoke Dravidian language. They were all long-headed. By the time they entered India they had become quite civilized. It is said that at one time these people had spread their civilization in the whole of north, central, western and perhaps in East India. It can be estimated from Brahui language which is spoken in Baluchistan that it was an extensive abode of the Dravidians sometime. There are evidences to show that the people of this race lived in the entire north India at a certain time.

The words 'Tamil' and 'Dravid' have probably been derived from the words 'Drumila' or 'Dramija'. Lycyians of Asia Minor have described themselves as 'Trimmile' in the inscriptions. Herodotus says that the Lycyians had come to India from an island named Crete. In the historical books the name of the pre-Hellenic people who inhabited this island before the Greek civilization, has been called 'Termilai'. It is possible that the Dravidians who had come from the eastern Mediterranean region might have brought their racial or national name 'Tarmilai' and it might have changed into Tamil later on.

According to Mahajan[6] V.D.,"The Dravidians had kings who dwelt in strong houses and ruled over small districts of country. They had minstrels who recited songs at festivals; and they seemed to have had alphabetical characters written with a style on palmyra leaves and a bundle of leaves was called a book; they acknowledged the existence of God whom they styled Ko or king-a realistic title known to orthodox Hinduism. They created to his honour a temple which they called ko-il, God's House. They had laws and customs but no lawyers or judges. Marriage existed among them. They were acquainted with the ordinary metals with the exception of tin, lead and zinc, with the planets which were ordinarily known to the ancients with the exception of Mercury and Saturn. They had medicines, hamlets and towns, canoes, boats and even ships, no acquaintaince with any people beyond the sea, except in Ceylon, which was then perhaps, accessible on foot at low water; and no word expressive of the geographical idea of island or continent. They were well acquainted with agriculture and delighted in war. They were armed with bows and arrows, with spears and swords. All the ordinary or necessary arts of life, including spinning, weaving, and dyeing existed among them. They excelled in pottery, as their places of sculpture show.

Scholars point out that the Puja ceremonies along with flowers, leaves, fruits and water are the result of the Dravidians. Aryans were accustomed to the Homa rites or sacrificial fire. In course of time, the Puja rites were adopted by the Hindus also. According to Prof. Mark Collins, the Sanskrit word Puja was a Dravidian Pu or flower. If Homa was a Pasu-Karma or a religious service involving the slaughter of animals, puja was a flower ritual or flower service. According to Charpentier, the word Puja has been derived from a Dravidian root called Pusu which means "to smear". The smearing of sandal paste or blood forms an important item in the Puja ceremony.

It is pointed out that the name Shiva is at least partly of Dravidian origin. In the Dravidian language, Shivan means red and this God was described by the Aryans as Nila-Lohita or "the Red one with blue (throat)." Shiva is stated to have drunk poison and kept the same in his throat which became blue. Shambhu is another title of Shiva and this is compared to the Tamil words Shembu or Chempu which means copper or the red metal. Likewise, the Vedic God Rudra has been identified with Shiva. The Dravidian God Murukan is stated to resemble Kumara or Skanda, the son of Shiva. The worship of the Linga was also due to Dravidian influence. Garuda as the vehicle of Vishnu is partly a divine eagle of the Aryans and partly of the Dravidians. The worship of the Monkey-God was also borrowed from the Dravidians."

According to Wheeler, "The religion of the Dravidian people, which lies under the crust of Brahmanism, is interesting from its extreme simplicity. 'Snake Worship' says Balfour "is general throughout Peninsular India, both of the sculptured and of the living creature. The sculpture is invariably of the form of the Nag or cobra, and almost every hamlet has its serpent deity. Sometime this is a single snake, the hood of the cobra being spread open. Occasionally the sculptured figures are nine in number, and this form is called the `Neo-nag', and is intended to represent a parent and eight of its young; but the prevailing form is that of two snakes twinning in the manner of the Esculapian rod'. Speaking of the village gods, Meadows Taylor says: "The worships of Grama Devatas or village divinities, is universal all over the Deccan, and indeed, I believe throughout india. These divinities have no temples or priests. Sacrifice and oblation are made to them at sowing time and harvest, for rain or fair weather, in time of cholera, malignant fever, or other disease or pestilence. The Nag is always one of the Grama Devatas, the rest being known by local names. The Grama Devatas are known as heaps of stones, generally in a grove or quiet spot near every village, and are smeared some with black and some with red colour."

Origin of the Dravidian race: Kanaksabhai Pillai has expressed the view that the Dravidians originated from the mongoloids. They came to India from Tibet and Nepal.

Dr. Caldwell opines that the Dravidians came from Central Asia.

According to most of the scholars, the Dravidian race originated from Semetic civilization. Both are long-headed. Worship of woman and marriage rituals are also similar amongst them. Colonel Holditch holds the opinion that the Dravidians had captured some region of Mesopotamia quite earlier. Later on, they came to India through the route of Makran coast.

Mr. Sewell[7] has given evidences to support this view. We find a racial change as we move from west to east upto the Indus valley which begins from Kish, The nose of a skull recovered from there is long and thin. A similar type is found in ul-uved where the nose of the skull is somewhat small and broad. Similar skulls have also been found in Mohenjo-daro. Here the difference is more marked. It is evident that this change occurred due to the admixture of regional races. The Australian type people lived in Mohenjo-daro earlier.

(A) Archaeological Evidences

Human skeletons recovered during the excavation of the cities of the Indus valley: Like other civilization, besides many useful things for human living, several statuettes, human skeletons and skull have come to hand, which were minutely examined and it was made known who the founders of the Indus valley civilization were.

Harappa : Three cemeteries have been unearthed during excavation here which have been named R-37, Cemetery G and Cemetery H.[8]

1. Cemetery R-37

" No 'royal burials' have yet brought to the Indus civilization the macabre splendour which those of Ur have lent to Sumer. Meanwhile, a more commonplace cemetery, the so-called R 37 of Harappa, has illustrated the burial-rites of the average Indus citizen. South of the Harappa citadel on slightly rising ground, fiftyseven graves of the mature Harappan period were identified between 1937 and 1946. With rare exceptions, the bodies were extended from north to south, the head towards the north, and lay in graves each large enough to contain also an average of fifteen to twenty pots, occasionally as many as forty. Personal ornaments were sometimes worn by the dead: shell bangles, necklaces and anklets of steatite or paste beads, copper finger-ring, an ear-ring of thin copper wire. Furthermore, toilet and other objects were occasionally included: handled copper mirrors, mother-of-pearl shells, an antimony stick, a large shell spoon. In one grave a pottery lamp and bones of a fowl were found at the foot. But on the whole, the grave-goods were of a poor order, and it is clear that, as explored, the cemetery represents the average citizen of the later period of the civilization... The statistics of the scientific investigation conducted regarding human skeletons of the Harappans recovered from the graves have been published. Of the 36 crania and mandibles from cemetery R 37 sufficiently preserved for study, 15 represent adult males, 19 adult females, and 2 juveniles. A majority of them are grouped in two main classes: 21 adult skulls in Class A, and 10 adult skulls in Class A I. with 4 unclassified and one aberrant. The last is a male skull marked by excessive massiveness, broad head, and large dimensions of certain metric characters. The remainder are dolichocephalic, A I slightly more so than A, which is liable to have pronounced supra-orbital ridges and low receding forehead. Without emphasis, Class A is compared with the ' Proto-Australoid', 'Caucasic', Whilst Class A, which is of slighter build, recalls the conventional ' Mediterranean', Indo-European'. In height the mean measurement of Class A males is 5 ft. 8-9 ins., i.e. relatively tall, of Class A I, two or three inches shorter. The age of adults at death ranged mostly between 20 and 40, with a bias towards[9] 30.

2. Cemetery G

Cemetery G has been found on the south-eastern outskirts of the mound. Here a tightly packed mass of human skulls, intermixed with a relatively small number of human bones, some animal bones and Harappan pottery have been discovered. Of all the crania, 23 crania are unbroken whilst others are in a broken state. These dead bodies were not buried but were thrown in a pit and were covered with the dust. Many of them bore marks of injury and cuts. Out of them 6 were men, 4 women and 4 unrecognisable. The remaining six were children. Out of these only 10 skulls were alright which have been divided into two groups of five each A and BI. Group A. had long heads and those of class B-1 were round headed strangers who never lived there. As the skull found in Area G were found lying piled up upside down and most of them bore marks of injuries, it appears that the round headed had launched a sudden attack on the long headed people. The long headed were the earlier inhabitants of Harappa.

3. Cemetery H : earlier stratum II

There were 25 skeletons out of them 11 are adult men, 8 adult women, a girl of 14 years and two children ageing 6 and 12 years. The sex of remaining could not be ascertained. Out of these 13 adults were considered worthy of investigation. They were divided into 3 groups 5 round headed were named B_2, 3 long headed A-1 and one long headed woman having broad nose was given the name A. Type A and A-I are longheaded and similar to those of cemetery R-37. B_2 have bigger heads as compared with those of B-1 of cemetery G. The frontal bone is bent backward which is evidently different from B-1. The average crania length of B-2 is 188.62 mm whereas that of B-1 is 177mm. Kragman has described B-1 as Alpine type and B_2 as Alpine and an admixture of Alpine. Similarly, from the burial jar of upper stratum of H, the skulls of the people of R-37 type and B-2 type have been found."

Mohenjo-daro

If we turn now to Mohenjo-daro, we are thrown back principally upon the groups of Indus citizens who were massacred in the streets during the ultimate attack on their city, and were dug up and published years ago by Marshall, Mackay, Sewell and Guha.

Dr. Guha and others have recognised four types of races after conducting a careful scrutiny of 26 skulls recovered from Mohenjo-daro.

1. Three skeletons of the first type whose heads measure 66.02 are related to the long-headed people. They have been recognised as proto-Australoid.
2. Six skulls, maximum in number, having average measurement 66.2 have been recognised as long-headed Mediterranean.
3. There is only one skull of the third type which has been described as one of the Mongolian branch of the Alpine.
4. Fourth type of skull is that of a child and is of Alpine type[10].

According to Martimer Wheeler[11], "The proto-Australoids were, if the measured example was average, a small folk with long, narrow skulls, a somewhat broad nose, and a tendency towards prognathism. The 'Mediterraneans' had moderately long skulls, rather short nose with narrow, high-pitched bridge, and fine regular features. The height of one of the men was 5 ft. 4.5 ins., and of two of the women 4 ft. 9 ins. and 4ft. 4.5 ins. The type is widespread over western Asia and the coastal tracts of Europe and may well lie at the back of the early developments of agriculture and of social organization; in other words, here, as at Harappa, it more likely than not represents the formative element in the Indus civilization. The single Mongoloid, regarded as 'quite characteristic', was presumably an intruder from the hills such as may be found today in any sub-Himalayan town or village, or may have come from farther afield-from Turkestan, Assam or China. The broad headed 'Alpine' type may be recognized today as a minority element in the Indian population and, as Piggott points out, was represented at Sialk in Iran in the fourth millennium B.C."

Both Dravidians and Australoids have dark skin approximating to black, dark eyes, black hair, either straight wavy or curly, but not woolly or friezely, thick lips, low nose with wide nostrils, usually short stature, though the Australoids are somewhat taller than the Dravidians[12].

Chanhu-daro

The only skull found at Chanhu-daro in the one season's work had been placed in a large storage jar with a conch shell beside it and several copper and bronze implements. No other portion of the skeleton was present, not even the mandible, and it had evidently been interred in the jar sometime after death. This skull is that of a young woman, long headed, but with a broad flat face and wide nose-a blend of diverse ethnic strains, Mediterranean and Negroid. The shape of the jar and the character of the objects buried with the dead appears to be of the Harappan age[13].

Lothal

Chatterjee and Kumar[14] have made the following observations in the case of the Lothal skulls (eight) and other skeletal remains measured by them:

The living stature varied from very tall to medium, and the majority of the skulls were medium-headed (mesocranial). The presence of long-headed (dolichocranial) and broad-headed (brachycranial) types were comparatively low among them. The characters of nose were broad and flat among both the male and the female, and the average nasal index of the male was 57.44 and that of the female 55.58. The majority of the facialis were broad and lone (leptene) in the case of the male. The characteristic feature of the orbits was low (chamalconch) in the case of the male, while in respect of the female it was of medium type (Masoconch). But the presence of high orbits was also there. They have classified racial groups as follows:-

1. Large and rugged, long headed type (Proto-Nordic), Aryan skull No. 2, 8, 9, 11 or four in number having head measurement 75.11. They belong to the second group of Sialk and Uved.

2. Medium-headed smooth type (Proto Mediterranean) skull No. 14, 17, 18 having cephalic measurement 85.44. They belong to the 4th period of Sialk.

3. Broad headed type (Alpino-Armenoid) has been found only one.

At the base of the Indus valley population there existed, according to Guha and piggott. "An autochthanous hyperdolicho-cranial element represented by the Veddoid or Australoid ethnic group. But it is the 71 index dolichocephalo (mediterraneans) who were predominant in the mature Harappan phase at Harappa, Mohenjo-daro and Chanhu-daro. A mesocephalic Alpine is said to have migrated to the Indus valley some time later than the 71 index dolichocephalo and made an attempt to settle down at Harappa (Cemetery G) during the mid-Harappan phase. In the post Harappan phase (Cemetery H, Stratum 1) there was a fairly large population of the Alpine strain (Mesocephalic or low Brachycranial). In addition to these groups there was a small Brachycranial element both at Harappa and Mohenjo-daro."[15]

But aforesaid anthropological reports of examinations of skeletal remains have been disproved by a group of scholars, who re-examined them at a much recent date. Which I am not ready to accept. What is the pitfall in their work is well explained in Vol II of this series chapter VIII pp 216-218.

But famous dental anthropologist Kenneth A.R. Kennedy has solved this problem most successfully by using technique of dental anthropology and has retained the previous view as such. (See detail, on page 339)

Apparently the Indus valley civilization was the result of the physical efforts of the Proto Australoids and the mind of the Mediterraneans. In the medieval period Brachycranial Alpino Armenoid invaders tried to settle. The proto-Nordic Aryan appeared in Lothal at a time when the Indus civilization had almost decayed. The late Harappan settlement of Indus valley civilization is believed to have declayed between 2000 B.C. and 1750 B.C. While Lothal is said to have decayed in 1600 B.C.[16]

Statue

At Mohenjo-daro a stone statue has been recovered which is described as being, that of a priest by Mackay and that of a Yogi (mystic) by Ram Prasad Chanda. This male figurine has a beard but the upper lip is clean shaven. The right hand bears an armlet like ornament and there is a painted or embroidered shawl round the body. The ancient Sumerian and Babylonian priests wore such dress.

The eyes of the figurine are half-closed and are located in the lower part of the nose. It appears that there was some inlaid matter in the eyes.

A comparison of the facial expression of the Sumerians and that of the Indus valley people is significant. Sporting a long beard, the upper lip cleans shaven, long hair tied into a bun at the back of the head in a faminine way were the fashions in vogue among the upper classes of the erstwhile Sumerians. Sometimes they had their faces clean shaven. The facial expression and the hair style of the figurine found at Mohenjo-daro belongs to this type.[17]

Mr. Piggott is also of the view that this figurine is Alpino or Aremoid or Sumerian type that existed in SIALK Iran. Another figurine of this type has been found in SIALK which is ascribed to jamdat Nasr and is of Sumerian type.[18]

Among the bronze figurines, there are small 'minor' works but these include the most remarkable of the authenticated Indus figurines, the dancing-girl from Mohenjo-daro without the missing feet and ankles, this charming little statuette is 4.5 inches high, it was found 6 ft. 4 ins. below the surface in a house in HR, Area and though presumably not of the latest period, cannot be regarded as very early. The right hand rests on the hip, the left arm, covered almost entirely with bangles, hangs loosely and the posture of the legs is easy. The head provocatively tilted, is a skilful impressionistic rendering of a prognathic 'aboriginal' type, with large eyes, flat nose and bunched curly hair, but whether as has been suspected, a Baluch native is indicated, or whether, the derivation is rather from South India, with which the Indus civilization was certainly in contact, is indisputable.[19]

Terracotta figurines of the mother goddess excavated in Crete are not dissimilar; it seems, to those from Mohenjo-daro and to others excavated in 1926-27 at Buxar in Bihar from a site 52 feet below the present surface and 13 feet below the Maurya stratum; which rather suggest the extension of the Indus valley culture to the Ganges valley.[20]

Ethnic features of South Indians in the Sumerian Figurines:

The most primitive civilization of Iraq was that of Akkad and Sumer. Regarding the figurines excavated at the sites of these civilizations Dr Hall writes, "The ethnic type of the Sumerians are strongly marked in their statues and reliefs, but while we compare them with those of the present south Indians we find them decidedly Indian type".[21]

Same view has been expressed by A.C. Dass, "Obviously the figurines recovered during excavations in Indus valley sites have a glimpse of the Australoid and the Sumerian (Mediterranean) type of people. Their faces resemble those of the figurines found in Sumer."

Rituals and Customs:

Here we shall throw light on the similarity among the Pre-historic Minoan civilisation of Crete island which is situated in the Mediterranean sea, Indus valley civilisation and the Dravidians of South India which corroborates Dr Hutton's view that the Sumerians after leaving the Mediterranean region first settled down in Mesopotamia and thence moving onward settled down in the Indus valley where they founded a civilization of high order. Later on, they were driven away by the Aryan invaders towards South India. They are still living there and they carry on their ancestral rituals and customs (of Crete island).

Bull-grappling sports:

The credit of the discovery of this cultural relationship between the two countries goes to Dr C.L. Fabri who, as early as 1935, published a note on it in Archaeological Survey of India's Annual Report for the year 1934-35 under the caption, "The Cretan Bull-Grappling sports and the Bull-sacrifice in the Indus valley civilisation." This article was published in 1935 in the annual report of the Archaeological Survey of India for the year 1934-35 A.D. (pp 93-100).

The material evidence round which this discussion gravitates is furnished by a number of seals and seal impressions found in the excavations at Mohenjo-daro. They include two steatite seals and three terra-cotta sealings. For drawing comparisons between the legendary scenes on the above seals and the Cretan parallels Dr. Fabri[22] cites a number of examples of frescoes, reliefs and sealings from the Minoan Palace at Knossos in Crete. :-

"The main points of comparison are that in the Minoan Crete a ritual was performed in honour of the Mother Goddess in which dare-devil young acrobats, men and women, participated. At great risk of their lives they grappled with and vaulted over the sacred bull in the arena and ultimately sacrificed the animal to the goddess." While dealing with the Indian evidence he observes,

"Like the Cretan, the Indus ritual also consisted of two parts, namely, (1) the bullgrappling games and (2) the subsequent sacrifice of the bull to the Mother Goddess". So far as Cretan examples are concerned I fully agree with his explanation of the details. But his interpretation of some of the main features of the Indus seals does not completely accord with the actual details as delineated on them."

An Interpretation:

Referring to Indus figure Dr Fabri says, "the left hand sealing can be divided into two halves, the left half showing a tree, a platform, a pillar and a bird is of the utmost importance and constitutes the crowning corroboration of all my comparisons in this article; and in the right half of this sealing is shown a bull, in charging attitude, lowering its head. A portion of this sealing is broken off, yet a hand and the arm of an acrobat above the horns are distinctly visible. Here is a person about to catch the horns of the bull exactly like the lady on the left of fig. (of Cretan). A second acrobat is shown, again as on the Cretan examples, alighting on the back of the bull with skilful jump no doubt in order to gain fresh purchase for the final landing in the arena. The performer is in every respect identical with those of the Minoan sports."

The final phase of the ritual drama was the offering of the dead body of the bull to the shrine of the goddess. The goddess is symbolized by the Holy Tree and in front of it is an obelisk surmounted by the double-axe on which is perched the sacred dove.

The same tradition prevails at present among the Dravidian races in South India. The rituals of bull fight are prevalent even at present among the lower caste of Tamil Nadu. J. H. Hutton writes, "Among the lower classes of the TamilNadu are the criminal tribes known as Kallar and Maravar, more or less professional cattle thieves who have a notable bull cult very suggestive of the Mediterranean, whether of ancient Mycenae or of modern Portugal. Bulls with sharpened horns are driven to fury, and the young man who wishes to distinguish himself and prove himself a desirable match for the lady of his choice, must jump on the bull's back and recover a cloth from its horns."[23]

Some of the features of south Indian culture suggest not merely Asia Minor (e.g. the fire-walking ceremonies such as are common in Southern India and formed a feature of the worship of Artemis in Cappadocia), but Crete.[24]

The above cited examples prove the undisputable relationship among the Crete, Sumerian, Indus valley civilisation and the Dravidian races in the southern India. At the same time it is also confirmed that the real founders of the Indus valley civilisation were Sumerians (Mediterranean) or Dravidians.

Other similarities between Indus valley and Mesopotamian civilisation

Other main similarities between the two civilisations are given below[25]:

1. **Pig tales in head dresses of gods:**-There is always presence of a

pig tails in the middle of horned head dresses of figures of Indus Valley gods. Such like head dresses, having pig tails have also been used in Mesopotamia during; the dynastic age.

2. Stool or dais with Bull's legs :- Indus seals generally display a god seated on a high bovine legged dais or thrones resting on the legs of a lion or a bull formed an essential part of the household articles in ancient Egypt or Mesopotamia.

3. Use of flat bricks :-Flat bricks have been in use in Mesopotamian architectural skill from ancient times to Jamdat Nasr period. In the Indus valley civilisation too flat bricks have been used from the beginning.

4. Invention of wheel:-The Sumerians invented the wheel and employed it in driving a chariot or for making pottery. In the fourth Millennium B. C. the Sumerians melted copper and moulded a variety of articles. The Potter;s wheel chariot and the art of moulding metallic utensils had been already known to the Indus valley people since ancient time.

Indus Script

During the excavations of Indus valley sites among the archaeological finds the chief discovery is that of seals of which each has something or the other impressed in Indus script. Numerous scholars have endeavoured to decipher the words impressed on about 400 seals. According to S.R. Rao "The early syllabic-cum-alphabetic writing of the Indus people was disciplined into an alphabetic system by 1500 B.C. (2000 B.C .)"[26]Naturally the question arises whether this script originated in India or it was a foreign product imposed and planted on the Indian soil. But for its confirmation it is essential to mention that all the letter-impressed seals so far recovered from the excavations at the pre-historic remains bear the same script. The hieroglyphics impressed on the seals of the upper or the lower strata are fully developed and mature nor their structure reveals their development by degrees. This shows that during the entire period of Indus valley civilisation there thrived a uniform mature civilisation in the Indus valley and its founders also belonged to the same race. During the excavations at Mohenjo-daro and Harappa, there have been found continually the remains of settlements of seven or eight strata. The writings on the seals found in the settlements of the lowest stratum are quite similar to those recovered from the settlements of the uppermost stratum. From this we can guess the span of time which must have been required to reach this stage of maturity through progress by degrees. In the opinion of Sir John Marshall there is no exaggeration in fixing a minimum of one thousand years period for this purpose. From this estimate the beginning of this script can be easily traced back to the early period of fourth millennium B.C.[27].

Langdan and Smith are of opinion that Indus script is neither related to the ancient Sumerian script nor to the ancient script of Elam. In the opinion of the former scholar the letters of this script bear more resemblance to the Egyptian hieroglyphics than with the pictorial and cuneiform scripts of Sumer. Inspite of all this the strokes and accent signs of the Indus script are distinguished in their style which is absent in the hieroglyphics of foreign lands.[28]

A number of Indian and foreign linguists are trying to decipher the Indus script. Among them the names of S.R.Rao, Iravatham Mahadevan, Ashko Parpola and Yuriya Knorozov are worth mentioning. Among the Indian scholars we shall first of all consider the research made by S.R. Rao formerly associated with the Department of Archaeological Survey of India. He claims to have deciphered the Indus script and says that the signs of the script are not word-based but sound based (phonetics).

According to him, it is not difficult to indentify basic signs because such signs have been repeatedly used for forming compound words without the use of any other signs and this script has the pecularity of having utilised compound words repeatedly like the old Aryan languages. This script which comprised of 62 basic signs including hieroglyphics was in 1600 B.C. disciplined in the alphabet of 26 letters. Its consonant symbols are based on the consonant symbols of the Sumerians and Phoenicians, both of which are written from right to left. The greatest contribution of the Indus valley people is to provide an order to alphabet.[29]

According to S.R. Rao, "They spoke an Indo European language which shows close affinity to Indo-Aryan in vocabulary, semantics and phonology. The occurrence of names of rulers and chiefs (Baka, Taraka, Ashtaka, Pancaka, Laba, Gara, Apa, Trika, Apta, Mana and Dasa, whom the Vedas consider as gods, Asuras and Rishis) and of countries (Malalha Melukha, Sapta-apa= Saptsindhu and odra), sacrifices (Ekaha, Pancaha, Saptaha) and divinities (Ka, La, Ha, Ta, etc.) suggests that the Harappans were the progenitors of Vedic Aryans.[30]

Among the foreign linguists, the name of Yuriya Knorozov, a Russian Professor may be chiefly mentioned. He is a famous linguist of Russia who in 1965, after 15 years' work had cracked the secret of the Maya Script of Central America. After that the Indus valley script caught his attention. Helped by a team from the Soviet Institute of Ethnography and using computers, Knorozov and his colleagues now claim they can well decipher the script excepting a few incomprehensible words.

In this connection the news of his discovery was published in the Sunday Times, a London daily paper dated 13th April 1980 which contains a reference to the renowned Russian paper Isvestia dated 30 January 1980.

According to this article published in the newspaper the Indus Valley civilisation was indigenous to the subcontinent not brought by invaders. In this way, he supported the diffusion theory that civilizations developed separately at several points of the globe rather than spreading from a central point.

This script runs from right to left and if there is a second line, from left to right. Until now all attempts to decipher it have failed though the Hungarian linguist Dr. G.De Hevesy pointed out remarkable similarities between this script and the Ester Island writings. Prof. Knorozov writes, "I and my colleagues are convinced that the Indus valley people did a lot of writing on palm leaves or other materials, including small wooden boards, some of which have been found, but with the writing effaced. writing instruments such as brushes and inkpots have been found. Some day archaeologists may discover some texts, better preserved in caves. But at present all of us have to go by the inscriptions, carved on stone or seals, only the tip of the iceberg. The inscriptions are in fact on vessels or statuettes brought by the worshipers to the temples or on the sanctified relics handed over by the priests to the worshipers, and used as amulets or talismans."

It is further reported that Knorozov first of all established that the inscriptions consist of the name or title of a god followed by a calendar formula recording when the particular sacrifice was made. This calendar formula is followed by the symbol of an auroch, goat, tiger, capricorn, ox and a yet undeciphered animal, each representing one of the six seasons of the year.

From the discovery made by Knorozov and his team the most extraordinary fact is that the priest astronomers had a highly developed calendar which combined lunar and solar observations. They also had a chronology recording 5, 12 and 60 year cycles which took into account the movements of the sun, moon and jupiter. In the third millennium B.C., the Indus Valley people knew five large planets and could calculate the time it took Jupiter to go round the Sun. Little wonder that ancient India had the reputation of being the home of Philosophers, astronomers and mathematicians.

But the Soviet experts' fundamental discovery is that the Indus Valley script uses a Dravidian language which is akin to the Tamil, Malayam and Kanarese of Southern India today. The script is therefore, completely indigenous and proves that the Aryan invaders, far from bringing a higher civilization, destroyed the very fine established one.[31]

To support my thesis another assertion may be quoted from Proto Indika.[32] Parpola and his colleagues believe, "The number of the interpretations offered can serve as proof; in other words, the greater the number of Dravidian interpretations, the more reliable the definition of the Proto-Indian language as a Dravidian. However, it is possible on equal grounds to maintain that the Proto-Indian language is close to Sanskrit, because a relevant group of researchers has offered a still greater number of "Sanskrit" interpretations. The classic way of checking, cross-reading, was never employed".

Obviously due to this reason it will be incorrect to call the Indus Valley script any other than Dravidian.

The scholars of the globe have been for many decades looking forward to the day when Indus Valley script will be deciphered because that will determine its real founders. In my view Yuriya Knorozov, the Russian linguist, has already decided the issue by calling it Dravidian. The whole world is apprised of his research and conclusion. The script also clearly proves the fact that the founders of the Indus Valley civilisation were Sumerians and Australoids whom the scholars have called Dravidians.

Linguistic Evidences : Kolarian language is spoken by a very small number of people who are also scattered. But the Dravidian languages are spoken over a wider area. These are spoken not only in the entire southern part of Godavari but there are signs of its being partially spoken throughout India such as Brahui in Baluchistan towards the North-West, Malto in Raj Mahal hills. Besides its words and accents are partly in use throughout India. This clearly shows that there was a time when it was spoken all over the Indian peninsula. J.H. Hutton gives an account of its' origin "No certain affinities have been established outside India, but it seems likely that these languages entered India from the north-west coming perhaps from Asia Minor, or at any rate from that direction, via Mesopotamia. The physical type particularly associated with these languages is probably closely related to that which is predominant in the Mediterranean, though it is generally found now in a state of mixture with other types, particularly with a round-headed type suggestive of Assyria, Armenia and the Iranian plateau. There are many cultural parallels between south India in particular and the older civilizations of Mesopotamia, Assyria, and Crete (See pp 32-33) and it is possible that many waves of immigration have taken place, all more or less of the same type of people. Probably the earliest of these were of a more or less unmixed long-headed type, the later comers being increasingly mixed with round headed peoples from the high-lands of Asia Minor and perhaps Iran.

At some later date, probably in the third millennium B.C., when there seems to have been much disturbance of races and peoples in the southern Russian steppe and in Iran, a wave of round-headed people seems to have come in from the north-west and passed down the west coast as far as Coorg. From there some no doubt trickled through what is now the Mysore state into the Tamil-speaking area of southern India, missing the Malabar coast of south India, and reaching the Telugu-speaking Andhra country just south of the Godavari river in even less force than the Tamilnadu. A section of these round-headed immigrants seems to have crossed India to what is now Bengal, probably moving south of the Yamuna and Ganges rivers for most of the way. It is possible that these immigrants introduced what is now known as the outer band of Indo-Aryan languages and it is possible that they were also the first to introduce a patrilineal form of succession, but these are very much matters of conjecture."[33]

The sweetness and other properties of Telugu language resemble those of the Italian language. The Telugu language spoken in aristocratic circles contains the properties of the languages of south-eastern Europe.

The Brahui Language of Baluchistan is Dravidian:

The Brahui of Baluchistan belong to Khan clan. Dr. Hutton[34] puts his view,"The true Baloch type is brachycephalic and the Baloch clans are patrilineal, but the Brahui, the other important indigenous people of Baluchistan, were probably long-headed originally and traced their descent and kinship through the mother.

They speak too, a Dravidian language completely different from Balochi and allied to those in southern India. It is no doubt an isolated remnant of what was once the general linguistic stock of northern India as it is now of southern."

But certain scholars have rejected this view. They hold that probably during the Kushan period some Madrassi troops were deployed here. The excavations have also yielded their skulls. It appears that this language is their legacy. Here, the Brahui speaking community is related to the Khan community while the Dravidian race is quite a separate and distinct one.

But the above view of the scholars does not appear to be correct. George Grierson, who was the director of the Survey of Indian Languages, throwing light on the history of the Brahui community and other inhabitants, writes - "This language is spoken in the Sarowan and Jhalawan provinces of Baluchistan and also in certain parts of Sind province (Karachi, Shikarpur and the Northern frontier region of Sind). The Brahuis maintain that they are the original inhabitants of Baluchistan. The Persians must, however, have invaded the country at a very early date. The cultivating class in the middle and westerly parts of the Khanat or Kalat are at the present day the Tajiks whose mother tongue is Persian. The Jats have occupied the south-east of Khanat the province of Los with the plains extending towards the Indus and almost the whole province of Kachh Gandav. The last settlers were the Baluchis who came from the south-west. They were not able to dislodge the Brahuis from the mountains, and, therefore, took possession of the north-east and of the tract between Sind and Kachh Gandav. The Brahuis are,.however, still considered as the dominant race".[35]

Obviously, the entire Baluchistan and its eastern regions were once inhabited by Brahui speaking people. The speakers of this language over such a wide area cannot be the remnants of several military troops. Undoubtedly, they are the remnants of the Indus Valley civilisation who once inhabited the entire region who could not be dispossessed of this difficult mountainous terrain by the later numerous invaders. This racial dissimilarity of Brahuis may have developed due to their continued sexual relations or blood affinities with the Baluchis for thousands of years. In this context it will do well to quote Sudhakar Chattopadhyaya. He writes :

"The above observations are no doubt interesting, but we cannot possibly leave out the question of language altogether, especially when dealing with ancient ethnology. We know that a superior culture dominates over an ethnic group of inferior culture. But if we find an inferior culture oasis in a superior culture region the natural presumption is that the first one belongs to a different group whatever the cephalic index of its members be, for such a change in head shape might have occurred as a result of later admixture. Thus the Brahuis of Baluchistan may be assigned to the palae-Mediterranean type of an early age. Similarly, Dardas may be regarded as Proto-Iranians. However, in any case we must be on our guard lest we depend too much on languages ignoring the physical characteristics altogether, though, as already stated, we cannot discard totally the possible linguistic backgrounds, however, restricted that might be, of ancient ethnological groups."[36]

Of some importance in this regard is David Mc Alpin's recent work which gives some evidence for us to believe that in antiquity there was a Proto-Elamo-Dravidian language family which covered all Southern Iran and extended into the Western portion of South Asia (Mc Alpin, 1975). The cultural historical implication of such a linguistic tie would seem to be important and far reaching.[37] It is clear from this that Brahui is a remnant of the same linguistic belt.

G.M. Vongard Levin and M.V. Gurov[38] have discovered in the archaeological findings that in the earliest phases of these languages i.e. which belong to the Age of Dravidian civilization in or about the 4th millennium B.C., contain such words as prove that at the dawn of the history of mankind these people were socially much advanced. They were good traders and inhabited the hilly region of North-western India. In these findings remnants of certain words have been traced which are interpreted as a type of crocodile, baboon, the blood-sucking giant lizard. These creatures are found towards the south of the Kabul river. There are also names of ten such trees as are available in the foot of the Himalayas in dry hills and in the north of the Punjab. This clearly shows that the Dravidians once inhabited the North-Western hills. Later on they extended their dwelling region to the Indus Valley. From there they went to central India and later on to Southern India. That is why the names of a majority of Dravidian castes have been derived from words meaning hill or mountain dwellers or hilly **(Paharia).**

From the archaeological researches of the Dravidian languages we arrive at definite conclusion that the Harappan civilization was founded on lofty and extensive indigenous development and was not the result of sudden growth. These new conclusions are not derived from the archaeological researches alone but are also based on studies of the Indus valley script and civilization conducted by the Russian great scholars.

J.F. Hewitt has observed, "Though the Aryan languages of the Vedic and Zend writings were admixture of other languages taken from outside at a later stage, yet the thought, moulded in them had taken birth in ancient Aryans. This union of the two elements is shown by frequent use of their words spelt with the cerebal linguals. DA, DHA, GHA, DHA, N which are not found in any of the European Aryan languages, but are fundamental letters of the Tamil-Dravidian dialects of Southern Indian and the Afghan Pustu. The existence of these letters in Sanskrit proves that the native language of Northern India which preceded it, must have belonged to the Dravidian type. But the interfusion of these alien races is not marked only in Indian Sanskrit, but also by the evolution of religious rituals and thoughts; for Aryans, little are other ancient races, based on their state policy on the belief that no people who had not the gods of the land on their side, could maintain a stable government in any country."[39]

From the above, it is apparent that the Dravidian language sometime in the past was spoken all over the Northern India. Words not only of Dravidian language but also of Munda language are found in the Sanskrit languages of Northern India. Sharat Chander Roy holds that there is evidence to prove that the Munda languages were once spoken throughout the Gangetic valley. In the languages of pronominalized Himalayan group (Tibet-Burma type group of languages) there are traces to suggest that they are related to the Munda family. The Munda languages, and the Kanarese the language spoken around Shimla have a number of truly similar properties.[40]

These views are supported by Asko Parpola also. He writes : "Comparison of different languages has shown that the Brahui language is dialectically related with Karukh. This is a North Dravidian language which is spoken from Nepal to Orissa and all the way to Bengal. So they together once formed a large dialect area and it can be surmised that even in the intervening area, where Indo Aryan is now spoken people spoke a related Dravidian language".[41]

It appears that after the devastation of the Harappan cities the Harappans wherever they might have gone, they were mostly separated from their clans and tribesmen so that owing to the paucity of means they took to rural life instead of urban living and a majority of them adopted cultivation, others resumed their old crafts which they partially carried on in the past and were associated with agriculture such as carpenters or blacksmiths, the makers of agricultural implements. When the Aryans here adopted agriculture as their profession, they automatically adopted the words of the language of their predecessors relating to agriculture and their original form. Given below are some examples of such words.[42]

	Mundari	**Santali**	**Sanskrit**
Plough	si, siu	si	si-in, sita (R.V., iv, 57, 6 and 7)
Sickle	datrom	datra	datra (R.V., viii, 78, 10)
Cattle	go	go	go
Cattle-shed	godha	-	goshtha
Cotton	ka-asom	kasakom	karpasa (later Sanskrit)
Yoke	arara	-	arara
Rice	mandi	-	manda
Straw	busu	-	busa
Sheep	mindi	-	mendha
Milk	toya	-	toya
Tree	daru	-	daru

But these Aryan words have been inflected and constructed according to Santali grammar, the grammatical system in Sanskrit having greater power of resistance. If, as Sir Henry Maine[43] says, "The occasional removal of the arable mark from one point of the village to another is in India a feature of non-Aryan rather than of Aryan tillage".

According to Sharat Chander Roy there is not only linguistic evidence, rather most of the non-Aryan male names and castes mentioned in Rigveda are found even at present among the Munda people e.g. Sambar, Kunara (I-51-6), Asurbala (II-11-20), Kuyava (VII-19-2, I-104-3), Dasyu, Danu (I-51-5, II-14-5) etc.[44]

On the basis of the archaeological and linguistic evidences given above it can be asserted that founders of the Indus valley civilization were the Austroloids, and Sumerian type people, not the Aryans, as some historians think. For a clear cut proof, we have the horse argument. In this regard Asko Parpola puts forward his[45] views. : "The Indo-Aryans had from the very beginning been a nomadic people in whose life the horse had played a major role. It is generally thought that the Indo-Europeans probably were responsible for the tamming of the horses, probably somewhere in the South-Russian steppes. So, if the ancestors of the Aryans already had horse in their culture, this is all the more so far the Aryans and we can read this in the Rigveda also. The Sanskrit word "Asva" which means, 'horse' is cognate with the Latin 'equus'. So we know that this animal was there in ancient Indo-European civilization. But in the Harappan seals, in which there are so many different animals depicted, we do not have any picture of horse. If the Indus people had been Aryans, I am quite sure, there would have been many representations of the horse.

Secondly, the bones found in the Harappan civilization do not give any unambiguous evidence for the existence of horse in the Indian sub-continent before about 2000 B.C. But then there is a very interesting development. As Mr. Mahadevan mentioned, the Aryans are thought to have come to India earlier. I agree with this contention although I think it was a different wave altogether, an earlier wave than the Rigvedic Aryans. But from 2000 B.C. we start getting not only horse bones but also representation of horse in terracota in sites in Baluchistan and Indus Valley." We will prove later (on PP 64-65) that these immigrants were round headed Alpines not nordic Aryans.

Evidently the Indus valley civilization was not the creation of the Aryans but it definitely belonged to the non-Aryan Australoids and Sumerian type of people. The scholars hold the view that it is the Australoids who were the ancestors of Sumerians (Mediterranean type, See Australoids in this chapter). The interfusion of the Dravidians and the caucacians today has reached to an extent that it has become extremely difficult to identify them separately. But Sir Huxley is of the opinion that it is the Australoids who are Dravidians[46]. These people are identified by their dark complexion, flat and wide nose, short stature and a rather awkward face. Description of such people repeatedly appears in the Rigveda where they are described as the enemies of Indra and are called Dasyus or Dasas who fought with the Aryans and were defeated and annihilated after a long struggle.

Description of Non-Aryan Dasyus and Dasas in Rigveda

Anasa or flat nosed

"O Indra ! you separated one wheel of the sun and created another wheel in order to endow wealth on Kuts. You killed the small-nosed Dasyus with a weapon and those (Mridhravach) who talked roughly during the battle."

R.V. V-29-10

PRĀNYACHCHA KRAMA VRAHAḤ : SŪRYASYA KUTSĀLYĀNYADVA RIVO YĀTVEAKAḤ I
ANĀSO DASYŪN : RAMRAṆO VADHEN NIDURYOṆ ĀVRAṆO MIRADHRA VĀCHAḤ II

The above verse describes Dasyus as **Anasa** (without nose) or small nosed just as the Dravidians are flat nosed.

Similarly in another verse the Dasyu king Vritra has been referred to as one having a broken nose. This clearly shows that the people living with the Aryans were in fact Dravidians who had flat noses.

Even today the Sudras of low caste in Uttar Pradesh (U.P.) are addressed as Anas (noseless) with a view to humiliate them.

Dark complexion

"O Indra ! You killed Pipru and the mightly Mrigya for Rijishvi the son of Vidith. You put to death five thousand monsters (Assuras) of dark complexion and you shattered the enemy cities as people tear away worn out clothes."

R.V. IV - 16 - 13

TYĀM PIPRUM MRIGAYAM SHUSHUVĀNS MRIJISVANE VAIDATHINĀY RANDHIAḤ I
PANCHĀSHAT KRISṆĀ NI VAPAḤ SAHASRĀ'TKAM NA PURO JARIMĀ VIDARDAḤ II

-"You punished the rule-breaker for the learned man and annihilated dark-skinned (enemies)".

R.V. I - 130 - 8

M'ANAVE SHĀSADAVRATĀN TVA CHAM KRISHṆĀ MARANDHAYAT I

-"O Fire! when for the sake of Puru you rose and burnt the enemy cities, the frightened dark-skinned subjects fled away discarding their food."

R.V. VII - 5-3

TVAD BHIYĀ VISHA ĀYANNA SIKNI-RASAMANĀ JAHAT ĪRHBHOJNĀN I I
VAISHVĀNAR PŪRAVE SHOSHUCHĀNAḤ PURO YADGNE DARYANNADĪDEḤ II

-"O invoker ! Invoke properly the energised perfect Soma which is a drug like water loitering after killing the dark complexioned Asuras".

R.V. IX- 41-1

PRAYE GĀVO NA BHŪRṆAY-RUTVEŚĀ AYĀSO AKRAMUH I
GHNANTAḤ KRISHṆĀMAPA TVACHAM - II

In this way, in Rigveda the Aryans have called their enemies Dasyus and dasas, dark skinned. Undoubtedly the Aryan followers of Soma, Aditya and Indra had to fight the dark skinned people of India. This difference of complexion clearly shows that there was a separate race. The Nordic Aryans had fair complexion while the Non-Aryan 'Dasyus' and 'Dasas' had dark complexion. That is why the Persians call the Indians dark-skinned people just as the word 'Hindu' means black, the word Indian in persian means black. The fair complexion and the dark complexion stand for high and low status in society. Just in the same way the fair complexioned were regarded as the rulers and the dark skinned were considered as common folk.

Mridhravach (Rough or unintelligible language)

O Indra ! you killed the small nosed Dasyus and killed in a battle the rough talkers.

R.V. V-29-10

ANĀSO DASYUN : ARAMRIṈO VADHEN NIDURYOṈ ĀVRAṈAN MRIDHRA VĀCHAḤ I

"Then Indra overpowered the Mridhravachas enemies (those who talked roughly or grumbled as may be interpreted from the Dravid language)"

R.V. VII-18-9

SUDĀS INDRĀḤ SUTUKĀN: AMITTRĀ-NARANDHAYANMĀNUSE VADHRIVĀCHAḤ II

By virtue of his might Indra broke the Dasyu cities and gave to **Anuputtra** Tritsu. O Indra! be kind to us so that we may be victorious over the Mridhravachas

R.V. VII -18-13

VYĀNAVASYA TRITSVE GAYAM̃ BHA-GJEṠM PŪRUM̃ VIDATHE MRIDHRAVĀCHAM II

Evil-doers and garrulous, **Mridhravacha** Panis undevoted and humiliating non-performer of Yajnas, the Dasyus are certainly defeated by Fire (Agni).

RV VII-6-3

NYAKRATŪN GRATHINO MRIDHRAVĀCHAḤ PAṈĪN:R SRADDHĀNI AVRADHĀN:AYAGYĀN" II

Captured that monster : Later on Indra cut off the feet with his thunder and killed Vrittra of limitless glory and the rough talker.

R.V. V-32-8

APĀDAMANTRAM̃ MAHATĀ VADHEN NI DURYOṈ ĀVRAṈAṄ MRIDHRAVĀCHAM I

From the above, it is obvious that the languages of the Dasyu-Dasas and the Aryans were different. Sayan has interpreted - Mridhravacha meaning hostile rough words whereas Geldner puts it as - impure language.

The question arises that even the Aryans must have used wrong and Rough language for their own - brothers, but here the word Mridhravach has been repeatedly used for Dasyus or Dasas or even for a particular person who was called 'Dasyu' or 'Dasa'. The fact is evident that the non-Aryan Dasyus and Dasas spoke a language (Dravidian) - distinct from Aryan's which was rough and - incomprehensible for the Aryans, remnants of which are available in Brahui language even at present in the Baluchistan region of Pakistan.

In Rigveda (X-22-8) it has been clearly stated "We live among the Dasyus. These people do not perform Yajnas and do not have faith in anyone. They have different customs. They are not worthy of being called human. O destroyer of enemies Indra ! Destroy these people".

The above mentioned conclusions can be summed up in the following sequence :-

The human crania and skeletons discovered in Indus valley cities on scientific examination evidently show that with a few exceptions the extent of population here resembled the Australian and Mediterranean type. This fact is confirmed by the statuettes discovered during excavations.

A comparison of the frescoes of the Minoan palaces found in Crete island, the figurines impressed on the seals found in the Indus valley and tradition of bull grappling sports among the Dravidians (Tribes) of South India, proves a remarkable similarity among them which is a self-speaking proof of the fact that the inhabitants of Crete, the Mediterranean people, the inhabitants of Indus valley and the Dravidians of Southern India all belong to one race who even today have the same customs and rituals which they had 4 to 5 thousand years ago.

Similarly, the remnants of Dravidian languages in Northern India such as Brahui language, "Malta" language in Raj Mahal Hills and the presence as well as absorption of its words in all the Aryan languages reveals that sometime Dravidian speaking people inhabited the entire Northern India.

Prof. Yuriya Knorozov, the renowned Russian linguist who had disclosed to the world the secret of Maya script of Central America; by dint of strenuous labour with the help of computers and the cooperation of a whole Institute, has successfully deciphered the Indus Valley script also by concluding that just as in Northern India the Aryan languages viz. Hindi, Panjabi and Bengali are related to Sanskrit language, similarly the Dravidian languages of southern India viz. Tamil, Malayalam, **Kaneri** were related to that language which was written in Indus script, has astounded the world and also revealed to them that the founders of Indus valley civilization were Dravidians who had dark complexion, short stature, curly hair, small flat nose and spoke Dravidian language incomprehensible to the Aryans and who have been repeatedly described in Rigveda as **Dasyus** and **Dasas** who had fought a war with the Aryans. Undoubtedly both the people contributed to the thriving of Mesopotamian and Indus Valley civilizations but it is impossible to tell whose contribution was richer. Some scholars are of the opinion that the contribution by the Australoids was mainly physical while that by the Mediterranian type people was chiefly intellectual and cultural.

References

1. Risley, H.H. 'The people of India'. PP 33-34.
2. Hutton, J.H. 'Caste in India'. PP 1-7.
3. Guha Dr B.S. ibid. P-26.
4. The Mundas and their Country. P XII.
5. Hutton, J.H. P-3.
6. Mahajan Vidyadhar, 'Ancient India'. PP 21-23.
7. Sewell and Guha, MASI No. 35. PP 56-81 (1932).
8. Wheeler, RE.M, "Ancient India'. Vol. III PP-83-85 BASI (January 1947) and Bose N.K. and others "Human skeleton from Harappa". ASIC (1963). PP 58-59.
9. Wheeler Martimer, "The Indus Civilization". PP 67-68.
10. Rao, S.R. 'Lothal and the Indus Civilization' PP 154-155
11. Wheeler, M. P 72.
12. Bahadur, K.P. 'Caste and Tribes, Culture of India' Vol. IV Preface VIII.
13. Mackay, E., 'Early Indus Civilization' P 153.
14. Chatterjee, B.K. and Kumar, G.D. 'Racial elements in post-Harappan Skeleton remains at Lothal'. AOMM-1963. edited by Bala Ratnam pp 104-110.
15. (a) Piggott Stuart, 'Prehistoric India'. P 147.
    (b) Guha B.S. 'Racial elements in the population' PP 638-640.
16. (a) Rao, S.R. PP-6-7.
    (b) Chatterjee B.K. and Kumar, G.D. P-108.
17. Shastri Kedar Nath 'Sindhu-Sabhyata Ka Adi Kendra, Harappa' P-47.
18. Piggott Stuart PP 148-149.
19. Wheeler, M. P. 90.
20. Hutton, J.H. P 152.
21. Dr Hall, 'Ancient History of Near East'. P 173.
22. Cited by Shastri K.N. 'New Light on the Indus Civilization', Vol. I (1957), PP 36-39 (Atma Ram & Sons, Delhi)
23. Hutton, J.H. PP 11-12.
24. Hutton, J.H. P 152.
25. Shastri Kedar Nath, PP 53-60
26. Rao, S.R. P 133.
27. Shastri, Kedar Nath, "Sindh Sabhyata Ka Adi Kendra, Harappa. P-217.
28. Shastri, Kedar Nath. P-216.
29. Daily Tribune 21 Nov. 1979.
30. Rao, S.R. P - 133.
31. Yuriya Knorozov's article, "Cracking the Indus Valley Code", Published

in "The Sunday Times, April 1980 (London)
32. Knorozav Y. 'Proto Indika'. P-16.
33. Hutton, J.H. P-5.
34. Hutton, J.H. P-41.
35. Grierson, George A.G. LSI Part IV. P-619 (Moti Lal B.Dass. Delhi)
36. Chattopadhyaya Sudhakar 'Racial affinities of Early North Indian Tribes', P-XII Introduction.
37. Possehl L.Gregory, ACI, 1979 p-255.
38. Science Today, Jan. 1982, P-26.
39. Hewitt, J.F., 'The ruling races of Pre-historic time'. P-135.
40. Roy, S.C. 'The Mundas and their Country', P-XII Introduction.
41. 'Front Line' Feb. 7-20, 1987, P-98.
42. Vishwanathan, S.V. 'Racial synthesis in Hindu culture'. P-58.
43. Village Community, P-109.
44. Ibid, PP 21-23.
45. Front Line, Feb. 7-22, 1987. P-99.
46. Census Report of India, -1901, Vol. I, P-508.

Chapter III

The End Of The Civilization

The different causes

Scholars do not agree on the causes of destruction of Indus valley culture. Some of them, however, do agree on the natural causes, while others on historical causes. Sir Martimer Wheeler[1] is of the opinion, that for a civilization so widely distributed as that of the Indus no uniform ending need be postulated. Circumstances which affected the sub-montane lands of the central Indus may be expected to have differed appreciably from those, which it encountered south or east or the Indian desert and in the watery coastlands of the Rann of Kutch. And the evidence at present available indicates that such was indeed the fact. Stuart Piggott[2] observes," In Indus valley enquiry has quite naturally tended to centre upon the great city Mohenjo-daro itself, where the later levels are familiar in a rough-and-ready fashion. And the verdict of those have dug into and through them is unanimous : they represent progressive degeneration. One thing at least is clear about the end of Mohenjo-daro : the city was already slowly dying before its ultimate end. Houses, mounting gradually upon the ruins of their predecessors or on artificial platforms in the endeavour to out-top the floods, were increasingly shoddy in construction, increasingly carved up into warrens for a swarming lower-grade population. Flimsy partitions subdivided the courtyards of houses. To a height of 30 feet or more, the tall podium of the Great Granary on the western side of the citadel was engulfed by using structures of poorer and poorer quality. Re-used brickbats tended to replace new bricks. The city, to judge from excavated areas, was becoming a slum.

Reasons for this decline in civic standards may be guessed, though guesses cannot carry us very far. Impoverishment of the surrounding farmlands by over-cultivation, by the destruction of neglect of irrigation-channels, by over-grazing, has been postulated. The untiring consumption of major vegetation implied by the firing, age after age, of millions of bricks may, even with the aid of hill-timbers, have helped to bare the land and may possibly, to some small extent, have reduced the transpiration of moisture. I have suggested that Mohenjo-daro was steadily wearing out its landscape; alternatively, Mohenjo-daro was being steadily worn out by its landscape. But all this is conjecture.

What is not conjectural is the intermittent impact of deep and prolonged flooding, in excess of the annual swelling of the river by normal rains and snow-melt. Something has been said of this above. The basis of the problem is that : it would appear from the records of the principal excavators (who unhappily recorded their observations with a baffling inadequacy) that at Mohenjo-daro periods of occupation were interleaved by three main phases of deep flooding, which may have succeeded similar phases in the depths not yet reached. At a number of points this abnormal flooding can still be detected in the form of deep deposits of silty clay, thick layers of collapsed building-material mixed with clay, and compensating mud-brick platforms upon which the inhabitants had at different levels sought to rebuild their town after flood disaster."

Postulation of creation of a lake by Dr Dales

It has further been observed that these flood-deposits are silty clay of still-water origin, as distinct from those of the freely flowing, seasonal floods normal to the river-system. They are in fact the result, not of down-river flow, but of the periodical ponding-back of the river by obstruction in the lower valley; in other words, of up-river encroachment.[3]

The whole problem is now in the hands of the hydrologist and the geologist and may be left there for a while. It may, however, be noted that a new stimulus was given to this research by the observations of G.F. Dales along the Makran coast in 1960. Dr Dales[4] Writes, "The Harappan stations, now some miles inland, made sense only in relation to a former coastal trade and that raised beaches, now also inland, created a consistent picture, if it may be assumed that their present position is due to uplift within the last three or four millennia. His comment is that 'the coast is in an active geological zone and indications are that it has been gradually rising for thousands of years.' comparable observations have been made independently and developed by R.L. Raikes; and the current postulate (under further investigation) is that during, and possibly before, the period of the civilization there were intermittent spasms of tectonic uplift across the Indus valley somewhere above Amri and well below Mohenjo-daro. There is reason to suppose that the neighbourhood of Sehwan, 20 miles above Amri, was just such a centre of periodical disturbance capable of creating a barrier and a resultant northward lake possibly as much as 100 miles in length. From time to time this lake, reinforced perhaps by an exceptionally high annual river-flood, might be expected to penetrate the dam and so shrink to something like the original river-bed; initiating a phase of rejuvenation of the Indus channel. Amri itself would appear to have been seaward of this dam, possibly in brackish water at the head of an estuary; at any rate, Casal found marine molluscs there in his Periods I-II, i.e. in the pre-Harappan and mixed Amri-Harappan Phases.

Again and again the lake had advanced upon them up the valley, spreading slowly perhaps but relentlessly. Eventually we may envisage the city as an archipelago of insulted habitations on heightened foundations in an inland sea. And then when after who knows how long a time? The lake subsided once more through regressive earth movements or through the openings of a broken dam, the islands were enlarged by the exposure of silt and debris. It is easy to imagine the accumulative demoralization of the citizens and the gradual worsening of civic standards".

Rejection of Dr Dales' view by H.T. Lambrick

But Sir H.T. Lambrick does not accept this view of George F. Dales in absence of solid proofs. And, whatever proofs are given they are neither correct nor reliable. He[5] rejects above theory on the following grounds :

"It is incumbent on the critic who views the matter in this light to propound his own interpretation of the data. Accepting that natural Indus silt of some kind is present in the ruins of Mohenjo-daro at various heights up to twenty-nine feet above the existing flood-plain, how did it get there ?

The site of Mohenjo-daro before any excavation had been undertaken, consisted of several large mounds of grey-white earth, with a pinkish tinge from the burnt brickbats scattered over them or protruding from the surface, among occasional bushes and shrubs (Marshall, 1931). In other words, it looked just like dozens of other old sites in Sind though on a larger scale than most of them. How were these masses of grey-white earth piled up over ruins of man's habitation and handiwork in the plains of Sind-pre-historic like Chanhudaro : Buddist like Kahujo-daro near Mirpur Khas, medieval like Tharri Mohbat? (Majumdar 1934: pl. IVb. opp. p. 26 : Cousens : 1929 : J. Sind Hist. Soc. 1946:62). After allowing a proportion to be the debris of disintegrated mud walls, etc., a vast quantity from some other source must have contributed to produce the characteristic configuration of these mounds. If we ascribe it to lacustrine-flood-sedimentation, we have to postulate individual uplift mechanisms at work virtually everywhere in Sind; and are next obliged to ask ourselves, were the similar mounds over ruined habitation sites in Bahawalpur and the south-west Punjab the result of yet other lakes, and further spheres of tectonic uplift? And we must not forget that Dr. Sahni requires uplift of this kind down stream from Budh-jo-Takar, to produce the phenomena at that place.

Clearly, some other influence must have been at work, and the obvious one is the wind, periodically whipping sand, silt and dust off the surface of the grey-white alluvial plain, and depositing it in every hollow or interstice among the ruins. Over the Centuries rainfall, with further disintegration of the mud buildings, consolidates the mound into the form which is such a familiar feature in the Indus plain. The important fact must be borne in mind that wind-borne silt naturally tends to be composed of the lighter grains; and when these are consolidated by rain, the texture of the resulting "silty clay" (or "clayey silt"?) is liable to resemble very closely the substance resulting from deposition in a lake or by a very slow-moving river flood.

Or take the detached sand-hills standing on the flood-plain of the Indus; those, for instance, about the latitude of the hypothetical barrier. These surely are accumulations of wind-borne silt from the banks and islands of the river exposed at its cold-weather level. Many a village in Sind has been obliterated, in modern times, by air-borne river silt."

So, it is clear that silt available in the upper strata or on top of Mohenjo-daro is a result of long process of wind borne silt deposites.

Major change in course of river-Theory of Lambrick

Further, Mr. Lambrick[6] puts his own theory in the following lines:

"At this point I may outline my own theory of the cause of the final ruin and extinction of Mohenjo-daro. I conceive that an avulsion and major change of course by the Indus took place considerably up stream of the city. The new bed being (ex hypothesis) lower than the old one and, say, thirty miles away to the eastward, close to the Western flank of the Khairpur hills, inundation spill thereafter did not approach within twenty miles of Mohenjo-daro, and the surrounding country, starved of water, immediately began to deteriorate. This theory is not susceptible of proof. But there is strong circumstantial evidence in its favour:

(1) A drastic change of course had become prima facie probable from the very fact of the Indus maintaining the same general course past Mohenjo-daro for 900 years or so, with the consequent build-up of its bed.

(2) There is a historical instance, recorded by the geographer strabo, of this actually occurring in part of the plain dependent on the Indus. That acute observer, Aristobulus, came in 326 B. C. upon a tract which had recently been reduced to ruin in this manner. He explains exactly what the Indus did and what the results were (see Strabo, xv, i, 19)."

Rise in the level of flood plain : Supporting viewpoint of Raikes

Above theory of Mr. Lambrick gets the support of R.L. Raikes[7]. He writes:-

"A flood in this context is taken to mean abnormal river flow at such a rate of discharge that the capacity of the river bed is exceeded so that excess flow has to be accommodated by the flood plain. Silt is solid matter carried in suspension by the river and comprises particles of clay, true silt, and even fine sand when the velocity of flow is high enough. Generally speaking, the excess flow would, except locally, move very slowly in the general direction of flow of the river. Only in the original channel would consistently high velocities be experienced. Over the flood plain the velocity would be low and would depend on the gradient, the depth, and the roughness. Of these factors the depth would be most subject to variation. In a river such as the Indus, variations in gradient and roughness would be marginal. Even at a depth of only one foot or flood plain flow, and even at the remarkably flat gradient of the Indus valley, there would be an appreciable velocity, though it might be low enough to ensure that some of the suspensed silt would be dropped.......... These inundations have caused a general rise in the level of the Indus flood plain that has buried the earlier Harappan levels under at least 30 feet of silt. The lowest level explored so far does not necessarily go back to the earliest occupations of Mohenjo-daro, but it does not make much difference to the present argument whether this level is dated to 2500 B.C. or somewhat later. The topmost Harappan occupation level coincides approximately with the flood plain level so far as the "lower and outlying parts of the city" (Marshall 1931:1) are concerned:

this is of course the most recent Harappan level, that which corresponds most closely with the end of the culture. Taking the archaeologists' estimate of approximately 1000 years duration, a very strange fact emerges: during 1000 years of occupation of the city, 30 feet of silt were deposited; during the subsequent nearly 2500 years, no further silt has been deposited."

Apparently, its reason was the same, that its course took place a major change, considerably upstream of the city and there after inundation spill never approached its old bed.

Final end due to some human attack

Similarly, it can be said that most of the Indus cities south to the Mohenjo-daro were ruined on account of uncontrollable activities of the Indus. Although the city of Mohenjo-daro suffered for degenerations on account of aforesaid reason, but it cannot be denied that it definitely met its final end due to some human attack. The citizens, who in the long run engraved their precious ornaments and other belongings in the last phase, had divided the rooms into small ones to accommodate the increased population, who had installed pottery kilns in the habitation area, must have surely fallen prey to some human attack. They were attacked all of a sudden and were massacred wherever they were . Human skeletons found in streets or in stair cases reveal the story of such a tragic end.[8]

It has of late been fashionable to decry the witness of sprawling groups of skeletons which are liable to encumber the later strata of Mohenjo-daro. There are five groups and one individual, and all were found at a high level. Unfortunately, the older excavators did not record stratification with any regard to precision, and in the absence of precise record it cannot be affirmed without shadow of doubt that the remains are all exactly contemporary. But in three instances-numbers (i)-(iii) in the subjoined list—there is in fact no doubt. The six occurrences according to M. Wheeler[9] are as follows:

(i) "A public well-room in the DK area was the scene of a tragedy which involved four deaths. The well was approached from the higher level of the adjacent 'Low Lane' by a short flight of brick steps. 'On the stairs were found the skeletons of two persons, evidently lying where they died in a vain endeavour with their last remaining strength to climb the stairs to the street'. One of them was probably a woman. It appears that the 'second victim fell over backwards just prior to death'. Remains of a third and a fourth body were found close outside. 'There seems no doubt that these four people were murdered ... It can be regarded as almost certain that these skeletal remains date from the latter end of the occupation of Mohenjo-daro and are not later intrusions. The fact that some of the bones of one of these skeletons rested on the brick pavement of the well-room and that the skull of another lay on the floor of a (brick-lined) sediment-pit (adjoining the entrance) prove beyond doubt that both well-room and pit were in actual use when the tragedy took place. And these were of the latest architectural period of the site.

(ii) In HR area, House V, the skeletons of thirteen adult males and females and a child, some wearing bracelets, rings and beads, were found in attitudes resembling simultaneous death. The bones were in bad condition, but it was noted that one of the skulls bore 'a straight cut 146 mm. in length' which 'could only have been done during life with a sharp and heavy weapon, such as a sword, and that this was in all probability the cause of death'; and another skull showed similar signs of violence. The relative level of this group is fortunately revealed by an oblique photograph taken at the time but only recently published; it shows the skeletons at the topmost architectural level.

(iii) In 1964, on the second day of his excavation on the western fringe of HR Area, Dr dales found five sprawling skeletons between walls of the latest period in 'a very thick accumulation of collapsed brick, ash and broken pottery'. They were not buried in any normal way but the victims of some disaster. They lay at a dog-leg bend in a lane and may well have been sheltering here. They represent three men, a woman and a child. Here at least there is no doubt as to their date at the extreme end of Mohenjo-daro.

(iv) In a lane in VS Area lay a group of six skeletons, including a child,but details are not recorded.

(v) In another lane, in HR Area, lay a single skeleton, though the circumstances are again obscure.

(vi) A group of nine skeletons in DK Area, amongst them five children, lay in strangely contorted attitudes and crowded together. It was thought that the bodies might have been thrown pell-mell into a hurriedly made pit but the excavator (Mackay) goes on with the baffling observation that for convenience sake the burial-place is termed a pit, but it had no defined walls nor even showed traces of having been dug. Once more, where are we. There were two elephant tusks with the party, and Mackay suggests that the skeletons were remains of a family, some of them ivory-workers, who tried to escape with their belongings at the time of the raid but were stopped and slaughtered by the raiders. The corpses had then been hastily covered as so much debris, without funeral-rites. As to period, one skeleton was wearing a bracelet of Indus type; the bones lay over a mass of broken masonry of intermediate III Phase and were therefore later than that; and the excavator's conclusion, for what it is worth, was that it was quite possible that the tragedy took place in the Late I-A Phase.

The surprising and significant thing about this last group is that it is the only one which is thought to have been deliberately covered, however, vaguely, shortly after death. Particularly in the East, where decay is rapid, bodies are not left lying about amongst inhabited houses. The general inference from the thirty-eight derelict corpses at Mohenjo-daro is that from the moment of death the place was uninhabited. The absence of skeletons (so far) from the citadel may imply that the raiders, whoever they were, occupied and cleared this commanding position for their own momentary use. For the rest, it may be suspected that sporadic fires in the sacked city kept predatory animals at bay.

Looking back on the macabre scene we may perhaps conclude that, since seventeen of these skeletons seem definitely to belong to the latest occupation and the remainder present the same aspect and have not been found in inconsistent circumstance, we have here in fact the vestiges of a final massacre, after which Mohenjo-daro ceased to exist."

Rejection of theory of human attack

The massacre, according to some scholars[10] seems to be a part of a human attack on the city and the invaders were none else than Indra and his followers, the Aryan speaking people from the west. A detailed description of such an invasion is given in the Rigvedic hymns. But George F. Dales[11] is not ready to accept such a hypothesis. He discards any of such views on the following grounds:-

"It is still premature to talk in terms of absolute dates-the entire chronology of South Asia down to the 6th century B.C. is a web of pluses and minuses of hundreds of years- so, on purely chronological grounds, we cannot even establish a definite correlation between end of the Indus civilization and the Aryan invasion. But even if we could, what is the material evidence to substantiate the supposed invasion and massacre? Where are the burned fortressess, the arrowheads, weapons, pieces of armor, the smashed chariots and bodies of the invaders and defenders? Despite the extensive excavations at the largest Harappan sites, there is not a single bit of evidence that can be brought forth as unconditional proof of an armed conquest and destruction on the supposed scale of the Aryan invasion. It is interesting that Sir John Marshall himself, the Director of the Mohenjo-daro excavations that first revealed the 'massacre' remains, separated the end of the Indus civilization from the time of the Aryan invasion by two centuries. He attributed the slayings to bandits from the hills west of the Indus, who carried out sporadic raids on an already tired, decaying, and defenceless Civilization.

What of these skeletal remains that have taken on such undeserved importance? Nine years of extensive excavasions at Mohenjo-daro (1922-31)—a city about three miles in circuit— yeilded the total of some 37 skeletons, or parts thereof, that can be attributed with some certainty to the period of the Indus civilization. Some of these were found in contorted positions and groupings that suggest anything but orderly burials. Many are either disarticulated of incomplete. They were all found in the area of the Lower Town - probably the residential district. Not a single body was found within the area of the fortified citadel where one could reasonably expect the final defence of this thriving capital city to have been made.

It would be foolish to assert that the scattered skeletal remains represent an orderly state of affairs. But since there is no conclusive proof that they all even belong to the same period of time, they cannot justifiably be used as proof of a single tragedy. Part of this uncertainty results from the unsatisfactory methods used by the excavators to record and publish their finds. But even allowing for this serious methodological shortcoming, it is possible to re-evaluate the published evidence and to come to some definite conclusions concerning the massacre myth.

The most celebrated group of skeletons, the photograph of which is usually published to provide visible proof of the 'massacre', was found in the area of room 74, House V (HR area) (see Marshall 1931. Pl. XLIV, a and pl. XL VI a). The interpretation of this grisly discovery was not even agreed upon by the excavators themselves. Hargreaves, who did the actual excavating, states that because four of the fourteen skeletons were found above the ruins of the southern wall of the room, the entire group belong to a date subsequent to the decay of the building and thus to a period posterior to the abandonment of the latest stage of the city. Marshal, the over all director of the excavation, says on the other hand "this does not seem to be proven". He points out that the building belongs to the Intermediate period of the city and that this entire area was covered over and rebuilt in the Late period (the assumed Late period remains were not preserved at this part of the city; it is probable they had eroded away). Marshal suggests that the skeletons could belong to the interval between the Intermediate and late periods,"though the possibility of their being posterior to the Late period may be admitted."............ During the removal of the thick accumulation of debris covering a courtyard of the Intermediate period (House III, HR area), incomplete remains of three skeletons were found. Their location in the debris shows, however, that they did not belong to the time of the courtyard but to sometime after it had fallen into disuse and had been filled in, possibly in preparation for the buildings of the Late period. The excavator suggests that it represents a Late funerary deposit and does not intimate any connection with a final massacre, of the city's population. Those who have so stated have misread the archaeological evidence.

One reads about" the slaughtered Harappans' who lay unburied amid their streets. This melodramatic description was prompted, in part, by the reported find of six skeletons in a lane between two houses in the VS area of Mohenjo-daro. And yet, the excavator stated in his report that" from their position they appear to be posterior to the adjacent remains," They were covered with loose earth, free from bricks and other debris that would indicate any violent destruction. There is no suggestion in the report that they were lying on the actual street surface. Marshall suggests again that they were probably burials of the Late period that just accidentally penetrated down between the building walls bordering the lane—the lane itself having been long before covered over. Had the skeletons really been found directly on the street surface, there would still be no case for a final 'massacre' because the lane belongs to the Intermediate period of the city.

Deadman's Lane in the HR area of the city was the scene of another well publicised but mythical street slaughter. One fragmentary skeleton (part of a skull, the bones of the thorax, and the upper arm of an adult) was found lying on its back diagonally across the narrow lane. But this incomplete skeleton was not resting directly on the walking surface of the lane. It appears to have been in the debris that accumulated between the walls of the building facing the lane sometime after the lane had fallen into disuse. The lane itself belongs to the Intermediate period of the city. This area was rebuilt during the Late period and houses covered the location of the earlier lane. The excavator suggests that this partial skeleton was interred under the floor of a house of the Late period. Thus, it was just accidentally located in the proximity of the lane and was not associated with it at all.

Another celebrated group of victims consists of nine skeletons that" lay in strangely contorted attitudes and crowded together (Block 10A, DK area)". Earnest Mackay, the excavator, expressed considerable doubt about the date of these remains. They were reportedly found at a level corresponding to the early part of the Intermediate period, For "convenience sake," Mackay termed the find-spot a burial pit although he admitted that he noticed no definite walls for the "pit" nor any traces showing that the area had been dug. Only two objects were found with the skeletons— an ivory comb that is not like the known Harappan period combs, and a copper bracelet. On the evidence of bracelet, Mackay dates the remains to" the period of the occupation of the city." The technical report on the skeletal remain states that they probably do not represent a massacre per se because many of the skeletons were incomplete, represented by only a few fragments of cranium and odd bits of bones.

Mackay suggests that these were the remains of a family who tried to escape from city with their belongings at the time of a raid but were stopped and slaughtered by the raiders. their bodies were then "thrown pell-mell into a hurriedly made pit." He says it is "quite possible" that the tragedy took place in the final period of the city but can offer no supporting evidence. That at least five of the nine skeletons were of children prompted the anthropologist who studied the remains to conclude that the raiders nursed a consistent hatred of the people of Mohenjo-daro as a whole, and total extermination appears to have been their endeavour.

Finally, in bringing this rather macabre account to an end, mention must be made of the lone bit of evidence from Mohenjo-daro that could conceivably be used as positive evidence of some murderous tragedy during the Late period of the city. In what we might call the "Well Room Tragedy" (DK area, G section) two skeletons were found on a flight of stairs "evidently lying where they died in a vain endeavour with their last remaining strength to climb the stairs to the street." But the circumstances surrounding this tragedy are unknown and it would be presumptuous to cry massacre on this bit of evidence alone.

Thus stands the evidence in the case against Indra and the Aryans, or to be less specific, against the idea of a final massacre by whom ever you prefer. The contemporaneity of the skeletal remains is anything but certain. Where as a couple of them definitely seem to represent a slaughter in situ, the bulk of the bones were found in contexts suggesting burials of the sloppiest and most irreverent nature. There is no destruction level covering the latest period of the city, no sign of extensive burning, no bodies of warriors clad in armour and surrounded by the weapons of war. The citadel, the only fortified part of the city, yielded no evidence of a final defence."

Above views of Dr Dales cannot be certified to be unchallengeable. There are innumerable instances in history when many of the cities were captured without a direct attack on them. If there was at all any attack, it is not always possible to trace out its archaeological evidences. History bears ample evidences to the fact that to capture Delhi most probably all the battles were fought many miles away from the city. Battles of Taraori (1191 and 1192 A.D.) and Panipat (1526 and 1556 A.D.) are most famous among them. If the king of Delhi ever met with defeat in the battle, the city was almost abandoned before the invaders could reach there. The invaders had to fight no battle there. Instead they massacred the few remaining inhabitants. Such examples of minor massacre have been traced out in Mohenjo-daro also under similar circumstances. It will not be justified to think of finding out the remains of wars such as bodies of warriors clad in armor and surrounded by the weapons of war, arrowheads, racked pieces of chariots etc. In Rigvedic description in the reference of Panis (Chapter X P-228) it appears from the conversation of Panis and Sarma that efforts were made for reconciliation before war. Panis stole cows of Indra, who through his messenger Sarma, requested for the release of same. It is also apparent from this account that Indra remained encamped at a far off place instead of attacking directly. It is just possible war must have been fought at a distant place before abandonment of city as the ten kings war was fought (see P.P 151-52 & 114) at the bank of Ravi somewhere near the city of Harappa.

It is crystal clear from the evidence available from Mohenjo-daro that it is not possible to reach any final decision about the causes of demise of all Indus Valley culture. hence we have to look for other sites from the north-nuclear region.

The Northern Nuclear Region

The Northern Nuclear Region comprises a considerable area. In the west it includes much of the modern states of east Punjab, Haryana and parts of northern Rajasthan, and in its eastern half the Doaba of the Ganges and Yamuna rivers. Indeed the former area consisted at one time of the Doaba of the now dry Sarasvati and Drishadvati rivers, and the latter with the ancient kingdom of Matsya, Kuru, Surasena and Panchala, and the whole of the area may therefore be compared with the ancient Aryavartta, the home of the Aryans of Indian tradition, also known as Brahmavarta.

Dealing first with the western half of this region, we find a curiously complicated situation, The earliest settlements yet known there belong to the Early Indus period. These appear to have been augmented during the Mature Indus period by a number of colonies, while existing settlements show indications of culture contact with the Harappans. A number of sites belonging to the post-Harappan period have been excavated, and these suggest that there may well be several regional variants of pottery style. A good example is Mitathal, excavated by Suraj Bhan. Here period I is the final stage of Early Indus and is culturally closely parallel to Kalibangan I; period IIA shows the blending of this local style with Mature Harappan elements, indicative of some sort of Harappan presence; period IIB shows a further direct development which its excavator names Late Harappan and which shows clear cemetery H affinities. It appears probable that all the variants belong to a broader cultural unity, indicated in the pottery by the presence of a redware, sometimes with painted decoration and with a number of notably "Harappan" forms surviving. This pottery has been called locally by various name; 'Bara ware' Late Siswal ware, Ochre coloured pottery etc. We would prefer to all these local variants under the one style, Redware of Harappan tradition. The distinctive Redware of cemetery H is closely related to that found at Bara and other sites near Rupar, north-west of Chandigarh, and at Sanghol in Ludhiana district. It has also been reported at a number of sites to the east as far as the Yamuna and southwards into Rajasthan, where it is probably represented by the early period at Jodhpura. The relations of this pottery are still not clearly established. Surprisingly reminiscences of the painted decorations of Tepe Giyan IV are found at Bara and Mitathal IIB. These incline us to expect that the phase belongs to the first half of the second millennium. As this region is of such importance, and as this period probably coincides with the foundation of the early settlements of Indo-Aryan speaking tribes in the area, it calls for special attention, and further research of all kinds. The period coinciding with the end of the Harappan civilization in the north of the region, in the Punjab, is of a rather different character from that of Sind, and may well prove of fundamental importance to our understanding of later Indian civilization.

When we consider the causes of demise of Harappa city itself, we cannot reach any conclusion, because most of the archaeological evidences from the upper strata have been looted by the dwellers of near by Harappa village[12]. George F. dales[13] throws light on this subject as follows: "The city of Harappa itself and lesser sites in the Indus valley to the north of Mohenjo-daro do not seem to have ever suffered significant flooding. Instead they give the appearance of having been abruptly abandoned, after which they stood empty for centuries. Such a pattern is certainly compatible with the invasion hypothesis. It is also compatible with a situation in which the Harappan state's weakened heartland to the south was unable to send help to the inhabitants of the northern frontier when they were threatened. The people who presented the threat could quite well have been hill raiders rather than Aryan invaders. An archaeological fact must also be taken into account in any effort to reconstruct the Harappan demise. The northern Indus sites show no evidence of a decline in material prosperity before their abandonment but quite the opposite is true of Mohenjo-daro and other southern sites. What does this contrast signify?"

It seems that evidences available from northern sites can give clue of civilization of invaders who attacked northern Indus towns and extinguished the culture. We will discuss on this topic in detail in the next chapter.

References

1. Wheeler. Sir Martimer, "The Indus Civilization". P 126 (Cambridge, 1968).
2. Piggott stuart, AI No. IV P 28, New Delhi (1948).
3. Raikes R.L. 'The Mohenjo-daro floods-Antiquity' XXXIX(1965) PP 196-203 and Raikes. The end of the ancient cities of Indus civilization. AA Vol. 66, No.2, 1964. P 284-299.
4. Dales G.F. 'Harappan out post on the Makran coast in antiquity' XXXVI (1962), PP 86-92.
5. Lambrick, H.T. "The Indus flood plain and the Indus Civilization", edited by Possehl L. Gregory, ACI P 319.
6. Lambrick, H.T., "The Indus flood plain and the Indus civilization", ACI, P 321 edited by Possehl. Gregory.
7. Raikes, R.L."The end of the Ancient cities of the Indus", cited by Possehl L.G. P 300.
8. Dales George, F. "New investigations at Mohenjo-daro," Archaeology-18 No. 2 (1965) P 147.
9. Wheeler, M. PP 129-130.
10. Piggott Stuart, "Prehistoric India" PP 239-240.
11. Dales George F. "The Mythological Massacre at Mohenjo-daro" PP 294-296. ACI edited by possehl L. Gregory.
12. Piggott Stuart, P 230.
13. Dales George F. "The Decline of the Harappans", P 311. edited by Possehl L.G. ACI.

Chapter IV

Who Were The Invaders? An Archaeological Review

The Black and Red Ware culture

To bring out the fact as to who were the invaders, it is neccessary to read the Harrapan's successive cultures. The Black and Red ware culture was the earliest among them. To begin with we take this culture first.

According to famous Archaeologist S.R. Rao[1], "The original inhabitants of Lothal, whose racial affinities we do not know, were advanced culturally. They knew the use of copper and produced superior earthen wares of thin fabric on a fast wheel. The presence of mica in the clay and the delibrate application of pinkish red slip over the vessel resulted in a micaceous red surface on account of which the ceramic ware has got its name. The shapes were limited to the round bottomed jars and bowls. The type fossil was convex sided bowl with a stud-handle which the Harappans copied later in their own fabric. The micaceous red ware vessels were painted in black over a light red surface with plant motifs horizontal zig zags, loops and intersecting lines, the painting being limited to the rim of bowl and the neck of jar. The indigenous style of painting influenced the Indus (Harappan) style considerably. A more important contribution made by the indigenous potter is what is known as the 'inverted firing technique'. Whereby the vessels came out of kiln partly black and partly red (i.e. black inside and red outside with a black top. In Wheeler's words 'The upper portion of the pot is thus in contact with the reducing agents present in the combustible material and turns black while the lower portion is exposed to the air and turns red as a result of oxidization). This technique was copied by the Harappans and their successors. The Black-and-Red ware, as the product of this technique is called, became the chief ceramic ware of the chalcolithic folk of central India and the Deccan in the second millennium B.C. and the culture trait of the megalith-builders of the south in the first Millennium. It serves as an important link between the Harappans and their successor in the Indian subcontinent"

Vibha Tripathi[2] throws light on the shapes of B and R ware pottery. "Black and Red ware occur at the site Sardargarh in considerably large quantity. The shapes follow closely the Painted Gray ware (PGW) forms."

This is siginificant to note that this culture was also adopted by Yadavas as proved from and noted at Ahar in Banna's valley. They mixed up with indigenous people and carried the above pottery traditions wherever they went. A detailed account of period and the area covered by this culture is given here from Vibha Tripathi[3];

"B-and-R occurs along with PGW at most of the sites. But before we define the precise nature of the association of the two wares we have to examine the distribution, both in time and space of B-and-R. It first shows itself in the Harappan context and continues through the chalcolithic assemblage in eastern India, pre-PGW deposits (Atranjikhera and Noh), pre-NBP levels in Bihar, PGW and outlives PGW up to the early Historical period (in Gujarat and Deccan). Black-and-red ware, thus , has extensive distribution both in time and space.

Below, we shall examine in brief the zonal features of the ware and study B-and-R in connection with PGW culture and pottery tradition. Srivastava (1971) has classified the entire B-and-R yeilding region into six zones. They are :

Region A (Gujarat)

Sites	Lothal, Rojdi, Rangpur, Prabhas-Patan, Amra and Lakhawal
Date	2400 B.C. to 800 B.C. with survivals at Rangpur and Prabhas-Patan
Painting	On the exterior
Region B	(South-eastern Rajasthan and Madhya Pradesh)
Sites	Ahar, Gilund, Eran, Awra, Manoti, Navadatoli, Nagda and Besnagar
Date	2000 B.C to 800 B.C. with survivals at Eran, Navadatoli, Nagda and Besnagar
Painting	On the exterior as well as on the interior
Region C	(Eastern U.P., Bihar and West Bengal)
Sites	Kosambi, Rajghat, Sohgaura, Sonpur, Chirand, Pandu-Raja- Dhibi
Date	1600 B.C. to 800 B.C. with survivals at Sonpur and Chirand
Painting	Generally on the interior
Region D	(Punjab, western U.P, northern and north-western Rajasthan)
Sites	Rupar, Alamgirpur Hastinapur, Atranjikhera, Sravasti, Noh, Gondi, Ghosla
Date	1000 to 800 B.C
Painting	Absent
Region E	(Maharashtra and northern Mysore)
Sites	Bahal, Prakash, Bahurupa, Nevasa, Nasik, Jorwe, Daimabad, Tekkalkota, Hallur
Date	1700 to 600 B.C, with survivals at Bahal, Prakash, Nasik and Jorwe
Painting	On the interior as well as on the exterior
Region F	(South Mysore, Andhra Pradesh, Madras, Kerala and Orissa)
Sites	Brahmapuri, Maski, Piklihal, Kesarpalli, Nagarjunkonda, Sisupalgarh
Date	1200 B.C. to 100 B.C
Painting	Absent

The foregone detail of distribution both in time and space shows that user of above ware first settled in the west and from there they further moved towards north-east and beyond in the far east up to Bihar and Bengal. They also moved towards south.

This culture has been noted between Ochre Coloured Pottery and Painted Grey Pottery culture at three sites i.e. Atranjikhera[4], Noh[5] and Jodhpura[6].

Foreign element in Black and Red ware culture, presence of iron

It is interesting to note that traces of iron have been noted in this culture against the previous view that P.G.W. was the first iron age culture and iron was first brought by Aryan invaders from the west. In support of this view Vibha Tripathi[7] puts evidences "Iron has now been reported from the pre-PGW deposit i.e Black and Red ware culture levels at Noh. This would further strengthen the hypothesis that these were the people who came from the west to settle down in the Sarasvati-Drishadvati valley. Their knowledge of iron was later imported to the P.G.W. people. Although we require further evidences to present boldly the above hypothesis. At present such a possibility is not altogether untenable."

Black and Red ware culture at Ahar.

The B and R ware was first noted at Ahar village in Udaipur district, located on the bank of river Ahar, a tributary of the Banas. This culture is represented by a 20 feet thick deposit.

Vibha Tripathi gives detail of pottery forms & painting of this culture, "Shapes commonly occurring are incurved or straight sided bowls, shallow dish -stand and a globular jar with a high narrow neck. Characteristic of the Ahar ware is the painting executed on it in white. The favourite designs are wavy or straight lines, dashes, concentric arcs, cross-hatched, lozenges etc. Associated with B and R ware at Ahar are ceramics like a sturdy brown ware, a coarse red ware and another variety of pottery with black painting on a whitish or yellowish surface and a coarse grey ware appearing a little later...... The Ahar culture is dated 1725 + 140 B.C. by C 14 datation. It continues up to 1200-1000 B.C."[8]

According to Sankalia[9], the archaeological remains of B and R ware culture of Banas valley (or Ahar culture) include some highly characteristic pottery, beads etc which indicate the existence of a significant element of west Asian complex. The examples which are relevant to our study are as follows:-

(a) The hallow stemmed bowl in Grey Ware is similar to those found at Tepe Hissar and Geoy Tepe.

(b) The stepped dish-cum bowl are similar to those found at Shah-Tepe.

(c) The animal headed handles of some earthen pots are similar to those found at Troy.

(d) Potting techniques and decorations, such as applique and punctured ornament, ribs along the shoulder and neck, grooved and incised designs are similar to those found on Shah tepe pottery.

(e) Correspondence between the light incised patterns on the terracotta beads or spindle whorls from Troy or Anatolia in general and the one with an incised pattern and bead from Ahar and an identical one on bead from Anau.[10]

Sankalia[11] has, therefore, particularly remarked "It would not be quite strange if some folk movement from western Asia, starting in about 2000 B.C. had reached south eastern Rajasthan."

Dr Sankalia[12] also putshis remarks cited below on the basis of the Puranic evidence, "The Narbada valley was inhabited much before the Mahabharta war. It suggests that the post Harappan chalcolithic cultures of central India and the northern Deccan were colonised by the Aryans in the wake of their early settlement in India. This period has been dated to 1700-1000 B.C. ... But Thapar(1970 p 153) thinks that "This part of Rajasthan was inhabited not by first wave of Aryans but by Saurseni language, speaking people". But he is not sure as to which branch of the Aryans is represented by these people, Asmakas or Assokas or by the Yadavas and Haihayas of the Puranic Tradition".

Excavation of Prabhas-Patan, its relation with puranic Tradition and Yadavas

According to puranic Tradition Prabhas-Patan (Som Nath) was related to Yadavas. This site is situated in Kathiawar near modern city of Veraval near the coast of Arabian sea at the bank of river Heron and is related to B and R ware culture. The deposits with B and R ware are assumed to start in Ist millennium B.C. still however by about 7th-6th century B.C. the B and R ware using people might have occupied this spot[13]. Nanavati[14] throws light on its relation with Puranic Tradition:

"Prabhas was the holiday resort of the Yadavas. The Pandavas also came here. So this place is essentially connected with the Yadavas. If one believes that in the tradition of Yadavas migrating from Dwarka and moving in this region a few remarks seem to be pertinent.

Looking to the divergent opinions of the Puranic Chronology at least one thing seems to be clear that if the date 3101 B.C. of the Mahabharata war be accepted, archaeological evidence is totally divergent, and both cannot be compromised. The other opinion of Pargiter that the Mahabharata war was fought round about 950 B.C. be accepted the picture becomes more clear. In the latter case the chronology of Prabhas suggests that in this period the material evidence of Iron Age is obtained. This material culture will not be out of context. The evidence of Prabhas is too meagre but it certainly suggests a slight overlap of Chalcolithic and Iron Age cultures. There is no evidence of heavy destruction but the mingling of cultures may lead one to infer that Raivataka and pre-Yadava population was probably of Chalcolithic culture. The marriage relations and struggles of mythology represent this overlap and later the establishment of a more widespread culture. In this part of the country this culture could be identified with the Yadavas. There "peculiar feature" as noted by Dr Jani is "the considerable admixture they had with the non-Aryans" (Chronology of Gujarat,p 24) seem to reflect the social features of the then existing society. These early Yadavas seem to use the materials that were found in many parts of Western, Central, Southern and Eastern India. This Culture is similar to that found at Maheshwara where Haihayas, a branch of the Yadavas ruled.

The problems of the Red and Black Ware, and even the introduction of Iron in India require much further work. The different tribes associated with Yadu seem to follow this tradition.

Looking from this angle the excavations at Somnath suggest that the Krisna legend and early Yadava movement might be identified with the early iron age of India, and that the pre-Yadava elements here were in the chalcolithic stage of culture. If Krisna migrated to this region he also opened up a new chapter in the culture of this region."

Who were the Yadus etc.?; Rigvedic evidences

According to Rigveda Yadus etc were non sanskrit speaking non Aryan tribes. R. Shaffer[15] observes direct evidence" These people (Yadus, Turvasa, Anu, Puru and Druhyu) were not Sanskrit speaking Aryans. According to Rigveda the Anus, Druhyus, Yadus, Turvasas and Purus attacked the Aryans at Parushni (Ravi), so they must have been native tribes hostile to the Aryans. And in the Rigveda Anu means a non-Aryan; Druhyu is considered a derivative of 'druh' 'be hostile to'. Turvasa is a derivative of 'Turv' to over power' No derivation has been of Yadu and we may infer that it was a native name .... And the Mahabharta (Adi 79-42) states-explicitly that the sons of Turvasas are the Yavans and that the sons of Anu are Mlechhas". In Rigveda the description of the Purus as Mrdhravac seems to strenghten the view that their language was different from the Vedic Nordics. Hence they were a non-Aryan Tribes. These five tribes lived to the west of the river Indus. In the ancient period, the river Indus divided this region into two linguistic zones-The western Iranian, the eastern Dardic" Chattopadhyaya puts forth linguistic evidences supporting above view," Dardistan the present home of the Dardric language includes from east to west, Gilgit and Kashmir, the Indus and the Swat Kohistan Chitral and Kafiristan... Philology also shows us that they must once have covered nearly the whole of the Punjab."[16]

In the background of the above linguistic evidences and 10 kings' war we should now note the presence of the Harappan people, who, as we shall see later on, did not disappear under the pressure of the Aryans, as it was commonly believed. It appears that the Harappans and the Yadus etc. lived side by side at the time of Rigveda in peace and war.[17]

The Racial Type: Ethnical evidences

In the Rigveda, the Vasistas are described as Svetyam or white, Kanvas as svavo or krishna dark (VII-33-1 and X-31-11). The appearance of black Rishi in the Nordic Aryan society is indeed a land mark. R.P Chanda[18] thinks that there were two sections of the sacerdotal class, Brahmanas by descent, Brahmnas by adoption and they were of different physical type. He further connects the black Rishi with tribes like Yadus and Turvasas... He[19] thinks that the Purus, Druhyus and Anus mentioned in the Rigveda along with the Yadus and Turvasas, may have come from western Asia (Assyria) and were probably of the same physical type as the Mitannis and the Hittites having dark or brown colour.

In the Rigveda (X-62-10) Yadus and Turvasas are dubbed as Dasas. They are also brought into special relation with the Parsus (VIII-6-46) or Parshavas or Parthavas. The word Dasas shows that their position was similar to original inhabitants. Their relation with Parsus does mean they were Iranians.

The Proto-Iranian broad heads belong, as already stated to three different groups. The Alpines (from their association with that European region) Dinaric (from the Dinaric Alps which stretch from Dalmatia to Croatia) and the Armenoids. Some scholars think that Tribes like Yadus, Turvasas, Anu, Druhyus and Purus belong to the Alpine group and in India they became ultimately mixed up with the Nordics.[20]

As stated by Sir REM Wheeler[21] and N.K. Bose that the bones and skulls of Alpine and Alpine mixed people have been found in cemetery 'G' and 'H' in Harappa. Here actually dead bodies had not been buried but thrown into pit and covered with soil. Because these skulls were lying in the form of heap at one place and most of them had signs of cut mark, so it is presumed that round headed had attacked the long headed all of a sudden. The long headed were indigenous Harappans and round headed Alpines. It is to be noted that cemetery H and G related to mature Harappan period, whereas Aryan invaders appeared at the end of this culture. It is clear from the above that Yadus were proto-Iranian Alpine people and were present in India before the arrival of nordic Aryans.

In some of the Puranas we get the following account— Yadavas are born from Yadus and Bhojas from Druhyus and Mlechhas from Anus[22]. As such Yadus of Rigveda are Yadavas of Puranas and later History (MBH-Adiparva sect 85. Verse 3533).

Movement of Yadus from Western Asia

According to a Rigvedic account (VI-20-12) Indra brought in safely over the sea (Samundra) the Turvasas and Yadus from a distant land.

According to vedic-index the Term Samundra does mean lower portion of Sindus. As such these tribes came through south west border or Bolon pass from west.[23]

Recently A.K. Sharma has claimed to have discovered the bones of true horse (Equus caballus Linn) at Surkotada (Circa 2100-1700 B.C.) and at Kalibangan also bones of true horse have been reported [24]. It shows arrival of a new foreign element using domestic horse in this period (See chapter IIP.41).

The only other people non-Indo Europeans known to have sacrificed horse are the Assyrians; for according to Aynard under the Assyrian empire white horses were 'some times' sacrificed to the gods.[25]

It can be proved from the above that not Aryans but non-Aryan Alpine Assyrian-Iranians horse using people have entered the Indus valley and beyond in Gujarat and Bana's valley before 2000 B.C.

It has already been shown in the foregone pages that according to Sankalia some of the pottery forms of B and R ware culture of Bana valley show certain similarities with similar forms in the sites of Iran and Western region. As already stated that R.P. Chanda[26] thinks that all the five tribes in question may have come from western Asia(Assyria) and were probably of the same physical type as the mitannis and the Hittites having dark or brown colour. That is why Krishna the black hero of Yadus and his associates have been mentioned in Puranas as Asuras (from Assyrians[27] Rigveda II-30-4, X-157-4, X- 53-4, X-138-3).

The association of the Yadus and Turvasas with Indra in the Rigveda shows evidently that they belong to a separate branch of the Aryans from the Avestic Iranians.... evidently the 'S' Speaker like the Yadus and the Turvasa were expelled by H. speaker and the former then migrated to Indus valley.[28]

E.J. Rapson[29] observes "We must seek the disturbing racial influence in some earlier tribal immigrations of which no other memorial now remains. The invaders probably belonged to the broad headed Alpine race, which inhabited the plateaus of western Asia (Anatolia, Armenia and Iran) and they would seem to have come into western India as the Dravidians also most probably came through Baluchistan before dessication had made the routes impassable for multitudes.'

The Harivamsa records a confused tradition how the Yadus came to settle in Anarta and Surastra, while branches of them were scattered in different directions far and near (Chanda IC 28- 29). Thus the presence of the broad headed race can be accounted for in the area. B.S. Guha observes that the broad heads drifted along the western littoral from southern Baluchistan through Sind, Kathiabar, Gujarat and Maharashtra.[30]

According to Sudhakar Chattopadhyaya, "Later on the Matsya occupied the Alwar, Jaipur, Bharatpur region. Their capital was Viratnagar, modern Vairat 40 miles north of Jaipur. It has already been shown that they were a branch of the Yadava tribe and hence broad heads... The Sursenas occupied the present Mathura district. The classical writers refer to Sourasanai with their cities Mathura and Kleisobara and the river Jomanes (Yamuna) flowing through it. Ptolemy refers to Madousa the city of the gods. They were a branch of the Yadavas (broad heads).[31]"

Above description of movement and settlement of Yadavas corresponds with the area where from earlier black and red ware culture has been traced out.

We can summarise the conclusions derived from the above discussion as follows:

(1) It is evident from archaeological and other evidences that B and R ware culture was earlier than later Harappa (O.C.P.) culture and sometimes parallel to OCP and PGW. Beginning period of B and R ware culture is earlier than 2000

B.C. where—as PGW culture flourished during 1500-500 B.C.

(2) Puranic and Rigvedic accounts support this view that this culture was related to Yadus or Yadavas.

(3) Yadus were S speaker Alpine round headed Iranians who were originally Assyrians.

(4) The above facts get the support of text books, linguistic and ethnological evidences also.

Horse[32] appeared in Indian continent before 2000 B.C. and also proofs of sacrificial rituals have been traced out at Kalibangan and Lothal at some later period, but these findings created a problem for historians because these evidences prove that Aryans had arrived in this period in the plain of Indus as well as in Rajasthan and Gujarat although accepted period of their arrival is at a later date.

But this anomaly is now automatically cleared when it is proved that much before arrival of Nordic Aryans the horse user Yadus etc. had already stepped in India and established themselves before 2000 B.C.

Ochre-coloured pottery

The first immediate successive culture of Harappa is Ochre Coloured pottery. This culture has been recognised as later Harappan culture, Bara ware, late Siswal ware and Red Ware of Harappan tradition. In this regard famous archaeologist and historian S.R. Rao[33] throws light as follows: "Most of the Harappan settlements in the Sutlej valley are later in date and the ceramic wares found there in lack the overall decoration of the mature Harappan phase in the Indus valley proper...... The echo of the gradual degeneration and devolution of the Harappa culture can be heard through the Sutlej and Ghaggar valleys as far east as Atranji-Khera in the Ganga-Yamuna doab. Here, as in Saurashtra, the Harappan stragglers had discarded certain characteristic Indus pottery types including the vase beaker, pedestalled goblet and perforated jar. The thin slip applied over the jars and dishes is found to have disappeared owing to waterlogging. This degenerated Harappan ware is found at a number of sites including Baragaon, Hastinapur and Ahichhatra besides Atranji-Khera below the Painted Grey Ware (PGW) levels, and has been labelled as Ochre-coloured pottery (OCP) in view of the fact that an ochreous wash comes off when the sherds are rubbed with a finger. A careful study of this ware in all its aspects has shown that it was not confined to the upper Ganga valley, but extended beyond into the Sutlej valley too. So far, as many as ninety sites of OCP have been located within an area of 300 kms to 450 kms from Bahadarabad (near Hardwar) in the north to Noh (near Bharatput) in the south and from Katpalon (near Jullundur) to Ahichchatra. The most significant evidence comes from Baragaon where pottery types such as the storage jar with clubbed rim, flat dish with beaded or beaked rim, dish-on—stand, and vase with globular body occur in the so-called, OCP in a typical Late Harappan context noted for its stone weights, and terrocotta cakes, Baragaon is therefore said to represent 'a derivative Harappan Culture mixed with elements drawn from such sources as Cemetery H and Jhukar cultures. Incised decoration is a Jhukar element present at Baragaon and Bara while the occurrence of flask types and the star and fish motifs at Ambakheri reminds us of Cemetery H culture. At most of the OCP sites the basic element in the cultural assemblage was Harappan, a fact confirmed by the excavation at Ambakheri also. Another interesting feature of these sites is that they are of short duration with 0.5 to 1.5 metre- thick occupation deposit. Undoubtedly they represent the temporary camp-sites or small village settlements made by the Harappan refugees while they were on the move from the Indus valley to the Ganga-Yamuna Doab. As they moved farther and farther eastwards from the Ghaggar valley, they discarded the chert blade, stone weight and even 'terracotta cakes', and adopted local ceramic traditions. This explains the introduction of vessels with loop handle Occasionally they resorted to painting as at Atranji-Khera where a few black-on-red painted sherds are encountered. In the light of the new evidence the term 'OCP' should be substituted by the term 'Late Harrappan' in describing the pre Painted Grey ware Culture of the Sutlej valley and Ganga-Yamuna Doab. The red ware by which it is distinguished was at times, fired to ochre-colour and the slip also disappeared owing to waterlogging. Even where it is not waterlogged the surface treatment of the Late Harappan ware is too Poor to stand weather action. From the excavations at Atranji-Khera we know that the users of this ware lived in small villages and their dwellings had thatched roofs. They knew the use of copper, which is attested to by the presence of a copper bangle at Baragaon and the terracotta crucibles with traces of copper at Atranji-Khera. At the later site storage jars and roughs were also used, and hearths were built with handmade bricks. The Late Harappa Culture-complex of the Sutlej and Gangetic valleys which subsequently lost its identity completely should be assigned to the period 1700-1500 B.C."

Above view gets the support of Vibha Tripathi's also. She[34] puts forward her views:

"The slowly accumulating evidence indicates that the upper Ganga plains were inhabited by the Ochre Coloured Pottery (OCP) using people immediately before the beginning of the Ist millennium B.C. This culture is now associated with the Copper- Hoards as demonstrated by Lal and Wahal (1971 PP 46-49) from the excavations at Saipai... The OCP associated with the Copper- Hoards immediately precedes PGW in the Doab. There is a possibility on some sites that there was an intervening culture represented by the B-and R ware. Such is the evidence produced by Noh and Atranji-khera. But generally PGW follows OCP culturally on most sites in the Doab and even outside the region in Rajasthan, Punjab, etc." So it is evidently proved that it is later Harappan culture.

Arrival of a new element in Shahi Tump

In South Baluchistan there seems no recorded evidence of burning in the later settlements, but it must be remembered that here little excavation has been done. At one site, however, a small tell at Shahi-tump, near Turbat, a cemetery had been made in the ruins of an abandoned village of the Kulli culture, which can also be equated with the presence of Harappa folk in the region by means of fragment of a clay toy cart of Characteristic type. So the Shahi-tump cemetery is later than the Kulli culture and some phase of Harappa. In the area excavated by Stein twelve inhumation burials were found, and an additional seven groups of grave-goods with no recognizable human remains.

According to Piggott[35], "The inhumations where identified all appeared to be of complete bodies lying on their backs or sides with the legs flexed. Grave-goods in most instances consisted of groups of pots, but copper or bronze tools and ornaments, stone beads and alabaster cups also occurred. Two burials, Stein's A And B, had richer grave-goods than the others. The skeleton discovered in burial A seems to have been that of a man buried crouched on his right side; in the grave there were more than fifty pottery bowls, cups and beakers, a copper stamp-seal, a stone pestle, a bead of ruby like stone, a stone blade and a group of twelve marine shells (Natica asellus) against the skull. Burial B (certainly male) had again a wealth of pottery vessels stacked in 'nests' of up to five bowls, a necklace of lapis, agate and onyx beads, a copper spearhead and a heavy, shaft-hole copper axe. The presence of animal bones, some charred, in certain of the vessels accompanying these and other burials suggests that funeral bakemeats had been deposited with the corpse.

The pottery from all the burials is consistent and characteristic. The ware is very good, hard and thin, varying from grey to pinkish and sometimes having a clear, yellowish-buff colour. The commonest form is a shallow bowl, usually with a rather sophisticated foot-ring, and allied forms are deeper bowls which may attain a considerable size, or be represented by small cups of similar profile...........The nearest parallels to this pottery come from the cemetery of Khurab near Bampur, 150 miles to the west over the Persian frontier, the date of which appears to approximate to that of Kulli and Harappa. At Khurab the vessels were very similar to pots from the Mehi cemetery (Belonging to the latest phase on that site, even possible dating from after its abandonment). As a whole, the Khurab and other cemeteries near Bampur are likely to belong to the centuries around, or probably just after, 2000 B.C.. But ultimately, the shahi-tump and similar wares are descended from the pottery of the Buff-ware group best represented in Susa I and other sites in Fars, and at greater remove, from that a Samarra.... Of the other objects from the cemetery, the copper spear and shaft-hole battle-axe from burial B indicate that this is the grave of a warrior. The spear-head, 9 inches long, has no mid-rib and recalls Harappa types, but the stoutly-made axe, with a shaft-hole 1.2 inches in diameter, seems to derive from Sumerian and Akkadian prototypes, while its nearest parallels, significantly enough, come from the graves of chieftains of barbarian tribes beyond the fringe of the oriental urban civilizations at Maikop and Tsarskaya in South Russia. In the loosely-knit structure of semi-nomadic barbarian society, spread over the steppe and along the frontiers of the more settled communities in Mesopotamia or Persia, such types, ultimately originated by Sumerian metal-smiths, would have a wide and often rapid distribution.

The copper stamp-seals from Shahi-tump, five of which were found, are even more explicit in their western relationships. They are all of one distinctive type, and it is significant that the only other example from Baluchistan comes from the final phase of the Sohr Damb at Nal, and is perhaps to be associated with its destruction by burning. They are all circular, with a simple pattern on their faces built up in compartments by projecting strips of metal, and seals of generally similar type have been found in Hissar II b and III b. in Anau III and at Susa, in a context which suggests a date about 2000 B.C. or a little later. And, as we shall see shortly, at least one similar seal is known from Sind where it is later than the Harappa period. The evidence is therefore strongly in favour of regarding these metal objects in the Shahi-tump cemetery as indicating a date after 2000 B.C. and associated with movements from the west.

Do these objects represent trade or migration ? To anticipate the further evidence discussed below, the latter seems to more likely, and since the pottery represents a local tradition, it seems likely too that migration was one of persons travelling light, bringing with them only the portable property of seals, spears, and battle-axes. Can these be warbands. enslaving or marrying the local women, who would make the pots, and is the Shahi-tump cemetery in some way related to the sacking of the Baluchistan villages? Skulls are slender evidence and deductions from their measurements must be used with caution, but the anatomist who examined the skull of the Shahi-tump man buried with the spear and axe reported that it showed traces of mixed origin and in certain respects tends to approximate to the Caspian or Nordic type of skull. Unfortunate though the second adjective is in a modern context, it does at least seem probable that the Shahi-tump cemetery was that of newcomers to the region, rather than that of the old population, with a few novel types of seals and weapons acquired by trade."

It seems that it was an earlier wave of Aryan invaders or a mixed race pushed by Aryans themselves from Iran towards south east.

The Jhukar Culture

This culture has been traced out on the remains of deserted town of Chanhu-daro. These remains prove that new-comer settled here after the town had been vacated and deserted as a result of some heavy blows of Indus floods. Mr Stuart Piggott[36] gives detail of the Jhukar sites:

"The site of Jhukar has given its name to this characteristic intrusive culture in Sind, which appears at all three sites stratified above and in the ruins of deserted Harappa settlements, but it is at Chanhu-daro that the largest body of evidence occurs. In the ensuing description, therefore, attention will be directed mainly to that site, with amplification where necessary from the other finds. The stratification at Chanhu-daro can be expressed as follows, following normal practice in these matters :

Chanhu-daro Ia	Harappa Culture
Chanhu-daro Ib	
Chanhu-daro Ic	
Chanhu-daro II	Jhukar Culture
Chanhu-daro III	Jhangar Culture

This settlement was one of squatters among the Harappa ruins of the IC phase, and while there seems to have been some rough rebuilding of house walls with brickbats robbed from other parts of the site, other huts seem to have been made of some perishable walling, such as matting, roughly set round a rectangular brick floor, which in one instance was some 17 by 8 feet overall. These brick floors might also be interpreted as stances for tents, and at all events they suggest rather squalid and not very permanent settlement on the site. Fireplaces are an interesting innovation, sometimes roughly built into doorways or niches of ruinous house walls or made of small rectangular or curved settings or bricks on edge.

The material culture represented among these primitive habitations includes abundant and characteristic pottery, stamp-seals, amulets; beads; metal tools and pins; bone awls and a pottery head-rest. It is altogether a curious and distinctive assemblage, contrasting strongly with that of the Harappa Culture it supplants, and yet not without clear contact with it. The pottery is a buff ware, with a varied repertoire of ornament painted on it in black and red. The forms include small-footed jars and bottles of types which have general parallels in Baluchistan, but the offering-stands and saucers with a looped pattern on the edge must derive either from Harappa or from the Kulli Culture in its Harappa-influenced phase. The range of ornament is quite varied, and employs geometric and stylized plant forms which in general have a strong resemblance to the trees on Kulli ware. Other simple geometric patterns accompanied with broad horizontal bands of plum red recall the Amri style; close-set chevrons in black and bright red can be paralleled precisely on a sherd from Zayak in south Baluchistan, where other patterns too can be matched the multiple loops and ball-and-stem motifs of Jhukar, for instance, occur at sar-Parom and Jai-damb. And one of the two animal representations at Chanhu-daro is really not unlike one from Periano-ghundai in North Baluchistan........... A most interesting contrast and comparison with Harappa is afforded by the Jhukar seals and allied amulets found abundantly in Chanhu-daro II. The seals are made of pottery faience, stone, and metal, and are totally different in their ornamental motifs from the well-known Harappa series; they also lack any inscriptions. But they are stamp-seals (usually circular, exceptionally square) within the great Western Asiatic family of such objects,and certain parallels can be noted. One of the faience seals has a pattern precisely comparable with that on the copper seals from the Shahi-tump cemetery; the treatment of animals on two others recalls Sumer and Elam rather than anything Indian; an interlaced coil pattern on another seal is best paralleled in Hittite contexts in Asia Minor, and this region produces many other less precise parallels for the types of seals and double sided amulets in Chanhu-daro II. Whatever may be said of the pottery, the Jhukar seals are foreign to India, and imply newcomers from the west, not unconnected with those who buried their dead at Shahi-tump. A copper shaft-hole axe provides another link with the Shahi-tump cemetery, and the series of pins offers a contrast to the Harappa customs of dress, which did not include garments held with this type of fastening. There are seven pins with the head rolled over in a manner know in Sumer since Early Dynastic times at least, but this type significantly makes its appearance first in the IIIb phase of Hissar. Of the other types of pins, it is difficult to say much except that one is vaguely reminiscent of type found in Sialk IV................. The picture given by the Jhukar material is not dissimilar from that of the less abundant relics from the Shahi tump cemetery. In both cultures the pottery appears to represent a more or less indigenous type in a late stage of evolution or divolution, but the smaller portable objects, such as seal, beads, metal implements, and weapons, and habits of dress implied by the use of pins, all suggest the arrival of new blood in the region............. At three sites in Sind where the Jhukar culture has been found, we can feel only that we are witnessing the arrival of barbarians, either as the destroyers of the Harappa civilization of following hard in the wake of the first raiders. It is their portable objects that are significant and which give the clue to their origins; here for once we can relegate pottery to a secondary place in estimating the content of these allied cultures."

Who were the Jhukar people, is still an unsolved question. But we find certain traces of these people in later period with the movement of later Harappans or the OCP using people, towards East and North-east, mixed up with others at Baragaon and Bara.[37]

Cemetery 'H' Culture

According to Stuart Piggott cemetery H culture is definitely a foreign element, He[38] observes:

"Unquestionable evidence of the arrival of new-comers at Harappa after the main phase of occupation of the city is, however, afforded by the large cemetery H' itself of two periods, both of which have been shown by the recent excavations to be later than the R 37 cemetery, of Harappa age. This later cemetery was situated in a natural hollow, which, at some time after the disuse of the cemetery, was filled up level with debris which contained a mass of Harappa potsherds, and it was into this debris, at a point some 120 yards to the north-east of cemetery R 37, that the graves of cemetery H were dug. It is characteristic of the conservatism of the Harappa culture that no significant change in the types of pottery could be detected between the layers underlying the R 37 cemetery, the cemetery itself, or either of the two debris-layers overlying it. But with cemetery H the change is abrupt and decisive.

The earlier burials in cemetery H (Stratum II) are extended inhumations, normally lying north-east and south-west, with the legs slightly flexed, and at an average depth of six feet beneath the present surface. About twenty-four such burials were found in the area excavated: some were claimed as dismembered or fractional, but it is not clear whether these were not sometimes the result of ancient disturbance. The burials are sometimes accompanied by the remains of food offerings-in one grave an entire dismembered goat had been laid with the dead man-and large numbers of pottery vessels were always present. In only two graves were any other objects found: a woman with a gold bangle on her wrist, and the three remaining teeth in the skull of another looped round with gold wire-for security or decoration as wheeler rather sardonically remarks.

The later burials in cemetery H (Stratum I) were only some two to three feet below the present surface, and consisted of true fractional burials in large pots, without any accompanying grave-goods or offerings. The bones in many instances showed that the bodies must have been exposed after death for some time before burial, when only the skull and a few long bones were selected for deposition in the cemetery. About 140 such burials were found, and a dozen of these were of babies, buried whole and crouched up in the funeral jars. These jars were closed at the mouth by lids of broken pots. The pottery from both strata of the cemetery is dissimilar from that of the Harappa Culture, and although certain characteristic forms are confined to the upper and lower strata respectively, this distinction is functional rather than cultural, and the technique of ware and painting is essentially the same in both phases of the cemetery. We can then regard it as a whole, and as the product of one culture despite the change in burial customs:."

Dr H.D. Sanskalia[39] gives a detailed description of cemetery 'H' pottery, technique of manufacturing and objects painted on them :

"First, a workmanship finer than that witnessed in the Harappan, and this in all the aspects of the potter's art : (a) preparation of the clay, (b) potting, and (c) baking. The Harappan was already known for its thick, well-baked pottery. In addition to all this, the cemetery H pottery is painted. And there are not just haphazard, unconnected patterns and designs, geometrical and natural paintings depicted on the large pots of Stratum I indeed relate a story, may it be mythological. But these are our earliest full-fledged paintings, important both from the point of art and the story they relate. Whether the paintings were done by the potter's wife (whose work this is usually believed to be) or the potter himself or some one else, the whole story must have been first sketched out and then carefully transferred on the broad shoulder of the pot. And the artist knew how much space each actor in the story was to be accorded, and accordingly drew it or him, small or large, full or in outline. The exact interpretation of the story or stories these paintings relate, will remain problematical until some more data, and in particular writing (which can be read), of the Cemetery H Culture is found. Vats very hesitatingly has drawn our attention to certain passages in the tenth mandala of the Rigveda. The eleborate painting on a burial pot was meant to portray what was believed to be a dead person. The hound on the left hand scene, may, like the two hounds of Yama, be the hounds of Hades and that the right hand scene, where the cattle are now decked with triden crest, depicts them in 'the Abode of Bliss' after they have passed through the intermediate Hades. The goat between the two scenes was a sort of 'path-finder' and a defied intermediary, an inference which may be drawn both from its large size and the crests on its horns (Vats 1940 P 238.)

However, Vats was careful enough to observe that though the paintings recalled some of the rites, rituals and beliefs contained in hymns 4-16, 18 of the tenth mandala of the Rigveda, still there was one vital difference. The Rigveda describes cremation rites, whereas these paintings are connected with post-exposure fractional burials.

At the moment one cannot press this parallelism between the two beliefs, any further, but they are pregnant with great possibilities, which are briefly discussed here

If in the future it can be proved that the Cemetery H belongs to Aryans or the people described in the Rigveda, then it might be said that they had some hand in destroying the Harappan civilization, for, as Wheeler has said, these are the only people who are known to succeed immediately the Harappans. Secondly, whether they can be accused of this great event or not, their pottery was finer than that of the Harappans, and thirdly, their potters could relate the story of the dead so well and in such a short space... However, certain forms are quite rare or unique, for instance, (Type F) squat food plates or dishes-on-stand and (Type G) vessels with elongated body and flaring neck and a ring base. In fact, the ring base, dishes-on-stand and such other distinctive features are almost absent in Indian pottery from the early Historic period and later (Gordon 1958:84). These characterize the prehistoric pottery of the Western Asia as already noted by Vats, and occur in the Harappan and the chalcolithic pottery of western and central India Thus, genetically the Cemetery H pottery is foreign-oriented. Even among its plain dishes, saucers and flat covers, we miss the familiar Indian thali (a flat dish with rounded corners and straight or inturned edge). These are absent even in the Harappan, but seem to appear for the first time at Navdatoli and later in the Painted Grey Ware. Likewise, vessels with conoid and ring base, and large lids with a handhold figure in the Harappan but are rare or absent later. The same may be said about its dishes- on-stand. All those from Harappans whether having a bowl or saucer-like upper part, have a long stem whereas those from the Cemetery H have a short stem with mouldings. Thus if any relation has to be inferred between the Cemetery H people and their way of life, it will have to be with the later Indian people and their lifeways.

And for this comparison there is no better repertory of Harappan pottery than the Cemetery R 37 at Harappa. Here one finds a bowl or dish-on-stand with mouldings, large lid with a prominent handhold saucers and dishes and slender vases or flasks with elongated concave-convex sides, and a small base, but not as narrow in the Cemetery H. However, these seem to be the direct ancestors of the Cemetery H flasks (All in Wheeler 1947. a).

In short, in the present state of our knowledge, the Cemetery H people culturally and racially do not seem to be far different from the Harappans.

It is impossible that the makers of this beautiful painted pottery should be confined to the area around Harappa. At least the whole of the Punjab, northern Rajasthan and probably Sind should have been the home of the Cemetery H people. Some of the points here raised for the first time were anticipated by Bridget and Raymond Allchin (1968 :149) but not taken to their logical conclusions, they seem to agree with Vats that the cemetery H culture was the final stage of the Harappans and continued with it, but that it must indicate the presence of foreign conquerors or immigrants. This might indicate a cultural fusion which may be represented by the cemetery H culture itself. They further thought that the pottery showed some affinities with ware from Tepe Giyan Strata II, III and Djamshidi II and Susa D all dated to Circa 1500 B.C."

In support of the above view of a foreign attack, S.S. Sarkar[40] puts evidences from Northern extension of cemetery- "Towards the fall of the 1930-31 (exploration work) season the cemetery was extended to the North. Here the first stratum yielded the same type of jar burials but the second stratum, which towards the southern side had been yielding complete burials, opened out a number of fractional burials only. The type of pottery accompanying the bones was however similar to that of the southern end. It appeared that at this period, there was some sort of disturbances which affected the burial customs of the second stratum people. The northern extension was found to cease at this end as the building walls were exposed and the total area of this extension was probably less than one fourth the area of the main cemetery. The people of the first stratum, as can be guessed from the skeletal remains and the burial jars, were much larger in number than that of the second stratum. The results of excavation at this end suggest, in the opinion of the above writer a period of clash between the two people and it appears that the people of the first stratum dominated over the people of the second stratum. The latter seem to have left their last trace at this corner of the cemetery and they had probably, to leave, the cemetery for the people of the first stratum here. In this extension the number of funerary pottery are fewer than those found in the main cemetery. Remains of only five individuals have been identified from the skeletal remains and they were very meagrely represented by the bones. They appear to be the remnants of the individuals killed in their struggle with first stratum people although the fractional nature of the burials is very much striking. It appears rather improbable that the first stratum people prevailed upon those of the second stratum, being their conquerors, to adopt the fractional burial. It may be that these individuals were not so carefully buried as the others in the main cemetery, because if they were really engaged in a warfare they could hardly pay any attention to the killed."

It is evident from the above details that the people of the first stratum used to expose the dead bodies to be eaten up by Vulture before burial and whereas the early people used to bury the whole body. As such the tradition of disposal of dead bodies of both was different from each other. The people of second stratum who seem to be Harappan of later age did not use to cremate their deads. But Sir John Marshall is of the opinion that there was also tradition of cremation in the Indus valley in bronze age. There are very few examples of (fractional) burials after partial burning of dead bodies. There are sufficient examples of complete burials of body in Harappa which was most probably a general tradition in Indus valley. Proto-Australoids and mediterraneans type are very few in number in these cemeteries whereas Alpines and mixed Alpines are abundant (see chapter II). Cemetery H culture has also been found out in Sanghol, Rupar, Bara, Baragaon, Ambakheri and Kotla Nihang etc.

Movement of Indo-Aryans from West; Grey ware Culture

It is quite necessary to trace back the path of movements of Indo Aryans in the west to link with their entrance in to India in respect of archaeological evidences and chronology. Bridget and Raymond Allchin[41] drew a picture of presence and movement of Indo-Europeans in the South of Russia as follows," Interest was early centred upon in identifying the original homeland of the speakers of the Indo-European languages and various views were put forward. Since 1871 there has been general acceptance that this early homeland must have been somewhere on the steppes of Eurasia, from the frontiers of China in the east to those of Western Europe in the west, and we must conceive of already widely dispersed Indo-European speaking tribes inhabiting these regions, and gradually separating from one another. It is generally agreed that the steppes were also the homeland of the wild ancestors of the horse, and that this animal was exploited and then domesticated by the human population, who learned both to ride and to harness the horse for draught purposes. Gimbutas has recently suggested that archaeological traces of these people may be found in the Early, Middle and Late stages of what she has named the 'Kurgan culture' (after the Characteristic Kurgan or barrow type of graves), which can be identified during the late fourth and third millennia as occupying the steppes to the west of the Urals. Their way of life was dominated by stock breeding, with horses outnumbering cattle. They practised metallurgy, having a characteristic range of copper and bronze tools and weapons. They or their neighbours seem to have invented the spoked wheel and the horse drawn chariot. Recent Soviet archaeological research supports the earlier view that the domestication of the horse may have taken place first in the South Russian steppes before the end of the fourth millennium and spread thence eastwards into the Kazakh steppes around the end of the third millennium. These eastward moving tribes were probably the ancestral speakers of the Indo-Iranian languages, and may be identified with the archaeological timber grave-Andronovo culture. In the east they must have come in contact with an earlier population. Thus we may expect the Indo-Iranian branch of the Indo-European family to have become separated from the other branches at the latest, during the third millennium, and, further, before the end of the millennium we may expect the Indo—Aryan and Iranian tribes to have become separated from each other. Both these developments may well have taken place considerably earlier.

The next development is still not clearly understood but it would appear that some where around 2000 B.C., or perhaps a century or so earlier, or later, some of the tribes moved southwards into the lands long occupied by agricultural communities. The causes of this movement, as indeed of the similar movements of the Mongols and other Central Asian peoples in later times, are not altogether clear increasing desiccation of Central Asia has often been invoked, but the evidence for major climatic change at this time has not been substantiated, although there are indications of minor fluctuations of climate, both regional and general."

Archaeological evidences

The foregone views are not sufficient to lead us to any definite conclusion For this purpose, we have to take into consideration archaeological evidences that have been traced out so far in the aforesaid region.

Shashi Asthana [42] gives an account of archaeological evidences to prove the presence and movement of Indo-European races in South Russian steppe region and Iran-" A number of plain Grey Wares in Iran, central Asia and north west India which are also said to have been associated with the upheaval of a new people, the Aryans and their movement into India but none of them could be definitely associated with the known, contemporary Indian ceramics. At Tepe Hissar (Schmidt, Excavations at Tepe Hissar,Damgham), Tepe Giyan (Contenau and Ghirshman Fouilles du Tepe Giyan pres de Nehavend 1391 et 1932) and Shah Tepe (Arne, Excavations at Shah Tepe, Iran) a plain, Burnished Grey or Black ware suddenly appears in an otherwise continuing red or Grey Painted pottery tradition. Although Allchin (The Birth of Indian civilization, Penguin books, London, 1968) feels that the Indian neolithic-chalcolithic Burnished Grey ware was associated with this ware, particularly one from Shah Tepe, yet, as has been already indicated, not all scholars agree with him. At Sialk also in cemeteries A and B a plain GW occurs (Ghirshman Fouilles du Tepe Sialk), Another GW occurs at Anau (Pumpley, Explorations in Turkestan, Prehistoric Civilization of Anau I & II) and other places in south Turkmenia, USSR, but all of them neither form a single tradition nor their traditions entered into the Indo-Gangetic plains. Recent discovery of a Plain Grey and plain Red Ware in Gandhara graves (Dani, Timargarha and Gandhara Grave culture: A.P.Vol.III) also does not help us much since they have definite parallels at Hissar and other places in northern Iran and central Asia, they have absolutely no paralleles in the Indian mainland. All that the occurrence of these Plain Grey ware shows is that there was wide-spread intrusion of peoples in sites located in the area from northern Iran to the western bank of the Indus in the Swat Valley region and many of them used a variety of Plain Grey Wares". It can be concluded from the above evidences that GW using Aryans moved from Hissar and reached Gandhara region during this age.

Dates of their movemnt

To reach a definite conclusion it is also necessary to take into consideration dates of their movement from far north east Iran to the south east ward, and the north region of Indus system, the border land of Swat Valley.

G.S.Ghurye[43] throws light on the subject in these words:-

"European scholars have unearthed a Burnished Grey Pottery at Tureng

Tepe, in strata, which by C-14 dating must be about 3000 B.C. would place the presence of Indo-European in the north-eastern part of Iran from Tepe Hissar, described as "the north-eastern entrance to Iran, north and east to Tureng Tepe and the Iranian boundary, "about the last centuries of the fourth millennium B.C. (Archaeology 1969 PP 10-17). B. Morton Smith, only a year earlier, had stated that PGW which is associated, according to him, with iron, had come on the Iranian plateau with the Medes in the thirteenth century B.C. (Archaeology 1968 P 159). According to Deshayes, "F. Guyler young Jr. has brilliantly proved that the ware of Khorvin and the related ware from the Zagros district must be ascribed to the Medes who probably settled in north-west Iran as early as the middle of the second millennium B.C.' and that Burnished G.W. so characteristic of Indo-Europeans, appeared "at the beginning of the Early Bronze Age in all the northern areas of the Near East".The presence of burnished Grey Ware at Tureng Tepe, therefore, bespeaks the presence of Indo-Europeans there and on the plains of Gorgan in which Tureng Tepe lies. Deshayes has further observed that the GW is "practically confined to the plains of Gorgan with the exception of an advance post at Tepe Hissar on the northern edge of the Iranian plateau". As the strata can confidently be dated about 3000 B.C., the coming of the Indo-Europeans in Iran can reasonably be ascribed to an invasion or immigration from a region north-east of Iran or north of the north-eastern boundary of Iran and that too almost from the time before 3000 B.C.... Dr Deshayes and Dr Sylvia Matheson have pointed out that the Turkmenian steppe had begun to be deserted probably about 2000 B.C. Tureng Tepe retaining some of its inhabitants till about 1700 B.C. or 1600 B.C. Dr Matheson (Persia; An Archaeological Guide PP 68-98, 1972) more positively has further stated that by the latter date the thinned local population no doubt already dominated by Iranian invaders from the north, were producing new shapes in wheel-thrown grey pottery". She further observes on the significance of the Grey-ware; "Recent studies of this ware have been connected with the movements of the Iranians who uptil now were believed to have entered Iran through the north-west Caucasian passes. Now it is thought that the earliest of the new comers had already settled in the west as early as the second half of the second millennium, and from the fact that they appear to have adopted north-eastern pottery forms, most of them at least can be presumed to have reached the plateau from this (north east) direction". So it is confirmed that these people began to move from Tepe Hissar and Tureng Tepe between 2000 BC— 1600 BC.

The Swat Valley Culture or Gandhara Grave Culture in Pakistan

We now turn to the northern valleys of the Indus system where a local Neolithic culture had long been established. There is surprisingly little evidence of any trade contacts or cultural influence from the Indus plains reaching this area during the Mature Harappan period although in the Ghaligai cave a brief Early Indus influence seems to have been in evidence. Allchin and Bridget[4] gives detail of findings of Gandhara graves. "At a certain date, as yet not definitely established, an interesting development takes place, not only in Swat but in many neighbouring valleys Dir, Chitral and the Indus itself. This is the appearance of a large number of cemeteries having a distinctive range of grave goods and evidently remaining in use over many centuries. These are the cemeteries of the so-called "Gandhara Grave culture". They first became known from the work of the Italian mission in Pakistan, and their work has now been augmented by excavations of the Peshawar University Department of Archaeology. Considerable material about the graves has been published, but there is still a need for synthesis as the different accounts appear to be mutually inconsistent on some matters. In these circumstances we must accept that any attempt to classify the graves or their contents must be tentative. The principal sites so far published are Katelai I. Loebanr I and Timargarha, all in Swat.

The broad chronology of the graves, both in terms of cross-dating parallels with sites outside India and Pakistan, and in terms of the dozen or more radiocarbon dates so far published, appears to cover a wide spread. Katelai I produced five samples dated between 1500 and 200 B.C., from Timargarha two samples give dates of 1710 and 1020 B.C., while from Barama two samples were dated to 800 and 430 B.C.

The graves consist for the most part of an oblong pit sometimes with dry stone walling and generally with stone slabs to form a roof. The pit is often dug in the floor of an upper larger pit. which was filled with soil and charcoal after the burial and often surrounded by a rough stone circle. Children's remains were sometimes placed inside a smaller cist with stone slabs for walls. The great majority contain inhumations with one or two skeletons. The body was laid on its side with legs drawn up and arms raised and bent. A minority of the graves contained cremated ashes, sometimes gathered in pottery cist or box-urn with flat lid, or large urn with a face decoration consisting of applique and cut-out features. Some burials were of collected bones. The grave goods included large quantities of distinctive plain pottery, either buff-red or grey, and of a distinctive range of forms. These included tall champagne goblets, pedestal cups, beakers with flared mouths, bottles with tall narrow necks occasional jugs with raised lips spouted pots some with small handles and one curious triple pot on three stem rising from a base. There are also some times terracotta figurines of distinctive type, generally flat tablets with rough human form, applique breasts and highly stylized heads, some with incised necklaces and eyes. Metal objects include those of copper or bronze, most commonly pins with decorated tops, and much more rarely objects of iron. Of special interest was the discovery of two horse burials in separate graves, presumably alongside their masters, and a bronze model of a horse. all three from Katelai. Another important find was an iron ckeek-piece of a snaffle bit from Timargarha. The obvious comparisons for all these classes of objects and for the graves themselves are not to be found in India or Pakistan, but in Iran and the Caucasus. Many parallels can be found for the pottery, in Tepe Hissar III. Hasanlu IV. Shah Tepe. Marlik, Sialk Cemeteries A and B, and the cemeteries of

Lenkoran and Talish. The copper or bronze pins may also find their nearest parallels in these sites. Stacul has shown that the graves may be divided into four groups of which only the last, associated with the thin-sided grey and red ware, produced iron tools. Thus there seems good reason to think that a fair proportion of the graves predate and arrival of iron in this area.

As in the western region, here too there have been some unassociated finds of metal objects. In 1958 Professor Jettmar photographed the residue of a large hoard of bronze objects discovered shortly before at a spot far up the Indus valley, high in the Gilgit Karakoram. This included several good specimens of trunnion axes of a similar type, along with shaft-hole axes narrow necks. This hoard also suggests Iranian contacts during the second half of the millennium. It may be argued-however improbably-that the stray items of copper and bronze found in these western border regions indicate trade contacts rather than movements of peoples.

A somewhat perplexing surface find is a golden stag from the Hazara district of the Punjab, now in the Peshawar museum. This piece has a distinctly Caucasian appearance and may be compared with many examples, made in various metals from such sites in the south-west Caspian area as Talish, Samthavro and Lenkoran, and from Marlik, where they date from B.C. 1450-1200 B.C. The age of this piece is open to debate. M. Bussagli has assigned it to the Animal style of the Scytho-Sarmatian period, and dates it according to the last centuries B.C. (La Civilta dell'Oriente, 4 PP. 137-8, and P I-191)" It is crystal clear from the above detail that G.W. using Indo-Aryans have reached Swat valley between 1700 B.C.—1500B.C.

The Grey Ware Culture in Indian Territory

Grey ware culture have been dug out on some of the later Harappan (OCP) sites in north east of the Indus system and beyond in Saraswati and Ganga Yamuna valley. We have already denoted in previous pages that this culture is related to the Indo-Aryan speaking people hence we give here a detailed description of it.

The Grey Ware pottery

The Grey ware is so close to PGW in fabric, form etc. that if the painting is removed from the later the two would be indistinguishable. Vibha Tripathi[45] gives a detail of G. W. pottery". The fabric of Grey ware is generally very fine. Though there are a few shreds of medium to coarse fabric also. The clay is free from impurities and is very well fired, which gives a uniformly grey surface to the ware. Generally the section is very thin and the colour of the pots varies from light to steel grey.

Prevalent forms in GW are, like PGW bowls and dishes, Lal (1954-55, P 44) while describing the GW points to its close similarity with PGW. But besides the bowl and dish shapes of PGW type, other shapes like Vases and basins some of them decorated with stamped and incised potteries like Red ware of this period have been found to occur frequently in GW.

Stratigraphically a grey coloured pottery has occurred since the earliest protohistoric period. It occurs in Harappan and post-Harappan contexts and then with PGW and also continues in the post-PGW context (NBP ware phase). However, the shapes and the fabric are different in each period of its occurrence. During the succeeding phase (NBP ware) the GW still represents the shapes of dishes bowls etc. but the fabric has deteriorated.

The distribution of the GW is more extensive than the plain GW. At sites specially in the eastern region, where PGW either occurs in a very small number (Vesali, Kosambi etc.) or is represented by its associated wares alone (Rajghat, Gulrihva Ghat, Prahladpur etc.) plain GW occurs in a fair quantity. During this period the shape, texture etc. of GW (at above sites) is close to PGW.

Common shapes

Bowls of the following types are seen in this fabric. A bowl with a vertical internally sharpened rim, straight sides and a convex base is seen at Hastinapur. It has a fine fabric and is treated with a smooth slip, both externally and internally. The shape is exactly like the PGW. Such bowls are seen at other sites like Allahpur, Chak and Sardargarh. A deep bowl with a slightly inturened externally clubbed rim in fine fabric is noted at Hastinapur. A bowl with an oblique clubbed rim and slightly convex sides in GW is seen at Allahpur, Rupar Alamgirpur and Sardargarh........ Dish is another important shape in the plain GW. Some of them have very fine fabric-identical to PGW type. The types of dishes demonstrated at Hastinapur are represented at most of the sites. A dish with a vertical featureless rim, straight sides and a Carination at the base is seen at Hastinapur......... Another variety has got slightly tapering sides and a prominently sagger base."

Manda

Now we look forward for G.W. Sites from N.West direction to east. The first site in west yet excavated in India is Manda. This ancient site lies on the right bank of the river Chenab, a tributory of the Indus, on the foothills of Pirpanjal Ranges. It is situated at a distance of 28 K.M. north west of Jammu. Its excavation work was done under direction of J.P. Joshi, who[46] gives a detailed account of archaeological findings:

"**I-A sub period.** This sub-period is marked by the arrival of Harappans represented by a deposit of 1 to 1.4 metres. It further consists of two different ceramic tradition (1) Pre- Harappan Red Ware and (2) Harappan Red Ware.

(1) Pre Harappan pottery is Red Ware with coarse fine and medium fabrics. This is reminiscent of the predefence phase at Harappa and Kalibanga I. A rusticated ware (mostly jar fragments) is available which is akin to Kalibanga I Fabric B. A ware deeply grooved on the inner surface, possibly in the form of basins or troughs. (2) Above the pre Harappan pottery lies the deposit of Harappan

Red Ware, which consists of medium to fine fabric with painted, unpainted and incised decoration. The shapes are represented by bowls, dishes-on-stand, cup with footed base, goblets, beakers, basins and jars. The design repertoire consists of only horizontal bands in black pigment.

I- B sub period: It is a deposit of 1.6 to 1.7 metres consisting of two layers. There are four distinct ceramic traditions in this assemblage (1) Harappan Red Ware, (2) Gray Ware (3) a small quantity of thick Burnished Gray ware and (4) Black slipped ware.

Harappan Red ware is represented by jars, dishes and dishes-on-stand. The GW is represented by bowls and dishes. Straight sided bowls also occur in this ware. Iron has not been found in this sub-period... An overall estimation of the ceramics suggests that the GW generally associated with PGW is seven to 19 per cent.Thus there is an interlocking of these two ceramic traditions (Joshi, 1978; Madhubala, 1975), evidently showing the overlap of the two cultures at this site.

Period II and III

The next period designated period II has a deposit of 1.7 to 2 metres, closely following period II is period III with Kushan pottery both incised and plain. This site remained most probably deserted up to 18th and 19th century when the fort and Sheesh Mehal were built by Raja Gulab Singh.

In Sequel

(1) It is significant that this northern most site of the Harappan civilization in India has both pre-Harappan and Harappan remains together in period IA. Similar position has been noted in Kalibangan.

(2) At Bhagwanpura and Dadheri the late Harappan sub-period is immediately followed by an overlap sub-period with late Harappan Red Ware, Grey Ware and the PGW. But in sub period IB at Manda the mature Harappan period is immediately followed by the overlap of late Harappan ware and GW. By way of corrolation it appears that the earlier two layers of sub period IB of Bhagwanpura are equivalent to sub period IB at Manda. At both places Black slipped ware is also available.

(3) The Bara and cemetery H elements which are available at Bhagwanpura and Dadheri are absent in sub-period IB of Manda.

(4) Another interesting feature which has come to light in period IB Manda is the presence of two traditions of Gray ware (a) Gray ware (b) Burnished thick Gray ware................. These wares are associated with Late Harappan pottery but without goblets, beakers and terracotta cakes. At this point the evidence from Bhagwanpura IB is significant. Here a plain GW preceds by two layers the PGW which is then associated with Late Harappan Ware. At Bhagwanpura the Burnished Thick GW is not present.

Thus, it appears that the Late Harappans came into contact with a Gray ware using people in the first instance and then with PGW people. The time lag is not much but it is meaningful."

CHRONOLOGY

Joshi further gives detail of chronology of habitation zone,"No material for absolute dating is available at Manda; however, on the basis of Pre-Harappan wares the beginning of subperiod IA can be dated to slightly earlier than about 2350 B.C. and the end of ca. 1750 B.C. The spiral-headed pin suggests a date of ca. 2100 B.C. for the middle levels of sub period 1A. The beginning of subperiod IB is then a little earlier than the middle of the second millennium B.C.. Manda subperiod IB anticipates an overlap of Gray ware with Late Harappan wares. This compares well with Bhagwanpura-IB (earlier levels) where only Gray ware has been found. As seen in table of TL dates (P-87) from Bhagwanpura may support the view.

On the basis of the finds at Manda Subperiod IB and Bhagwanpura Subperiod IB (earlier levels) it can be concluded that there was a phase of Plain Gray ware anterior to Painted Gray Ware (Thapar in press). Both these subperiods have been found to interlock, individually or together with the Late Harappan in Jammu, Punjab and Haryana. Since this picture is emerging in a region which is geographically well known in the Vedic period it appears that one may be nearer to an identification of the culture with one of the waves of the Indo Aryans. This is confirmed by both geography and Chronology (i.e. the middle of the second millennium B.C.)

B.B. Lal has dealt in great detail with the problem of the Indo-Aryan movement. One would like to agree with him when he says, "The full picture has yet to emerge but hopefully will emerge" (Lal in press)."

Further J.P.Joshi[47] writes about Three minor sites, Dadheri, Nagar & Katpalon," The excavations at Dadheri District Ludhiana, Punjab have yielded a threefold sequence in cultural deposit of six metres. In Subperiod IA the Late Harappans built a settlement of huts and mud-walled houses over solid rammed mud platforms. Evidence of a mud wall running east-west in an oblique fashion with a length of 1.7 metres and a width of 0.59 metres has been found. Post holes suggest that people were also living in huts. Evidence of a flood during this period was also recorded. The Late Harappan is represented by a sturdy red ware, both painted on plain. The shapes include jars, dishes-on-stand etc. The design repertoire consists of horizontal bands, criss cross patterns filled in at the arches, hatched iozenges, etc. A large jar with a painted and incised design is one of the most fascinating finds from this level. A considerable amount of incised pottery with a Pre-Harappan lineage has also been found.

Small finds include faience bangles, terracotta wheels, beads and a painted bull. Copper objects and beads of carnelian and lapis lazuli were also present

The pottery obtained from Subperiod IB included Painted Gray Ware, Gray

Ware, Black Slipped Ware, an associated Red Ware and Late Harappan Ware. The percentage of Black Slipped Ware is much more than that found at Bhagwanpura in a similar context.

The antiquities include faience bangles, beads of semiprecious stone, terracotta wheels and a copper ring. No iron has been found.

In Subperiod IB the excavations have revealed evidence for interesting house types. At first the people were living in semicircular huts as attested by the discovery of post holes. Three oval structures of burnt earth, perhaps of religious character also came from this phase. These structures probably had a domed roof. In the next stage the houses were built with mud walls...........The site was deserted for a long time after Sub-period IB. However, a few sherds of Kushan affinity have been found but no regular habitation as such could be discerned by the present excavation in Period II. The latest Period III represents medieval times.

KATPALON AND NAGAR

Excavations at Katpalon District Jullundur, Punjab have brought to light a sequence of three cultures in a deposit of six metres. In Period I, PGW has been found interlocked with the Late Harappan Culture. An oval structure in a dilapidated condition was also found in this period. Other finds include copper and antimony rods, terracotta beads and wheels. Late Harappan Ware, Painted Gray Ware and Gray Ware were also there. The succeeding periods, after a break, are Kushan and medieval.

At Nagar Jullundur district, Punjab has a cultural deposit of five metres. A sequence of three periods has been brought to light. Period I yielded Late Harappan Ware, Painted Grey Ware and Grey Ware. Two oval structures and post holes indicate round and semi circular huts. Otherfinds include copper objects; bone styli; terracotta animal figurines and ear ornaments in addition to bangles and beads.

Period II is the early historic and Period III belongs to medieval times."

BHAGWANPURA

Excavation work of this site was done under direction of J.P. Joshi[48]. He gives a detailed report of explored site. "The site at Bhagwanpura District Kurukshetra, Haryana is situated on the right bank of River Saraswati. Excavations at this site, in a cultural deposit of 2.7 metres revealed Late Harappan Culture in Subperiod IA. In Subperiod IB the Late Harappan was found interlocked with the Painted Gray Ware Culture.

SUBPERIOD IA

The occupation of Late Harappans in this subperiod was built over raised mud platforms, evidently to protect the habitation from the floods of the Sarasvati. One such mud platform, measuring 4.25 by 10 metres, was exposed in one of the trenches. This platform was provided with a landing step. After an accumulation of 70 to 80 centimetres of deposit the occupation was damaged by a gigantic flood; however, the Late Harappans continued to live at the site.

An analysis of pottery from this Subperiod indicate; that : (1) there is a Red Ware both plain and painted, (2) an Ochre colour Ware is present but comes mostly from the flood effected trenches, (3) there is an incised Ware with a variety of designs, some of Pre-Harapan lineage, (4) pottery of Bara type is present, (5) Thick Gray Ware, generally associated with Harappan and Late Harappan assemblages is present, and (6) there are some pottery shapes of Cemetery H. The Shapes include dish-on-stand, bowls, dishes, jars with everted rims, flanged neck basins, drooping dishes and button based goblets and cups. Besides the usual geometric and vegetal designs, pipal and banana leaves are also painted on pots. The entire pottery corpus appears to be an amalgam of various ceramic traditions, for example, one can compare the shapes with Bara, Bahadarabad, Atranjikhera, Hulas, Siswal IIB, Daulatpur and Raja Karan-ka-Qila.

The antiquities of this subperiod include a terracotta bull with long horns and pinched up hump, a gray to black terracotta consisting of the leg portion of a deity or a human figure, and two more anthromorphic figurines, wheels with hubs, bangles, copper rods and pins, faience beads and bangles, beads of semiprecious stone and bone pins etc.

SUBPERIOD IB

Though no stratigraphic break could be discerned, this subperiod is marked by the continued occupation by the Late Harappans and the arrival of Plain Gray Ware using people followed by the PGW using folks. After an accumulation of this overlap culture, some of the habitation was washed away by a flood. This calamity did not prevent both the Late Harappans and the PGW using folks from continuing to live at the site. However, it has been noted that the Late Harappans gradually diminished; but they did not vanish till the end. This may be due to the superiority of the PGW people who slowly entrenched themselves at the site in the late levels of Subperiod IB. During this period of overlap three phases of structural activity could be identified.

At first the people were living in round or semi-circular thatched huts. Inside one of the huts we found four saddle querns and different types of pestles on the floor. This may indicate that the house belonged to a corn grinder.

An oval structure of highly burnt earth with a northeast to southwest orientation is also associated with this phase. The structure measures 2.75 by 1.25 metres and has a 10 to 50 centimetre thick wall and inner depth of 50 centimetres. A large number of pieces of burnt earth, a few potsherds in a sturdy Red Ware and some dome-shaped terracottas, perhaps belonging to the collapsed roof of the structure, were found inside the structure.

In the second structural phase a complete walled house complex with a thick (0.7 to one meter) wall was found. This appears to be a well planned house with 13 rooms. There is a corridor between two sets of rooms and a courtyard on the eastern side. Ths size of the rooms varies from 1.6 by 106 metres to 3.35 by 4.2 metres. Copper objects, faience bangles and beads, terracotta ghatta-shaped beads, bone styli-terracotta figures. PGW plain Grey Ware vessels and Late Harappan pottery were found in this building. A statistical analysis of the pottery revealed that two to five per cent of the total corpus was Late Harappan in the rooms of the houses. This shows some social contact between the two groups of people. Two oval shaped structures, size : (1) 1.8 by 0.85 metres, (2) 1.6 by 0.92 metres, are also associated with this phase........ Besides the continuance of Late Harappan pottery and antiquities, Subperiod IB yielded Plain Gray Ware in the early levels followed by PGW. PGW is associated with a Red Ware and a limited quantity of a Black Slipped Ware. A PGW with designs in thick lines is also availbale from the early and middle levels of the subperiod. The design repertoire is very rich in the PGW tradition. It includes dots, slashes, horizontal bands, wavy lines, concentric circles, intersecting circles, net designs, honeycomb design, fish scales, lotuses etc. A unique maltese cross and a set of intersecting circles forming a six-or four-petaled flower have come from Bhagwanpura IB. Gray Ware shapes are : bowls, dishes and straight-sided bowls and basins. It has been noticed for the first time that a few Late Harappan shapes (e.g. bowls, basins, dishes, jars and dish-on-stand) were copied in the Gray Ware.

Other important finds of this subperiod include terracotta anthropomorphic figures with parallels to objects found in the Gandhara Grave Culture - I in Pakistan. There is a one-wheeled anthropomorphic figure, wheeled incised terracotta rams, birds, dogs, wheels with or without hubs, hopscotches, decorated dishes, ear ornaments, dabbers, violin-shaped Gray Ware mother goddess used as pendants, bone and ivory needles, pins and styli and one sytlus with black pigment on its tip. Some of the bone pins have a very fine polish. Glass bangles in sea blue, white and black are the most impressive finds. Copper bangles, rods, and some indeterminate pieces have also been found. A seal with incised graffiti of Harappan lineage is also available. A large number of terracotta ghata-shaped beads, incised biconical beads, decorated faience beads and semiprecious stones deserve special mention. A bull-shaped carnelian pendant, although found on the surface, is most exquisit. Remains of Equus Cabalus Linn is another important discovery."

TL DATES FROM BHAGWANPURA

Dr.K.S. Nambi[49], Dr.R. Sasidharna and Dr. S.D. Soman of the Health Physics Division, Bhaba Atomic Research Centre, Bombay, kindly undertook the task of TL dating material from Bhagwanpura (Nambi, Sasidharan and Soman 1979). To aid comparative study and build up hypotheses, extracts from the report are reproduced below:"The Red Ware (RW) mentioned in the report is the Late

Harappan Red Ware and Gray Ware (GW) also includes Painted Gray Ware.

TL AGES OF BHAGWANPURA POTTERIES

Among the 18 samples excavated, GW occur only in the first six layers (up to a depth of about 1.3 m); the red wares are seen less frequently in these layers, but occur exclusively in all layers beyond 1.3 m depth. Below figures show the TL ages obtained for the GW and red wares collected from differenct layers. Bhagwanpura being an ancient site in the domain of the famous Indus Valley Civilization, one is reminded of the overlap phase between the late Harappan and PGW cultures that is datable to circa 1500 B.C. to 1000 B.C. (ASI, 1978) which is quite close to the TL ages mentioned above."

Table of TL dates (ages estimated) for the Bhagwanpura potteries

Sample code	Depth of find (meters)	TL age year BP* (Std error, predicted accuracy)
BPR -1	0.3	3830 (± , ± 13%)
-2	0.8	311 (± , ± 15%)
-3	0.8	2710 (± , ± 15%)
-4	0.55	4038 (± 4% , ± 13%)
-5	0.55	3814 (± , ± 14%)
-6	0.55	2617 (± 1% , ± 16%)
-7	0.55	1344 (± , ± 13%)
-8	0.9	1235 (± , ± 15%)
-9	1.1	2649 (± , ± 15%)
-10	1.15	2742 (± , ± 16%)
-11	1.18	2434 (± , ± 17%)
-12	1.3	4868 (± , ± 12%)
-13	1.4	3241 (± 9% , ± 13%)
-14	1.6	3532 (± 4% , ± 12%)
-15	2.1	4141 (± 12% , ± 15%)
-16	2.25	5460 (± , ± 15%)
-17	2.4	4696 (± 3% , ± 17%)
-18	2.45	3024 (± , ± 15%)

*Date of measurement : 1978 After J.P.Joshi. Chart I

It has already been said that OCP is a later Harappan culutre. This culture is followed by G.W. at Manda and Bhagwanpura and at Dadheri, Katpalon and Nagar intermixed with P.G.W. This is also being followed by P.G.W. culture at sites like Sanghol, Alamgirpur and Allahpur and with a small gap at Ropar and Hastinapur. It shows that Harappans came in contact with new comer G.W. and PGW using people at these sites. Here the word contact can be termed as attack of new comers on the Harappans. Here the most important is the finding of G.W. on mature Harappan without break of sequence at Manda. This is to be noted that change of mature Harappan in to late Harappan indicates degeneration of Harappan culture and this degeneration apparently must have occurred due to invasion and destrcution by new comers.

As already proved these Grey Ware using new comer invaders were Indo-Aryans. This fact is supported by Rigvedic accounts too given below.

Geographical horizons in Rigveda

Geographical horizons as given in the Rigveda are the northern zone of Harappan culture a region north of Mohenjo-daro, Harappa city and other small sites in the north west and east. A detail of the above is given by Bridget and Raymond Allchin[50] as follows : "In the west it is bounded by the western tributaries of the Indus, the Gomati (modern Gomal), the Krumu (modern Kurram) and the Kubha (modern Kabul) rivers. Other rivers are mentioned even to the north of the Kabul, notably Suvastu, the modern Swat. This latter signifies fair dwellings and may therefore indicate Aryan settlements in this beautiful valley. The centre of Rigvedic geography is the Punjab. The rivers most often referred to are the Indus itself, the Sarasvati and the Drishadvati and the five streams which collectively gave their name to the Punjab (Punjab, five waters), the Sutudri (Sutlej), Vipas (Beas), Parushni (Ravi), Asikni (Chenab), and Vitasta (Jhelum). The eastern horizons are the Jamuna river and the Ganga (Ganges) which is mentioned only in one of the latest hymns. These must have been the confines within which the first generations of Indo-Aryans setteld. It is the sacred heartland remembered later as Brahmavarta or Brahmarsidesa."

As already shown through archaeological evidences that the western region was occupied by the G.W. using people and eastern region was in the occupation of PGW using people .

Description of Aryan invasion in Rigveda

It has already been proved that a new element who used Gray Ware appeared in north west of Indus system, eastern Panjab and old Sarswati valley, just above the Indus Valley culture without break of sequence It does mean coming of or invasion of Indo-Aryan in this region. Rigvedic Hymns contain detailed description of such an invasion.

There is repeated description in the Rigveda that its composers and their followers attacked the Sapta Sindhu or Hapthindu (VIII -24-27) region and city and Citadels of original inhabitants. The cities were burnt to ashes and the inhabitants were massacred. These cities are called 'Pur' 'Pur' is a word of frequent occurrence in the Rigveda and later meaning rampart 'fort' or stronghold. Elsewhere a fort made of stone (Asmamayi) is mentioned. Some times strongholds of iron (Ayasi) are referred to, but these are probably only metaphorical. Autumnal (Saradi) forts are mentioned apparently as belonging to the Dasas. It may be that the forts in that region were being occupied either against Aryan attack or against inundation caused by oveflowing rivers. Forts with 100 walls are also spoken.[51]

In the Rigveda Indra is shown to be pouring the vials of his wrath only on those Dasas and Dasyus, who are residents of the cities (Puru) and Citadels (Ninya).

Description of destruction of Forts

Indra smote ninety-nine Castles of Shambar for his Aryan devotee Devdasa.

R V. II-19-6

DIVODĀSĀYA NAVATIM̃ CHA NAVENDRAḤ PURO VYAIRACH- CHHAMB. RASYA I

He smote to the ground the hundred Castles, impregnable to Sambara the Dasyu. R.V. VI-31-4

TVAM̃-SHAT-ĀNYAV SHAMBARASYA PURO JAGHANTHĀ PRATĪNI DASYOḤ I

O Indra ! You shattered to pieces seven Castles of Shardasur with your thunder bolt. R.V.VI-20-10

SAPTA YATPURAḤ SHARM SHĀRADĪRDARDDHAN DĀSĪAḤ PURUKUTSĀY SHIKSHAN I

O Indra ! you smote the Castle of Dasyu named Pipru and by annihilating the Dasyus in the war defended Rijiswa. R.V. I - 51-5

TVAM̃ PIPRORNRIMANAḤ PRĀRUJAḤ PURAḤ PRA RIJISHVĀNAM̃ DASYUHATYEṢAVĀRVITHĀ II

Praise of Agni for burning Cities and Citadels

Many cities were put to fire. The composer of Hymn praises the Agni for this act.

O Indra and Agni ! you together vanquished ninety Castles of the foes in one stroke and decimated Dasa's wives. R.V. III - 12 -6

INDRĀGNĪ NAVAI PURO DĀSAPATNĪRADHŪNUTAM I SĀKAME KEN KARMAṆĀ"

Indra and Agni stopped the Dasyus from abducting the sage Dabhit outside the castle and burnt their arms and weapons to ashes. R.V. II-15-4

SA PRAVOL HIRNPRIGTYĀ DABHĪ TERVIDSHVA MADHĀGĀ YUDHAMIDDHE AGNAU I

Massacre of Dasyu and Dasas by Indra

O Indra! you saved Kuts by duelling with Shushna; got Shambar defeated by Atithigva; trampled the demon named Arbudh; you have taken birth only to annihilate the Dasyus. RV 1-51-6

TVAMKUTSAM̃" SHUṢṆAHATYE ṢVĀVITHĀ'RANLHAYOTITHIGVĀY SHAM BARAMIMAHĀNTAM̃ CHIDARBUDAM̃ NI KIRAMĪḤ PADĀ SANĀ DEV DASYU HATYĀY YAJNISE II

Indra assumed strength and pride by killing the Dasyus foes of his devòtee.

R.V. I-103-4

UPAPRAYAN DASYU HATYĀYA VAJRĪ YADDHA SŪNUAḤ SRAVASE NĀM DADHE/

When he (Indra) executed Dasyu and routed a number of his castles.

R.V. X-99-7

SA NRIATAMO NAHU SO'SMATSU JĀTAḤ PURO'BHI NADARHAN DASYU HATYE'

O Indra ! Endow us with a son who should be of uncommon performance, the destroyer of Dasyus and their castles.

RV X-47-4

DASYUHANAM̃ PŪRBHI DAMINDRA SATYA MASMABHYAM̃ CHITRAM̃ VRIS ṆAM̃ DĀḤI

Indra (Purandra)the killer of Vrittra and the destroyer of the enemy's castles; put to death all the dark complexioned Dasis.

R.V. II-20-7

SA VRITRA HENDRAḤ KRISHṈA YAUNĪḤ PURANDRO DĀSĪ RAIRAYAD 'VI/ I

Forts of stone and iron or copper

Indra presented to the host Devdas the giver of charity in Yajna 100 forts of stone. R.V. IV-30-20

SHATAMA SHMANMAYĪNAḤ PURĀMINDRO BYĀSYAT, I DIVODĀSĀYA DĀSH ÙSE II

When Indra took thunderbolt in his hand he killed the Dasyus and smote their iron forts. □R.V. II-20-8

PRATI YADASYA VAJRAM̃ BĀHVOR DHURHATVĪ DASYŪN PUR ĀYASĪR NI TĀRĪT I

Inside these forts were amassed all kinds of wealth of the Dasas[52] which Indra captured after destroying them. These forts, citadels and cities may have a cosmic symbolism, yet they are manifestly replicas of actual towns, habitations and settlements with which the authors of the hymns must have been familiar.

Curiously enough the cities of the Indus civilization answer to the description of the cities of the Dasyus in the Veda. Right from Kotdiji to Harappa, Mohenjo-daro, Chanhu-daro, sutkagendor, Makran, Alimurad, Kalibangan, the defensive walls were built of stone blocks, mud bricks and baked bricks.

We can say that above records of memories of sudden attack of Aryans have been preserved in the Rigvedic descriptions. There is also description of wars and victories of Indra and his charioteer followers, on black coloured, of short stature, flat nosed, Mridhravach Dasyus and Dasas whose descriptions have been given in chapter II. Of course faces of non-Aryans were ugly but their houses and towns were full of gold which attracted Indra. The non-Aryan civilization was far ahead. They were also very strong but as already mentioned in chapter III their civilization was already on the decline due to countless disastrous activities of Indus and various other natural reasons, particularly in the region of south of Harappa. That is why they fell prey to the Aryan invasion and were defeated. As a matter of fact, it seems that southern people due to above deterioration failed to help their brethern of the north in troubled water.

The Painted Grey Ware Culture

The PGW, with its highly evolved technique of manufacturing, shows an excellent fabric, firing and finish. It is wheel turned thin pottery.

The colour commonly found in PGW, as evident from its name is gray. It varies from ash gray to battle-ship gray. Buff gray is also found though not very commonly. Other shades which are met with are brownish and reddish gray. But in every case the core is gray.

Common findings of this ware are bowls of different variety such as straight sided, tapering, convex sided, hemispherical, incurved sided concave sided etc. and dishes of Limited variety, some lota type with flat bottom pots are also available. Vibha Tripathi[53] gives an account of area covered by PGW Culture & its sites:

"The PGW sites are confined to a geographical horizon, which roughly comprises modern Punjab, Haryana, northern Rajasthan and western Uttar Pradesh. This PGW Zone is bounded by the Sutlej in the West, the formidable deserts in the south west and the Aravali ranges in the south and the river Chambal in the south east and in the north again by the hilly tracts of Himalayan ranges.

On the west the ware is reported from Sardargarh on the Indo-Pakistan border. "The position regarding its occurrence on the Pakistan side is not clear. However, sherds of the PGW type are reported from Lakhiyopir in Sind..... The distribution of the PGW extended from Harappa in Punjab, where it is represented by stray surface finds and a line of sites on the dry bed of Ghaggar in north Rajasthan, eastwards across the watershed of the Ganges and the Indus to the Ganges-Yamuna Doab............. Some important sites of PGW culture are as under-Ahichhattra in district Bareilly, Alamgir, Allahpur and Hastinapur in district

Meerut, Atranjkhera in district Etah, Khalona in district Agra, Noh in district Bharatpur, Mathura, Tilpat, Indrapat, Kampil, Rupar, Sardargarh, Sravasti, Ambakheri, Bagpat, Barnowa, Bisrakh, Dakha, Kailapur, Kaithara, Kanauj, Kaseri, Nurnagar, Rai, Sarasava, Baghaula, Bhagwanpur, Chandpur, Chhat, Dhir majra, Panipat, Pehowa, Raja Karan-ka-Qila, Bairat etc."

Mr B.B. Lal is of the view that the Aryans, who put an end to Indus Valley civilization were the people represented by the Painted Grey Ware culture. He[54] gives four points in support of his theory:-

(1) PGW has been found to occur in the lower levels of a large number of sites associated with the Mahabharta story.

(II) The distribution of this distinctive ceramic fits with the geographical face of Vedic literature, being virtually co-terminous with the land Brahmavarta and Brahmarsi Desa held holy in Aryan literature.

(III) The people who occupied the Ghaggar, traditionally an early home of the Aryan in India in the wake of the Harappans used the PGW.

(IV) A considerable part of the PGW settlement at Hastinapura was washed away by a heavy flood resulting in the desertion of the township for the time being. The occurrence of the skeletal remains of the horse though in the late levels of PGW strata, has also been emphasised as a significant evidence.

But the above view is not accepted by scholars like Leonard Woolley[55] and G.M. Bongard Levin[56]. Mr G.M. Bongard-Levin holds that the decline of the Harappan civilization was due to some internal causes rather than the invasion of the Vedic Aryans. On the other hand, D.D. Kosambi has very plausibly suggested that the Painted Grey ware should be associated with the Purus or the Kurus. In his words, "Kuru land clearing and occupation can only be associated with Hastinapur II and the excellent Grey Painted ware. Archaeologists puzzle over this pottery, for calling it 'Aryan' leads to contradiction in that many indubitably Aryan sites produce no trace of the Grey Painted Ware. If the Grey Painted Ware be labelled not just Aryan, but specifically 'Puru' ceramics, the main difficulty is resolved.[57]

The Kurus in the ascendant

Dr Buddha Prakash[58] gives a detailed account of origin of Kurus. "The Kurus, as a people, are not mentioned in the Rigveda. In VIII, 3. 2.12, there is a reference to Pakasthaman Kaurayana, a generous donor. His patronymic shows that his father was Kuruyana. In X.32.9. we find a mention of Kurusravana Trasadasyava, son of Mitratithi and father of Upamasravas. X.33.4 shows that he was dead by the time the hymn was composed. In X.98, 5-7 there is a reference to Arstisena Devapi and Santanu, whom the Aitihasikas, according to Yaska, identified with two Kauravya princes. Though these notices prove that the name Kuru was known to the composer of some hymns of the Rigveda, the fact that the tribe of the Kurus or the land called Kurukshetra is conspicuous by absence in it indicates that it did not play any important part in that age. In the Rigvedic period, in the territory of the Drishadvati, Sarasvati and Apaya, later known as Kurukshetra, on account of the association of the Kurus, the Bharata kings are said to have kindled the sacred fire; (Rig. III- 23).In the Apri hymns Sarasvati is mentioned with Bharati, the glory of the Bharatas. In the Vajasneyi Samhita the Bharats appear in the place of the Kuru-Pancalas (Vajasneyi samhitas XI 3- 3).

But in the Atharvaveda and Brahmana texts, the Kurus became prominent and are usually-associated with the Pancalas (A. Veda XX-127-7). They are said to be in occupation of the territory,through which the rivers Drishadvati, Sarasvati and Apaya flowed, and which, consequently came to be known as Kurukshetra (Jaiminiya Upanisad Bharamana III-7-6; VIII.7; Kausitaki Upanisad IV-1; Gopatha Brahmana 1-2-9). It was the home of later Vedic culture. Its speech was best and purest and its mode of sacrifice was ideal and perfect (Pancavimsa Brahmana XXV- 10", Satpatha Brahmana IV-1-5-1; Aitareya Brahmana-VII-30).

Besides the Kurus; there are references to the Uttarakurus in Brahmana literature (Satapatha Brahmana III. 2-3-15). In the Aitareya Brahmana (VIII.14) it is stated that the people, living beyond the snowy regions, like the Uttarakurus anointed their kings for Vairajya, who, as a result, are called Virats. At another place in the same text (VIII.23) Vasistha Satyahavya is stated to have anointed Janamtapi Atyarati, according to the ritual of Aindra Mahabhiseka, who, in consequence, went over the whole earth and conquered it upto the oceans. There upon Vasistha Satyahavya demanded his fees. Atyarati replied that when he would conquer the Uttarakurus, he would confer the whole empire on him and himself become a commander of his army. Satyahavya retorted that the country of the Uttarakurus was the land of gods, which nobody could conquer, and, since he had deceived him, he would snatch every thing from him, As a result, Atyarati lost his prowess and Susmin, son of Saibya, killed him."

The Uttarakurus

In the Mahabharta, the name Uttarakuru is used in contradiction to Daksinakuru[59].

The distance between their countries can be measured from the marches of Arjuna described in the Sabhaparvan. After crossing the White Mountain (Svetaparvata)he marched through Kimpurusavarsa and reached the Manasarovara lake in the country of the Hatakas, dominated by the Gandharavas[60].

From there he entered into the region, called Harivarsa, beyond which lay the land of the Uttarakurus. Else where,in the Epic, the region to the north of India, corresponding to Svetaparvata and Kimpurusavarsa is called Haimavata, and the site of the Manasarovara Lake is indicated by the mountain Hemakuta, beyond which is said to be Harivarsa[61]

The Kailasa range, running parallel to the Ladakh range, 50 miles behind it, is thus, the dividing line between Haimavata and Harivarsa. Beyond Harivarsa, including the territories of Tibet, lay the idyllic and Utopian land of the Kurus.

called Uttarakuru. This was the land of mystery and solitude, where nothing familiar could be seen[62] and it was useless to wage war[63].

Yet Arjuna is said to have reached its frontier and conquered the northern Kurus living there[64].

According to the Epic, Uttarakuru lying to the north of the Himalayas, was a land of idyllic pleasure and bucolic beauty. Thus, it cannot be the bleak, mountainous country of the Himalayas. It rather represents the region to the north of it, watered by the Tarim and its tributaries. Chinese travellers and pilgrims have testified to the prosperity and richness of these regions and the religiosity and righteousness of their people and Indian writers have described their luxury, wealth and bliss by the terms Manikancanavarsa, Gandharvaloka etc.

(Buddha Prakash,Uttarakuru Bulletin of Tibetology Vol.II, No.1 (March 1965, p 27-34.)

The migration of the Kurus

Dr Buddha Prakash[65] gives an account of migration of Kurus cited below:

"In Tibetan texts, Uttarakuru is known as Jhangdaminan (N.C. Sinha Uttarkuru in Tibeten Tradition-Builetins of Tibetology Vol. II No. 1 March 1965 PP 35-38). According to a Tun-huang document entitled, "The Religious Annals of the Li country" this land lay in the direction of the Tarim Valley somewhere in eastern Turkestan (F.W. Thomas, Tibetan Literary texts and documents P 318, f,n,II cited by Sinha P 37). The change of climate and inroad of sandy vaste, perhaps, led to the dispersal of the Kurus from there. One of their sections reached Iran, swept through the corridor between the southern foot of the Elburz Range and the northern pasture lands in the basin of Lake Urmiyah and, beyond that, in the steppe country in the lower basin of the rivers Aras and Kur, adjoining the west coast of the Caspian sea. From there, they travelled on still further westward over the watershed between the basins of the Aras and the qyzyl Irmaq (Halys) and debouched into the Anatolian Peninsula to settle in the region, called the Kuru Plain, Koroupedion, after their name, which, like its Indian counterpart, Kurukshetra, was the scene of memorable battles, like those between Seleucos Nicatar and Lysimachus in 281 B.C. and the Romans and Anthochus III in 190 B.C. which decided the fate of empires in that region (K.J. Baloch Griechische Geschichte Vol. IV, Part II PP 458-71). Another detachment of the Kurus found its way to Luristan and joined the early Achaemenids, as is clear from the fact that two kings of the Parsuwas Ansan branch of the Achaemenian family of Iran were named Kuru. A third wing of these people swung to the south-east and through Bactriana and the Hindu Kush moved into the Panjab and occupied the Sarasvati-Yamuna region. It is significant that one section of the Kurus called Pratipeyas, is known as Balhika (M.B. II-63-2112). It is also likely that either there was an infiltration of people from Uttarakuru along the Himalayan routes, or, after the settlement of the Kurus in India, the tradition of their coming from the North-West was forgotten and a connection between their Indian abode and their Urheimat beyond the Himalayas was established through Himalayan routes that were regularly in use."

The Kurus were also an Indo-Iranian people, Pelliot has shown that, in ancient times, the Iranian people lived in Chinese Turkestan. His remarks are as follows;

"We know now that Iranian people once covered an immense territory extending all over Chinese Turkestan, migrating into China and coming in contact with the Chinese. The Iranians were the great mediators between the west and the East, conveying the heritage of Hellenistic ideas to central and eastern Asia and transmitting valuable plants and goods of China to the Mediterranean area. Their activity is of world-historical significance."

(Paul Pelliot, Influences Iraniennes en Asie central et an Extreme orient (Paris 1911) cited in Berthold Laufer Sino-Iranica (Chicago 1919, P 185).

Otto Maenchen-Helfan has, also shown that the Yuo-che an Iranian people were in occupation of the northern states of the Tarim basin long before the foundation of the Kusana Empire, as can be gathered from the name of the places, Kutsi, Ku-shih and Kao-chang, which were known to the Chinese already in the early Han period. (Otto Maenchen-Helfen-The Yue-chih problem re-examined-Journal of the American Oriental Society Vol. 65 (1945) P 77.

Archaeological proofs of movement of these people have been noticed in the aforesaid region. Shashi Asthana** gives an account of their movement, "At some sites outside India, near- paralleles of the PGW has been discovered by Wace at. Tsani Tsangli and Zerila in Greece, Thessaly (Wace and Thompson-Prehistoric Thessaly Cambridge, 1912) and also at Shah Tepe in northern Iran (Arne, Excavations at Shah-Tepe Iran Pls XIV-317-19 and XLVI-328-338 etc. 1947). The Greek specimens may suggest the presence of the Aryans in that region also, although it is far-fetched idea. A plain fine GW from Shah Tepe and a variant PGW from the south of Lake Urmia in Iran (Lal B.B. 'Ancient India Vol. 10 & 11,p 147) and Siestan (Lal Ibid P 147) bear a close resemblance with the Hastinapur pottery. The discovery of this type of pottery in Siestan, south of lake Urmia. and at Shah Tepe, Tsani, Tsangli and Zerila may point to a route by which the authors of the PGW, probably different groups of the Aryans, came to India. It can be presumed that a wide area of west Asia. and Southern Europe was under the impact of a similar culture. It may, however, be clearly understood that it is only a surmise and the resemblance may only be the case of parallelism."

(Thapar' The Aryan: A reappraisal of the problem' India's contribution to world thought and culture PP 156-158)

The Decline of the Kurus and their association with the Painted Grey ware.

In India the Kurus mixed and merged among the Puru-Bharatas and lived in association with the Pancalas. Later on, however, their relations worsened and the movement of other Iranian people from the north-west put an end to their supremacy. The story of the decline and fall of the Kurus forms the central plot of the Mahabharta. After the battle of Hastinapura, the capital of the Kurus is said to have been washed away by a flood in the Ganga, compelling the king Nichachhu to shift the capital to Kosambi. The mound of Hastinapur still shows the traces of this flood and, just below the flood-level in period II, we find the Painted Grey ware (see detailed report on following pages).

Among the domesticated animals, the horse (equus caballus linn) occupied an important place. Tools and weapons were mostly of copper, though, in the upper levels of the period, iron slags are also met with. This culture can be associated with the Kurus, who are known to be in occupation of the Hastinapur region in the period before the flood in the Ganga, mentioned above.

Mr Ghurye gives an account of pottery found at Hastinapur II as follows."As regards the pottery the more common types of pots of the Polished GW stratum period i,e, Hastinapur II were bowls and dishes with convex sides and round or saggar base. Most of them were turned on the wheel.. The pots had painted designs on them. Among the designs'Swastika' deserves special mention. Corrugations on stems another type of decoration which is met with in even earlier strata at Ahar in Rajasthan and at Navdatoli in Madhya Pradesh appear here in an early level of this period."[67] However, a detailed report of excavations work of mound of Hastinapur is given ahead.

The Mound of Hastinapur and Mahabharta period

The old mound of Hastinapur is situated on the dry bed of Ganga (Budganga) in the tehsil of Mawana District Meerut. Now-a- days the Ganga flows at a distance of 5 miles east of the above mound. First of all excavation work of this mound was taken up by B.B. Lal[68] of department of Archaeological Survey of India.

There have been found remains of five continuous strata of habitations. The gaps between two strata of habitations are of those periods when the sites remained deserted. The date of third period of habitation is sixth century B.C. This is the same period when the Gautam Buddha and his contemporary king Udayan of Kosambi lived. Under this stratum begins that period (second) which is known as dark age in Indian history.

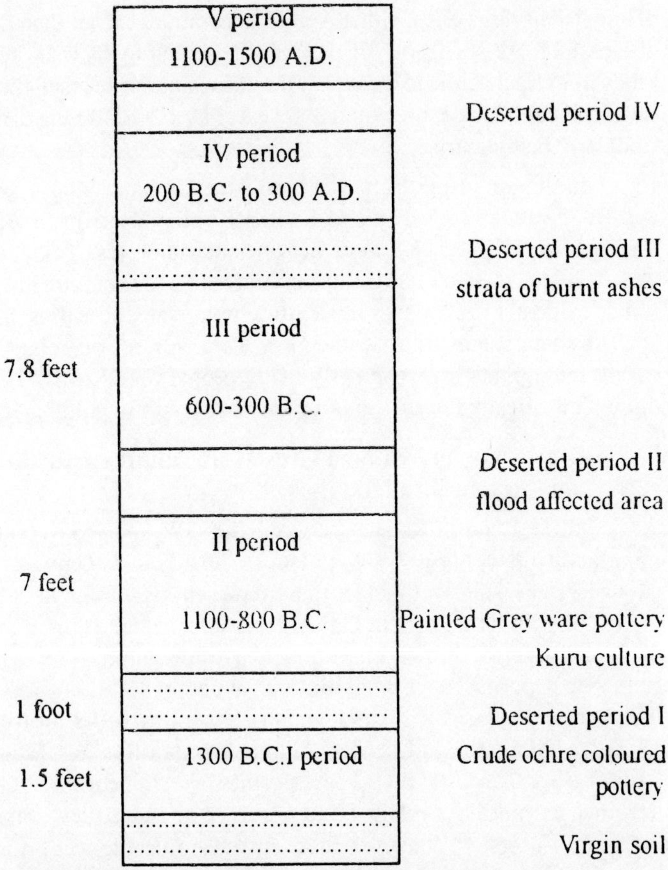

1. Rough sketch of stratification of Mound of Hastinapur

The second period has a great significance. Between this stratum of 7 feet and habitation of Ist stratum one foot of remains seems to be of that period when this site was deserted for the first time. From the remains of 7 feet of second period have been found by the excavator shards of Painted Grey ware pottery. Copper arrow heads, spearheads, sickles, nails, rods, knives, glass bangles, terracotta toys and bone owls etc. From the remains have been found houses of mud brick plastered with mud. The end of habitation of this period was caused by a disastrous flood, which destroyed the largest part of the town. From the deposit found of strata, excavator has come to the conclusion that (1) the users of Painted Grey ware pottery of period II were Vedic Aryans (2) and the remains of this mound are related to the Hastinapur of Mahabharta period.

The excavator is of the opinion that the population of II period lived for a period of 300 years. Its beginning took place at about 1100 B.C. and it ended in about 800 B.C. as a result of disastrous flood in the river Ganges. According to him the population of period III also lived for a period of 300 years or it began in 600 B.C. and ended in about 300 B.C.

According to Puranas a disastrous flood came into Ganges during the reign of king Nichachhu. Nichachhu lived 18 generations earlier than the king Udayana of Kosambi. As per theory of pargitar by assuming 18 years reign of every 18 kings from Nachachhu to Udayana, the excavator has reached the conclusion that this flood cannot be earlier than 800 years (18 x18 + 483 the date of Nirmana of Budhha)[69] before christ.

In this way right from Sietan to lake Urmia & Shah-tape in Iran, Rupar and Bhagwanpur in Sutlej and Sarswati Valley, Hastinapur in north Ganga. Yamuna Doaba in east Kosambi near Allahabad in west. Panipat. Bagpat, Tilhat etc., the cities related to Mahabharta, traces of above culture have been found. It stands evidently proved that this culture was related to Kurus, as such theory of D.D.Kosambi stands true. So the Grey ware culture was related to Aryans. the earlier immigrants, whereas PGW using people were Kurus. However, we now discuss the already referred to difference between two cultures in detail.

Grey Ware and Painted Grey Ware cultures Two different Waves of Indo-Aryans invaders

There is no difference between the GW and PGW pottery as regards manufacturing technique, shapes (fabric form) etc, excepting that the latter is painted. But inspite of this fact these represent two different cultures. Here, we discuss this difference in detail. In order to understand it thoroughly it is essential that some light is thrown on B and Red ware culture. As evident from Pre-Harappan deposits from Lothal this type of pottery technique was contribution of indigenous people which was later on adopted by invading tribes like Yadus. These Yadus were round headed Alpine Assyrian-Iranians. who reached Indus Valley earlier than 2000 B.C. These people were ethnically a different stock from long headed nordic Aryans. After arrival in India they got mixed up with indigenous people. Wherever these mixed up people went, they carried with them the same tradition of pottery. This culture flourished in west Gujarat in period between 2400-800 B.C. in south east Rajasthan and Madhya pradesh between 2000-800 B.C., in U.P., Bihar and West Bengal between 1600-800 B.C. In Punjab, Haryana and North West U.P. between 1000-800 B.C.

Now we turn back to the main point and giving a detailed account of distribution of OCP, GW and PGW cultures sites in different districts of Punjab after J.P. Joshi:[70]

"A survey of the explored sites in Punjab, a region which is close to Jammu, suggests that there are a number of Late Harappan sites in additon to those known at Ropar, Kotla Nihang Khan and Charr-marr-da-Theh. The distribution of these purely Late Harappan sites is; one in Amritsar, three in Jullundur, five in Ludhiana, five in Ropar and six in Patiala. Late Harappan Pottery is found along with Painted Gray ware and Gray Ware at one site in Amritsar, two in Jullundur, six in Ludhiana, twelve in Patiala, one in Ropar and two in Sangrur. Late Harappan pottery with Gray Ware is available at eight sites in Gurdaspur, four sites in Jullundur, five sites in Ludhiana, five sites in Patiala, two sites in Ropar and two sites in Sangrur. Sites with only Gray Ware number eight in Amritsar, ten in

Gurdaspur, one in Hoshiarpur, four in Jullundur, two in Ludhiana and two in Patiala. Pure PGWsites are three in Amritsar, six in Jullundur, four in Patiala,fourteen in Ropar and two in Sangrur. Painted Gray Ware with Gray Ware sites number two in Amritsar, one in Hoshiarpur, two in Jullundur, ten in Patiala and one in Sangrur.

The exploration suggests that there are separate sites with the Gray Ware which is generally associated with PGW. These are in District Gurdaspur, where Painted Gray Ware as such is not available. There are presently ten mounds in Gurdaspur with this Gray Ware; however, it is known that as one moves towards the east in the districts of Amritsar, there are eight mounds yielding Gray Ware, four in Jullundur, one in Hoshiarpur, two in Ludhiana and two in Patiala. Thus, the survey shows that separate mounds of Gray Ware become fewer and fewer as one moves from west to east. It has also been observed that at present Painted Gray Ware with Gray Ware and associated Red Ware occurs from Amritsar towards the east. It has been noticed that there is a concentration of Painted Gray Ware sites in District Ropar with four in Patiala, six in Jullundur, two in Sangrur and three in Amritsar (none in Ludhiana). Patiala District has the largest number of sites with both Late Harappan and Painted Gray Ware (Madhu Bala, 1978)"(No such data could be collected from Pakistan).

It is crystal clear from the above account of distribution of G.W. sites that the centre of abode of these people was northern heart land of Indus system whereas PGW using people lived in Sutlej Valley and beyond in Saraswati and Ganga Valley

As a result of heavy push from the PGW using people the GW using people in addition to the west also moved towards the east i.e. in eastern U.P. and few parts of north-west Bihar. In support of the above view, Vibha Tripathi[71] puts some archaeological evidences, "The distribution of the Gray Ware is more extensive than that of the plain Gray Ware. At sites, specially in the eastern region, where PGW either occurs in a very small number (Vaishali, Kosambi etc.) or is represented by its associated wares alone (Rajghat, Gulrihva Ghat. Prahladpur etc.) plain Gray Ware occurs in a fair quantity. During this period the shape, texture etc. of Gray Ware (at above sites) is close to PGW."

So it is crystal clear from the above archaeological evidences that B & R ware culture prevailed in Western India, Gujarat, south eastern Rajasthan, south western and eastern U.P., Bihar and West Bengal. Whereas GW using people lived in North West India or north Indus system and predominantly in eastern U.P. The PGW using people dominated in Madhya Desha i.e. eastern Punjab, Haryana and north west Uttar Pradesh.

Linguistic evidences

But to our surprise, when we take for consideration the linguistic theories of Dr Hoernle and George Grierson, based upon surveys of Indian languages and their scientific studies and analyse, we reach strikingly at the same conclusion. In the words of Dr Hoernle[72] "Indo-Aryans invaded India twice. First wave entered

CHARTS OF DISTRIBUTION OF DIFFERENT CULTURES IN DIFFERENT DISTRICTS OF PUNJAB FROM WEST TO EAST

	Gurdaspur	Amritsar	Jullundur	Hoshiarpur	Ludhiana	Ropar	Patiala	Sangrur
Late Harappan		1	3	00	5	5	6	
Late Harappan +Gray Ware	8		4		5	2	5	2
Gray Ware	10	8	4	1	2		2	
Late Harappan + GW + PGW		1	2		6	1	12	2
Painted Gray Ware		3	6			14	4	2
GW + PGW		2	2	1			10	1

Chart No. I

CHART SHOWING DISTRIBUTION OF DIFFERENT CULTURE ON DIFFERENT SITES

	Pre-Harappan	Harappan	Jhukar	Cemetery H	OCP	W&R Ware	GW	PGW
Manda	+	+			+		+	
Nagar					+		+	+
Dhaderi					+		+	+
Katapalon					+		+	+
Sanghol		+		+	+			+
Bara				+	+			
Rupar	+	+		+	+			+
							Margin in OCP & PGW	
Kotla Nihang				+	+			
Bhgwanpura					+		+	+
Kali Banga	+	+						
Banwali	+	+			+			
Shishwal								
Baragoan		+			+			
Amba Kheri					+			
Hastinapur					+			+
							Margin In OCP & PGW	
Alamgir		+			+			+
Atranjikhara					+	+	+	+
Jodhpura					+	+		+
Nuh					+	+		+
Allahpur						+		+

Chart No. II

and settled in Panjab. They came along with their families. At a letter date (after 1500 B.C.) another wave of them invaded India. They could not trace the route through Kabul valley, hence came through Gilgit and Chittral passes and entered the middle land, which extended from Himalayan range in the north up to Vindyachal in the south and in the west from Sirhind up to the junction of Ganga-Yamuna in the east. The second group developed their traditions on the bank of Saraswati and Ganga Yamuna. The habitation region of first one was treated as of low dignity whereas the land between Sarswati and Drishadvati (Brahmabarta) was thought to be sacred."

The opinion of Dr. Hoernle is based on the scientific studies of Indian languages. He is of the opinion that Panjabi, Rajasthani and Hindi of eastern region (Bhojpuri) were the languages of the first group and western Hindi that of the second group.

Dr. Hoernle[73] also argues, "Certain differences within the modern Indo-Aryan languages of India proper might be explained by reference to two main waves of immigrants an earlier represented by an outer band of languages (Bengali, Oriya, Marathi, Sindhi, Kashmiri) and a later represented by a central group of languages, comprising mainly Hindi, Rajasthani and Panjabi. "This theory has not been universally accepted, but some scholars have believed that the languages of outer band might represent elements surviving from an earlier, possibly "Pre-Vedic wave" while those of the central group might represent a"later vedic wave" of other perhaps more plausible theory, would make the outer band languages; earlier wave of vedic group itself.

Sir George Grierson puts his theory with a slight difference. He was director of Linguistic Survey of India. As such he had a thorough knowledge of Indian languages. He concludes that western Hindi and Kashmiri, Panjabi, Marathi, Bengali, Asami and Uriya languages have a vast difference, although other languages are close to each other. In fact in the beginning of linguistic history of India Indo-Aryan dialects must have been divided into two groups; one language of the middle region another group of languages of outer skirt. It is evident from the above discription that GW & PGW regions were infact two different groups of languages or peoples.

Ethnical evidences

It is said that it is very difficult to tell the clear cut reason of physical difference of people of east of Sirhind from that of the Panjab. If there would not have been process of division of Panjab (into Haryana and Panjab) this difference could never have come to notice. The people of one group would have slowly mixed up with the others and the scientific researches and general thoughts could have failed to explain whatever could be explained now that there is certainly a line of ethnical differences somewhere near the Sirhind.

Similarly B.S Guha[74] observes about movement of broad heads through the south west region of India; "That the broad heads drifted along the western littoral from south Baluchistan through Sind, Kathiawar, Gujarat and Maharashtra." This indicates towards third group of B & R ware region.

It is to be noted that Mr Guha was a famous anthropologist as also Director of Anthropological Survey of India. His opinion is based upon scientific researches. Dr. D.C. Vaidya has also reached the same conclusion after a deep study of great epics and puranas. He is of the opinion that Pandavas and their relatives were the representative of second wave of Aryans and in the battle of Kurukshetra the second group defeated the first one. There was tradition of polyendry among them, owing to the difficulty of route, they could not bring their women with them. The physical difference of people of Panjab and that of Ganga Valley also gives indication of the same fact.

Evidences of Sanskrit text books including Rigveda

The aforesaid view also gets the support of Mr. R. Shaffer[75]. His observation is based on thorough studies of sanskrit literature. In his own words "In another migration the Iranians were the first to descend the Sarayu. They (Yadus etc.) were followed by the Indo-Aryans who forced the Iranians to scatter east and West. Where they became the eastern and western Manavas, the earliest race in India. A second wave of Indo-Aryans, forced the first Indo-Aryan to flee to the west, less rich lands of Punjab and it is from the later that we have the Vedic literature".

Rigvedic Evidences

S. Chattopadhyaya[76] observes, " If we study the history of the battle of the ten kings, we arrive at some interesting conclusion. The Bharata king Sudasa seems to have fought two battles one on the Parusani or the Ravi and other on the Yamuna; in both he was victorious (VII-18-20). His western enemies were Puru, Yadu and Turvasa, Anu, Druhu, Alina, Paktha, Sivi and Visanin,. His eastern enemies were Aja, Sigru and Yaksu, evidently totemistic proto-Australoid tribes"...From Bharatas and ten kings battle we can draw an ethnological map of the Rigvedic age as under :

I- to the west of Ravi.

1- Proto Iranian broad heads using Iranian or Dardric speech

2- The harappans-consisting of the Mediterraneans, proto- Australoids and proto-Nordic (They were not a part of Harappans, but were present there as an earlier immigrants i.e. first wave) and Mongoloids.

II. East of Yamuna

1. The proto Australoids

2- Sino Tibetan elements

III. From Ravi to the Yamuna

The Nordics, if the Bharatas and the composer of Rigveda can be so described.

IV. North of Bharata territory.

The broad head Dardrics

From the above ethnological map it can be concluded that Dardric speaker broad head Alpine were in the west, Nordic Aryan were in the centre and Australoids and Sino-tibetan elements were in the east in the Rigvedic period.

Some of the Iranian broad headed people had also been pushed east ward. We reach this conclusion from another Rigvedic account (VIII-96-13,14,15) where Indra and Brahaspati had to fight with Krishna; the black (hero) leader of Yadus[77] at the bank of river Ashumati (Yamuna).Indra and Brahaspati killed Krishna along with his ten thousand warriors.

When we investigate more deeply about the territory of kings who took part in the ten kings war, we reach a more surprising conclusion. Among the kings who took part from the east one was Yakshu. According to Buddha Prakash[78] the word Yakshu is a Variant of Akwasa, akkaka or Yakaku, Yakshu, Ikshvakus and these Ikshvakus were related to the first wave of Aryan immigrants When the second wave of Aryans came through Chitral and Gilgit and attacked the eastern region of Panjab, a part of earlier group was pushed back to westward and another one towards east. One of the eastern part was Yakshu who were later on known as Ikshvaku. These people were pushed further more in the eastern direction by the second more powerful group (see Shaffer's view). As a result of which they settled in the region called Kosala Videha and Vaishali Mr pargitor[79] has informed that first historical kings who appeared in the Sanskrit literature were Ikshvakus and Nabhanidishth. These Ikshvakus were the same to which famous king of Ayodhya Rama belongs.

Finally it can be concluded from the above discussion that long headed Indo Aryan Nordic people entered India in two large waves, whereas another earlier wave which came from Assyria and Iran, was a different race called Alpines and were round headed. This conclusion gets the support of archaeology, linguistic, ethnology and text books evidences.

According to some scholars the'Early Vedic age' probably lasted down to 1500 B.C. and was followed by a second Mature Vedic age during which the compilation of the hymns into the Samhita took place. This may have lasted for some two or three centuries and probably coincided with the second major influx of Indo-Aryans from Iran. There after we enter the third or the Late Vedic stage which continued from 1300 B.C. down to 600 B.C. The famous Rigvedic kings like Devdasa, Sudasa and Trasadasyu must have lived about 1300 B.C. The third king of the Puranic dynasty is Pururva the Aila, who immediately followed the two mentioned above. Above dates strikingly compromise with the C-14 dates of GW& PGW cultures (See PP 83-87.)

Conclusion

In order, however, to reach the conclusion as to who were the human invaders, we have to re-examine the archaeological evidences of successive Harappan culture once again.

The first culture is B & R ware culture. This culture has been dug out in South Gujarat, South eastern Rajasthan, western Uttar Pradesh, Madhya Pradesh, Bihar, Bengal, Punjab, Maharashtra and some parts of southern India. The users of this pottery came from north West Iran and Assyria and were related to Yadavas, the round headed Alpines.

After Harappans we find degenerated late Harappan culture, known as Ochre coloured pottery. This culture has been found at a number of sites in Upper Ganga, old Sarswati and Sutluj Valley. Its life span is between 1700-1500 B.C.

Next we met with a new element in Shahi tump, who used a pottery of pinkish and yellowish buff colour. The other belongings such as spear-heads, shaft hole copper axe, beads, ornaments and seals seem to be of western origion. Seals of similar type have been found in Hissar IIB and IIIb in Anau III and susa in a context which suggests a date about 2000 B.C.

Another new element appeared in Chanhu-daro in Sind on the remains of Harappan culture, known as Jhukar culture. Although technique of pottery is of foreign origin but its paintings are local. Whatever may be said of pottery, but Jhukar seals are foreign to India. It is apparent from these seals that these new exotic traits were closely related to those from Iran or central Asia.

Similarly a new foreign element has also been traced out in cemetery 'H' in Harappa city itself. In addition to pottery of Harappan type this is painted and paintings depicted on some funeral jars reveals a story which is very close to that described in Rigvedic hymns. According to S.S. Sarkar, the people of Ist stratum of this cemetery used to expose the dead bodies to be eaten up by vultures before burial, whereas earlier people used to bury the whole body. So, earlier people were original Harappan inhabitants and Ist stratum new comers were invaders.

It is quite clear that all the aforesaid successive cultures do not give us any surer clue of invasion of Indo-Aryans on Indus Valley culture. For this purpose we have to trace back the path of Aryan movements in west and further link their entrace in India in respect of archaeology and chronology.

Life span of Indus Valley civilization has been fixed by scholars between 2700-1700 B.C. On the other hand European archaeologists have unearthed a Burnished GW pottery at Tureng tepe in a strata which has been dated by C-14 dating technique about 3000 B.C. This will place the presence of Indo-Europeans in the North Eastern part of Iran from tepe Hissar as early as 3000 B.C. This Gray ware culture has been connected with Aryans by scholars.

Further Dr. Deshayes and Dr. Sylvia Matheson have pointed out that Turkmenian steppe had begun to be deserted probably about 2000 B.C. Tureng tepe retained some of its inhabitants till 1700 or 1600 B.C.

So it is clear that the Gray ware using people moved from northern eastern

Iran towards south or south eastward at about 2000-1600 B.C. who appeared at the same time in Swat Valley i.e. in Dir, Chitral and in north Indus Valley. Swat Valley or Gandhara graves culture, flourished between 1600 and 400 B.C. According to A.H. Dani its first two periods represent the Vedic period and IIIrd represents the Mahabharta period. As such Gandhara graves using people were first Indo-Aryan immigrant. The Swat Valley is virtually northern region of Indus system. It means Aryan invaders had reached in this period in the quite north of Indus cities at the same period (1700-1600 B.C.) when the Indus cities were suddenly destroyed or abandoned.

The city of Harappa itself and lesser sites in the Indus Valley to the north of Mohenjo-daro do not seem to have ever suffered significant flooding instead they give the appearance of having been abruptly abandoned after which they stood empty for centuries. Such a pattern is certainly compatible with the invasion hypothesis. These northern Indus sites show no evidence of decline in material prosperity before their abandonment, but quite the opposite is true of Mohenjo-daro and other southern sites. What does this contrast signify? It signifies that the towns situated in North including Harappa fall prey to some human activities.

On the basis of the findings at Manda[80] period IB and Bhagwanpura IB it can be concluded that these sub-periods have been found interlocked with Harappan and Late Harappan respectively with Gray ware. Interlocking of both the cultures at above noted sites does mean, attack of new comer Nordic Indo-Aryans on the original inhabitant Harappans. On all the other sites except Manda, Harappan pottery has been found in achre coloured condition i.e. in a degenerated condition. This degeneration occurred due to invasion from West and migration of poor Harappan refugees towards east. So archaeologically it is proved that Gray ware using Aryans invaded the Harappans and destroyed their culture.

Not only this picture of invasion is emerging in a region which is geographically well known in the Vedic period, but also this invasion gets full support of Vedic accounts too where it is repeatedly mentioned that the composers of Rigveda and their followers invaded the Sapta Sindhu region and destroyed the cities and citadels of black coloured flat nosed Dasyus and Dasas, massacred them in countless numbers. This invasion of Vedic aryans confirms by both geography and chronology i.e.middle of the second millennium B.C.[81].

Above theory gets the support of Mr A.H. Dani[82] he gives five points in favour of his theory- (i) the geographic scene of archaeology and its history opens in the same region that is in the north West region, beyond the Indus, which is generally known as Gandhara region; (ii) the chronological period of both refers to same dates, that is the middle of the second millennium B.C. (iii) The knowledge of copper or bronze technology is seen at this time, The word 'Ayasa' in the Rigveda-definitely stands for a metal which in all likelihood is copper; (iv) the methods of the disposal of the dead, first by the extended methods and later by cremation and complete inhumation, are also similar. The references in the Rigveda and Atharva-veda clearly show that the early Aryans practised these modes of disposal of the deads; (v) The literary evidence brings the Aryans from the western region. the archaeological evidence also connects the Gandhara grave culture with the plain Grey Ware of the west, that is northern Iran and central Asia.

Objection to above Theory raised by B.K. Thapar

But B.K. Thapar [83] does not agree with the above views of invasion of Aryan from west.

He produces archaeological evidences in support of his view : "In Thessaly besides the straight sided bowls no other forms much less the distinctive Indian dish with incurved sides was available. One of the bowls had in addition, at mid hight, a sloping lug painted on the upper surface, a feature altogether absent in the Indian examples. The painted patterns consisted of thick rim band with regular spaced vertical horizontal bands, rim bands joined by oblique lines with dots etc. The designs in each case showed a disciplined style with no blurring. This evidence, though alluring, failed to carry conviction, largely because of no chain of transmission of the pottery tradition could be built between the two region viz. Thessaly and India. Likewise the suggested similarity in fabric of fine Gray ware from south of lake Urmia with the Painted-Gray Ware from the Ganga-Yamuna Doab and the Sarswati valley seems to be more-apparent than real for it is not supported by any close correspondence in characteristic pot forms excepting the corrogated stem, the complete shape in the Indian assemblage remains unknown. The occurrence of a few PGW sherds of the patent Ganga-Yamuna Doab fabric on some sites in Siestan including Lakhiyopir in Sind however provides some weight to the hypothesis but has remained-geographically separated from the known area of distribution of the ware in India. Similarly the apparent resemblance between the PGW of the Doab and that of the Shahi Tump does not seem to be fully consistent in form and decoration etc."

As such Thapar's archaeological evidences can be summed up as under :-

(i) There is a dissimilarity in forms and fabrics of pottery of Urmia lake and India.

(ii) There is a break of continuity or chain between the two regions.

Hereby we consider the first question i.e. dis-similarity in form and fabrics of pottery. This dis-similarity is not altogether. There is resemblance in two patterns; as in Thessaly in Manda and Bhagwanpura Gray ware is represented by straight sided bowls and dishes.[84]

However, above insignificant dis-similarity in pattern is due to the following reasons : (i) change in food habits of users of pottery and (ii) change in region or new contacts due to migration.

While Aryans were still in Russian steppe region, they were mainly depending on hunting. But in addition to the game, barley and milk were also part of their food. But when they reached the Indian territory their food habits were also changed due to inclusion of new items into their food. The most important of them was rice, which requires a dish of larger size, having higher straight sides to eat, comparative to those being used in their original land of habitation. Similarly, comparative to cold region more water is required to quench the increased thirst in a hot weather region like India, accordingly size of bowl or glass like pot will also increase and shape also be changed.

Now we take the second point for consideration : Different waves of Indo-Europeans moved from their original home land in Russia towards south and south east in the Iran. As much as farther they moved they came in contact with similar number of new folks or original inhabitants of different races and culture using different pattern of pottery and in the same ratio they also adopted shapes of new pottery and forgot their own. In other words longer the distance they travelled higher the number of pottery shapes they adopted and forgot their own, that is why whenever they appeared in Manda in Jammu & Kashmir and Bhagwanpura in Kurukshetra only straight sided bowls and dishes were retained[85] from their legacy of original shapes and rest were forgotten rather they adopted some of Late-Harappan pattern[86]. So, it is clear that this dis-similarity was on account of natural process and should not be taken so seriously as Mr. Thapar has taken. Further, this can be clarified by putting up the example of changing of red ware Harappan pottery in to ochre coloured, even at a distance of 100 miles or so travelled from Harappa to the district of Amritsar, where from a site[87] of ochre coloured pottery has been traced out. Whereas the distance travelled from the steppe region of south Russia to the Indo-Gangetic plain was many thousands of miles.

S.R.Rao[88] throws light on such change of Harappan pottery :"As the Harappans moved farther and farther east wards from the Ghaggar valley they, discarded the chart blades, stone weights and even terra-cotta cakes and adopted local ceramic tradition. This explains the introduction of vessels with loop-handles.... The late Harappan culture complex of Satluj and Gangetic valley which subsequently lost its identity should be assigned to the period 1700-1500 B.C. ... In Saurastra too the Harappan strugglers had discarded certain characteristic Indus pottery types including the base beaker, pedestalled goblet and perforated jar."

This is very interesting to note that this ochre coloured pottery changed to such an extent that its variant could not be recognised as later Harappan even after a long period of 50 years and scholars gave different names to this changed pottery such as Late Siswal Wares, Baran Ware, copper hoards culture[89], ochre coloured pottery etc. So it is crystal clear that above change in pottery form has no meaning and stressing on it will be simply an unscholarly attitude and as such this view is liable to be rejected.

Now we take the second problem that is the break up of continuity. It has already been shown that GW Cultures of different tradition right from Tureng Tepe up to Swat Valley of Gandhara graves have been accepted as an Aryan culture[90]. But it is learnt that there is a break in continuity in Pakistan between

Swat Valley and all the way direct up to Indo-Pak border touched by district Gurdaspur in Punjab, except Manda 28 K.m. West of Jammu. Either Pak government has not carried the excavation work in this region, if carried, any report to this effect has not been obtained so far. But there is 100% probability of their existence. When we take a survey of potential of GW sites in different districts of Punjab, the result so found is very interesting. Number of sites increases from east to west and decrease in the reverse direction. (direction is slightly north west to south West). There are two sites in district Patiala, two in Ludhiana, four in Jalandhar, eight in Amritsar and ten in Gurdaspur[91].

It is quite clear from this potential of GW sites increasing towards west in the same direction of route which was followed by most of the invaders including Alexander the Great. But on the other hand, in case of late Harappans, number of sites is increasing from west to east in the reverse direction and this is the sign of their fleeing towards east due to pressure of invasion by the horse riders. As a matter of fact these sites were temporary camps in their way to safe rescue which is proved from the very thin layer of their occupation deposits[92] (0.5 to 1.5 metre thick deposit). From increasing of potential of GW sites towards West, we can derive following results; (1) if the excavation work is done definitely there will be more and more sites in the west in the district of Sialkot and beyond. (11) the centre of abode of GW people was north west of the Indus system. (111) There is sufficient ground to say, if work done and report received from Pak, the continuity will definitely be covered up to Swat Valley or Gandhara graves.

If efforts are made, it will bring fruit and the problem will be solved completely to the entire satisfaction of Mr. Thapar, however the findings of site of Manda in the west of Jammu in Indian territory in hilly region to the north of suggested route is a sign of definite continuity than probability.

In sum, however, the evidences from Gandhara graves, Manda in Jammu, Dadheri and Nagar in Punjab, Bhagwanpura in Sarswati Valley are reasonably consistent in implying that at some period likely before 1500 B.C. the long established cultural traditions of north western India were rudely and ruthlessly interrupted by the arrival of new people, the horse rider Indo-Aryans from the west. At Harappa we know from the evidence of the rebuilding of the citadel walls that the inhabitants were on the defensive in the last days of the city. Rigvedic accounts of Aryans and non-Aryans war at Haryupeeya (Chapt V p 114) and defeat of Panis and release of cows at the hand of Indra (Chapt X PP 228-29) is evident to the above mentioned invasion on the Harappan cities.

This movement of people, this sack of the ancient cities by the outer barbarians is something not confined to India alone. It is the period that sees the rise of the Hittite to empire in Asia minor, while archaeological evidence of folk movement are clear in Assyria and again in north Persia.

The Kassite rulers of Babylon at the opening of the Sixteenth century bore what were probably Indo-Aryan names, as did the Mitannin rulers of the succeeding

Centuries. A treaty of the Hittite king subiluliuma and the Mitannin Mattiuaza of C 1380 mentions the Aryan gods Mitra, Indra and Varuna (In-da-ra-uru-v-na or v-ru-na Mi-t-ra-Na-sa-at-ti-i-ia) all familiar from the Rigveda[93] itself and among the Bogazkoui tablets is a Treatise on horse training by Kikkuli of Mitanni using chariot racing terms in virtually pure Sanskrit. As far as known, during the first half of the second millennium B.C. the Iranian speaking tribes were still located further north in the southern parts of central Asia, Sogdia and Bacteria, while the Indo Aryans fanned out across Iran and also eastwards in to India proper[94].

References

1. Rao, S.R.'Lothal and the Indus Civilization'. P54.
2. Tripathi Vibha, "The Painted Gray Ware; An Iron age culture of northern India". P 29.
3. Ibid PP 50-51.
4. IAR 1962-63, 1963-64, 1964-65, 1965-66, 1968-69.
5. IAR-1962-64 PP 28-29, 1968-69, 1970-71.
6. IAR 1958-59, P 74.
7. Ibid P 56.
8. Tripathi Vibha.PP 57-58.
9. Sankalia, "Excavations at Ahar". P223.(Poona, 1969)
10. Sankalia,'Prehistory and Protohistory of India and Pakistan (1974 P 418.)
11. Sankalia, "Excavations at Ahar". P 223.
12. Mentioned by Tripathi Vibha, PP 120-121.
13. Nanavati, J.M. 'Som Nath'. P 18.
14. Nanavati, J.M. (1956). PP 88-89.
15. EAI PP 17-18, mentioned by Chattopadhyaya S. "Racial affinities of early North Indian Tribes" P 3.
16. Chattopadhyaya, S. PP 3-4.
17. Chattopadhyaya, S. P 5.
18. Chanda, R.P. "The Indo Aryan races". IC 25
19. Chanda, R.P. IC 33.
20. Chanda, R.P. IC 33, CF 76.
21. (a) Wheeler REM "Ancient India", Vol. III PP 83-85 (January 1947) BASI
    (b) Bose N.K. and others "Human Skelcton from Harappa". ASIC (1963) PP 58-59.
22. Chattopadhyaya, S. PP 67-68.
23. Chattopadhyaya P 2.
24. Sharma, A.K. Evidences. of horse from the Harappan settlement at Surkotada', Puratattva No. 7, PP 75-76. and Sharma and Joshi's artical,'Exploration in Kutch and excavation at Surkotada' JOI, Vol. XXII, Nos. 1-2 (1972) PP 135- 136.
25. 'Animals archaeology', P 54. cited by Ghurye 'Vedic India' P 325.
26. Chanda, R.P. IC 29-33.
27. Rao, S.R. P 159.
28. Chattopadhyaya, S. P. 46.

29. CHI, Vol. I. P 40.

30. Chattopadhyaya, S. P. 87.

31. Chattopadhyaya, P 84.

32. Parpola Asko. 'Front Line', Feb. 7-22, 1987. P 99.

33 Rao, S.R. PP 182-183.

34. Ibid. P 3.

35. Stuart Piggott, 'Prehistoric India'. PP 215-221.

36. "Prehistoric India" PP 221-226.

37. Rao, S.R. P 183.

38. Ibid. PP 231-232.

39. Sankalia, H.D. "Cemetery 'H' culture". PP 324-327. ACI Edited by Possehl L. Gregory.

40 Sarkar, S.S. 'Aboriginal Races of India'. PP 143-145.

41. Bridget and Allchin Raymond, "The Cambridge Archaeology, the rise of civilization in India and Pakistan", P 300.

42. Asthana Shashi, 'History and Archaeology of India's contacts with other countries', P 134

43. Ghurye, G.S. "Vedic India", P 8 and 13.

44 Ibid. PP 236-241.

45. Tripathi Vibha . PP 80-81.

46. Joshi, J.P. and Madhubala "Manda; a Harappan site in Jammu" PP 186-195. Edited by Possehl L.G. "Harappan Civilization".

47. After Joshi, J.P. and Madhubala. PP 192-193.

48. After Joshi, J.P. and Madhubala. PP 19[illegible]-192.

49. After Joshi, J.P. and Madhubala,PP 193-194.

50. Bridget and Allchin Raymond. P 306.

51. Mackdonell A.A. and Keith A.B. "Vedic Index of names and subjects" Vol. I P 538

52. Rigveda I-130-7

BHINAT PURO NAVATI MINDRA PŪRVE DIVODĀ SAȲ MAHI DĀSHUS̄ENRITO
VAJRE N̲ DĀ SHU ŚE N RITO, I
ATITHIGVĀY SHAMBARAM̄ GIRERUGRO AB̄ABHARAT I
MAHO DHA NĀ NI DAYAMĀN DJASĀ VISHVĀ DHANĀ̃NYOJASĀII

53. Tripathi, Vibha . p 8.

54. Lal, B.B., 'Proto historic investigation; AI No. 9 (New Delhi) p 88 and also excavations at Hastinapur and other explorations in the upper Ganga and Sutlej basin. 1950-52', AI No. 10 & 11, New Delhi, 1954-55, P 151.

55. Woolley Leonard,'History of Mankind (Vol. I) Pre-history and the beginning of civilization'. p 411-412.

56. V. Balabushevich- 'Some problem of history of India'- Paper presented by the U.S.S.R. delegation to the XXVI- International Congress of Orientalists (1963) p 3. Mentioned by Dr. Buddha Prakash, p 73.

57. Kosambi, D.D. 'The Autochthonous elements in the Mahabharata - JAOS. 84 (1964) p 44.

58. Dr. Buddha Prakash, 'Rigveda and the Indus Valley Civilization' PP 115-117.

59. MBH I-102-10

UTTARA KURUBHIḤ SĀRDHA DAKSHI NĀHKURAVASTA THĀ I

60. MBH II-25-5

SARO MĀNASA MĀSĀDYA HĀṬKĀNABHITAḤ PRABHUN I
GANDHARVARAKSHITAM̐DESHAM̐ VYANJAYATPĀṆḌAVASTATAN" II

61. MBH VI-7-6

IDAM̐ TU BHĀRATAM̐ VARŚA TATO HAIMAYATAM̐ PARAM I
HEMKŪṬATPARAM̐ CHAIVA HARIVARŚA PRACNAKSHATE II

62. MBH II-25-12

PRAVIŚṬASHCHĀPI KAUNTEYA NEN DRAKSHYASI KINCHAN
NA HI MĀNUŚDEHENA SHAKYAMATRĀ BHIVĪKSHITUM II

63. MBH II-25-11

TTARAḤ KURAVO HYETE NĀTRA VUDDHAM̐ PRAVARTATE I

64. MBH V-27-8

DISHAM̐ HYUDĪ CHĪMAPI CHOTTĀRANKURŪN I
GĀṆḌĪVADHANAVAI KARA THO JIGAYA II

65. Dr. Buddha Prakash, PP 118-119.

66 Asthana Shashi,'History and Archaeology of India's contacts with other countries'. P 93.

67. Ghurye, G.S. P 390.

68. Lal, B.B. "A1" No. 10 and 11.

69. Lal, B.B. 'Hindustan Times', 27th feb. 1955. 'Hastinapur excavation and the Aryan Problem'. mentioned by K.N. Shastri, 'Sindhu sabhyata Ka Adi kendra Harappa'. P 229.

70. After Joshi, J.P. and Madhubala. P 190.

71. Ibid P 81.

72. Dr. Hoernle 'Expansion of Aryan's in India', mentioned by V. Mahajan in his book 'Prachin Bharat ka Itihas', p 79.

73. Mentioned by Chanda, R.P. IC 75.

74. Guha, B.S. quoted by Chattopadhyaya, S. P. 87.

75. EAI PP 43-44.

76. Racial affinities of early north Indian tribes. PP 5-6.

77. Kosambi, D.D. 'The Culture and Civilization of Ancient India', P 114.

78. Dr. Buddha Prakash. pp 102-105.

79. Mentioned by Ghurye, G.S. P 4.

80. Joshi, J.P. and Madhubala PP 186-192.

81. Bridget and Allchin Raymond. P 306.

82. Dani, A.H., 'Timargarha and Gandhara GraveCulture', AP Vol. III .P 52.

83. Thapar, B.K. 'The Aryan : A reappraisal of the problem'. ICWIC-PP 156-157, AS of India, New Delhi.

84. Joṣhi, J.P. and MadhuBala, pp 188-192.

85. Joshi, J.P. and Madhu Bala, PP188-192.

86. Joshi, J.P. and Madhu Bala. P 192.

87. Joshi, J.P. and Madhu Bala. P 190.

88. Rao, S.R. P.183.

89. Asthana Shashi, P. 82.

90. A-Ashthana, Shashi, P. 134.
    B- Dani, A.H.Vol. III.

91. Joshi, J.P. and Madhu Bala. P. 190.

92. Rao, S.R. P. 183.

93. This sequence is exactly the same which is given in Rigveda X-125-1
    AHAM̃ MITRĀ VARUṆOBHĀVI BHARMY AHAMINDRĀGNI AHAMSHINOBHA II

94. Bridget and Allchin Raymond. P 301.

CHAPTER-V

Date Of Indus Civilization And Its Description In Rigveda

The date of Rigveda's composition is commonly admitted to be 1500 B.C. but the evidences given below prove it to be earlier;

Forts constructed on high altitude

As mentioned in the foregoing chapter the Harappans made their abode in forts which were subsequently annihilated by Indra. As described in Rigveda these cites (Pur) were founded on mountains;

"O Indra! you shattered the enemy fortresses for Puru and Devdasa; endowed abundant power on 'Atithigva' by dint of your radiant force and sent 'Shambar' rolling down the mountain."[1]

It has already been said that all the cities and forts of Indus Valley were founded on lofty platforms. The huge mound of Mohenjo-daro being 70' high looked like a mountain to the visitors. Similarly the cities of Harappa, Kalibanga, Satkajendor were founded on lofty clay platforms.

Towards the north-east of the great bath at Mohenjo-daro there is a mansion measuring 2230' x 78' which must have been the residence of high officials. In the southern part of the fort is constructed a 90' long assembly hall; there are two parallel godowns measuring 52' x 20' each. The presence of such palatial buildings in cities and forts basically affirms what has been mentioned in Rigveda i.e. Indra devastated the sky high or Luxurious Pura (city).

Hari-yupeeya

Harappa the type site of Indus Valley civilization lies at a distance of 15 miles in the south-west of the Montgomery district in Pakistan. At present, there is a large village close by that bears the same name. This mound has a circuit of about three miles. Possibly this place was once known as Hariyupeeya mentioned in the Rigveda VI-27-5 and VI-27-6.

VADHĪDINDRO VARSHIKHASYA SHE SO'BHYĀVARTINE CHĀYMĀNA YA SHI KSHAN !
VRICHĪVATO YADHARIYŪPĪYĀYĀM HAN PŪRVE ARDHE BHIYA SĀPARO DART" I I I(5)
TRINSHACH CHHATAM VARMIN INDRA SĀKAM YAVYĀ VATYĀM PURU HŪT SRAVASYĀI
VR ACHĪ VANTAḤ SHARAVE PATYAMĀNĀḤ PĀTRĀ BHINDĀNĀ NYATHĀNYĀYAN(6)

As per scene Indra wiped out the remnants of the Varaskikhas atHariyupeeya on behalf of Abhyavartin Chayamana, an Aryan chief. The tribe destroyed was that of the Vricivata whose front line of 130 panoplied warriors was shattered like an earthen pot by Indra on the Yavyavati (Ravi) river, the whole opposing army being ripped apart 'like old clothes'; the rest fled in terror. Such vigorous language describes some actual fight at Harappa, whether between two Aryan groups or between Aryans and non-Aryans. The description of Vricivats tribe is not available anywhere else in the Rigveda. But its relation is said to be with vrcin who was a non-Aryan foe of Indra. In other words, it was place of victory of Aryans upon non-Aryans. This view gets the support of Wheeler and D.D. Kosambi[2].

The mother goddess and the fertility cult

A familiar figure from the Indus Valley is that of a mother-goddess associated with a fertility cult. Terra-cotta figurines of this goddess are very common from all Indus sites including Mohenjo-daro and Harappa. The commonest type is a standing figure adorned with a wide girdle, often with a loin- cloth and almost always with a necklace and an emphatic head dress, which is generally fan-shaped above, sometimes with a shell-like cup or pannier[3]. The cult of mother goddess is concomitant with the growth of agriculture in neolithic times and is attested over wide areas of the world. In Vedas this goddess is known as Aditi, Viraj, Vasupatni, Visvarupa, Vaisvadevi, Vaisvadhaya, Kevali etc. She is the great principle of motherhood identified with universal nature or infinity. She is described as intact (anarva), Widely expanded and extensive belonging to all men and producing heaven and earth, the mistress of the cosmic order[4] (rta);

"The daughter of Daksha Prajapati is the mother of gods".

RV V-59-8

MIMĀTU DYAURDITIRVĪTAYE NAḤ SAM̄ DĀNU CHITTRA VSASO YATANTĀM, I

"Aditi was born of Daksha! O Daksha! your daughter has given birth to gods who are immortal and praise worthy. She is undoubtedly a symbol of mother and the bearer."

RV X-72-4,5

ADITE RDAKSHO AJĀYAT DAKSHĀDVADI TIḤ PARI, I

ADITI HARYA JANIṢṬA DAKSHA YĀ DUHITĀ TAVA, II

TAM̄ DEVĀ AN VAJYĀ YANTA BHADRĀ AMRIT BANDHAVAḤ" II

May Aditya who satisfies and nourishes all, satisfy our minds. May Soma the lord of luxuries grant us luxury!

May Aditya who treats us favourably guard us. May we also begetting brave descendants sing hymns of high praise in the Yajna.

R.V. II-40-6

DHIYAM̄ PŪSĀ JINVATU VISHVAMINVO RAYIM̄ SO MO RAYI PATI RDADHĀTU, I

AVATU DEVYA DITI RANARVĀ BIRAHAD VADEM VIDATHE SUVĪRĀḤ" II

Pashupati seal of Mohenjo-daro (Trimurti and Pashupati Nath)

We take up the representation of the three headed figure on a seal[5]. The figure's head is crowned with a three-pointed headdress of two horns and a central fan-shaped structure. Its arms, covered with bangles, are outstretched with the hands resting on the bent knees. Around the neck and completely covering the chest are a series of triangular necklaces or torques, and round the waist is a band, beneath which there seems to be the erect phallus. Surrounding the figure are animals; an elephant, a tiger, a rhinoceros and a buffalo. Below the seat are two deer. Marhsall identifies the figure with Siva[6]. The following arguments may be advanced in support of this view; (1) the figure is three-faced and Siva is known as **tristrsa** and trivaktra, (2) he is seated in a yoga posture and siva is called Yoga-dhyaksa mentioned in the Mahabharta[7].

The Three-headed God

The three-headed god, called Dasa here, is described as the son of Tvastr in Rigveda x, 8- 8,9[8]

"Well-skilled to use the weapons of his father, Aptya, urged on by Indra, fought the battle.

Then Trita slew the foe seven-rayed, three-headed, and freed the cattle of the son of Tvastr.

Lord of the brave, Indra cleft him in pieces, who sought to gain much strength and deemed him mighty.

He smote the three heads from his body, siezing the cattle of the comniform son of Tvastr.

Here, as well as in Rigveda II-11-19, the three headed son of Tvastr is named as Visvarupa:

"May we gain wealth, subduing with thy succour and with the Arya, all our foes, the Dasyus.

Our gain was that to Trita of our party thou gavest up Tvastr's son Visvarupa. II- —11-19[9]

Visvarupa Tvastra

(The three headed god identified with Visvarupa Tvastra)

P.R. Deshmukh[10] is of the opinion that the god on the seal, mentioned above, represents the three headed six-eyed god described in Rigveda(x-99-6)

SA: IDDĀSAM̃ TUBĪRAV PATI RD NŚA LAKSHAM̃ TRISHĪ RŚ Ā N̲AM̃ DAMANYAT, I

"Lord of the dwelling he subdued the demon Who roared aloud, six eyed and triple headed".

The head dress of horns

Besides the three heads, the figure of the god is shown to be having a pair of horns. On two other seals also we fina the same type of headdress. To quote Macay, "seal no. 222 depicts a figure seated in what may be called a Yogi attitude with the heels pressed together on a low dais, whose legs represent those of a bull.

The headdress is a twig with leaves like those of a pipal. The horns, if indeed, they are horns, are definitely separate from the head, they are, moreover, represented as fastened to the base of the twig. The figure has three faces, one in front and two in profile. On seal 235 there is a somewhat similar figure. The stool is omitted, however, and the figure is apparently seated upon the ground. The headdress consists of two horn-like objects, between which there appears to be a spike of flowers. A pigtail hangs down on one side of the head which has one face only in profile, facing to the right[11].

In Rigveda I. 33.12,[12] the chief Susna is called sringin (horned) and in VII. 18.7, one of the tribes, taking part in the Battle of Ten Kings, is known as Visanin probably because its members or warriors wore horns on their heads. The horns in question are apparently of the bull, as we can infer from the expression vrsasipra (having the headdress shaped like that of a bull), used in Rigveda VII. 99.4.[13].

The horns and the bull

The horns of the bull are symbolic of the bull himself, who figures prominently on the Indus seals. On no less than 388 seals, we find the bull with one horn only, though, owing to the difficulty of drawing in perspective, one horn is supposed to be behind the other, as is clear from seals no. 234 and 359, where the same animal is shown to be possessed of two horns. On many other seals[14], there is the short-horned bull with its head lowered as if about to charge and with a manger or food-vessel below the head. On nos. 135 and 655, however, and the unusually shaped seal no. 229, the manger is missing. On about 25 seals are figures of the grand Brahmani bull[15] with massive body, burly hump, flowing dewlap and long curved horns. In the Rigveda the bull symbolises many gods. For instance in X.-31-8[16] Surya is represented as a bull supporting the heaven and the earth; in I.33.13 the vajra of Indra is called a sharp bull; in X.28.2 Indra himself is described as a sharp-horned bellowing bull; in III.55.17 Parjanya is compared to the bull roaring in other regions; in VII.3.3 Agni is associated with a bull, but newly born 'in II.33.15 Rudra is addressed as a tawny bull;

The three-headed bull

The figure of the god with three heads, surmounted by the horns of the bull, has its counterpart in that of the bull with three heads looking back, forth and down. In one figure the three heads of the bull are those of unicorn, ibex and bison[17]. This is an exact representation of Rigveda III. 56.3[18]

"The Bull, who wears all shapes, the triple-breasted or three-uddered with a brood in many places. Ruleth majestic with his triple aspect, the Bull, the Everlasting one's impregner."

The three aspects may be the triple bond of the bull mentioned in Rigveda IV. 58.3. This Vrsabha Visvarupa is but another form of Tvastr Visvarupa depicted on the seal in question.

Language of the Richas

In the opinion of scholars not only the battle of ten kings is described as contemporary of Rigveda but the war had continued even with the original inhabitant the Dasyus and Dasas throughout most of the period of its composition and the Aryans had not yet completely conquered the Non-Aryans which the eulogisers had been witnessing."O Indra ! By virtue of our invocations. protect our armies by routing the foes and make the invasion by the enemy forces futile, destroy those who obstruct the activities of the performers of Yajnas. O Indra! end our enemies with your might, who coming from far and near cause violence in front of us; crush their boldness and put them to route".(Rigveda VI.25-2-and 3).

"O Indra! we augment your might by invocations and make an offering of Vajra (mace of stone). You defeat those Dasas by virtue of your sunlike radiance."

(Rigveda II-11-4)

From the above examples, it is obvious that the sages who composed the Vedas being the eye-witnesses knew fully well the defeat of Non Aryan Vrcivant's sons by Abhyavarti the son of Aryan Chayaman and Indra in the war which took place in the city. Hariyupeeya constructed on colossal clay platforms in Indus Valley. Similarly, they had personally witnessed the Harappans worshipping Matridevi (Mother goddess) and Pashupati Nath or else they were fully aware of it since only then their description could be so direct and exact. They also knew that the Non-Aryan Susna wore a horned head dress. In the same way from the numerous incidents mentioned in Rigveda it is apparent that these belonged to the period of sage authors.

Dating of Indus Valley civilization

Till recently the date of Indus Valley civilization was determined on the basis of contemporary finds from archaeological excavations in Mesopotamia i.e. the period determined for the Mesopotamic starta-was also considered to be the period for the like articles found in the Indus Valley. For example, seals, weights, ornaments and metallic and clay utensisls were subjected to intensive study and comparison to decide whether they were the products of same hands or workshops. Had this fact been confirmed the inhabitants of both the civilization would have been considered as belonging to the same period. On the basis of such comparative studies the date of Indus Valley civilization was determined to be approximately 2400-1750 B.C. But now because of the later researches and the new scientific dating technique of Carbon C-14, this period is considered to be 2500-1700 B.C.

Comparative study:

In the words of M. Wheeler[19] some of the relevant seals which may be dated, however, vaguely, in the Persian Gulf, Southern Mesopotamic and Assyria are described below:-

1. Gadd no. I pre-sargonid (before c. 2350 B.C.); squarish steatite seal with rounded corners and button back of Indus type; on the face an Indus bull with

lowered head and belly-band, but lacking the usual Indus definition and facing the reverse way from the Indus type, as it were a copy from an Indus sealing; above, an archaic cuneiform inscription regarded as pre-Sargonid but of uncertain meaning. Looks like an adaptation from an Indus type. From Ur, unstratified.

2. Gadd no. 16, Pre-Sargonid or Sargonid (about 2350 B.C.); circular steatite seal with button back; bull with lowered head; above, an inscription in Indus characters; rough workmanship and ascribable to Type II (above). Found in the filling of a tomb-shaft ascribed to the elusive second Dynasty of Ur but regarded by Frankfort as of the Akkadian period.

3. Gadd no. 15, probably Sargonid; similar bull, above, crowded signs including some of Indus type with other. unknown features. From Ur, at a depth and with objects which suggest a Sargonid date. Ascribable to Type II(above); clumsy Indus style, to be regarded as a Persian Gulf Variant.

4. Sargonid; square steatite seal of normal Indus type, with 'unicorn' and Indus inscription. From Kish, 'found with a stone pommel bearing an inscription clearly not earlier than Sargon of Agade' S. Langdon in Journ. Roy. Asiatic Soc. (1931), PP 593-6.

5. Sargonid; cylinder seal, probably 'glazed' steatite; elephant and rhinoceros, with crocodile over. No inscription but clearly of Indus workmanship. From an Akkadian house at Tell Asmar. H. Frankfort, Cylinder seals (1939), p 305; and Tell Asmar, Khafaje and Khorsabad seals (or. Inst. Chicago communication, no, 16, 1923), P 51.

6. Sargonid; square alabaster seal with button back; on the face, concentric squares with bead-pattern between outermost squares. Cf no. 7 below: This type of seal is un-Babylonian but is comparable with Marhsall, III, pl. CXIV, 516, and at Tell Asmar, where the example was found, is at home with the Indus objects from the same Akkadian stratum Frankfort, Tell Asmar etc., P 52.

7. Sargonid or slightly earlier; square terracotta seal; concentric squares, CF no. 6 above. From Tepe Gawra VI, which extended to the beginning of the Sargonid period. E.A. Speiser, Excavations of Tepe Gawra (Am.Sch. of Or. Res. Philadelphia), 1 (1935), PP 163-4.

8. Probably Sargonid ; square steatite seal of nomal Indus Type with unicorn and Indus inscription. From Kish, below the pavement of Samsuiluna, son of Hammurabi, Mackay in journ. Roy. As. Soc. (1925), PP 697-701; S. Langdon, ibid. (1931), P 593.

9. Larsa period; seal inadequately described, bearing Indus script. From Lagash, au niveau des objects de 1' epoque de Gudea ou des restes de 1' age de Larsa. H.de Genouillac in Rev. d' Assyr. XXVII (Paris, 1930). P 177.

10. Gadd no. 6. Probably Larsa period : stone cylinder seal; palm-tree confronted by humped, bull with dot-in-circle eye reminiscent of bulls on Kulli pottery (CF. No. 12, below); beneath the bull's head a heap of fodder behind. a scorpion with

two snakes and above, a horizontal human figure with rayed head. Found at Ur in a vaulted tomb which is apparently that described by the excavator as 'a Larsa tomb which had been hacked down into' a wall dividing two apartments in the north-west annexe added by Bur-sin, King of Ur. to the funerary building of his father.

11. Gadd no. 12, very doubtfully Kassite (1500 B.C. or later) : circular seal with button back bearing three striations between four dots-in-circle; on the face, a human figure with a yoke form which hang two objects that have been regarded as skins or pots, the man being identified as a water-carrier. Above are two star-like forms. The objects hanging from the yoke may rather be fishing-nets, each net containing a fish; cf, a net-carrier on a potsherd from Harappa, again with star-like forms in the background (Vats, II, Pl. LXIX,16). From 'upper rubbish, Kassite level' at Ur-very dubious stratigraphy. The seal can be classified with Persian Gulf Type III and would be at home in the Larsa period, a little before or after 1900 B.C.

12. C. 2000-1750 B.C. : fragment of cylinder seal of 'white stone'; head of large-eyed bull of Indus or Kulli type - cf. no. 10 above.From Hama, Syria in 'Level H'. H. Ingholt, Rapport preliminaire sur sept campagnes de fouilles; Hama en Syrie (Copenhagen, 1940), P 62 and pl. XIX.

After the discovery of many such seals and their comparative study it stands revealed that the Indus Valley Civilization had trade relations with such other civilizations prior to 2400 B.C. which lasted till 1750 B.C.

Dating through chemical action of carbon C-14

The Scientists have discovered the principle of carbon C-14 according to which a radioactive matter carbon C-14 or radio carbon is continuously being mixed with carbon dioxide present in the atmosphere. It has been discovered that this process is constantly going on in all organisms throughout life. At a particular time after the death of that particular organism C-14 starts decreasing as radioactive particles are constantly released at a fixed rate. The rate of release of these particles can be determined by the fissions with the help of an instrument known as Gieger counter. After the passage of a certain period the radioactivity of any object is halved and again at the end of like period it is reduced to one fourth. In this way its radioactivity goes on diminishing. Half of the total life period of radioactive carbon is utilised in making calculatoins. According to some scientists one half of the life of C-14 is 5730 ± 40 while others put it at 5568 ± 30 and for dating purposes both are employed. If the proportion of release of carbon C-14 of some ancient remains (charcoal,bone etc.) is correctly calculated then it becomes possible to tell the date of the death of that organism or date of the burning of that wood. Such dates are calculated from the wood charcoal[20].

Since recently this scientific method has been employed to determine the period of Indus Valley Civilization. Dates have been calculated from the C-14 wood charcoal found during excavation after subjecting it to laboratory experiments. These Lumps of wood charcoal have been recovered during excavations conducted at Kotdijji, Mohenjo-daro, Kali Banga and Lothal sites. The dates of these lumps have been determined after their examination in the Tata Institute of Fundamental Research, Bombay[21].

In the following table, the dates are based upon a half life of 5730 ± 40 that in brackets on a half life of 5568 ± 30. For counting period before christ dates have been given after deducting 1950 years ± 40 and ± 30 means dates can vary between 40 and 30 years.

Site	Level	C 14 dates
Kot Diji, 25 miles N.E. of Mohenjo-daro	Layer 14, the Lowest 'Kot Dijian' (pre-Indus or non-Indus) Layer but two	2605 B.C. ± 145 (2471 B.C. ± 141)
,,	Layer 5, Late 'Kot Dijian'	2330 B.C. ± 155 (2211 B.C. ± 151)
,,	Layer 5, Late 'Kot Dijian'	2250 B.C. ± 137 (2133 B.C. ± 141)
,,	Layer 4A, Latest 'Kot Dijian' pre Indus Layer	2100 B.C. ± 138 (1975 B.C. ± 134)
Mohenjo-daro	Charred grains found long ago and ascribed to a late level	1760 B.C.± 115 (1650 B.C.± 110)
Kalibangan, dist Ganga-nagar, 100 miles S.E. of Harappa	Lower middle levels of Harappa culture, index no. TF-145	2060 B.C. ± 105 (1945 B.C. ± 100)
,,	lower middle levels of Harappa culture, index no. TF-147	2030 B.C. ± 105 (1915 B.C. ± 100)
,,	Middle levels of Harappa culture, index no. TF-151	1960 B.C. ± 105 (1850 B.C. ± 100)
,,	Middle levels of Harappa culture, index no. TF-139	1930 B.C. ± 105 (1825 B.C. ± 100)
,,	Late levels of Harappa culture, index no. TF-150	1900 B.C. ± 105 (1790 B.C. ± 100)
ROJDI, in dist. Rajkot, N. of	It is thought that Rojdi IB equates with Lothal A III B□	1970 B.C. ± 115 (1860 B.C. ± 110)

Lothal	period IB, index no. TF-200.	
,,	period IB, index no, TF- 199	1745 B.C. ± 105 (1640 B.C. ± 100)
Lothal	Indus phase III, three samples, index nos. TF-22, 26,27	2010-2000 B.C.±115 (1895-1880 B.C.± 120)
,,	Indus phase IV, index no. TF-29	1895 B.C. ± 115 (1790 B.C. ±110)
,,	sub-Indus phase V, index no. TF-23	1865 B.C. ± 110 (1755 B.C. ± 105)
,,	Sub-Indus phase V, index no. TF-19	1800 B.C. ±140 (1700 B.C. ± 135)
,,	Indus phase late II, index no. TF-133	1895 B.C. ±115 (1790 B.C. ±110)
,,	indus phase early,II, index no. TF-135	1555 B.C. ± 130 (1455 B.C. ± 125)
,,	Indus phase late I, index no. TF- 136	2080 B.C. ± 135 (1965 B.C. ± 130)
Lothal BV AB	Period of decline	1900-1600 B.C
,, AIV AB		2200-1900 B.C.
,, III AB	Pre-growth period	2200-2000 B.C.
,, II AC		2350-2200 B.C.
,, I		2450-2350 B.C.
Mohenjo-daro	latest mature Harappan level on edge of HR Area P-1176 Ash	1966 B.C. ±61 (1851 B.C. ± 59)
,,	p-1177 Charcoal	2062 B.C. ±66 (1945 B.C. ±64)
,,	p-1178 A Charred straw	1967 B.C. ±61 (1852 B.C.±59)
,,	P-1179 Charred wooden door-jamb	2083 B.C. ± 66 (1963 B.C. ± 64)
,,	P-1180 core of wooden door-jamb	1993 B.C. ± 63 (1878 B.C. ± 61)
,,	P-1182A Charred straw	1864 B.C.±65 (1752 B.C. ± 63)

Specimens of C-14 of Mohenjo-daro were examined in the Radio Carbon Laboratory of the University of Pennsylvania in 1965 A.D.

From the dates obtained as above the dates of the beginning till maturity and the end of Indus Valley Civilization can be expressed in the following table[22].

1.	Pre-Harappa Culture: (Rana Ghundai III, Damb Sadaat II Kulli (?), Aamri I, Sothi and Kot-Diji cultures	2700-2500 B.C.
2.	A. Harappa culture (mature phase)	2500-1900 B.C.
	B. Late Harappa culture (decadent phase)	1900-1700 B.C.
3.	Transmutation of the Harappa Culture in Gujarat	1700-1600 B.C.
4.	Post-Harappa culture in Gujarat (Lustrous Red Ware)	1600-1300 B.C.

Wheeler holds that Mohenjo-daro came to an end sometime between 2000 B.C. and 1900 B.C. It is a fact worth recording that an extremely horrible flood came in about 2000 B.C. which totally devastated the Harappan civilization of Lothal. There was another flood in 1900 B.C. which completed the annihilation of this city. Thus the date of destruction of Mohenjo-daro, Lothal and Kalibanga can be taken to be 1900 B.C. while Lothal continued to be inhabited till 1600 B.C. The beginning of this civilization in this way can be fixed in about 2700 B.C. and the end between 1900 B.C. and 1700 B.C. as during this very period the savage races emering from the steppe region of Russia brought havoc in Egypt, Mesopotamia and Iran, and during this very period they appeared in Swat Valley in north and gradually advancing invaded the cities of Indus Valley and ruined them one after the other, clear reference to which is available in Rigveda. It is evident from the above that the date of Rigveda's composition or few of its hymns can be fixed earlier than 1500 B.C., even up to 1700 B.C.

References

1. RV I-130-7, See Chapter IV, of this book.
2. (a)Wheeler, M. "The Indus Civilization" ed. III, P-27.
   (b)Kosambi, D.D., "The culture and civilization of ancient India", P79
3. (a)Wheeler, R.E.M. P 73.
   (b)Marshall, "The thousand syllabled speech", Vol. I, P 49.
4. Aggarwal, V.S., "Vision in long darkness" (1963). P 95.
5. Wheeler, REM. P 73.
6. Marshall, "Mohenjo-daro and the Indus civilization". Vol. I, PP53-56.
7. M.B.H. XIII 17-7- to 13 and (XIII-14-16 to 65) (Gorakhpur edition)
8. R.V. X-8-8

SA PITRYĀṄVĀYUDHĀNI VIDVĀNINDRA ŚIT ĀPTYO ABHYAYUDHYAT I
TRISHĪRŚĀṈAM SAPTARASHMI JAGHANVĀTVĀŚTRA SYACHINNIḤ SASRIJE TRITOGAḤ II

R.V. X - 8-9

BHŪRĪDINDRA UDINAKSHANTAMOJO VĀBHINTSATPATI- RMANYAMĀNAM i
TVĀŚTRASYACHI DVISHVARŪPASYAGONĀMĀCHAKRĀ-ṈASTRĪṈ ISHĪR ṆĀPI RĀVAK ii

9. R.V. II- 11-19

SANEM YE TA ŪTIBHISTARANTO VISHVĀḤ ISPRIDH ĀRYEṈDAS YŪN I
ASMABHYAM̄ TAT TVĀŚTRAM̄ VISHVARŪPA MARAND- HAYAḤ SĀKHYASYA TRITĀYA II

10. Deshmukh, P.R. The Indus civilization in Rigveda.P.41.
11. Mackay, E. 'Further excavations at Mohenjo-daro', Vol. I, P 335, Vol. II Plate LXXXVII No.222-235.
12. R.V. I-33-12

NYĀVIDHYADILĪ VISHASYA DIRALHĀ VI SHIRNGIṈAMABHINACHCHHUŚ ṈMINDRAḤ.I
I

13. R.V. VII-99-4

DĀSASYA CHID VRIŚASHI PRASYA MĀYĀ JA GHNA THURNARĀ PRITANĀJYEŚU. Ī

14. Mackey, Vol. I, Plate No. LXXXII, No. 689-701.
15. Marshall, Plate CXI, 329-340.
16. RV X-31-8

NAITĀVADENĀ PARO ANYADASTUKSHĀ SA DYĀVĀPRI-THIVĪ VIBHARTI I
TVACHAM̄ PAVITRAM̄ KRIṈUT SWADHĀVĀNYADĪM̄ SŪRYA NA HARITO VAHANTI II

17. (a) Mackay, E. 'Further excavations at Mohenjo-daro'II plate No. XCI XB.
    (b) Marshall III, plate C XII-382
18. RV III. 56-3

TRIPĀJASYO VRI ŚBHO VISHVARŪPAUTA TRYUDHĀ PURUDHA PRAJĀVĀN, I
TRYANĪKAḤ PATYATE MĀHINĀVĀN TSA RETODHA VRI ŚABHAḤ SHASHVATĪNĀM" II

19. Wheeler, PP 117-118

20. Baker, Harold,'Radio carbon dating, its scope and limitation in entiquity, 32 (1958), PP 253-263.

21. Wheeler, M. PP 122- 124.

22. Rao, S.R.'Lothal and the Indus Civilization', P.7.

CHAPTER VI

The Aryan Races And Problem Of Their Original Home

The Aryan Race

The word 'Arya' in Sanskrit and most of the Indian languages derived from Sanskrit means,'free born' or of noble character, or a member of the three higher castes. The word, as with so many others, changed its meaning, through the centuries[1].

The word 'Arya' is constituted in Sanskrit from root 'RK' (Rik) and all the different words (gan) which have 'RK' root mean 'to go'. As such, Arya means 'straggler' (nomad).It seems they did not like to construct permanent houses to live in. Usually they lived in huts (Mandapas). Although with the passage of time their off shoots, have started living in houses, yet it is still a tradition that yajnas are performed in huts or Mandapas only[2].

According to Penka[3], the word 'Arya' does mean a race of long head, long (prominent) beautiful nose and wide body.

As per B.M. Apte[4], Arya is the name of high caste Hindu, a man of first three varnas which is differnent from Dasyu.

Who were the Aryans ?

In his admirable thesis "The Home of the Aryans," Max Muller[5], the father of Aryan theory, declared that if we speak of Aryan race at all we should know that it means no more than X+Aryan speech. The problem thus originated on a purely linguistic basis. Looked at from this point of view, the term Aryan may signify two or more different ethnological groups using some form of Aryan speech. To be more concrete, let us take the long head Nordics of North Europe and the broad head Scythians of Central Asia. Anthropologists will maintain that they belong to two different racial groups. But the fact is that both used some form of Aryan speech and on this ground, according to Muller's theory, both should come under the same (i.e. Aryan) groups.

Another band of scholars, Penka and his followers, modified the theory and for x+Aryan speech, they propagated the new Aryan thesis as race + Aryan speech, and today it is maintained that this race is the Nordic one. Thus, from a purely philological problem, Aryanism became a dominant theme in the hands of the ethnologists. But as students of history, we may put the reverse question: Why should we place the Nordics of Europe only in the category of race? A Stein states that he saw several characteristics of Aryan features among the people of Central Asia, dominated by broad heads, who are, however, in a very low stage of civilization[6]. The tribes inhabiting this region were first known to the Chinese through the Reports of Chang-K'ien which was incorporated later on in ch. 123

of Shi-Ki of T'si-ma-t'sien,the Herodotus of China.According to this source,the people occupying the tracts from Ta-Yuan (Ferghana) westwards as far as the country of An-si (Parthia) talked different dialects, but their manners and customs being in the main identical, they understood each other. They had deep-set eyes, most of them wore beards... A later authority states that they, excepting the inhabitants of Yu-tien, had high noses, while the commentary on the Shi-Ki, 123,4, states that the Yueh-Chi, a tribe of this region, were pink and white in complexion. The description seems to convey the idea that the population belonged to the so-called Indo-European group which thus included both long and broad heads and as the people understood each other, the various dialects of this region apparently originated from a common stock. The Yueh-Chi spoke a modified form of the Iranian tongue. Thus if instead of Nordics, we put the Scythians in the category of race in the formula x (or race) + language = Aryans, there can hardly be any objection against it. This shows that the Aryan problem is primarily a problem of philology and only secondarily a problem of ethnology.

Indo-European languages and Aryans

Sir William Jones[7], who was a judge by profession in Bengal, was fond of learning and comparing different words of different languages, having same meaning. He (in 1786) was astonished to know that there is a remarkable similarity between many wards[8] of Indian (Sanskrit), Iranians and European languages. And later scholars have established affinities between Sanskrit, Iranian, Armenian, Slavic, Lethic, Greek, Latin, Celtic and teutonic languages.

This marked resemblance between the words for blood-relations like mother, father, brother, sister etc. in all the Indo-European languages has now been labelled by the scholars as 'Indo European'. This discovery, rather hypothesis led the scholars to visualize further the existence of a common home where the ancestors of the speakers of these languages lived in the dim past much before migrating to other places. They hypothesized that the Aryans while moving into distant lands got divided into several groups. They designated these groups as Indo-Europeans, Indo-Aryans, Hittites, Kassites-Mitannians and so on, particularly on linguistic grounds[9].

In detail these languages[10] fall into two groups on this basis (1) those that preserve the original guttral sound, and (2) those that sibilize it. The first group of languages is called the chentum or centum (Kentum) group and the second the satem ((satam) group. The first group includes all the European members except Lithuanian and other Baltic languages, the slavic languages and Albanian, the Hittitte and tocharian. The second group comprises, Sanskrit and allied languages of India, Iranian, Armenian, Albanian and the Balto-slavic.

The Indo-Aryans were S speakers whereas Iranians were H. speakers. From Latin developed the Romance language group (Italian, Spanish, French, Rumanian etc) in southern Europe, from teutonic German, English, Swedish etc. and from the slavic Russian and polish etc.

Different Theories of original home land

Thus the basic concept of the generic unity of the languages, spoken by these people gave rise to divergent theories regarding the original home of Aryans enumerated below which can be divided into following groups:

(1) Theory of Central Asia

(2) Theory of Arctic region

(3) Theory of Tibet

(4) Theory of India

(5) Theory of Europe

Max Mullar's Theory of Central Asia

It has been a prominent theory that early home of Aryan was central Asia. German scholar Max Mullar[11] on the basis of comparative studies of different languages, has mentioned in his book 'Lecture on the Science of Language' that the ancestors of Indians, Iranians, Greeks,Romans, Germans and Celtic tribes lived in a common home in distant past. He reached this conclusion after comparative studies of languages of these people. Sanskrit words Pitar and Matri, Iraninan Pidar and mother (Madar), English father and mother, latin Pater and Mater seems to be variations of two common words. These were the words being used daily in families and not the merchandise words. It is clear from the above that these words could have been adopted by these people only when they lived together. Prof. Max Muller is of the opinion that main branch of Aryans went towards north west. Aryans of Europe went through the path of south of Caspian sea and Asia minor to Greek and Italy. One branch of them reached India through the passes of north and west.

Prof. Muller[12] has given a final pronouncement on the subject. "If an answer must be given as to the place where our Aryan ancestors dwelt before their separation.. I should still say, as I said forty years ago, somewhere in Asia and no more". At all events'somewhere in Asia' is more vague and therefore, more probable then vactria, which was his earlier and more definite selection.

There is a myth in the zend Avesta that man was first born in Airiyana vaejo and Iranians migrated from there to Iran... We get information from the writing of clay tablet of Babylonia in 2100 B.C. that use of horse was new among the ass-user Babylonians. They called the horse 'ass brought from east' or 'ass brought from hills'. It is thus clear that the Aryans came from a nearby place from Iran and established Kassite's rule in Babylon[13].

The Theory of Arctic region (Lokmanya BG Tilak)

Indian scholar B.G,Tilak [14] maintained that original home of the Aryan was Arctic region. He has put above theory in his book'The Arctic home of Aryan'. From the contention that by and by the earth is becoming cold, Tilak has reached the conclusion that at some time in remote past arctic region was suitable for habitation and was the early home of Aryans. Tilak scrutinized the whole sanskrit text deeply and reached above conclusion. There is mention of six months days and nights in the Rigveda which can be seen in the north Arctic ocean region.

Tibetan theory

Swami Dayanand has established this theory in his book 'Satyarth Prakash' that original home of Aryans was in Tibet. But this theory has not been accepted by the scholars.

Theory of India

Bengali Historian A.C.Dass has propounded a theory as such "Sapta Sindhu' region or the Panjab was the original home of Aryans. There were seven rivers flowing in this region: Sindhu, Jhelam, Chinab, Ravi, Beas, Sutluj and Sarswati. He is of the opinion that we get the gesture of the region from the above geographic situation. India was connected with Asia through land route and Aryans migrated to west from Sapta Sindhu. Mr. Dass[15] has put forward his theory in the following words: "Original home of Aryan was Sapta Sindhu region which includes beautiful Valley of north Kashmir and Gandhara region in the West. Sapta Sindhu, as the ancient Panjab used to be called, was entirely cut off from southern India by a sea which covered the modern Rajputana and extended as, far as far east as Assam. An arm of this sea ran up to the present lower Valley of the Indus to the point where she was joined by her Tributaries. Thus there were three seas on the three sides of the Sapta Sindhu on the other side it was connected with the Western Asia and through the path of Gandhar and Kabul, one after other wave of Aryans went to Western Asia and Europe..Because the first wave of Aryan had reached far west in the Europe and other waves following them were pushing ahead as such they left Sapta Sindhu far behind and for ever." But this theory has neither been accepted nor thought to be reasonable.

Another Indian scholar R.B. Pandey[16] has forwarded another view because in the Rigveda in the 'river prayer hymns' sequence in the name of rivers is from east to west that is why original home of Aryan was the central region i.e. the region between Ayodhya and Pratisthan (near Allahabad) where two Aryan royal families named Surybansi and Chandrabansi were born. But scholars have not accepted this view also.

Theory of Europe

Different locations in Europe have been suggested by different scholars.

1. According to Penka it was the Baltic region
2. According to Ceiger...Germany region
3. According to Tomaschete...Danub region
4. According to Bender... West of the Volga,specially Lithuania Poland, Ukraine and South Russia.
5. According to P. Giles....Austria-Hungary

In any case the theory has been advocated mainly on the following grounds:-

(a) In every branch of the Indo-Eurpean Languages (there is a cognate word for honey or an intoxicating drink) made from honey. This shows that the earliest Aryans must have lived somewhere in a bee-belt, but none of the Asiatic sites can claim to be so.

(b) The beech tree, which figures so much in early Aryan account, grows only in the temperate region and this does not fit with any known region in Asia.

(c) The 'silver birch' is made a special point in the thesis. It is pointed out that it has practically the same name from Iceland to India. But grows in Europe only north of the 45 degree and thus the birch tree alone furnishes a strong probability that the Indo-Europeans came from some where north of the 45° parallel and east of the Vistula (Bender).

(d) The discovery of the centum tocharian in eastern Turkistan, it is held, add further weight to the theory, These Tocharian documents are not older than 500 A.D. and the presence of the centum group in such a limited area cannot justify the conclusion that the vast number of centum speaking people migrated from that area.

Dr.P. Giles theory: In the Cambridge History of India, Vol. I, PP60-66, Dr P. Giles adds some new and interesting arguments in support of the European home theory. He maintains ," A comparative study of the vocabularies of the different Indo-European languages shows that in the original homeland, the Indo-Europeans were acquainted with oak, beach, willow, coniferous trees (birch etc.), while of birds they knew the goose; the duck and the eagle. Again, as they knew both the horse and the cow, the topographical features of their habitat must have been a varied one for 'the horse is a native of the open plain, the foal is able to run by its mother from the first day and accompanies her always in her wanderings. The calf, on the other hand, is at first feeble, unable to walk or see its way distinctly, and therefore, is hidden by its mother in a brake while she goes further afield to find suitable pastime. After thus giving his arguments, the learned scholar observes: is there any part of Europe which combines pastoral and agricultural country in close connexion, which has in combination hot low lying plains suitable for the growth of grain and rich upland pasture suitable for flocks and herds, and at the same time trees and birds of the character already described? There is apparently only one such area in Europe, plains of Austria & Hungary, the area which is bounded on its eastern side by the Carpathians, on its south by the Balkans, on its western side by the Austrian Alps and the Bohmer Wald, and on the north by the Erzgebirge and the mountains, which link them up with Carpathians.

It has already been stated that ancestors of Indians, Iranians, Greeks, Romans, Germans and English lived together at one place. They lived for centuries together at a place which was bound by high up hills or deep water and was cut off from outer world, that is why similarity developed in their languages. They lived there for centuries together and called themselves wiros. They also practised agriculture and were also known as Arya or Airya." So theory of Dr P. Giles is more acceptable than any other.

Indication of early home in Sanskrit Literature and Avesta

Rigveda

According to Rigveda (VI-20-12 and VI-45-1) Indra brought Yadus and Turvasas safely across the sea or river Indus. It means these people were brought from the west.

According to D.R. Bhandarkar[17] "In Rigveda (III-59-3, VI-32-3 and VII-95-4) the word Mitagyanu has been mentioned, perhaps this word is related to Mitanni. These Mitannis were in the north west of Elam, whose name has been mentioned in the inscription of Boghaz-kui.

In many passages, of Rigveda, Kesin horses are mentioned, where the word is taken every time in the sense of 'possessed of a mane'. This is meaningless and tautologous, because every horse is possessed of a mane. Besides, in some texts the word Kesin occurs by itself, e.g in Rigveda, III- 41- 9, where also it obviously signifies a horse. Just as Sindu was originally noted for horses, which were, therefore, called saindharva, the Kesin country may similarly have been the habitat of an equinine species, for which reason they were called Kesins. It may be further pointed out that the Satapatha Brahmana speaks of a people called Kesins...Evidently these Kesins seem to be the descendants of the Kassi or Kassites settled in India at the time of Rigveda.

Simillarly Gemini Upnishad Brahman mention the name of a king named Kesin-Darbha who established a branch of Panchala.

The Kassites, called Kashshu by the Babylonians, kassi by the Assyrians and Kossaioi by classical writers, inhabited that part of the central range of the Zagros mountains, which is now known as Luristan. They are first mentioned in the Elamite texts of the late third millennuim B.C. in the second millennium B.C. they penetrated into Babylonia and established the second Babylonian dynasty which ruled for 576 years (1700-1150 B.C). The first Kassite kings ruled in Babylonia simultaneously with the last kings of the first Babylonian dynasty. TheKassite kings were of Indo-European stock, unlike their subjects, who were of Asianic origin. Bedrich Hrozny treats them as people of Caspian stock. The names of their deities recall Indo-Eueropean gods, e.g Buriash=Greek Boreas, Shuriash=Indian Surya. Under them the horse became popular in Babylonia and was regarded as a divine symbol."

However, we do not get desired proofs and indications from this scripture due to cerain inherent defects which is explained by D.D.Kosambi[18] as follows:

"The Rigvedic hymns were properly edited, written down and commented in South India during the second half of the Fourteenth century. The text had till then been memorised syllable by syllable (as a few scholars in India still do to this day), but not generally committed to writing. It follows that not all Vedic tradition survived.Rigvedic action lay in the Punjab.The line of priests who maintained the tradition had lost all contacts with that region for many centuries,so that the names of localities often conveyed no meaning.Many important words even apart from names of places,rivers and people are still difficult to intrepret,for the language has changed. In addition to above there was another trouble with the Aryans. They were on the mov, the names of rivers and mountains often travelled with them. The Sarswati river, sacred in the vedas ,was once the Helmund in Afganistan(Harahvaiti in old Persian,Araqattu in Assyria) then a river in the eastern Panjab which dried after the Rigveda,probably by the first Millennium."

Hence historic value of Rigveda is smaller in comparison with Avesta and old testament of the Bible.

Ramayana

We now turn to the Ramayana account : According to the Sudhakar Chattopadhyaya[19],"The Uttara-kanda of Ramayana records the tradition that the Aila,Aryans according to Pargiter, came from Balhika, the present Balkh in N.E. Afghanistan. The story centres round Ila and is found not only in other epic but the Puranas as well. The story is rather fanciful and we need not go into all the details. It may be noted that Ila's father was Prajapati Kardama. The term Kardama may be connected with the Kardama river, modern Zarfsan, as proposed by Rapson in another connection. Ila is said to have left the country placing his first son Sasavindu on the throne while he himself came to Pratisthanapura, where, after his death, Pururava Aila ascended the throne. The story, though legendary in form, clearly preserves an old tradition referring to the coming of a batch of Aryans from Balkh, which, in the ancient period, formed a part of Iran. Pururava Aila may be regarded as an eponymous ancestor of the Purus who came to India through the Hindu Kush north-western passes."

The Papancasudani refers to the establishment of Kuru kingdom in India by a body of colonist from Uttar Kuru. As such above accounts of Ramayana and Papancasudani indicate coming of Aryans from the direction which is indicated by the archaeological evidences.[20]

Avesta

According to a description given in the Vendidad Airiyana vaejo was the home land of the Aryans.Sir Max Muller[21] writes on the subject:

"In the Vendidad which was created by Ahura Mazda for Yima appears to be interesting. It is stated that there was at first no heat or cold there, but afterwards "Angra Mainyu", who is all death, counter-created by his witchcraft the serpent in the river and winter. There are ten winter months there, two summer months, and those are cold for the water, cold for the earth, cold for trees. Winter falls there with worst of its plagues. Traditions maintain that when due to excessive cold the Aryans had to leave the country, they moved to Sughda (Bokhara) and Muru (Merv). They moved further to Bakhdhi (Balkh) and then to Nisaya (Nisa), Haryu (Herat) and finally to Vaekereta (Kabul). Then the countries where the Aryans finally settled were diveded into two groups : Harahvaiti (Arachosia), Haetumant (the Helmund) and Hapta-Hindu (Sapta-Sindhu) in the east, and Urva (Tus), Vehr-Kana (the Gurgan), Rhaga (Rei), Varena (Gilan) and other districts to the west.

It can hardly be claimed that every detail of the above account is historically correct. But it shows at any rate the belief that the forefathers of the Iranians originally lived in a region not far from Bokhara and Merv. The forefathers again left their home due to a climatic change causing severity of the winter months. The account further shows how the Aryans became divided into two branches, one entering India and the other into the highland of Iran Jackson identifies this 'airiyana vaejo' with Azerbaijan."

There are evidences of cyclic desiccation in the innermost Asia in that period (Chapter IV PP76-77,).

The Avestan Tradition agrees in two respects with the Indian accounts :

(1) The Rigveda clearly states that the Sapta-Sindhu country became the Cradle of the Aryans power in India.

(2) The Ailas, who are regarded as the forefathers of the Aryans in India came from Balhika, country of Balkh, the Bakhdhi of the Avesta.

Further Sudhakar Chattopadhyaya (P-46) observes :

"So, the presence of the Aryans in Iran is proved by the evidence of the Avesta which in its original form may be as early as the first millennium B.C. but which has later been edited several times. The language of the work is, however, archaic and akin to that of the Rigveda with which it shows some peculiar affiliation. At this stage it is not necessary for us to go into the contents of the work, but we may note that it gives us a picture of the Aryans who pronounced s and h. This characteristic is not to be met with in the language of the Aryans of India. Thus we find in the Indo-Iranian world two distinct types of Aryans, one using the s as h and the other using s as such. Not only this, in the Avesta, Ahura, who resembles Varuna is the highest God while other gods occupy positions subordinate to him[22]. In the Rigveda, on the other hand, Indra occupies the highest position. The association of the Yadus and Turvasas with Indra in the Rigveda shows evidently that they belonged to a separate branch of the Aryans from the Avestic Iranians. In other words, there appears to have lived two branches of the Aryans in Ancient Iran. Prof. Gray has observed that series of Aryan waves came to ancient Iran, the first to come pronounced the sharp sibilant, as s being followed by other waves pronouncing the same original sibilant, as h, Evidently, the s speakers like the Yadus and the Turvasas were expelled by the h speakers and the former then migrated to the Indus valley. The earliest appearance of the Aryans in Iran and Western Asia is proved by the Tel-èl-Amarna letters and the Boghaz-kui inscriptions of 1400 B.C. The Boghaz-kui record deals with horse breeding and acquaints us with numerals like aika, Teras, Panza, nava etc."

Stuart Piggott[23] gives detail of the Boghazkui records as such," The most exciting document is a treaty between the Hittite king Subiluliuma and the Mitannian Mattiuaza son of Dusratta, in about 1380, in which the latter invokes his gods as witness, in the formula ilani Mi-it-tra-as-si-il ilani U-ru-w-na-as-si-il ilu In-da-ra ilani Na-sa-at-ti-ia-an-na. These can only be the gods Mitra, Varuna, and Indra of the ancient Indian pantheon as recorded in the earliest Sanskrit religious texts (such as the Riveda) described later, and the last deity is likely to be the Nasatyas, an alternative name for the heavenly twins, the Asvins, in the same literature. This Hittite treaty does not, of course, mean that there were Indians in the Mitannian Kingdom at this time, but it does point to just that common stock of mythology among the Indo-Aryans."

D.D. Kosambi[24] had gone through the archaeological and linguistic evidences deeply and has accepted above view.

We may here note the interesting fact that although the Mitanni kings bore Aryans names the native Mitannian gods were un-Aryan. This shows that while the rulers belonged to an Aryan dynasty, the people over which they ruled belonged to an un-Aryan stock. The Hittites, on the other hand, were Aryans root and branch[25]. The presence of the Aryans can be traced still earlier. As early as 1760 B.C., the Kassites established a dynasty at Babylon. The Kassite leaders were also Aryan princes ruling over the un-Aryans. We need not go into further details of these three dynasties, but may note the salient facts :

1. That from about 1760 B.C., the Aryans began appearing in Western Asia;
2. That it is now almost certain that the Aryan princes of the Mitannis belonged to the Satem group while the Hittites belonged to the centum stock (for satem languages of the Mitannis, infra)
3. That the language of the Boghaz-kui records and the Tel-el-Amarna letters appears to be more archaic than the language of the Rigveda or the Gathas of the Avesta.

The above data would lead us to the conclusions : that the Rigveda is later than 1400 B.C., or that the Aryans of Western Asia were less cultured or less advanced in the science of language than the early Aryans of India though they were in fact the later migrants.

Aryans in the lower Volga region and south of Russia (Caspean sea region)

In the light of above facts, if we go back to the theory of P. Giles, it would appear that any tribe moving eastward from the home determined by him would at once come to the Tigris-Euphratis valley than straight eastwards to Iran and India. Why first to innermost Asia and then finally to Iran and India. But they were first noticed in lower Volga region. Mariya Gimbutas[26] puts archaeological evidences supporting the presence of Indo-Europeans in the aforesaid region :

"The lower Volga area, the region round the sea of Aral, Uzbekistan and Kazakhastan up to the Altai mountains, where a culture called Kurgan, after the Russian word for 'borrow', meant for burying the dead, is attested from the third millennium B.C., is the urheimat of the Indo-Europeans. This culture fully corresponds with the early stratum of Indo-European words concerning social structure, patterns of habitation, architecture (small rectangular timber houses), economy (predominantly stock breeding, farming on a small scale) and religion (horse sacrifice, sun symbolism etc.). None of the culture in the Balkans, in central and northern Europe, before the intrusion of the Kurgan peoples, shows this correspondence. This is the argument against the assumption of the Tripolye, Danubian and Funnel-necked Beaker culture being Indo-European'...I would like to see in the expanding Kurgan people the common ancestors of all Indo-European groups that formed in the successive centuries in Europe and the Near East. In the third millennium B.C., the Kurgan people, already divided into various tribes, speaking their own dialects, spread over the North Pontic area, Anatolia, the Aegean, the Balkans, central Europe, north-western Europe, the East Baltic area and central Russia, and destroyed the old European neolithic and chalcolithic cultures and the Early Bronze Age Aegean and western Anatolian civilizations."

Before dispersal they were present in the region of South Russian steppes. In support of above view stuart Piggott[27] puts linguistic theory developed by certain scholars:

"The most reasonable hypothesis, and one which seems best to satisfy the demands of philology and archaeology, is that originally put forward by Professor J.L. Myres and the Late Herold Peake, and developed by Professor Childe, which sees the Indo-European languages evolving among the earliest agriculturists of the South Russian steppes and the lands eastwards to the Caspian sea. On linguistic evidence this area had been favoured by such scholars as Schrader in the last century, and the archaeology as we now know it seems to provide the most satisfactory back ground of material culture in accordance with the hints given by the language itself. In this South Russian area the basic culture in the late third and early second millennium B.C. was that of agriculturists, perhaps partly nomadic but sufficiently sedentary for small cemeteries to be formed, presumably close to relatively stable settlements. They domesticated sheep and cattle and the horse."

D.D.Kosambi[28] throws light on further movement of ancestors of Indo-Europeans from aforesaid region. which fully corresponds with archaeological (see Chapter IV,PP 77-78), chronological and linguistic evidence:

"Two main Aryan waves started from Central Asia in the second millennium, the first about the beginning and the second towards the end. Both affected India, and probably Europe, too, Neither was a deliberate, planned, or directed movement. The pasture of the particular homeland (approximately modern Uzbekistan) was insufficient to support the cattle and their owners, perhaps because of a long dry spell. The migration was not always in a fixed direction. Some of those who penetrated into India recoiled, either because they were beaten back or were otherwise dissatisfied with conditions in new territory. This is shown by the characteristic Indian humped bull on some Hittite seals late in the second millennium. The Hittite language had an Aryan base; the word Khatti which means Hittite may possibly be connected with Sanskrit Kashatriya and Pali Khattiyo."

It is evident from the above description that Aryans were settled in the region south of Russia around the Caspean sea and from there they moved towards south west and east. In the south east they reached the Swat Valley where from their Gandhara grave culture has been dug out.

It is now a most probably decided fact that the Aryans were original inhabitant of some cold region,. that is why they were of fair colour having beautiful sharp nose, blue eyes, and of Tony hair and long structure. It is evident from the Rigvedic description (I-42-8) that they were not used to living in the hot weather region. According to Patanjali (Mahabhashya Sutra 2-2-6) Brahmans were of fair colour. and tony hair and others were of black colour.

'A' blood group which is related to Aryan has highest pressure in Europe. According to D.N.Majumdar[29] one of the ethnological features of white people of Europe is highest frequency of 'A' blood group. It shows that Aryan white people had their origin habitation some where in Europe or near the border land of Europe and Asia or South West Russia, Where from they moved and reached central Asia or Russian steppe region. It is also to be noted that 'B' blood group has relation with the non-Aryan Dravidians or original inhabitant Sudras and centre of origin of 'B' blood group is some where in India[30]. It is clear from this fact that Aryans cannot atleast be original inhabitant of India.

Aryans half civilized barbarian Shepherds

It is strange to note that Aryans who came from north west in India, were still in the first stage of civilization. But they destroyed the city civilization of Indus Valley, which was one of the oldest-great civilization of the world. Sir Isaac Taylor[31] throws light on their civilization in these words: "It is believed that the speakers of the primitive Aryan languages were nomad herdsmen, who had domesticated the dog who wandered over the plains of Europe in wagons drawn by oxen who fashioned canoes out of the trunks of trees, but were ignorant of any metal with the possible exception of native copper. In summer they lived in huts, built of branches of trees and thatched with reeds. In winter they dwelt in circular pits dug in the earth, and roofed over with poles, covered with sods of turf, or plastered with the dung of cattle. They were clad in skins sewn together with bone needles. They were acquainted with fire which they kindled by means of fire stricks or pyrites, and they were able to count up to hundred. If they practised agriculture, which is doubtful it must have been of a primitive kind... the only social institution was marriage, but they were polygamists and practised human sacrifice. Whether they ate the bodies of enemies slain in war is doubtful. They believed in a future life. Their religion was shamanistic, they had no idols, probably no gods properly so called, but reverenced in some vague way the power of nature."

Further Sir Isaac Taylor[32] writes in the same book about early life of Aryans in Greek-" Even as late as the time when the Homeric poems were composed the Greek princes lived in dirt and squalor. There were much heaps in the palace of Priam and at the door of the palace of Ulyssis. In the hall where the suitors caroused the hides and feet of oxen and the offal of beasts recently slaughtered for the feast lay upon the floor. When we read that at the funeral of Patrocles Achilles slaughtered with his own hand, twelve noble Trojan captives, four horses and two dogs and when we read the description of his dragging by the heels the body of Hector thrice around the walls of Troy it is manifest that the golden age imagined by the poets was in reality an age of brutal savagery. In the older Greek myths and legends we find traces of human sacrifice such as prevails at Dahome, of infanticide of the exposure of children of the capture and sale of wives which must be regarded as survivals from an earlier stage of barbarism.

We find traces of the same practices among other Aryan nations. Human sacrifice prevailed among the celts in caesar's time and among all the Teutonic tribes and did not cease in Iceland before the conversion of the scandinavians to christianity at the close of the tenth century... There is reason to believe that infanticide, human sacrifice and even cannibalism were practised in Britain, if not by the celts, certainly by the Iberians and Mr. Bateman affirms, as the results of his explorations among pre-historic graves that there is accumulated evidence to prove that wives were burnt on the funeral pyre of their deceased husbands. There can be no doubt that it was an early Aryan custom to kill the widow at her husband's funeral. Children were exposed, and infant daughters especially were put to death at the father's will. Among the Indians, the Iranians the Scandinavians, and the Massagetae, the aged were killed when they became an encumbrance. Even the people of Swiss lake-dwellings fashioned the skulls of their enemies into drinking cups, and the Greek Word Testa; which may be traced in Sanskrit and zend may indicate that the same savage custom was not unknown to the Indo-Iranians and the Greeks. The Sanskrit word'Gola'a round pot, reappears in Greek and the Latin' testa' in zend and Lithuanian."

It is proved from the Sanskrit literature that there was no tradition of marriage alliance among primitive Aryans that is why the nomenclature of their off-shoots was behind the mother's name such as from Prajapati Daksha among Diti were born, two sons Diti and Aditi and one daughter named Danu. After their settlement in India two royal families named Surya and Chandra were established in the Madhyadesha which were patriarchal in form and is thought to be a beginning of marriage life. There was a system of polyandry among second group of Aryan immigrants, the Kurus, who established their power on the land between Sarasvati and Yamuna. The story of Sunassepa is a solid proof to show that Rigvedic Aryan practised human sacrifice (see Chapter IX P-176).

The Aryan immigrants in India destroyed the cities of Indus Valley, symbol of city civilization, which was achieved by dint of hard labour of more than one thousand years. As a matter of fact they were neither of the knowledge of city civilization nor of its high value.

According to E.J. Repson[33] Aryans were half civilized, barbarian, fighter shepherds tribe.

Jacquatta hawkes and Leonard Woolley[34] put their view on the subject cited below- "The Aryan conquerors were a simple, not to say a barbarous people, pastoral nomads for the most part, some perhaps petty farmers, who had not even a word for brick in their vocabulary. They could destroy, but they could not rebuild just as the Saxon Pirates who settled in Britain, Shunned the Roman sites whose walls of massive stone seemed to their ignorance to be the work of devils, and when they in due course began to build did so under the influence not of Rome but of the contemporary architecture of the continent. So it was with the Aryan, Harappa and Mohenjo-daro were left to moulder into shapeless mounds".

Mr. S.V. Vishwanathan[35] throws light on the non Aryan Dravidian civilization and compare it with the Aryan civilization, as follows," Having settled for a long time in villages where the main occupations were agriculture and pasture, the Aryans specialised in philosophical and intellectual studies, and had very little inclination for manual professions (M. Senart' Caste in India January 1912, P 133). Hence the industries and handicrafts remained entirely in the hands of non-Aryans, as also the fine arts of sculpture and painting. The result was, as Fergusson (tree and serpent worship P 78) says that all literature of India was a Aryans. all her architecture non Aryan.

Even in Ramayana we have allusions to the art of portrait painting practised by the non Aryans. Indrajit deceived Hanuman by killing an image of Sita which could hardly be distinguished from the original, and a model of Rama's head produced before Sita looked such an exact reproduction of him as to cause intense grief in her. The Aryans explained away all this as being 'Maya' (illusion)."

Such many of masks have been traced out from the sites of Indus Valley civilization.

It is quite apparent from the above events of Ramayana that non Aryans were very much expert in the field of art and crafts. Whereas Aryans were still so backward that it was not possible for them to differentiate between the masks and their originals.

It is still more astonishing to know that Aryans could not establish urban life even after passage of 1000 years after their arrival in India[36]. Hastinapur was simply a large village made of sun backed bricks.

The state of civilization is duly confirmed by archaeological findings too. Vibha Tripathi[37] an archaeologist, throws light from archaeological findings from the sites of Painted Grey Ware culture- " The moderate size of the habitation (confirmed from excavations at Rupar, Atranjikhera (850 x 550 sq meter) and

Noh, where PGW habitation is confined to a certain part of the mound only) small houses constructed with mud, bamboo and reed, together with the absence of currency, weight, varied crafts and burnt bricks suggest a rural society. The Aryans of this age, had left their nomadic life and had started settled life in the houses made of mud plaster. A few plaster pieces with reed marks suggest that the "Wattle-and daub" method of constructing houses was known. On the floors are seen the post-holes attesting to the use of timber like cone and sissoo in house building. Village life of a settled kind during this phase is further evidenced by the availability of hearths in side the house at Ataranji-khera and Allahpur. The tool typology during the PGW phase is represented by spearheads, arrow heads, points,socketed tangs, axes, blades, rods, knives, sickle and a pair of tong and a few small things like pins, nails, and bits of broken metal objects. Most of these are hunting implements. A large number of animal bones obtained during the excavation, some of them with cut marks or charred, indicate that animal life was a substitute to a perhaps not too flourishing agriculture. Rice grains excavated at Hastinapur and Noh, and metal tools like axes and sickles, found at Noh and Atranji Khera, indicate that agriculture was known to the PGW people..... An important agricultural implement conspicuous by its absence is the plough share... It seems quite likely that the plough share of the PGW period may have been made out of some perishable material most probably wood. A wooden plough may not have been much of a handicap in cultivating fertile, soft, alluvial soil, deposited yearly by floods in the land of the Sarasvati Drishadvati, Sutlej, Ganga and the Yamuna........ At Hastinapur bones of humped cattle like cow, bull, buffalo and others like sheep and pigs have been found in a large number. On this basis Lal says it is evident that cattle breeding formed an important occupation of the people..' The bones found during excavations bear definite cut marks, some of them charred. Thus, it appears that the PGW people were fond of beef and pork also...Horse bones are the most significant animal remains excavated at Hastinapur. We learn from literary sources that on special occasions horses were sacrificed and their meat distributed among the participants. It was believed that it imparted some of the swiftness strength and vigour of the horse to the participants."

G.S.Ghurye[38] gives an vivid account on the base of Rigvedic description (Mandala I Hymns 162 and 163) of sacrificing a horse, roasting of whole body on the fire and carving its parts for distribution among the participants:

"Every little part of the animal, after it was slaughtered, was to be collected for being thoroughly and properly roasted on the fire. The fat that oozed out in roasting was also to be collected. That the Rigvedic people ate the flesh of the sacrificed horse or perhaps of any horse, is to be guaged from the singer's utterances: "They who observing that the Horse is ready call out and say, the smell is good, remove it; and carving meat, await the distribution". It is clear from stanzas 18 and 19 of the 162nd hymn that the sacrificed horse was roasted as a whole and the carving of it took place afterwards. The carver had evidently to be an expert animal-anatomist; for he is asked to carve the horse rib by rib, every one of the 36 ribs apparently having been individually and specifically named even in those times. However, the dissector cut out only 34 out of the 36 ribs,"each one being sacred to a separate divinity". What was done with those two left out is not indicated, and I should think that that was the only portion left for the human co-participants to make use of; How the killing of the horse is no killing but only reaching the horse to his Father and Mother, in order that he may, approaching the gods, bring "all-sustaining riches, wealth in good-kine, good horses, mainly offspring and freedom from sin" has already been mentioned. As a sort of an apology or as contrition of the conscience or/and as insurance against revengeful activity the singer assures the sacrified horse that the oblational activity will banish all the woes that the horse might have had"when someone seated, with excessive vigour, urging hath with his heel or his whip distressed it (162.17)."

The Aryan people lived a village life run up to the period of Grihya sutra[39]. This is apparent from the description given in above literature. Hopkins[40]draws a picture of their life as follows:-

"The Grihya Suttras practically recognise life only as lived in villages. In the Dharma Suttras, as these are later and have to do with wider relations, the town (pur, nagar) appears as a larger unit, though how much larger it is not easy to say: and when we remember that pur is after all only a stronghold or fort, and Nagara is anything larger than a village, we must be cautious of too ready belief in large cities. Everything indicates on the contrary that life was still chiefly that of small places and kings were only petty chieftains. There was not supposed to be any school or even studying done in town. The Dharma Suttra of Gautama, regarded as the oldest of extant Dharma Suttras, says expressly that one should not recite the holy texts at any time in a town: and it is assumed, as in the Grihya suttras, that such life as is described passes normally in villages. Even in the description of the royal residence the hall has a thatched roof. The king still stands up in propria persona and hits a thief with a cudgel, and, if the king fails to strike, the guilt falls on the king (Gaut, Dh. S., XII, 43). The commentators, apparently aware of the incongruity in applying such a rule to the kings of their day, attempt to restrict its application as intended for specially evil thieves (of gold); but it is in fact a general rule even as late as Apastamba (Dh. S. I. 25, 4) who says: "A thief shall loosen his hair and appear before the king carrying a cudgel on his shoulder. With that (cudgel) he (the king) shall smite him; if he dies his sin is expiated, but if the king forgives him, the guilt falls on him who forgives."

According to Apastamba Dharma Suttra (I-1-2-39-40) a Brahman student should wear panther skin, a Kshattriya of deer and a vaishya of cow. Similarly, according to the same book (I-1-2-33) a Brahman should wear the girdle of Munji (long reed) grass, a Kshattriya of bow string and a vaishya of wool thread.

It is clear from the above evidences that a few centuries before the Mauryan period Aryan people were living a village life and as and when there was urbanisation that was on account of efforts made by non-Aryan original inhabitants. Rajgiri was the first town, which was centre of non-aryans Magadhan power whose description in detail is given in chapter XII P-278 and after that second city was Patliputtra, centre of non Aryan Nandas and Mauryan dynasties.

As regards use of stone in masonry it still holds true, which was told by James Fergusson[41] a 100 years ago, "No (stone) building is known to exist or any cave possessing any architectural character whose date can be extended back to the time when Alexander the Great visited India... that nothing that can properly be called architecture is to be found there (in India) till considerably after ALEXANDER's time, and that the history of art in India begins with... the introduction of Buddhism as a state religion under Ashoka in the middle of the 3rd century B.C. that stone architecture commended in India only 250 years before Christ.

The only exception referred to by Fergusson, was the so-called thione of Jarasandha' on the Rajgir hills. This rude tower, built of masses of unhewn stones picked up from the rocky hillsides and fitted together without mortar, was he supposed, older than Ashoka's age. And he made the interesting observation that its form and structure "point almost undoubtedly to Assyria as the country from which its forms were derived, and the Birs Nimrud with its range of little cells on two sides seems only a gigantic model of what is here copied on a small and rude scale.

Here, however, I may note that nothing has been found to prove conclusively that this tower was erected before Asoka's epoch, or to support General Cunningham's conjecture that its stones were quarried out of the rude cavern behind it, which seems merely one of the many natural caves abounding in those hills. Nor can the adjoining rough stone-wall of the town of new Rajgir, the stones of which also bear no marks of the chisel, be placed with confidence before Ashoka's epoch, although the town itself is said to have been founded over a century previously. Indeed, one of the chief accounts of Ashoka alleges that the monarch at first resided at Rajgir and afterwards transferred his capital to Pataliputra.

Similarly, too with regard to the rock-cut inscription on the Elephant cave on the Khandagiri Udayagiri hill near Kalak in Orrissa- this inscription which Fergusson accepted as being about a century earlier than Asoka, has since been conclusively proved to be not anterior to Asoka's time. I have personally visited each and all of the above mentioned objects(the tower, wall, and caves) and have carefully examined them with especial reference to this question.

Nor do the references to the alleged earlier occurrence of the word for bricks' in Indian literature, which were put forward by Babu Rajendralal Mitra and others in trying to prove an earlier origin for stone architecture, shed any trustworthy light on the subject; for the books in question are very corrupt, having been freely altered and added to by the copyists, and are doubtful. At present none of them is in the form in which they were composed before Ashoka. In this way Mehar has fixed the period of Mahabharta, 200 B.C. in which 'brick' word has been mentioned. Similarly the time of Ramayana is later[42] (Quoted through Dowson's classical Dictionary of Hindu Mythology p 190)."

Recently, Dr. Buhler[43] has proved that Indian alphabet has been taken from Phoenician. Rapson[44] puts his remarks as follows:

"Both of the alphabets, now usually known as Brahmi[45] and Kharoshthi, are of Semitic origin; that is to say, they are derived ultimately from the same source as the European alphabets. They were introduced into India at different periods, and probably by different routes. Brahmi is found throughout the sub-continent and in Ceylon. The home of Kharoshthi is in the North-West; and whenever it is found elsewhere it has been imported.

Brahmi has been traced back to the Phoenician type of writing represented by the inscription in which Mesha, king of Moab (c. 850, B.C), records his successful revolt against the kingdom of Israel. It was probably brought into India through Mesopotamia, as a result of the early commerce by sea between Babylon and the ports of Western India. It is the parent of all the modern Indian alphabets.

Kharoshthi is derived from the Aramaic script, which was introduced into India in the sixth century B.C. when the North-West was under Persian rule, and when Aramaic was used as a common means of communication for the purposes of government throughout the Persian empire. That originally the Aramaic language and alphabet pure and simple were thus imported into Ghandhara as Buhler conjectured in 1895 (W.Z.K.M., ix, p 49) has been proved recently by Sir John Marshall's discovery of an Aramaic inscription of Taxila. When the first Kharoshthi inscriptions appear in the third century B.C., the alphabet has been adapted to express the additional sounds required by an Indian language; but unlike Brahmi which has been more highly elaborated, it still bears evident traces of its semitic origin both in its direction from right to left and in its imperfect representation of the vowels. In the third century, A.D. Kharoshthi appears more fully developed in Chinese Turkestan where its existence must be attributed to the Kushana empire. In this region, as in India, it was eventually superseded by Brahmi".

So we can sum up the stage of civilization of Aryan people in a few words that they were half civilized barbarian, cow herders, hunters, clad in skin sewen clothes, unknown to any script, who lived in huts thatched with grass.

References

1. Kosambi, D.D.'The culture and civilization of ancient India in historical outline.' P. 72.
2. (a) Kosambi, D.D. 'Bhagwan Budha', P 20.
   (b) william, M. Monier's Sanskrit, English Dictionary.
3. Penka 'Origines Aricae' (1883), P 6.
4. Apte, B.M. 'English-Hindi Dictionary'.
5. Muller, Fredrich Max 'The home of the Aryans' cited by Sudhakar Chattopadhyaya in his book 'Racial affinities of early north Indian Tribes', PP 40-41.
6. Sir A Stein found in central Asia many tribes who, though in rather low stage of civilization yet bore pure Aryan features-white complexion blond and chestnut hair and prominent nose (Keane,' Man: past and present P 542-544).
7. A French missionary Coeurdoux in 1767 also reached to the same conclusion.
8. For example:

English	Sanskrit	Latin	Celtic	Teuton	Lithuanian
Father	Pitar	Pater	Athir	Fadar	-
Mother	Matri	Mater	Mathir	Muotar	Mati
Son	Sunus	-	-	Sunus	Sunus
Daughter	Duhitar	-	-	Dauhtar	Duhte
Brother	Bhratar	Frater	Brathir	Bropar	Bratru
Sister	Swasri	Soror	Siur	Svistar	Sastra
Fire	Agni	Ignis	-	-	-
Chariot	Ratha	Rota	Roth	-	-
Horse	Aswa	Equus	Ech	Ehu	Aszwa
God	Devas	Deus	-	-	Deiwas

After Ashthana Shashi "History and archaeology of India's contacts with other countries", P. 123.

9. Mookerji. R.K. 'Hindu civillization', P 66. (Part I, Bombay 1963)
10. Ghurye, G.S. 'Vedic India', PP 1 & 2
11. Muller F. Max. 'Lecture on the science of language'.
12. Muller F. Max 'Good words', August 1887 reprinted in 'Biographies of words', Mentioned by Isaac Taylor in his book 'The origin of the Aryans' P 31.

13. Cambridge Ancient History I,P 107. cited by Sudhakar Chattopadhyaya P 59.
14. Tilak, B.G. "The Arctic home in the Rigveda", PP 58-60 and 160.
15. Dass, A.C. 'Rigvedic India', XPP 538-539.
16. Pandey, R.B. "IHO" XXV, P 94 FF
17. Bhandarkar, D.R. 'Some aspect of Ancient Indian culture', PP 1-3.
18. Kosambi, D.D. "The culture and civilization of Ancient India ", P 78.
19. Chattopadhyaya Sudhakar 'Racial affinities of early north Indian tribes", P 52.
20. Law, B.C. 'Ancient Mid Indian Kshttriya Tribes, P 16, Calcutta (1924).
21. Muller F. Max. S.B.E. Vol. IV, 'The Zend Avesta', Part I, Vendidad Fargard, I-1 to 4.
22. Deshmukh, P.S. 'Religion in vedic literature. PP 168-69, Bombay 1933.
23. Piggott Stuart, 'Prehistoric India', P 250.
24. Kosambi, D.D. P 77.
25. Hrozmy, "Encyclopaedia Britannica', 14th Ed., S.V. Hittites.
26. The Indo-European Archaeological Problem, "A,A" 65 no 4 August (1963), 27, pp 815-25.
27. Ibid P 248
28. Kosambi, D.D. P 77.
29. Majumdar, D.N. "Races and culture of India," P 92.
30. Majumdar, D.N. ibid P 101.
31. Taylor, Isaac, "The origin of the Aryans" P 77
32. Sir Taylor, Isaac, PP 106-107.
33. Rapson, E.J., C.H.I., Vol. I (1922), 99.
34. History of Mankind, P 458.
35. Racial synthesis in Hindu culture, PP 184-185.
36. Thakur, B.S. 'Urbanisation in Ancient India', P 66.
37. The Painted Grey Ware---An iron age culture of Northern India, P 110-117.
38. Ghurye, G.S. P 52.
39. Muller F. Max. "S.B.E." Vol. XIV. P XIII. Period of Grihi Suttra is third to fifth century B.C. and 800 B.C. according to Majumdar, R.C. Vedic age.
40. Hopkins, E.W. "C.H.I.," Vol. I P 215.
41. JRAS VIII, PP 30 etc. 1843. Tree and serpent worship, 1968, History of Indian and eastern architecture, 1876- Indian Archaeology with special reference to Babu Rajinder Lal Mittra by J. Fergusson (1884) P 9. cited by L.A, Waddel 'Report on the excavation at Patliputtra, PP 63-64.

42. None of the epics, which is in present form was existing before 4th century A.D. Because their evolution, which is in the present form. took many centuries. Epic was neither written by one man or one generation, but by so many generations. Fundamentally, it is an ordinary historical event which has been expended by bards to please kings. Hopkins CHI' Vol. I, PP 230-33.

43. (a) A.A. Macdoneld has accepted above view and stated that alphabet was imported to India from Phoenicia (Israel) in 800 B.C. by the merchants which was used for maintaining account only for a very long period. "India's past", P 52 (b) G. Buhler,'Indian paleography'. PP 31-32.

44. Rapson, E.J. CHI, Vol. I, P 55.

45. Above alphabet must have come into existence in 500 B.C.
Dutta, N.K., 'The Aryanization of India' P 43.

CHAPTER VII

The War Between Aryans And Non-Aryans

Indra the Commander of the Aryans

The word Indra is a compound of two words IN+DRA, In means a warrior e.g. (SAH INĀ BARTTE ITI SENĀ) The meaning of the word DRA is chief or head in the Babylonian languages. Thus the word INDRA means chief or commander of the army. The first Commander of repute who assumed the name Indra was Shukra. After that this tradition might have lasted quite long. In Hindu mythology there is a story of Nahusha becoming Indra.

In the work 'Lord Buddha' the writer D.D. Kosambi[1] describes Indra as the Commander of the Aryans. Rigveda contains a description of **Parjanya the** rain-god. indra's features are also described-fair complexion, grey eyes, moustaches and long beard.[2]

The entire Rigveda is replete with eulogies of Indra and inspiring him by the fair complexioned Aryans (Sages) to fight against the dark-complexioned non-Aryans where non-Aryans have been called Dasyus and Dasas. It has been said in the last Chapter that Indra the Aryan god and Army chief became their eminent general in a short period. It is a fact that Indra was more of a commander or millitary chief than a venerable god[3] who was perfectly a human being who fought against the dark-complexioned Dasas and Dasyus.

We have already mentioned in Chapter V P. 114 that Indra had devastated Hariyupeeya (Harappa) for Abhyavartin the son of an Aryan chief named Chayamana after waging a war against its non-Aryan king Vricivata.

According to learned scholar D.D, Kosambi,[4]" One feat for which Indra is praised again and again is the 'freeing of the rivers,' During the nineteenth century, when nature-myths were made to account for everything including the Homeric destruction of Troy, this was interpreted as bringing down the rain. Indra was the rain-god who released the wasters pent up in the clouds. However, the Vedic rain god is Parjanya. The rivers Indra freed had been' brought to a standstill' by 'artificial barriers'. The demon Vritra lay like a great snake across the hill-slope. When this demon was smashed by Indra, the stones rolled away like wagon wheels,' the waters 'flowed over the demon's inert body.' This can hardly mean anything except the destruction of a dam. for all the figures of speech. The word Vritra as analysed by good philologists means obstacle or barrier but not demon as such. Indra was called Vritrahan, Vritra-killer, for this spectacular feat. The same word was transferred as verethraghna in Iranian to the supreme Zoroastrian god of light Ahura Mazda. The myth and metaphors give a clear account of the methods where by the Indus agriculture was ultimately ruined. (Some scholars are of the view that the ten kings battle described in Rigveda was also caused by these dams. The battle took place on the bank of Parshuni (Ravi river).) Indra has mentioned river Vivali which was flooded up to the banks. This fact is worth remembering that at some time the rivers of the Indus valley were utilized for irrigation purposes after constructing temporary mud dams on them. This possibly converted the land into swamps which hindered the Aryans in their taking the cattle herds for grazing over long distances. This destruction of the dams might have made it impossible for the inhabitants of Indus valley to dwell in cities."

Indra's confrontations with Dasyus and Dasas

From the repeated description of Indra and Dasyus and Dasas in Rigveda we learn that the invaders has to struggle for long in order to gain perfect control on the Dasyus and the Dasas. This was caused by the fact that the Aryan invaders coming from far off and remote places were outnumbered by the natives and early settlers of this region. Some of the incantations insinuating at this struggle are mentioned below:-

"He who created the world, settled the Dasa Varna in the lower caves, he, who conquers the wealth of the enemy is Indra". □(Rig II-12-4)

"O Indra! by invocations we enhance your power and present thunderbolt. You defeat those Dasyus like the radiance of the sun". □(Rig. II-11-4)

O Indra! the Vritra the demon who concealed in the cave astonished the space and the sky with his surprising power you killed him with your thunderbolt.

(Rig II-11-5)

'O Indra! we invoke your dependent who made the arrogant Dasyus flee. You destroyed Tvashtra's son Vishwarupa for the sake of friendship or Trita".

(Rig. II_11-19)

"You are the destroyer of the Dasyus and winner of wealth" (Rig. VI-16-15)

Causes of the war

(A) Indra took upon himself the task of subjugating the Dasas and the Dasyus

"Indra who weakens the enemy in the battle, endows the chariot wheel with power to gain speed. He keeps away from him who does not please Soma and blesses the Soma worshipper. Indra is the inspirer of the creation and the source of terror. He conquers the Dasyus". □(Rig. V-34-6)

(B) To enhance the power of Aryans

'Indra armed with thunderbolt sets out to annihilate the Dasas' forts. O Indra,! strike the Dasyus with the thunderbolt and enhance the might and glory of the Aryans". (Rig. I-103-3)

This was not only a motivation by the Rishis to Indra, commander of the

Army but also a guideline. Power can be increased and snatched only by destroying the enemies.

(C) To gain victory over the non-Aryan Dasyus and the Dasas

"You defeated the opponents with the support of your followers. Your invocations in the form of mantras effected the victory over the Dasyus". (Rig. I-33-9)

(D) Looting wealth

The Aryans were also tempted by the wealth of the inhabitants of the Indus valley to invade them time and again. The sages and Rishis motivated the Kshattriyas to attack the Dasyus and the Dasas to gain wealth for performing the rituals (fire worshipping).

'O Indra! you are the showerer when you devastated the cities of 'Shushanu' you had also deprived him of his riches. (Rig. IV-30-13)

'O Fire,! you gave away the booty you got from the wealth produced on the mountains (cities and forts founded on lofty platforms) to your worshippers. Be a murderer of the enemies like the brave. Face the foe who comes to fight."(Rig. X-69-6)

O Indira,! kill those who do not please Soma and are difficult to overcome because they cannot give you happiness. Give their wealth to us. He who invokes you deserves the possession of wealth". □(Rig. I-176-6)

'O Indra! the 'Kakat' people who are non-Aryans, of what use are the cows to them. Neither they milk them nor do they prepare 'ghee'. O Indra! bring those cows to us. Also let us have the wealth of those who lend wealth with a view to earn more wealth. □(Rig. III-53-14)

"He, who created the world, settled the Dasa Varna in the lower caves, he who conquers the wealth of the enemy, is Indra."

(Rig. II-12-4)

(E) Defence of the Aryan community

It is believed that Indra defended the Aryan community by killing the Dasyus and the Dasas.

"The horse, the sun, cattle wealth (cows) jewels, gold etc. all are a form of Indra's generosity. He has always safeguarded the Aryan community by destroying the sinners". □(Rig. III-34-9)

"O Fire! you honour the friends. Basugana has made you strong. You, in order to defend the dutiful (Aryans), have made the Dasyus flee from their place by dint of your rediance". (Rig. VII-5-6)

(F) To deprive the Dasas and Dasyus of their virtues

"O Indra! you divest all the Dasyus of virtues; you render those Dasas condemnable. O Indra ! and Soma! Kill the enemies by obstructing their aggression.

Accept the articles means for killing them. □(Rig. IV-28-4)

Obviously the skills of the Indus valley people such as properly organised cultivation, industrial occupations, trade etc. which had made them prosperous were banned and were debarred from doing any such work so that they might die their own death. I may term this action by the Aryan settlers a naked conspiracy against the Non-Aryans. In support of my view I may quote G.S. Ghurye[5]

"Ban was definitely launched on occupation although governing management was in absolute need of their growth but the social trend and circumstances banned them by hatching a conspiracy".

This view is also corroborated by the laws enacted by Manu against the Sudras (See Chapter 12).

(G) The end of Dasa community

Fire pervades all the people of seven regions and all the rivers. He dwells in all the three places equally. He killed the Dasyus for the sake of Mandhata the son of Yovanshva. May the fire the chief among the Yajnas destroy all our foes.(Rig. VIII-39-8)

'O Indra! endow us with a son who should be of uncommon performances, the destroyer of wise and healthy Dasyus and their castles.' (Rig. X-47-4)

O Indra! we enhance your power through invocations and offer you the thunderbolt. You destroy those Dasyus with your radiance like the sun. □(Rig. II-11-4)

"Then O Pururava! The gods invoked you when leaving for the fierce battle and killing the Dasyus". □(Rig. X-95-7)

Sovereignty can be seized only after annihilating the enemy. He can be made slave only after inflicting defeat on him. This explains why the Rishis often invoked the Aryan gods and the army chiefs to annihilate the Dasas.

The enimies of Indira-only urban non-Aryans (Dasyus and Dasas)

It is clearly known that the Aryan civilization was perfectly a rural civilization. On the other hand the civilization of the Indus valley non-Aryans Dasyus and Dasas was urban. They dwelt in towns with high ramparts and strong fortresses. Indra the military chief of the Rigvedic Aryans was the enemy of only those who lived in cities and strongly built forts i.e. the urban dwellers of Indus valley.

"O Indra! you murdered the Dasyu namely Pipru and the mighty Mrigya for Rijsva the son of Videeth and put an end to five hundred dark complexioned monsters. Just as people tear away worn out clothes, you ruined the cities of 'Shambra'. □(Rig. IV-16-13)

"That Indra armed with thunderbolt sets out to destroy the enemy forts"

(Rig. I-103-3)

"Among the Angirisas you had killed the monster named 'Bal' by your militant power and opened the gates of the cities". (Rig. VI-18-5)

Similarly, the following verses have already been mentioned in Chapter IV in support of above view.

Rigveda II-19-6, III-12-6, VI-31-4, IV-30-20, II-20-8, VI-20-7, II-31-4, I-33-12

The Asuras of Avesta

A study of the Vedas and the Avesta of the Zoroastrians reveals that the Indian Aryans and the zoroastrian (Parsian) Aryans were diametrically opposed to each other. As opposed to the Indian Aryans, the Zoroastrians held the Asuras as sacred and the god as Satanic. They named their diety. Ahur Mazda (The great Asura). The Aryans cremated their deads whereas the Zoroastrians exposed and buried them into graves. The Indian Aryans regarded Suras as gods and the Asuras as monsters. On the other hand to the Zoroastrians the Suras were the monsters and the Asuras were their gods.

Who these Asuras were has been a most important question with the Indologists. In A.K. Banarjee Sastri's view quoted by Sudhakar Chattopadhyaya[6] in his book "Racial Affinities of Early North Indian Tribes", they were Assyrians and were the authors of the Indus Valley civilization". D.R. Dhandarkar has corroborated this view on page 4 of his book "Some Aspects of Ancient Indian Culture".

The following observations by M.Haug (Religion of the Parasis, London 1878 pp 268-69) being interesting are worth noting:

"Asura is, in the form Ahura, the first part of Ahuramazda (Hormazd), the name of God among the Parsis; and the Zoroastrian religion is distinctly called the Ahura religion.... in strict opposition to the deva religion. But among the Hindus Asura has assumed a bad meaning, and is applied to the bitterest enemies of their Devas... but in older parts of the Rigveda Samhita we find the word Asura used in as good and elevated a sense as in the Zend Avesta. The chief gods such as Indra, Varuna, Agni, Savitri, Rudra etc. are honoured with the epithet 'Asura' which means 'living, spiritual', signifying the divine, in its opposition to human nature... In a bad sense we find Asura only twice in the older parts of the Rigveda (ii. 32.4; vii. 99.5)"

In these Richas the word Asura is applied to "Sons or man of the Asuras". But it occurs several times in 'Purush Sukta' but the scholars believe that this was appended at a later stage.

Dasyu

Meyer and Hillebrandt equate this word with the name of the Dahae, a tribe nearly akin to the Iranians in the Kirghiz, Turkman Steppe, which extends from the Caspian Sea beyond the jaxartes or Syr Darya.[7]

Mr. Kent holds that this name survived in Dahistan of medieval times, which was situated to the east of the Caspian sea[8]. From this Sukumar Sen concludes "The word Dahyu as Dasyu is an Iranian word meaning a country or a people like Parsi, Persia and Medes or Media". In Avesta the word dasyu is used as a common noun and it is also mentioned in the edict of Achaemania.[9]

Sudas and the Ten Kings War

D.D.Kosambi holds that the military events described in the later Rigvedic hymns seem to be historical since these are ascribed not to the god Indra but human beings, heroes or kings. The best known victory of this kind is the victory of king Sudas (pronounced Sudah) over the ten kings confederacy[10]. Sudas called descendent of Pijavana is also stated to be the son of Devdasa. Whether Sudasa was an Aryan or non-Aryan king, is a subject of controversy. Scholars do not agree on one point. G.S. Ghurye[11] opines- "The Tritsa Bharata king Devdasa, father of Sudas and a senior contemporary of Purukutsa, similarly was engaged in fighting against many persons, apparently not belonging to the Rigvedic Aryan community... so Sudas was also non-Aryan"

D.R. Bhandarkar holds that Rigvedic heroes, Devdasa and Sudas , who are said to have been assisted by the Vedic gods, were Dasas. As he[12] writes , "We may proceed one step further and discuss who by extraction Sudas was. He was, of course, the hero of the Dasarajna or the 'Battle of Ten Kings', fought on the Parusni, where there were Arya and Dasa allies on both the sides . But he was also the grandson of Devdasa Atithigva. And Hillebrandt[13] seems to be right in interpreting the name as the 'heavenly Dasa' and conjecturing that he was himself a Dasa".

Similary in his book 'Sudras in ancient India' R.S. Sharma [14] has referred to Sudas as a non-Aryan King. Views of D.D. Kosambi[15] on this issue are different. He puts forth his views cited below :

"The termination 'Dasa' is curious. In later Sanskrit, the name Devdasa may be translated 'servant of heaven', but originally Dasa or Dasyu applies to a hostile non-Aryan people. They had the special colour (varna, later on mean caste also) namely black (Krishna) which distinguished them from the Aryans, and hence can only refer to their darker complexion, as contrasted with the lighter skin-colour of the new comers. Only after repeated conquest does the word Dasa come to mean slave or helot (just as `slave' and `helot' both derive from, ethnic names), a member of the Sudra Varna, servant, or in the form Dasyu, `robber' or `brigand'. That so early a name of an Aryan king should end in Dasa means that there was some recombination between Aryans and non-Aryans soon after 1500 B.C. The tribe over which Sudas was chief is given as the Bharatas, or perhaps a speical branch of the Bharatas called the Tritsus. The modern offical name Bharat for India means `land of the Bharatas'. These Bharatas were definitely Aryans. Obviously, racial purity meant nothing to the early Aryans : adoption of the autochthones was always possible and practised."

Dr B.R. Ambedkar[16] is also in favour of this view of Kosambi. But

I am also of the view which is held by Kosambi that Sudas must have been a kshattriya ruler of Aryan tribe known as Bharata. This view is based on the following gound :

(a) He was a follower of Indra and Indra had been his ally in the war which fact has been repeatedly mentioned in Rigveda.

(b) The second undeniable proof of this is that in the description contained in the Rigveda the non-Aryan rulers possessed their own cities with ramparts and forts. But no where has Sudas been said to be in possession of his fortified towns and castles. The Rigveda contains description of only annihilation or capturing of forts and castles by him in which he was actively aided by Indra.

(c) There are many well known Aryan chiefs and Rishis having thier name ending with Dasyu or Dasas. Trasdasyu was son of Aryan Purukutsa (Rig IV-42-9) (for detail, see chapter 15). Similarly, Mahidasa was son of Aitreya Rishi and Itra.

The Battle of Ten Kings : The battle of ten kings with Sudas is a historical event of the highest magnitude in Rigveda. Sudas had defeated the confederacy of ten kings on the bank of the Parshuni (Ravi) river. □(Rig. VII-83-7)

DASH RĀJĀNAḤ SAMITĀ AYAJYAVAḤ SUDĀSAMINDRĀVARUṆĀ NA YUYUDHUḤ

Causes of The battle

Sage Vasista was the priest of Sudas, But the priest of Purukutsa, leader of 10 kings confederation, was sage Vishwamitra. The opponent of Sudasa's were Alan, Paktha, Bhalna, Shiv, Anu, Druhyu, Turvasa, Yadu, Puru, who were Aryans and Iranian tribes and Shamber, Vekarn, Bheda, were non-Aryan kings.

At first Vishwamitra was the family priest of Sudas. But due to some reason he deprived Vishwamitra of this honour and gave this place to the sage Vasista. Possibly this antagonised Vishwamitra against Vasista and he writhed in enmity and as a part of revengeful activity he instigated the opponent against Vishwamitra and Sudas. Consequently a terrific battle was fought in which Sudas was victorious.

Some scholars are of the view that the war was a set foot on the cause of River Ravi. Kosambi[17] opines:

"The cause of the Ten-Kings battle was that the Ten tried to divert the river Parushni. This is a stretch of the modern Ravi which, however, changed its course several times. Diversion of the waters of the Indus system is still a cause for angry recrimination between India and Pakistan. The 'greasy-voiced' Purus, though enemies of Sudas, were not only Aryans but closely related to the Bharatas. Later tradition even makes the Bharatas a branch of the Purus. The same clan priests in the Rigveda impartially call down curses and blessings upon the Purus in divers hymns."

The war : The priests on both sides invoked Indra and Varuna to help them with men, money and war material[18]."The ten confedrates rallied against him on the Parushni, and the Yaksus, Sigrus and Ajas lashed out at him on the Yamun. It was, perhaps, the rainy season, when the rivers were in spate and difficult to cross. But, somehow, under the energetic guidance of Vasista, Sudas succeeded in negotiating them."

Rigveda sings this victory as follows :-

'O Indra ! you enabled king Sudas to cross the Parushni river with its terrible current. You undid the curse of obstructing the traffic of the invocation by the current of rivers. (Rig. VII-18-5)

"The alliance of foes pounced at Sudas and diverted the Ravi in his direction by digging a ditch. But that plan of the enemy failed becuase the current of the flooded river flowed towards their own men and drowned them all". (Rig VII-18-8,9)

"This obstacle proved a boon for Sudas and marching forward he captured the seven enemy forts. (Rig. VII-18-15)

"Chief of the confederacy of the ten kings was defeated and made captive. In darkness his wife gave birth to a son, named Trasadasyu who later on rescused the family from decimation". (Rig. IV-42-8.9)

This victory converted the status of Sudas into paramountcy[19].. From a very miserable condition , he emerged into an imperial position.

Decline of Sudas : Because of the bravery of Trasadasyu the Purus became the adversaries of Sudas. From Jemini Brahman[20] we learn that the successor of Sudas community consigned to flames Shakti the son of Vasista. This turned Vasista his enemy and Sudas lost his power.

The warring communities, both Aryans and Non-Aryans

These great victories of Sudas turned the other rulers and chiefs his bitter foes. He was opposed by two confederacies. The details of the enemies are well described by Dr. Buddha Parkash in his book "Rigveda and the Indus Valley Civilization". I am quoting an excerpt from his book, reproduced below :

"We hear of two confederacies against him : the alignment of the Ajas, Sigrus and Yaksus under the leadership of Bheda on the Yamuna and the rally of Yadus-Turvasas, Bhrgus, Druhyus, Pakthas, Bhalanas, Alinas, Sivas, Visanins, Purus, and Anus under the guidance of Simyu, Purodas, Purukutsa, Kavasa, etc. on the Parushni. In that emergency Visvamitra and his family also deserted him and went over to his enemies. But, undaunted by these difficulties, he appointed Vasist as his priest and successfully encountred the opposition of his antagonists both on the Yamuna and on the Parushni".

The enemies of Sudas appear to be his own kith and kin. The poet speaks of his adversaries on the Yamuna as follows :

"Yamuna and the Tritsus aided Indra. Then he stripped Bheda bare of all his treasures. The Ajas and the Sigrus and the Yaksus brought in to him as tribute heads of horses." (Rig.VII-18-19)

"Among these peoples the Yaksus may be equated with the Akhaioi, known to the great poet Homer or the Akavasa, who invaded Egypt under Romses II.Later on they seem to have been known as Okkaka and Ikshvaku[21]."

The Yadus and Turvasas

As for the other opponents of Sudas, they were mostly ancient Indo-Iranian. In Rigveda it is mentioned: I got wealth in thousands from the Yaduvanshi Parsu's son Tirendra(VIII-6-46)

SHATAMAHAṀ TIRINDIRE SAHASRAṀ PARSHĀVĀ DADE RĀDHĀNSI YĀDVĀNĀM ॥

H.S. Nyberg[22] says,"The Parsu, in all probability stands for the people called Parthava or Parsava. Elsewhere they are bracketed with the Turvasa, who are probably the same as the Tura, who are mentioned with the Ariya, Sairima, Sainava, and Daha in the Avesta. They are counted among the Iranian people of the central Asian Steppes, who gave Zarathustra a good reception." Then they spread in different sections. In the words of G. Le Strange[23].

"A section of them accompanied the Sarmatians in their west ward migration north of the Caspian sea and another mounted the Iranian plateau and then moved south-east, for, in the Abbasid period, a district in eastern Baluchistan in the neighbourhood of the modern Khannate of Qalat, bore the name of Turan."

Even at present the southern part of the Kabul Valley is inhabited by a community named Turis. To quote Dr. T.L.Pennell[24].

"In the present century a community of Turis lived near the Suleiman Mountains in the Upper Valley of the Kurram river, immediately to the south of the Kabul Valley. These Turis are said to be pastoral nomads, who migrate twice a year between the summer pastures in the Kurram Valley and the winter pastures round Qalabagh on the west bank of the Indus north of the Salt Range."

Puru and Purukutsa

The name Puru is of Indo-Iranian origin which is mentioned as Pouru in Avesta and which occurs in the inscriptions, of the Achamenian emperors as king Puru. In Rigveda Sayana has interpreted the expression Puru to mean 'many'. The passage says,"O Man! you having numerous families, serve the gods. We pray before you through the words of Great Agni (fire). Other people too invoke him". (Rigveda 1-36-1). In another verse Puru is referred to as a favourite of fire (Rigveda VIII-5-3). The verse No. VI-20-10 in Rigveda mentions that help was given by Indra to the Purukuts in war against Dasas. It says, "You broke the seven winter (sardi)- castles where the Dasas took refuge. In this way help was given to Purukutsa. Of sweet tongue Purus, the foes of Sudas were not only Aryans, but also had relations with Bharatas. However, this relationship was not permanent. According to D.D. Kosambi[25] "The quarrel was of another sort than that between Aryan and non-Aryan. The Purus remained in the Harappa region and expanded their rule over the Panjab in later times. It was they who put up the strongest fight against Alexander in 327 B.C. The modern Panjabi surname Puri may possibly originate with the Puru tribe."

Among the adversaries one of the rulers is named Pakhata. Today they are known as Pakhtoons The Pakthas are the North-East Iranian people, known as Afghans, who call themselves Pakthana, Pashtana, Pathan, plural forms of the singular words'Pakhtun' and 'Pashtun', in the divers dialects of their language. Herodotus calls them Paktyes and locates them in the fourteenth taxation district of his gazetteer of the Achaemenian empire where the Bisutun inscription places the Harahvatiya (Harauvatiya) or the people of the Valley of the Harahvatis known as Arakhosia or Arachosia. Another name, given to them by the Greek historian, is Thamanaioi, probably derived from some word like the Persian 'daman,' meaning the skirt of a garment, and, by analogy a borderland' or march', a name still borne by the region between the Salt Range, the Solimauny Mountains, the Indus and Sungur in Upper Sind[26]. The Paktyes are also found in Anatolia, Herodotus groups them with the Armenioi in the thirteenth taxation district of the Achaemenian empire. Some place names and personal names in Anatolia also throw light on the establishment of these people in that region. A town at the neck of the Gallipoli Peninsula bore the name Paktye before the end of the sixth century B.C.[27], a mountain near Ephesus was called Paktyes by Strabo[28], a Lydian, whom Cyrus put in charge of Croesus's captured treasure and who took that opportunity to place himself at the head of a Lydian insurrection against Achaemenian rule, was know as Paktyes in the History of Herodotus[29]. Toynbee suggests that the plural form of Paktu was Paktuk, which lives in the Hellenized form Paktyike, and that the word Katpatuka, occurring in the inscriptions of the Achaemenians as the name of Cappadochia, signifies the Paktyes domiciled in Khatti[30]. Thus, we observe that the Pakthas were a wide-spread Indo-Iranian people living from Anatolia to the Harahvatis Valley."

There was another community Matasya a non-Aryan community which inhabited the Bharatpur region in the historical age.

The Druhyus are mentioned as related to Purus, Yadus, Bhrigus, Alinas, Bhalanas, Anus and Turvasis (Rigveda VI-46-8). Kuhn and Carnoy equate the Bhrigus with the Greek Phlagyai suggesting their affinity with the Phrygians[31]. According to Mackdonell, "Etymologically the word Bhargu means shining from the root `Bharg' to shine. This was originally a name of fire. Kuhn and Waber further identify the Bhrigus as fire priest with the Greek Phrygians. The Alinas stand for the later Alains or sumerians (Sarmatians). Zummer has located them in the north-east of Kafiristan[32]. The Bhalanas inhabited the East Kabulistan and the Bolan pass got its name from them[33].

The Sivas have been identified by the Greek writers as the Siboi. These people inhabited the area between Iravati and Chanderbhaga at present known as Jhang. Even today we come across a railway station midway between the Bolan and the Harnoi passes on way to Sakhar and Kota. The station is named Sibi.

Sibistan in the middle ages got its name from these people[34].

The tribe named Visanin probably got its name because they wore a horned headdress[35]. As is evident from the engravings on seals, an aristocrate class of Indus Valley also wore such like dresses[36].

The Greeks and the Persians also used to wear the headdress of horns as a mark of social status and divine attributes. One section of the Sakas, living on the northern section of the jaxartes, around and downstream from Tashkent, are called Tigrakhauda in the Achaemenian inscriptions in view of the pointed hoods worn by them. On the Behistun (Bisutun) relief of Darius, their chief Skunkha is shown as wearing this type of headdress. They were the neighbours of the Soma drinking sakas, called the Saka Haumavarga, located in Farghanah. Toynbee thinks that the medieval and modern Western hood was ultimately derived from the headdress of these Sakas. Thus, it is clear that the practice of wearing a horned or pointed headdress, which underlies the name of the tribe Visanin; shows its Iranian origin[37].

It appears that the opposite Tribes were mainly Iranians. The ten kings battle signifies the Iranian and Aryans sentiment mentioned in Avesta where the Aryan gods are Asuras and the Asuras are gods.

References

1. Kosambi, D.D.'Bhagwan Buddha' P.22 (Hindi) (Raj Kamal Prakashan, Delhi)

2. A. RV II-11-17 PRADODHU VACHCHHIMASRU ŚUPRĪṈĀNOYĀHI HARIBHYĀM SUTASYA PĪTIM।

B. Kretschmer-Compare it with Hittite Inor (as) it is an Asian loan word 'Vedic India' P.63. Loui's Renou translated by Philip Spratt.

3. The word 'Daeva' is derived from root Div which means. 'The Shining One' or the Glorious One. S.B.E. Vol. IV Introduction P. LXXX.

4. Kosambi D.D.'The culture and civilization of Ancient India', P 79.

5. Caste and Races in India, P 168.

6. Ibid P 8

7. Bhandarkar, D.R.'Some aspects of Ancient Indian Culture' P.4.

8. Kent, Ronald G. 'Language' XII P.298. Mentioned by Buddha Prakash P. 55.

9. Sen Sukumar 'Old Persian inscription' P.8.(University of Calcutta-1941.)

10. R.V. VII- 83-7

11. Ghurye G.S., 'Vedic India', P 204.

12. Bhandarkar D.R. P. 4.

13. Vedic Mythology Vol. I. P 97 FF

14. Ibid P 24.

15. Kosambi D.D. P 81

16. 'Who Were the Sudras? PP 133 and 142

17. Kosambi, D.D P 82

18. R.V. Vil 83-6 YUVAN HAVANT VBHAYĀS ĀJI THIVNDRANCH VASVI VARUNN CHA SATYE ।

19. R.V. VII-18-13 VI SADYO VISHVĀ DRAṄ HITĀNYEŚA MINDRAḤ PURAḤ SAHASĀ SAPTA DARDAḤ. ।
VYĀNAVASYA TRITSAVE GAYAM BHĀGJEŚM PŪRUM VIDATHE MRI DHRA VĀCHAM" ॥

20. Jai Bra. II-392

21. Dr. Buddha Prakash P 102.

22. H.S. Nyberg Die Religionen des alten Iran, PP 237-249-51 cited by Buddha Prakash P 102.

23. Strange G. Le 'The lands of the eastern caliphate,' PP 331-32

24. Pennell Dr. T.L.'Among the Wild Tribes of Afganistan Frontier' PP 55-56.

25. Kosambi D.D. P 82
26. Elphinstone M.' An Account of the Kingdom of Caubul'. Vol. II P. 55.
27. History of Herodotus, VI. P 36.
28. Strabo,'Geography' (Tr. Hamilton and Falconer). XIV 1.13.
29. Herodotus, OP. cit. I, 153-6.
30. Toynbee Arnold J.'A Study of History', Vol. VII, P 610. Ind. Vol. 14.
31. Mackdonell-'Vedic Mythology' P 140.
32. Zimmer-Altindisches leben-P 431, Mentioned by Buddha Prakash P 106.
33. Ibid P 431.
34. Law B.C.-Historical Geography and Ancient India-P 127.
35. Mackdonell and Keith-Vedic India-II P 313.
36. See Chapter No. 5.
37. Dr. Buddha Prakash P 107.

Growth Of Caste System

Brief History of the primitive Man

The earth came into existence approximately 4500 million years ago. The story of Man commences from the period one million years back when he descended from the trees and standing erect learnt how to walk. However, Homo Sapience could not appear on this earth till thirty to forty thousand years ago. The modern human beings are the descendants of this very Man. In the same period Man went on progressing and gradually learnt the use of stone implements and fire. This period of the development of the primitive man is termed Paleolithic Age. In fact the progress of man became rapid only ten thousand years back. This period is known as Mid-Paleolithic age. Later on he learnt farming and cattle rearing. The cultivation of crops brought about many changes in his life so that it marked the beginning of a new era. This period is known as Neolithic age.

During the end of stone age and in the beginning of the metal age when man learnt the arts of farming and cattle rearing, there was a rapid and surprising development of his civilization. when in a particular region on account of some causes if grass became scarce for cattle grazing, he naturally migrated from that area and settled at such places as could provide adequate fodder for his cattle. Similarly with the change of seasons it became impossible to stay at one place. The agriculture productivity fell low owing to the paucity of rains or became negligible. To overcome his ordeal he bade good bye to his first abode and explored new lands with favourable weather conditions to accumulate surplus yield in abounding rains. But this migration might not have been so easy as has been assumed. On the new land the earlier occupants who had been tilling the soil or rearing cattle must have offered stout resistance. There must have been stiff confrontation. If the earlier inhabitant was comparatively more skillful in the art of fighting than the new comers, he must have had to retreat and on the converse, if the new comers had been a more skillful fighter as compared to the original occupants, he must have been victorious over them. As a result of the confrontation some of the earlier occupants might have been killed some might have fled to save their lives while the remaining might have accepted subjugation or put into prison. In other words the valiant new conquerors might have enslaved the natives.

It appears that the entry of fair complexioned stalwart Nordic Aryans in about 1700-1600 B.C. was a similar type of event. They defeated the dark complexioned aboriginals in wars and captured the bushgreen fertile lands of Sapt Sindhu. Some of the dark complexioned aboriginals had fled to the Ganga-Yamuna plains and South India and settled there. Its proofs have been given in chapter XII. Perhaps those who had accepted the sovereignty of the Aryans without putting up any opposition or those who were defeated in the war might have been made slaves by the Aryans and forced to work in their homes as servants. Needless to say that the two groups were quite distinct so far. One of them was the Victor who claimed superiority while the other was the defeated one who suffered from inferiority complex[1]. Another conspicuous difference was that of complexion, fair and dark (also of handsome and ugly looks as well as physical build up) viz. the fair complexioned and with cherishing superiority complex were the victorious Aryans and having dark complexion, suffering from inferior complexity were the defeated non-Aryan slaves. In the beginning this was the fundamental difference which formed the basis of the caste system.

Aryan and Non-Aryan Two Varnas

Obviously, in the beginning, the Aryans and the non-Aryans were the only two varnas. This is to state that the two had basic differences both internal and external from the start. From the internal point of view the Aryan being the conqueror class developed the tradition of exploitation. Where there are two classes, the ruler and the ruled, the master and the slave, one enjoying full rights and the other utterly devoid, the growth of class consciousness is just a natural phenomenon. With the dawn of stability, the system evolved in keeping with these feelings and the society began to take shape. In fact the Aryans were always trying to trample upon the non-Aryan slaves. As such, the gulf between the Aryans and the non-Aryans went on widening till it became unbridgable. The two groups became quite distinct from each other. This view is supported by the opening verses of Rigveda:-"He who created the universe and settled the Dasa Varna in Caves, He is Indra".(Rig.II-12-4)

YENEMĀ VISHVĀ CHYAVANĀ KRITĀNIYO DĀSAM̃ VARṈAM DHARAM̃ GUHĀKAḤ I

Here the word'Dasa' has been clearly employed for the non-Aryan class which is in singular number that is to say that it stands for the entire Dasa community or the non-Aryan section treated as one class. In Vedas the non-Aryans are referred to by the words'Dasyus' or 'Dasas'. On the other hand the Aryan class has always been mentioned under the same name viz. the Aryan varna, as for instance:

"'They by killing the Dasyus have always provided defence to the Aryan Varna (colour)"(Rig. III-34-9)

HIRAṈYAMUT BHOGAM̃ SASĀN HATVODASŪN PRĀRYAVARṈMĀVAT I

Here also the word Varana has been used in singular. That is, the people who are termed as Aryans belong to one and the same class or Varana and not to more than one. According to Sayana the Aryan'Varana' means the upper three Varnas.

In Satpath Brahman it is mentioned that only the upper three Varnas are the Aryans. They only can perform Yajna (ĀRYA EVĀ BRAHMAṆ VĀ KSHATTRIYA VĀ VAISHYA VĀTE HI YAJANYĀH)[2]

Rigveda supports the above view:- 'Come close to Indra for the defence of the humans. May he subdue anger of the Dasas and endow with high progress the human caste'(the Aryans)(Rig I-104-2)

O TYE NARAINDRA MŪTAYE GURNŪ CHITTĀN TSADYO ADHYANO JAGAMYĀTI

DEVĀSO MANYUM̄ DĀSASYA SHCHAMNAN TE NA Ā VAUSHAN TSUVI TĀYAVARṆAM II

Here the word human stands for the Aryans. "We (The Aryans worshipers) dwell amidst the Dasyu caste. Their customs are different. They are not fit to be called human beings. Therefore O' Indra, the destroyer of enemies, destroy these people." (Rig X-22-8)

AKARMĀ DASYŪRABHI NO AMANTURANYA VRATO AMANUṢAḤ I

TVAM̄ TASYĀ MITRA HANVADHAR DĀSASYA ḌAMBHAYAḤII

Here the term Aryans and Dasyus have been employed to signify the two big divisions of humanity.

Again it is mentioned:

"O' Indra! these 'Kikat' people who are non-Arynas, of what use are cows to them? Neither obtain milk nor do they prepare'ghee' O'! Indra,! bring those cows to our Aryan worshipers. Also let us have the wealth of the usurers".

(Rig. III-53-14)

KIM̄ TE KRIṆVANTI KĪKAṬEṢU GĀVO NASHIRAM̄ DUHRE NA TAPANT I DHARMAM I

Ā NO BHAR PRAM GANDASYA VEDO NAICHĀ SHĀKHAM̄ MAGHAVAN RANDHAYĀ NAḤ II

The above examples make it clear that in the beginning there were two varnas, the Aryans and the non-Aryans of whom the non-Aryans have been referred to as 'Dasyus' or 'Dasas'.

Prof. Rapson[3] opines that first of all the colour discrimination between the Aryans and the non-Aryans led to the birth of the caste system. In its earliest form the society was divided into two classes-the Aryans and the non-Aryans.

Senart Emile[4] supporting the above view throws light in detail:

"The literature of the Brahmanas establishes the antithesis between Sudra and Arya, Arya embracing the three higher Varnas. A multitude of signs betrays between the two terms not merely inequalities of rank but the much deeper struggle of two religious traditions. The Vedic hymns reveal the struggle at its height.

The word varna, literally colour, is generally accepted as being in Sanskrit the name of the caste. In regard to this I shall have to make reservations. It is at any rate certain that it serves regularly to designate the four theoretic Varnas. This meaning is not known in the Veda. On the other hand, the word is there employed in two opposing phrases: Arya Varna and Dasa Varna, the Aryan race and the enemy race. They have still more transparent synonyms, such as black skin, the black people. In more modern literature, the black race (Krishna Varna) continues sometimes to be opposed to the Brahmanas. This antithesis is therefore the completely equivalent prototype of that which later came to be expressed by Arya and Sudra, Arya Varna and Sudra Varna.

Through whatever evolution its use may later have passed, the word varna was therefore first employed to distinguish between two different and hostile peoples; it characterized the one by the relative whiteness, the other by the blackness of its skin. It the Aryan Varnas signify in later literature the three castes reputed to be of Aryan stock, the expression was originally used in the singular: the 'Aryan Varna' was the collective designation of the whole light-coloured race of invaders.

It is therefore certain that the terminology of the system rests on a past which was different. It envelops in its network and fashions to its own ends divisions which originally were connected with quite different ideas, and terms which it has diverted from their first significance. Let us bear this warning in mind."

Only three Varnas among the Pre-Aryans

In the Purush Sukta of the tenth Mandal of Rigveda (X-90-11,12), the four Varnas are mentioned for the first time,otherwise prior to this we come across only three Varnas-Brahman, Kashttriya and Vaishya. The fourth Varna has always been referred to as Dasas, Dasyus or non-Aryans. It means that the society was still in the grip of chaos during the post war period and the Aryans had not completely subdued the non-Aryans yet. The Aryans admitted them to their society only after subjugating them completely both physically and mentally. In other words at the time the verses of the tenth Mandala were composed, peace had been restored in the society and the non-Aryan Dasyus and Dasas had been admitted to the society under the name of 'Sudras'.

A proof to the effect that before the Aryans came, there were only three Varnas among them, is found in the Zoroastrian scripture 'Avesta'. It has been found that the Aryans first of all established their colonies in Persia (Iran) and after that in India. probably the persian Aryans composed 'Avesta' soon after the Vedic Aryan Rishis had composed the Vedas. The first Varna was the Purohit (Atharva) who looked after rituals, the second Varna comprised of the soldiers known as charioteers (Rathaesthas). The masses formed the third Varna who were occupied with artisan, agriculture, cattle rearing, trade etc., Known as farmers and artisans (Vastria, Fshuyant and Hatis). This was the class that came to be called Vaishyas in India.

It establishes that the caste division existed among the Aryans, prior to their arrival in India and that they comprised of only three Varnas. That is why before the tenth Mandala of the Rigveda we find mention of only three Varnas.

V.M. Apte[5] is of the opinion "'The mention of only three Varnas before the Purush Sukta of the tenth Mandala of the Rigveda does not imply that before that the fourth Varna had no existence. The fourth Varna did exist but so far it had not been included in the Aryan social system. These probably constituted the survivors after their confrontation with the advancing Aryans and were later on included in the Aryan social set up. The defeated predecessors were of quite a different complexion as compared with those who were victorious. Thus, there arose the need for division of labour and functions especially in the case of the fourth Varna which was quite distinct from the earlier three. In this way, the fourth section consisted of artisans and servile class which was not much different from the third section. It is more than probable that along with the aboriginals, the inhabitants of the Indus Valley must also have had confrontation with the Rigvedic Aryans."

Obviously the Aryan community which was already divided into three Varnas before they settled here provided the first three Varnas and the remnants of the Indus Valley known as Sudras who had no rights but only duties to serve the upper three castes. The artisan and the servile class is a part of Sudra community of today.

At this stage of our discussion, a question is likely to arise-were there no social disturbances after the period of origin? The answer to this question is that in the beginning the laws were not so strong or rigid. Later, they became more and more strict with the passage of time and any flexibility became difficult. According to some scholars Rigveda contains such description on the basis of which it may be said (X-27-12 BHADRĀ BADHŪRMAVATI YATSU PESHĀḤ SVANYA SĀ MITTRAM BHANOTE JANE CHIT) That in that period the tradition of swayamvar existed and there was freedom of work. The poet's mother was a milk-mad who made dung cakes and the father was an apothecary. (IX-113-3)

In fact there is unanimous agreement of all scholars on this point that 'Intermarriages to a certain extent existed among the three Varnas of Aryans" (S.V. Vishwanathan "Racial Synthesis in Hindu culture". PP 52-1978).

Here the Swayamvar tradition does not mean that the Aryan damsels of fair complexion used to put garlands round the necks of non-Aryans slaves and accepted them as their spouses. Exactly in the same way the three Varnas of the Aryans enjoyed freedom of work or the choice of profession. There is no such example in the Rigveda as may support the view that a particular Aryan had adopted the profession of a slave which had become the sole profession of the non-Aryans.

In Rigveda the Vasistas (VII-33-1) are termed fair and the Kanvas dark (X-31-11) that is the presence of dark complexioned Rishis among the Nordic Aryans shows that even in the Brahman sect there had been interfusion of blood with the dark complexioned non-Aryans. Several scholars are of the opinion that before the advent of the Aryans broad headed Alpines had settled here who were related to Turvasas and yadus etc, whose remains have been excavated from the cemetry 'G' and 'H' of Harappa some of these people also had adopted priesthood known as black section of Rishis.'

We may reproduce here an excerpt from a famous sociologist and scholar Ram Prasad Chanda's book 'Indo Aryan Races[6] in support of above view:

"The Arya immigrants from Mesopotamia must have absorbed a good deal of Semitic blood in their Syrian home and were probably dark like the Semites. The Purus, Druhyus and Anus, mentioned in the Rigveda along with the Yadus and Turvasas, may have come from the same Quarters and were probably of the same physical type. The fair and fair-haired invaders who formed the nucleus of the Brahman caste came earlier (later as now proved) direct from the credle of the Arya folk in the far north and elaborated the Vedic sacrificial cult in their Indian home from the primitive worship of India, Varuna and the other gods of nature. They were probably akin to the Athirvans and magi of Ancient Iran, for the Iranians, like the Indo-Aryans, but unlike all other Indo-Germanic peoples, had and the parsis still have in their Dasturs, a hereditary priesthood. The ancestors of the Rishi clans probably came earlier. When later on the ancestors of the Rigvedic warrior tribes enetered India and came in contact with the Rishi clans, the former recognised the cultural superiority of the later and accepted them as their religious guides."

It appears that in the beginning the sons born of the slave girls by the Aryan Rishis also got some respect and they also after acquiring education became Rishis. But it was to a negligible extent like a drop in the ocean, if we may say so.

Caste Division

It is important to understand properly the system of caste division in the Hindu code by the Brahmani writers:

Dwij:

The dictionary meaning of Dwij[7] is twice born. As a matter of fact everybody is born but the Upnayana ritual is considered to be the second birth when in the earlier period one was admitted to studentship. Clearly it refers to any member of the first three Varnas of Hindu classes viz. Brahman, Kshattriya and Vaishya. Opposed to this is Adwij i.e. once born who has not undergone the Upnayana ritual.

Sudra:

This word is a compound of 'Suk + dra', 'Suk' means 'sorrow' and 'dra' means to be surrounded i.e. that person who is overwhelmed with sorrows[8].

According to Buddha those who were afraid of and were involved in inferior behaviour came to be known as Suda from which the modern word 'Sud' originated.[9]

In the time of Buddha the word 'Sudra' became synonym of Chhudra and this gave rise to the opinion that the word 'Sudra' was modified form of "Chhudra".[10]

The Hindi-Sanskrit dictionary compiled by the lexicographer Monium Willium defines 'Sudra' as a member of the fourth varna.

According to Taitreya Brahman the Sudras are descendants of Asuras (DEVYO VAI VARNO BRAHMANAHI ASURYA SHUDRAH). At another place in the same scripture, their origin is explained to be from nonentity (ASTO VAES SANBHUTAH YACHCHHUDRAH)[11].

According to Yajurveda 30-5 (TAPSE SHUDRAM) a Sudra is a person who earns his livelihood by the sweat of brow. As per Gautam Dharm Suttra (X-6,9), the Sudras are the non-Aryans.

According to several scholars of the west this is a word of Dravidian languages and it will be of no use to find out its etymon in sanskrit language[12].

Classification of Sudras

(i) Touchable

(ii) Untounchable

(i) Touchable : The unex communicated is termed as Sudras, in the primitive religious books. In the modern time they are also known as touchable Sudras. In English language, they are termed depressed classes or backward classes. They denote the section of society which has lagged behind. They include the servile class, tillers, cattle rearers, oil crushers, distillers, carpenters, copper smiths, gold smiths and metal workers, wood workers, weavers, bamboo workers, dyers, printers, corn porchers, tailors etc.

(ii) Untouchable: (ex-communicated): They are termed as Maha-sudra or the Scheduled Castes in English. This is so because the names of these communities appear in the schedule prepared by the Indian Government. Mahatma Gandhi gave them the name 'Harijans'. These are engaged in leather work, scavanging and other filthy professions.

Varn Sankara: The Brahmani writers hold that this Sudra caste grew on the basis of inter union of upper and lower classes (Varn sankarta). We may also call them hybrid castes of which one is Anuloma and the other is Viloma or Pratiloma.

Anuloma: When a child is born of a father being of higher caste and the mother belonging to a lower caste, he is known as Anuloma Varna-Sankara. This is the same class which is treated as backward or depressed class. We many cite a few examples from scriptures as follow:

According to Manusmriti:

(X-8) Born of Brahman father and Sudra mother will be Nishad or Parashar, fisherman.

(X-9) Born of Kshattriya father and Sudra mother will be ugra professing Chaubdari.

Parashar Smriti (XI-23): If the father is Brahman and the mother is Sudra who has not been ritualized the child will be Dasa and if the ritual has been performed then the child will become a barber. This is different from the origin stated in Manusmriti and reveals the hollowness of the Smrities. (XI-24) Kshattriya male and Sudra female--their union results in cowboy or Ahir. (This also does not tally with Manusmriti).

Viloma: When the father belongs to a lower caste and the mother comes of a higher caste the offsprings are the ex-communicated. Maha-Sudra or scheduled castes or Harijans. Some examples are given below:

Manusmriti (X-12)- The son of Sudra father and a Vaishya will be a Ayogava. wood-worker. Those born of a Sudra father and Kshattriya mother will be chhatta, will adopt the profession of catching and killing reptiles. A union between a Sudra and a Brahman woman will produce a Chandala.

In Chapter X of Manusmriti the origin of some Varn Sankar castes is explained like this:-

S.No.	Male		Female		Offspring
1.	Brahman	+	Kshattriya	=	Murdhvasitika
2.	Kshattriya	+	Vaishya	=	Mahishwa
3.	Vaishya	+	Sudra	=	Karna (Kaistha)
4.	Brahman	+	Vaishya	=	Ambastha
5.	Kshattriya	+	Brahman	=	Suta
6.	Vaishya	+	Kshattriya	=	Magadha
7.	Sudra	+	Kshattriya	=	Chhatta
8.	Vaishya	+	Brahman	=	Vaideh
9.	Sudra	+	Brahman	=	Chandala
10.	Nishad	+	Sudra	=	Pukkas
11.	Sudra	+	Nishada	=	Kukkat
12.	Chhattah	+	Ugra	=	Swapak
13.	Vaideh	+	Ambast	=	Vain
14.	Brahman	+	Ugra	=	Abrata
15.	Brahman	+	Ambasht	=	Abhir

It has been stated earlier that according to Avesta the Aryans comprised of three Varnas. The third varna which consisted of no other than common masses engaged themselves in agriculture, cattle grazing, artisan jobs etc. In fact the common people were called 'Vish' by the Aryans. The word 'Vaishya' is born of this root 'Vish'. It is obvious the Aryan Vishas followed the same pursuits as were later on in the case of Vaishyas and Sudras. It has already been said that the Aryans treated all non-Aryan Dasas and Dasyus as Sudras and entrusted them with the jobs other than trade and agriculture, such as artisan which they were doing already and servile jobs which they were forced to render after they were defeated in the war.

Apparently the Aryans had reserved the respectable professions of trade and agriculture for themselves. In Chapter X PP-227-40 we shall learn that among the Indus valley non-Aryans there was a section called Pani which had been a trading class since ages and they were more trained in this art and hence more prosperous then the 'Vish'. Their skill in trading and prosperity made them respectable. Secondly the greedy Brahmani Purohits always had their eye on their wealth[13] and riches. Therefore, the Purohits gave them respect and honour only to satisfy their own selfish interests. Apart from this the Panis resembled the 'Vaishyas' in their work. Therefore, it became difficult to distinguish between the two on the basis of profession. Gradually, the non-Aryan Panis started intruding into the Vaishya class and were partially mixed with them by the advent of the Muslims.

K.N Dikshit has corroborated these views. He says, "What did the Aryans do at the end of the Indus Valley Civilization? They absorbed the remnants of the Indus Valley people into two lower varnas such as traders, artisans and tillers."

From this at least one thing becomes crystal clear that excepting Brahmanas, kshattriyas and Vaishyas (not non-Aryan vanik) all the sections were certainly non-Aryans Sudras-To clarify this view we may here consider the origin of those controversial castes which are not included in the upper three varnas. The main among these are Marathas, Kayasthas, Soods, Yadavas and Rajputs. Of course some of these might have become part of the higher castes forced by circumstances[14] or some other reasons, the Dwij class is not even today prepared to admit their superiority. They are hanging in the balance.

YADAVA

It has already been mentioned in Chapter IV P-64 that the Yadavas were an Iranian tribe and they had come to India from the south western Asia through south Baluchistan or by the sea route[15] Several scholars hold that of the five communities (Panch janya) mentioned in Rigveda one was the Yadava or Yadu while other believe that they belonged to Kanvas and Vishwamittra etc, to the section of dark complexioned Rishis. In some provinces of India such as Uttar Pradesh and Bihar etc, this community comes in backward classes or Sudras. In a verse in Rigveda they are said to be at par with Dasas[16].

Similarly in Rigveda VI-20-15, IV-30-17[17], X-49-8 and VII-10-4,5 it is mentioned that Indra had helped them in crossing the ocean and included them in the Aryan society. That is to say they were not Aryans but they were later admitted to the Aryan society just as the Aryan sages had admitted the non-Aryans, Dasyus and Dasas to their four varna system by giving them the name of Sudra.

As described in the Rigveda, a colossal adventure of Indra which appears to have a historical basis, was a battle fought with a dark complexioned non-Aryan chief named Krishna. It is said that when Krishna stopped at Ashumati (Yamuna) with his army of ten thousand soldiers, Indra sent forward Marut an Aryan Vish and personally fought against Adaiveh Vish, with the aid of Brihaspati. Adaiveh Vish has been described by Sayana as dark Asur[18].

That Indra had said, "I have seen the dark Asur (monster). He wonders in the growth (Khar) on the bank of Ashumati. O Marudgana! fulfiller of all wishes, I too wish you may kill him in the war". (Rig. VIII-96-14).

DRAPSAMAPASH YAM̃ VISUṆE CHARANT MUPAHVARE NIPAYO ANSHUMATYĀḤI
NABHO NA KRISHNAMAVATASTHI VÃNSAMIŚYĀMI VO VRAŚṆO YUDHYATĀJAUII

On the bank of Ashumati the fast mover Krishnasur lives in radiant glory. Indra killed him along with his entire army with the help of Brihaspati." (RV VIII-96-15)

ADHA DRAPSO ANSHUMATYĀ UPASTHE 'DHĀRAYAT TANVAṀ TITVIŚĀ ṆAḤ I
VISHO ADE VĪRBHYĀ CHARANTĪ BRIHASPATINĀ YUJENDRAḤ SASĀHE II

Similarly, there is description of the killing of Krishangarbha in I-100-1. Sayana mentions the destruction of the foetus of the wife of an Asure named Krishna,

That Krishna was a non-Aryan chief of the dark yadav race has also been confirmed by D.D. Kosambi.[19]

Proofs of hostility between Krishna and Indra are also available in the later Sanskrit scriptures. Weber[20] has described the boyhood exploits of Krishna with the remarks, "Now christianity has reached India in any form whatsoever, there is similarity between the names 'Krishna' and 'Christ'. In southern India Krishna is called Krishna (Christhna) which has reached India in the form of story of the birth of Krishna whose mother was Devki. Devki means divine."

Regarding the story reaching India, learned writers hold, "First of all this story reached Egypt proof of which is found there in 430 A.D. Probably from there it reached India through the traders."

Mr Kennedy[21] writes that in 4th century A.D. the Scythians coming from central Asia carried the tale of a child god who was related to the birth of Christ. Here the story found appropriate atmosphere to grow and became popular. The name of this new child God had the echo of adult Krishna and got attached with him."

The above opinion is based on the fact that there are many similarities between the boy Krishna and Christ. Narad prophesied the death of Kansha at the hands of the last issue of Devki, in the same way a saint had prophesied the killing of Achrysis by his daughter's son Phareseus. Similarly the legends of Kali Dehan murder of Pootna are also synonymous with Christ.

In support of this, views of D.D. Kosambi[22] are produced below in detail-

"Krishna is really foreign to the Mahabharata, a later intruder in the epic. The legend says that he joined the Pandus in burning down the Khandava forest to clear the land. The ambiguous position of the Yadus in the Rigveda and Krishna's dark skin may be another step in the recombination of Aryans with aborigines, just as the irreconcilable Naga stories are a clear, step in that direction. Both types of stories would not be acceptable in one epic unless the audiences contained elements that derived from both types of people. The conflict with Indira had a remarkable consequence. Late in the fourth century, invading Greeks found that the worship of an Indian demigod whom they equated immediatedly with their own Herakles was the main cult of the Panjab plains, while 'Dionysos' continued to be worshipped in the hills. This Herakles was unmistakably the Indian Krishna. The Greek hero was traditionally a matchless athlete burnt black by the sun, who had killed the Hydra (a many headed snake like Kaliya) and Violated or wedded many nymphs. In addition, the manner of Krishna's death was more familiar to Greek myth than to the Indian. The Yadu demigod died of an arrow shot into the heel by the wild hunter jaras, really his half-brother. Indians still cannot understand how such a wound could be fatal. The stories of Achilles and so many other Greeks of mythological antiquity show that the peculiar death must have been due to a ritual killing connected with a poisoned weapon often wielded by the brother (or tanist) of the sacrificed hero. The other Indian god whom the Greeks recognised as conquering Dionysos can only be Vedic Indra, whose hard-drinking and hard-fighting character rages berserk through the Rigveda. The immense significance of this Greek report has been missed. It shows that although the Yadus were extinct, the cult of Krishna had already driven that of Indra out of the best-cultivated portion of the Panjab. Moreover, this occurred even though Indra-Dionysos (in the Greek record) had first brought knowledge of iron and metals, use of oxen for agriculture, and the art of house-building to India after his 'conquest'.

On the basis of the above proofs we are led to the conclusion that the Krishna of Bhagwat is perhaps a modified form of Christ and the Krishna of Rigvedic description is the non-Aryan god and chief of Yadu caste.

Dark skinned Krishna was a non-Aryan chief. Oldham[23] is of the view that, "Krishna was a non-Aryan of dark skin so much so that in the Indian school of painting this fact is still preserved and he is always painted as a blue skinned human. As far his ancestral history it is said that he was the incarnation of Vishnu. He was the son of Vasudev who was the great grandson of Aryaka who was a Naga chief. The word 'Nag' means 'serpent' and it was applied to those people who worshipped the serpents and who were mentioned in Sanskrit literature as Asur, monsters, Danavas and Dasas. These words are still used for the Dravidians of northern India not yet subdued.

Similarly, it has been said about Balram, the elder brother of Krishna that he was always under the protection of many hoods of cobras. He is considered the reincarnation of Shesh Nag. At his death his soul came out of his body in the form of a huge cobra (V.P. V-37-64)."

In Vishnu Purana (V-35-15,16) the Kuru says :- "Balramji ! whether you go or stay, we are not prepared to free Samba under your or Ugarsen's orders (15). Previously all the members of Yadu dynasty bowed to us but now why not doing so,inspite of being slaves you are passing orders like masters (16).

This view is also supported by Alberuni's[24] description where he writes, "There was born a son from the union of Vasudeva and sister of Kansha, the king in those days, in the city of Mathura. He was from a low born Sudra-Shepherd jatt family'

S.R. Rao[25] in his book 'Lothal and the Indus Valley civilization' writes,

'One thing is worth noting, It is that the two spindles of a particular type have been excavated at Lothal, and the spindles used by for spinning wool by the nomade tribes named Bharwars today, are of the same design and description. This tribe calls itself Yadavas of Maharashtra".

From this it appears that the Yadavas were connected with the Indus Valley civilization[26] and a chief of one of their clans lived in Mathura region. It is possible that in the stampade that followed the barbarous invasion by the Aryans, a group of Yadavas crossed the Indus river and went towards Baluchistan. Thus the incident mentioned in the Rigveda(VI-20-12 or VI-45-1) regarding Indra's rescuing the Yadavas from the ocean, clearly means that Indra brought back the Yadavas after crossing the ocean like river Sindhu where it meets the sea. Scholars believe that during that period a sea Journey by the Aryans seems improbable. It is contrary to the nature of the Aryans (Bodhayan Dharm Sutra I-1-24).

In a case, Masakkakne versus Ammakutte (ILR-1927-52 Madras I) cited by Dr Ambedkar[27] in his book entitled, "Who were the Sudras? in 1927, the Madras High Court had given the judgement that the Yadavas are a Sudra caste. In another case[28], while giving judgement regarding a caste case, the principle adopted was that all non-Brahmans are sudras unless they prove that they are Kshattriya or Vaishyas. This corroborates the view that all the 'Adwijas' (non Dwijas) must be Sudras. Such is the course of judicial pronouncements on the issue as to how to determine who is a Kshattriya and who is a Sudra. It is a most confusing medley of opinion which settles little and unsettles much. The Kayasthas of Bihar, of the Upper Provinces (now U.P.) and Benares are Kshattriyas, while the Kayasthas of Bengal are Sudras !! According to the Madras High Court all Mahrattas are Sudras, but according to the Bombay High Court, Mahrattas belonging to five families and 96 families are Kshattriya and the rest are Sudras!! The Yadava community to which Krishna belonged is popularly believed to be Kshattriyas. But according to the Madras High Court, the Yadavas are Sudras!!"

On the basis of the proofs already rendered it may be stated that the Yadavas were undoubtedly non-Aryan Sudras and not Aryan Kshattriyas as it is said in several parts of the country even today.

MARATHA

Now we shall consider the famous said Kshattriya caste of Maharashtra called Maratha of which Chhatrapati Shivaji was a descendant.

This is an open secret that Shivaji after conquering the several kingdoms of the Western Maharashtra by dint of his courage and power, had established his rule there and founded one fort. He thought of his coronation in order to declare his kingship. But the Brahmanas refused to perform his coronation saying that he was a Sudra. Shivaji's friends advised that the coronation must be held in strict accordance with the vedic tradition[29]. But he had to face a number of hurdles in the fulfilment of his desire. First, that no person other than the Brahmans could help perform this ritual while not a single Brahman was prepared to do so. Secondly, this ritual could not be held until his identity as a Kshattriya was confirmed. Thirdly that he had not undergone the Upnayan Samskar (the ritual of admittance) and in the absence of Upnayan this ritual of coronation was impossible. The Brahmanas under the leadership of Moropant Pingley who was Shivaji's Prime Minister refused to recognise Shivaji as Kshattriya. So much so that in this concern even the Maratha chiefs of Shivaji did not stand by him rather they also treated him as Sudra[30]. Balaji Avaji, Shivaji's friend and secretary was of immense help to him. He gave some money to Brahmans and got prepared the pedigree table of Shivaji which was connected with the Sisodiya dynasty of Mewar. He procured the services of a famous Brahman named Gaugbhat from Banaras in exchange for a large sum of money and it was then that the coronation ceremony of Shivaji would be effected.

But after that the Madras High Court in a case declared Shivaji' brother Benkaji (Ekogy) a Sudra and refused to treat him as a Kshattriya[31].

Obviously the Marathas are in fact Sudras and in no case Kshattriyas. That is why a brave Warrior like Shivaji had to submit to the authority of the Brahmans and he could achieve his aim only after paying a considerable sum of money in the form of charity.

Similarly, the controversial castes viz. Kayasthas and sood will also be proved to be non-Aryan Sudras in tenth chapter. Rajput castes also can be proved to be originally non-Aryans who turned Rajputs after giving away charity generously to Brahmans.

References

1. Ghurye, G.S. "Caste and races in India". P 173.
2. (A) JRAS Vol. II (1866) P 281 foot note

   (B) Satp Bra-Kanva Shakha, Adhavara Kand 1-6.
3. Rapson, E.J. CHI Vol. I, P 48.
4. "Caste in India", PP 120-135.
5. 'Were castes formulated in the age of the Rigveda'? P 35. BDCRI Vol. II (Nov. 1940), N. 1 & 2.
6. Indo Aryan Races IC 25 & 33.
7. Hindi-Sanskrit dictionary-Monium Willium.
8. Vayu Purana I-VIII-158.
9. Digha Nikaya III-95.
10. IAB. Vol. I, PP 138-139.
11. Tait Bra, I-2-6-7 and III-2-3-9 cited by J. Muir in 'Original Sanskrit text,' P 21.
12. Encyclopaedia Britanica, Vol.I
13. Rigveda III-53-14

    Ā NO BHAR PRAMGANDASYA VEDO NAICHĀ SHĀ KHAM MAGHAYAN RANDHAYA NAḤ II

    O Indra! bring the wealth of profiteer (Pani) for us.
14. Some non-Aryan kings entered into Dwijas through performance of Hiranyagarbhya ceremony. In this ceremony king had to lay quite naked in the golden vessel of womb like shape. Then Purohita remained enchanting slokas of child birth ceremony. The king by and by slipped out of it, who was given a Gottra of Dwijas by the Purohita and golden vassel of womb like shape was taken away by him in cherity.(prachin Bharat ki Sanskriti Aur Sabhyata (Hindi) P 210 Kosambi, D.D.)
15. Chanda, R.P. IC 25;26,27
16. Rigveda-X-62-10 UT DĀSI PARIVISE SMADRIṢṬĀ GOPARĪṆASĀ I YADURSTUVASHCHA MĀMHE II
17. Rigveda IV-30-17

    UT TYĀ TURVASHAYADU ASNĀTĀR SHACHĪ PATIH INDRO VIDVA N APĀRYAT I

    Both, Turvasa and yadus, who do not known how to swim, were brought to this side (of river) by the wise Indra the husband of Sachi.
18. Kosambi, D.D. "The Culture and Civilization of Ancient India". P 114.
19. JBBRASB. N.S. XXIII-43, Kosambi, D.D.

20. Weber, IA, Vol. XXX, 1901, P 286.
21. JRAS 1907, PP 989-90.
22. Kosambi, D.D. P 117.
23. Oldham, "The Sun & the Serpents". PP 78-80.
24. Albaruni Ka-Bharat. P 287 (Hindi).
25. Ibid P 107.
26. See chapter 15, (History of Abhiras)
27. Ibid P 188.
28. Ibid P 189.
29. Sarkar Yadu Nath, 'Shivaji and his time'. P 210.
30. Ambedkar B.R. PP 201-203.
31. 48 Madras-1 (1924) Maharaja Kolhapur versus Sundaram-Ayangar- Mentioned by Dr. Ambedkar, BR P 187.

CHAPTER IX

Various Theories Of Sudra's Origin In Sanskrit Literature

Rigveda

In the Purushusukta in tenth Mandala of Rigveda contains the first reference to the four Varna system. This is reproduced below :- Rig X-90-11,12

YATPURUṢA BYA DADHUḤ KATIDHĀ VYAKALPAYAN I
MUKHA KIMASYA KO BĀHŪ KA URU PĀD UCHCHETE II (11)
BRĀHMAṆOASYA MUKHMĀSHĪD BĀHŪ RĀJANYAḤ KRITAḤ I
ŪRŪ TADASYA YADVAISHVAḤ PADMAYĀM SHUDRO AJĀYATA II (12)

How many types of colossal beings grew from that Prajapati? who were their hands, feet, abdomen, mouth etc.? (11) Their mouth became the Brahamans, arms Kshattriyas, thighs Vaishyas and feet Sudras(12).

In this way the Aryan sages had imputed divine origin to caste system so that it may remain above enquiry or suspicion. How much supreme and most sacred the origin of caste system or its description in a scripture may be, it is almost meaningless to a student of history. Most of the scholars are of the opinion that the tenth and the last Mandala of Rigveda was appended at a later stage. (According to Keith, it dates back to the period between 1000-800 B.C.)[1]. The experts in linguistics hold that its language, usage and grammar is entirely different from the earlier sections (Mandals) while Risley believes that this addition has been done in the modern age.

Satpath Brahman II-1-4-11

MŪRATI VAI PRAJĀPATIḤ I IMĀMAJANMAT BHUV ITYANTRIKSHASY SVARITI,I
DAVAYETĀ VADRĀ JYIDSVA SARVA YĀVDIME LOKAḤ SARVE ṆEVĀDHĪYATE II

Saying "Bhuh" Prajapati created the whole Universe. Saying "Bhuva" he created air, with the word "Swaha" He created the sky and the entire creation came into existence in this way. Saying "Bhuh" Prajapati created the Brahmans. Saying "Bhuva" He created Kshattriyas and with the word "Swaha" Vaishya came into being. "Swaha" became a cause of creation of every thing uttering Bhuh He himself came in to existence, with the word "Bhuva" the seasons were formed and the cattle were formed with the utterance of "Swaha". In this way the whole world became perfect.

Regarding the human origin the following story related in Satpath Brahman is reproduced below (1-8-1-1 to 10):-

Water was brought to Manu, in the morning to wash his hands. As he was thus washing, a fish came into his hands, (2) (which spoke to him) 'preserve me; I shall save thee'. (Manu enquired) 'From what wilt thou save me?' (The fish replied) 'A flood shall sweep away all these creatures; from it I will rescue thee'. (Manu asked) 'How (shall) the preservation (be affected)?' 3. The fish said : 'So long as we are small, we are in great peril, for fish devours fish; thou shalt preserve me first in a jar. When I grow too large for the jar, then thou shall dig a trench, and preserve me in that. When I grow too large for the trench, then thou shalt carry me away to the ocean. I shall then be beyond the reach of danger.' 4. Straightway he became a large fish; for the waxes to the utmost. (He said) 'Now in such and such a year, then the flood will come; thou shalt, therefore, construct a ship, and report to me; thou shalt embark in the ship when the flood rises, and I shall deliver thee from it'. 5. Having thus preserved the fish, Manu carried him away to the sea. Then in the same year which the fish had enjoined, he constructed a ship and resorted to him. When the flood rose, Manu embarked in the ship. The fish swam towards him. He fastened the cable of the ship to the fish's horn. By this means he passed over this northern mountain.6. The fish said,'I have delivered thee; fasten the ship to a tree. But lest the water should cut thee off whilst thou art on the mountain, as much as the water subsides, so much shalt thou descend after it.' He accordingly descended after it as much (as it subsided). Wherefore also this, viz. 'Manu's descent'is (the name) of the northern mountain. Now the flood had swept away all these creatures; so Manu alone was left here. 7. Desirous of offspring, he lived worshipping and toiling in arduous religious rites. Among these he also sacrificed with the paka offering. He cast clarified butter, thickened milk,whey and curds, as an oblation into the waters. Thence in a year a woman was produced. She rose up as it were unctuous. Clarified butter adheres to her steps. Mitra and Varuna met her. They said to her, 'who are thou?' 'Manu's daughter', (she replied)' Say (thou art) ours', (they rejoined). 'No', she said,'I am his who begot me'. They desired a share in her. She promised that, or she did not promise that; but passed onward. She came to Manu. 9. Manu said to her, "Who art thou?' 'Thy daughter', she replied. 'How, glorious one,'asked Manu,'(art thou) my daughter?' 'Thou hast generated me; she said, 'from those oblations, butter, thick milk, whey and curds, which thou didst cast into the water. I am a benediction. Apply me in the sacrifice. If thou wilt employ me in the sacrifice, thou shalt abound in offspring and cattle. Whatever benediction thou wilt ask through me, shall accrue to thee'. He (accordingly) introduced her (as) that (which comes in) the middle of the sacrifice, for that is the middle of the sacrifice which (comes) between the introductory and concluding forms. 10. With her he lived worshipping and toiling in arduous religious rites, desirous of offspring. With her he begot this offspring which is this offspring of Manu. Whatever benediction he asked with her, was all vouchsafed to him. This is essentially that which is Ida. Whosoever, Knowing this, lives with Ida, begets this offspring which Manu begot. Whatever benediction he asks with her, is all vouchsafed to him'. (C.H.1.I PP82-89 AB Keith)

This legend is repeated in Chhandogya Upnishad III-11-4- and VIII-15-1 and Taitreya Samhita II-6,7,1 and 1-7-1,3.

Here not only the theory of origin of man given is different from the one in the Purush Sukta of Rigveda but also the author himself presents two different theories. The first theory is that human beings originated from the utterence of 'Bhuh, Bhuva, Swaha'. Later on the entire generation of Man (which include men of different races) is said to have descended from 'Ida' while the anthropological study of origin of man has proved that the inhabitation of the earth was composed of different ethnic groups e.g. Negritos, Nordic Aryans, Dravidians, Mongols etc. and all these different races cannot be believed to have ascended from a single human couple. Even Darwin's theory of origin of species 'is completely falsified here.

Taitreya Brahaman III-12-9-2

RIGBHYO JĀTAM̃ VAISHYAM̃-VACHARĀTA ICHAḤ I

This whole universe has been created by Brahma. It is a human saying that the Vaishya Varna originated from the invocations of Rigveda, the Kshattriyas from Yajurveda, and Brahman Varna from Sam Veda.

Here the author might have wanted to trace the origin of the Sudras to Atharvveda but he was not in favour of honorifying a non-Aryan slave. The same thing has happened in Satpath Brahman. Here too no theory is given explaining the origin of the Sudras.

Aitreya Brahman (VII-13-18): Aitreya Brahman contains the legend of Sunassepa. According to this legend:

Visvamitra is alluded to as being the Hotri-priest of king Harischandra, and as belonging to the tribe of the Bharatas. He is also addressed as Rajaputra, and his sons are called Kusikas. The outlines of the story are as follows: King Harischandra of the family of Ikshvaku having no son, promised to Varuna, by the advice of Narada, that if a son should be born to him he would sacrifice him to that god. A son was accordingly born to the king, who received the name of Rohita; but Harischandra, though called upon by Varuna, put off from time to time, on various pleas, the fulfilment of his promise. When the father at length consented, the youth himself refused to be sacrificed and went into the forest. After passing six years there he met a poor Brahman Rishi called Ajigartta who had three sons, the second of whom, Sunassepa, he sold for a hundred cows to Rohita, who brought the young Brahman to be sacrificed instead of himself. Varuna accepted the vicarious victim, and arrangements were made accordingly, Visvamitra being the Hotri-priest, Jamadagni the Adhvaryu, Vasista the Brahman, and Ayasya the Udgatri (tosya he Visvamitrohota Asij Jamadagnir adhvaryur Vasishtha brahma Ayasyah Udgata)". The sacrifice was not, however, completed, although the father received a hundred more cows for binding his son to the sacrificial post, and a third hundred for agreeing to slaughter him. By reciting verses in honour of different deities in succession Sunassepa was delivered: and at the request of the priests took part in the ceremonial of the day. The rest of the legend runs like this. Sunassepa got up and went towards Vishwamitra. Sunassepa's father Ajigartta said,"O sage, restore my son to me. Visvamitra replied, "No the gods have given him to me (DEVAḤ ARSĀTAḤ). Thus he became Viswamitra's son, Devarata. Kapiloma and Vabhariva were his descendants. Ajigartta tried to convince his son but he flatly refused to come to him. He told Viswamittra "O Prince, whatever his argument I shall never agree to be called a descendant of Angirisa". At this Visvamitra rejoined, 'Thou shalt be the eldest of my sons, and thy offspring shall be the most eminent. Thou shalt receive my divine inheritance; with this (invitation) I address thee'. Sunassepa answered, If(thy sons) agree, then for my welfare enjoin on them to be friendly, that so, a chief of the Bharatas, I may enter on thy sonship'. Visvamitra then addressed his sons, 'Do ye, Madhuchhandas, Rishabha, Renu, Ashtaka, and all ye who are brothers, listen to me, and concede to him the seniority'. 18. Now Visvamitra had a hundred sons, fifty of whom were older then Madhuchhandas and fifty younger. Then those who were older did not approve (their father's proposal). Against them he pronounced (this doom) 'Let your progeny possess the furthest ends (of the country) These are the numerous border-tribes, the Andhras, Pundras, Sabaras, Pulindas, Mutibas. Most of the Dasyus are sprung from Visvamitra. Madhuchhandas with the (other) fifty said,'Whatever our father determines, by that we abide. We all place thee in our front, and follow after thee'. Then Visvamitra was pleased, and said to his sons, 'Ye, my children who, shewing deference to me, have conferred upon me a (new) son, shall abound in cattle and in sons. Ye, my sons, the offspring Gathin, who possess in Devarata a man who shall go before you, are all destined to be prosperous; he is your wise instructor. This Devarata, O Kusikas, is your chief; follow him. He will receive you as my inheritance, and obtain all the Knowledge which we possess'.

I may reproduce Professor Max Muller's[2] remarks on this legend in his own words:

"So revolting indeed is the description given to Ajigartta's behaviour in the Brahmana, that we should rather recognize in him a specimen of the Un-Aryan population of India. Such a supposition, however, would be in contradiction with several of the most essential points of the legend, particularly in what regard the adoption of Sunasssepa by Visvamitra. Visvamitra, though arrived at the dignity of a Brahman, clearly considers the adoption of Sunassepa Devarata, of the famous Brahmanic family of the Angirisas, as an advantage for himself and his descendants; and the Devaratas as are indeed mentioned as a famous branch of the Visvamitras (Wilson's. V.P. P 405, 23). Sunassepa is made his eldest son, and the leader of his brothers, evidently as the defender and voucher of their Brahmanhood, which must have been then of very recent date, because Visvamitra himself is still addressed by Sunassepa as Raja-putra and Bharata-Rishabha". It must, however, be recollected that the story, as told in the Brahmanas, can scarcely be regarded as historical, and that it is not unreasonable to suppose that the incidence related, even if founded on fact, may have been coloured by the Brahmanical prepossessions of the narrator. But if so, the legend can give us no true idea of the light in which Visvamitra's exercise of priestly functions was looked upon either by himself or by his contemporaries. It appears improbable that the figure 100 should occur again and again viz. 100 cows, sons of Visvamitra. It may not be wrong to imagine that even if the related incidents are based on fact, these are coloured by the uncontrolled imaginative tradition of Brahmans. If this is so, it cannot present true views in the light of which Visvamitra had acted as a Purohit and which is not looked upon with disdain by the audience.

In the context of the above related legend prof. Weber has arrived at the following conclusions drawn from, a dissertation presented by Roth[3]:

"(I) The oldest legend about Sunassepa (alluded to in R.V. i.24. 11-13, and R.V. V-2.7) known only of his miraculous deliverance by divine help from the peril of death.

(II)This story becomes expanded in the sequal into a narrative of Sunassepa's threatened slaughter as a sacrificial victim, and of his deliverance through Visvamitra.

(III) This immolation-legend becomes severed into two essentially distinct versions, the oldest forms of which are respectively represented by the stories in the Aitareya Brahmana, and the Ramayana.

(IV) The latter becomes eventually the predominant one; but its proper central point is no longer the deliverance from immolation, but the incorporation of Sunassepa, or (with a change of persons) of Richika, into the family of the Kusikas. It thus becomes in the end of a family-legend of the race of Visvamitra.

Thus we neither can draw any conclusion based on history, nor any dynasty nor is proved that the Andhra, Pundra,Sabra, Pulinda etc. Dasyus are the progeny of Visvamitra.

Mahabharta (Calcutta edition) : According to Anushasan Parvan, 1955-2006 the origin of caste system is explained as follows :

Vitahavya's son invaded Devadas's Kingdom Kashi. In the war the entire family was killed. The troubled and the aggrieved ruler went to the cottage of Bhardwaj sage. There as a result of Yajna the king was blessed with a son : whom he named Pratardan. On growing up he took his father's revenge on the enemy. Vitahavya took shelter under the sage Bharigu. There the sage converted him into Brahman. Pratardan, therefore, who had been chasing him now had to abandon the chase and go back. Gritsamad was his second son; Devdas belonged to the sixth generation of his brother Kasa's dynasty.

Bhrigbhumi was born in the 12th generation of Kasa. Bhrigbhumi's father was Bharigu. The descendants of this Angiras in the dynasty of Bhrigu came to be Brahmans, Kshattriyas, Vaishyas and Sudras.

The Ramayana : The Ramayana[4] presents a different theory of the origin of the caste system. According to J. Muir[5] the story is reproduced below:

"The universe was nothing but water. In it the earth was fashioned. Then

Brahma Svayambhu came into existence, with the deities. He next, becoming a boar, raised up the earth, and created the entire world, with the Rishis his sons.. Brahma, the eternal, unchanging, and undecaying, was produced from the aether (akasa). From him sprang Marichi, of whom Kasyapa was the son. 6. From Kasyapa sprang Vivasvat : and from him was descended Manu, who was formerly the lord of creatures (Prajapati). Ikshvaku was the son of Manu and to him this prosperous earth was formerly given by his father. Know that this Ikshvaku was the former king in Ayodhya". Manu Kashyap Maharaj's wife produced all human beings, Brahmans, Kshattriyas, Vaishyas and Sudras. A similar story is also given in Vishnu Puran (1-4-3 to 9 and 47 to 51).

VISHNU PURANA :- Vishnu Puran[6] provides another theory of the origin of varnas which is given below:

First of all was born Harinyagarbha Brahma from his right hand thumb Prajapati Daksha was born. Daksha had one daughter Aditi. She gave birth to Vivshan and he produced Manu. Manu's sons were named Ikshvaku, Nrig, Dhrisht, Sharyati, Narishyant, Prashu, Nabhag, Disht, Krush, prishaghra. Desirous of having one more son he performed the Yajnas of Mittra and Varuna. But owing to wrong utterance in the Yajna a daughter named Ila was born. However, blessed by Mittra and Varuna, she turned into a male issue named Sudyumna. This enraged Ishwar (Mahadev) and she was transformed back into a girl. She began to roam in the hermitage of Soma (moon) son of Buddha and gave birth to Pururva.

1. Prishaghra son of Manu turned a Sudra because he had slaughtered a religious cow.
2. Kshattriya was born of Manu's son Krusha.
3. Nabhag's progeny was Vaishya.

Vishnu Purana[7] contains a description of the different parts of the earth and their inhabitants. Priyavarta the son of the self existent first Manu Brahm produced intelligent sons like himself viz. Bhrigu, Pulist, Pulaha, Ritu, Angira, Maricha, Dakshu, Attri and Vasista all born from his forehead. These are the Brahmans described in Puranas. But Sanandan and others who were created by Brahma were not connected with world and were impotent. They had all become enlightened and were free from desire and jealousy. In this way they were different from the created world. Therefore, great rage grew out of the mighty Brahma which could burn into ashes all the three Lokas, all the three Lokas began to glitter in the flames of fire. Then from his flaming knit eyebrows Rudra was born who was shining like the mid-day sun. He had a half male and a half female body, which was colossal and dreadful. "Divide thyself into two halves"- saying these words Brahma Vanished. On hearing this Rudra divided himself into two parts, one male and the other female. He further subdivided the male part into eleven parts, beautiful as well as ugly, civilized as well as wild. He sub divided the female part also into numerous parts which had two types of complexion-fair and dark. The Brahm created the self existent God who had been born of himself and was nothing besides Himself. Manu was the protector of creatures. Manu the self-existent God took the woman named Satrupa as his wife, He was liberated hardly from excitement, impurity. By him Satrupa Devi had two sons Priyavart and Uttanvad and two daughters Prasuti and Akuti who were blessed with the virtues of beauty and generosity. He married off Prasuti to Daksh and Akuti to Ruchi.

The above explanation of human origin differs from that given in the vishnu Puran IV-1 to 6 and 12 to 19.

MANUSMRITI: The theory of origin of Varna given in Manusmriti I-31 resembles the one given in the Purush Sukta of Rigveda. Manusmriti (I-8 to 12) explain the origin of universe :-

"He (the self-existent) having felt desire, and willing to create various living beings from his own body, first created the waters, and threw into them a seed. That seed became a golden egg, of lustre equal to the sun; in it he himself was born as Brahma, the parent of all the worlds. The waters are called Narah, for they are sprung from Nara; and as they were his first sphere of motion (ayana= path), he is therefore called Narayana. Produced from the imperceptible, eternal existent and non-existent caused that male (purush) is celebrated in the world as Brahma. After dwelling for a year in the egg, the glorious being, himself, by his own contemplation, split it in twain'. Out of these two parts Brahma created heaven and earth and in between them formed the sky, eight directions and a huge expanse of waters."

Chapter VII of Manusmriti contains a description of the origin of Anulom and Vilom Varansankar of the Sudras which is different from the theory of origin given in Prashar Smriti and its hollowness is self-explanatory.

Many castes were formed by degradation from the original varnas on account of non-observance of sacred rites. These are called Vratyas. Thus Vratya Brahmanas (X-21) were known as 1. Bhrijjakantaka, 2. Avantya, 3. Vatadhana, 4. Pushpadha and 5. Saikha-Vratya or degraded Kshattriyas (X-22) became 1. Jhalla, 2. Malla, 3. Lichchhivi, 4. Nata, 5. Karana, 6. Khasa, 7. Dravida (X-43-44), 8. Paundraka, 9. Odra, 10. Kamboja, 11. Yavana, 12. Saka, 13. Parada, 14. Pahlava, 15. China, 16. Kirata, 17. Darada, Degraded Vaisyas (X-23) became 1. Sudhanvan, 2. Acharjya, 3. Karusha, 4. Vijanman, 5. Maitra, 6. Satvata.

How artificial does seem the above theory of origin of Varna system ! It assumes somehow or the other the entire world population has descended from the four original varna. In this way even foreign nations like Chinese, Greek (Yavanas). Scythians (Saka) and Dravidians are assumed to have been born in the same varna in which Kshattriyas were born. Thus from the ethnic point of view they are closer to the Kshattriyas then to the other Varnas.

When we consider the different theories of the origin of Varna system as explained in various scriptures, we learn that the Brahmni sage group had differences of opinion among themselves i.e. they were opposed to one another. In fact such controversy, is possible and can arise only when the literature is based on conjuctures and imagination. Had they described the facts they had witnessed there must have been oneness and homogeneity[8].

J. Muir[9] holds, "The above passages are amply sufficient to prove that according to the traditions received by the compilers of the ancient legendary history of India (traditions so general and undisputed as to prevail over even their strong hierarchical prepossessions). Brahmans, Kshattriyas, and even Vaishyas and Sudras, were, at least in many cases originally descended from one and the same stock".

Controversy in Sanskrit Scriptures

According to Manusmiriti X-8, the issue of Brahman married Vaishya daughter is Ambasht and that of a Sudra daughter is Nishad or Parshwa.

In Vishnu Puran I-13-7 to 23(See chapter X Kayastha also) there is a story of king Vena. Mrityu's daughter Sunita was married to Anga. She gave birth to Vena who became a ruler. He banned all forms of Yajana and religion. The sages killed him with the sharp blades of Kusa grass when the sages rubbed hard his thigh a short-statured and broad faced man was formed. The sages ordered him to sit down (Nishida) and he became Nishad. From him sprung the Nishadas who settled down on the Vindhya mountains.

Both the above theories explain the origin of Nishadas differently.

Manusmriti X-43-44-Those Kshattriyas and Vaishyas in the absence of religious rites and the paucity of Brahamans for performing Yajnas or teaching Vedas, became Sudras. Mondrik, Audra, Dravida, Kamboja, Yavana, Saka, Darda and Khasa all turned Sudras.

Manu X-45- the castes excommunicated from the functions of Brahmans, Kshattriyas, Vaishyas are called Dasyus, notwithstanding whether they speak Malechchha language or the Aryan.

The Verse No. 45 means that the Dasyus are the castes out of four Varnas. If this is true, then the Dasyu community is different from the Sudras referred to in verse Nos. 43-44. How very controversial? This controversy is also present in Aitreya Brahman where in verse VII-17-18 Visvamittra says to his sons:-

"Let your descendants possess the furthest ends (of the country)", and the author of the Brahmana adds "These are the numerous border-tribes, the Andhras, Pundras, Sabaras, Pulindas, Mutibas. Most of the Dasyus are sprung from Visvamitra". Here the writer of this ancient Brahmana connects together certain tribes named either in Manu, or in the Mahabharata, as degraded Kshattriyas, with the appellation Dasyu, thus intimating that the latter was a general name embracing all the former. This view is further confirmed by the following lines of the Mahabharata (II-1031-1032).

DARADĀNSAḤ KAMBOJA RAJAYATVAKA SHĀSANḤ I
PRĀGUTTATA DISHAM̐ YE CHA VASANTYĀSRITYA DASYAVAḤ. II

"The son of Indra conquered the Dardas with the Kambojas and the Dasyus who dwell in the north-east region".

Dronaparvan of the epic Mahabharat

According to verse 4747 the soldiers destroyed the host, "converted the beautiful earth into a mass of mud with the flesh and blood of thousands of Kambojas, Sakas, Kiratas and Varvaras. The ground was covered with the shorn and hairless but long-bearded heads of the Dasyus and their helmets, as if with birds bereft of their plumes". Here the word Dasyu is evidently a general term for the tribes named just before. Some of these same tribes had previously been called Mlechchha in verses 4716, 4723 and 4745.

From the examples cited above, it appears that the authors of Puranas and Epics had a firm belief that all the human hierarchies settled around them had a common origin with them. Though at the same time they wrongly thought that these hierarchies have been excluded from the Brahmanical system. That is why they asserted their origin from their own kingdom and thus of the same origin as they had thought. The fact remains that they were not even distantly related to them

In Vishnu Puran IV-4-40 (P 547) Wilson has presented the following hierarchies of the dynasty of Raghu as mentioned in the Vishnu and Matsya Puranas and Ramayanas:-

Vishnu	**Matsya**	**Ramayana**
Kalmaspada	Kalmaspada	Kalmaspada
Asmaka	Sarvakarma	Sankan
Moolaka	Anarnya	Sudarshan
Dashratha	Nighana	Agnivaran
Ilavila	Anamittra	Sighrag
Vishwasaha	Raghu	Maru
Dalip	Dilip	Prashushruka
Dirghbahu	Aja	Ambrish
Raghu	Dirghabahu	Nahush
Aja	Ajapal	Yayati
Dashratha	Dashrath	Nabhag
		Aja
		Dashrath

The variation in the three hierarchies shows that the authors of these ...es, relied not on facts but only on the information they could get from ...d them.

Geological analysis of the Earth in Bhagwat and Vishnu Purana

The authors of the sanskrit scriptures and associated literature knew nothing about genesis and they relied mostly on conjectures and fancy. In the words of

Emile Senart:

"The authors or compilers of the puranas in reality knew nothing of any part of the world except that immediately around them. Whenever they wander away beyond their own neighbourhood, they at once lose themselves in a misty region of fiction, and give the most unbridled scope to their fantastic imaginations".[10]

Jambu Dwipa and Bharatvarsha

According to Vishnu[11]Purana the names of the seven continents are Jambu dvipa, Plaksha dvipa, Salmali dvipa, Kusa dvipa, Kraunch dvipa, Saka dvipa and Pushkara dvipa. These are surrounded severally by seven great seas, of salt water, sugarcane juice, wine, clarified butter, curds, milk and fresh water. Jambu dvipa is situated in the centre of these continents[12]. Again to quote Wilson:

"It fell to the lot of Agnidhra, son of Priyavarta, who again divided it among his nine sons[13]. In the centre of Jambu dvipa is the golden mountain Meru, 84,000 Yojanas high, and crowned by the great city of Brahma. ----- There are in this continent six-cross-ranges of boundary mountains; those of Himavat (Himadri, or Himalaya), Hemakuta, and Nishadha lying south of Meru and those of Nila, Sveta, and Sringin, situated to the northward. Of these, Nishadha and Nila are the nearest to Meru, while Himavat and Sringin are at the south and north extremities. The nine Varshas or divisions of Jambu dvipa, separated by these and other ranges, are Bharata (India), south of the Himavat mountains, and the Southern most of all; then (2) Kimpurusha, (3) Harivarsha, (4) Ilavrita, (5) Ramyaka, (6) Hiranmaya, and (7) Uttra Kuru, each to the north of the last; while (8) Bhadrasva and (9) Ketumala lie respectively to the east and west of Illavrita, the central region. BharatVarsha, and Uttara Kuru, as well as Bhadrasva and Ketumala, are situated on the exterior of the mountain ranges.

In those eight Varshas there is neither grief, nor weariness, nor anxiety, nor hunger, nor fear. The people live in perfect health, free from every suffering for ten or twelve thousand years. Indra does not rain on those Varshas, for they have abundance of springs. There is no division of time into the Krita, Treta and other ages".

There may have lived real people in Uttara Kuru as there is a reference to them in Aitreya Brahmana VIII.14.4.Elsewhere in the same work the Uttar Kurus are treated as belonging to the domain of mythology.

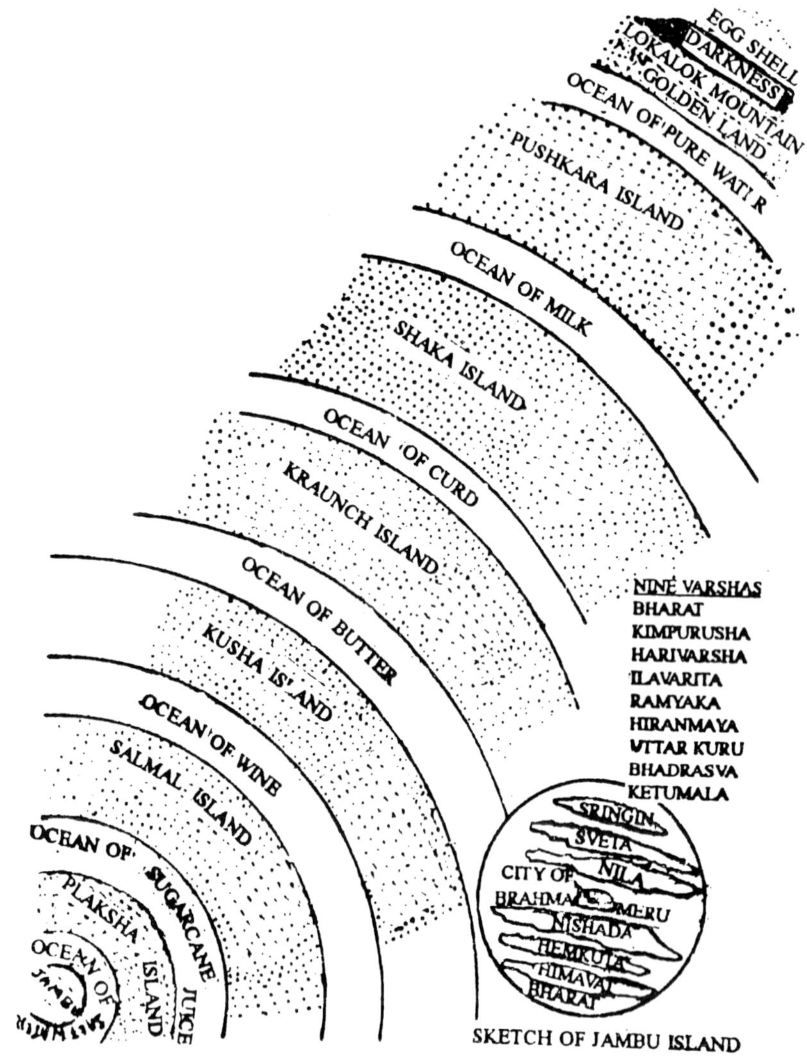

2. Rough Sketch Of Earth As Per Description In Puranas

No. of Islands and Oceans in different continents (Islands) as given by Albaruni

	Mastsya Purana		Vishnu Purana Commentary Patonjali		Indian name	
I	slands	oceans	Islands	oceans	Islands	oceans
1.	Jambu Dipa	Lavan or salt	Jambu, name of a tree	Chhar or salted water	Jambu	salt
2.	Shaka Dipa	Chhirodak or milk	Plaksha, name of a tree	Ichchhu or sugarcane	Shaka	Sugarcane juice
3.	Kusha Dipa	Gharati-mand or Butter	Shalmal, name of a tree	Sura or wine	Kusha	Wine
4.	Kronch Dipa	Dahi mand or curd	Kusha , name of a tree	Sarpis or butter	Kraunch	Butter
5.	Shalmai Dipa	Sura or wine of rice	Kraunch sangh	Dadhi or curd	Shakali	Curd
6.	Gomed Dipa	Ichhu seed or sugarcane juice	Shaka, name of a tree	Chhir or milk	Gomed	Milk
7.	Pushkar	Swadudak or Sweet water	Pushkar name of a tree	Swadud or Sweet water	Pushkar	Sweet water

After Albaruni ka Bharat P-175.

It is incorporated in the Mahabharata[14] that in the north of Nilgiri there is a Jamboline tree. The Jambu became famous by this name after that tree. It is 11000 Yojanas high, the length of its fruit is 2,500 Artni (the length from wrist to little finger). As the fruit falls on the earth it produces sounds of explosion and juice starts flowing out of the fruit. This juice assumes the form of a river that starts flowing and circling round the Meru mountain reaches the Uttar Kuru.

"The country to the north of the ocean, and to the south of the Himadri (or snowy range), is Bharata Varsha, where the descendants of Bharata dwell" (Uttaram yad samudrasya ilimudres chaiva dakshinam carsham tad Bharatam numa Bharati Yattra santatih)[15]. It is divided into nine parts (bhedah), Indradvipa, Kaserumat, Tamra varna, Gabbastimat, Nigadvipa, Saumya, Gandharva, Varuna; and "this ninth dvipa," which is not named, is said to be surrounded by the ocean "ayam tu navamas tesham dvipah, Sagara-samvritah,"and to be a thousand Yojanas long from north south. "on the east side of it are the Kiratas, on the west the Yavanas, and in the centre are the Brahmans, Kshattriyas, Vaishyas and Sudras following their respective occupations of sacrifice, arms, trade etc.'[16]

The Vishnu Purana contains a very short list of the tribes inhabiting Bharata Varsha (See Wilson, Vol. 11,PP 132 f.). It specifies, as the principal only the Kurus, Panchalas the people of Kamarupa, the Pundras, Kalingas, Magadhas, Saurashtras, Suras, Bharas, Arbudas, Karushas, Malavas, Sauviras, Saindhavas, Hunas, Salvas, Sukalas, Madras, Ramas, Ambashthas, and Purasikas. These tribes seem to be all confined to India and its Vicinity[17].

In Bhagvat Purana[18], Bharatvarsha is mentioned as Karambhumi while the other Varshas are abodes of the divine. "Of these, Bharatvarsha alone is the land of works, the other eight Varshas are places where the celestials enjoy the remaining rewards of their works, they are called terrestrial paradises. In them men pass an existence equal to that of the Treta age, living for the space of ten thousand ordinary lives, on an equality with gods, having the vitality of ten thousand elephants and possessed of wives who bear one child after a year's conception following upon sexual intercourse attended by all the gratification arising from adamantine bodies and from vigorous youth".

From the above description it is obvious that the authors of the myths (Puranas) meant to say that the inhabitants of Bharatvarsha are not only different from the dwellers of the dvipas but even in Jambu dvipa they have an exclusive identity. The word "Manusha" is applied only to the inhabitants of Bharat. This clearly shows that the human being of all the other places might have been of different races The words Manuja, Manava (of the dynasty of Manu) have been used for Kusha dvipa and Pushkar dvipa the continents. In a chapter translated by Colebrook[19] is mentioned,"Vishnu's Garud (eagle) had brought one chief of Dwijanas from Shaka dvip". Thus the Brahmans of Shaka dvipa became known in the Jambu dvipa.

According to this verse also there is racial affinity between the inhabitants of these two dvipas. It is to be noted that the descendants of Priyavarta became kings of all the dvipas and the varshas of the jambu dvipa. As per Vishnu Purana[20] Sahasrabahu Arjun son of Kritavirya was the ruler of the seven dvipas. If the ruler kings belonged to human races, the ruled inhabitants also must have been human beings.

Description of Earth's seven dvipas-As Vishnu Purana[21] describes Jambu dvipa surrounded by sea of salt water. The sea itself is bounded on all sides by the Plaksha continent. In this way there are series of continents and seas in a circular form. Jamu dvipa is circular and is in the midst of the entire system. It is elaborately described in the Shabhaparava chapter 28 of Mahabharata.

Plaksha dvipa is twice the size of Jambu dvipa. The character and conditions of its inhabitants are described as follows[22];

"In those seven provinces (which compose Plaksha dvipa) the division of time into Yugas does not exist; but the character of existence is always that of the Treta age. In the (five) dvipas beginning with Plaksha and ending with Saka, the people live 5000 years, free from sickness. In those five dvipas duties arise from the divisions of castes and orders. There are also four Varnas, Aryakash, Kurus, Vivasas, and Bharina, who are the Brahmanas, Kshattriya, Vaishyas and Sudras'[23] and whose worship is thus described: There Hari who is All and the Lord of all, and the creator of the world, is worshipped in the form of Soma by these Varnas the Aryakashas etc."

"The inhabitants of this dvipa receive different names in the Bhagvata Purana, being there called (V. 20,4) Hansas, Patangas, Urdhvayanas, and Satyangas, four castes, who, purified from passion and darkness by the touch of the waters of these rivers, live a thousand years, resemble the gods in their appearance and in their manner of procreation and worship with the triple Veda the divine soul, the Sun, who is the gate of heave, and who is co-essential with the Vedas".

Plaksha dvipa is surrounded by an equally wide belt of sea of sugarcane juice (VP II-4-20). This sea is surrounded by Salamal dvipa (V.P.II-4-24). This is divided into seven parts (V.P. II-4-30-31) called Varshas. These seven Varshas have a system of four castes. The castes which dwell there are severally the Kapilas, Arunas, Pitas and Krishnas (or the Tawny, the Purple, the Yellow, and the Black). These, the Brahmans, Kshattriyas, Vaishyas, and Sudras, worship with excellent sacrifices Vishnu, the divine and imperishable soul of all things in the form of Vayu, and abidning in sacrifice. Here the vicinity of the gods is very delightful to the soul".

This dvipa is surrounded by a sea of wine of the same compass as itself (V.P. II-4-33). The outer side of this sea is surrounded by Kusa dvipa which has an extent twice that of Salmala dvipa (V.P.II-4-34). In this set of Varshas (of Kusa dvipa) live Daityas, Danavas, Deva, Gandharvas, Yaksha and Kimpurushas, and other beings. There too, there are four Varnas, pursuing their proper observances, Damins, Sushmins, Snehas and Mandehas, who in the order specified are Brahmans, Kshattriyas, Vaishyas, and Sudras. In order to destroy their right (to reward) derived from the performance of these works, they worship Janardana in the form of Brahma, and so neutralize this direful merit which brings rewards".

Regarding the Kusa dvipa the Mahabharata[24] says :"In these (Varshas of Kusa dvipa), gods, Gandharavas, and living creatures, amuse and enjoy themselves. No one dies there. There are no Dasyus or Mlechchhas there. The people are fair, and of very delicate forms". The Bhagavata Purana V. 20,16, says, "The people of this Dvipa are called Kusalas, Kovidas, Abhiyuktas and Kulakas". Kusa dvipa is surrounded by a sea of clarified butter (ghee) of the same circumference as itself. This is surrounded by Krauncha dvipa which is twice the extent of Kusa dvipa (v.P.II-4-45).

In all these divisions divided by mountains of the dvipa, people dwell with the gods. There is no place for fear. These people are Pushkaras, Pushkalas, Danyas and Tishyas (V.P.II-4-53), who may be enumerated as the four Varnas respectively viz. Brahmans, Kshattriyas, Vaishyas and Sudras. (V.P.II-4-70). This dvipa is surrounded by a sea of curds. This set is surrounded by Shaka dvipa. The inhabitants of this dvipa are Mriga, Magadha, Manasa and Mandaga the first being principally Brahmans, the second Kshattriyas, the third Vaishyas and the fourth Sudras. They worship Vishnu symbolised by the sun.

"This dvipa is surrounded by the ocean of milk as by an armlet. This ocean again is encompassed on its exterior by Pushkara dvipa which is twice as extensive as saka dvipa".

"In this dvipa men live ten thousand years, free from sickness and sorrow, from affection and hatred. There is no distinction among them of higher and lower, of killer and slain: there is no envy, nor ill-will, nor fear, nor anger, nor defect, nor convetousness, nor other fault; there is neither truth nor falsehood. Men there are all of the same appearance, of one from with the gods. The two divisions of this dvipa have no rules of caste or orders, nor any observances of duty: the three Vedas, the Puranas(or,trade), the rules of criminal law and service do not exist. This (dvipa) is a most excellent terrestrial heaven; where time brings happiness to all, and is, exempt from decay, sickness, and all other evils."

Pushkare dvipa is surrounded by fresh pure clear water and is equal to itself in compass what is further (VP II-4-87). Further ahead there is a belt of golden earth but this is uninhabited. Further there are Lokalok mountain which is ten thousand yojanas in expanse and the same measure in height. This is enveloped in darkness. This darkness is covered by an egg shell. The shell of the mundane egg is outside the seven spheres comprising this system.

"These seven spheres have been described by me; and there are also seven Patalas: this is the extent of Brahma's egg. The whole is surrounded by the shell of the egg at the sides, above, and below, just as the seed of the wood apple (is covered by the rind)."

On scanning critically the Indian mythology we find there is lack of wisdom and the presence of childish imagination. It has been well observed, 'Indian mythology, when striving after sublimity, and seeking to excite astonishment, often displays an extravagant and puerile facility in the fabrication of large numbers. But, in the sentence last quoted, its conjectures are substantially in unison with the discoveries of modern astronomy ;or rather, they are inadequate representation of the simple truth, as no figures can express the contents of infinite space.

As for the origin of Varna system as given in the Sanskrit literature(Puranas)i.e. mythology, we may arrive at the following conclusions;-

1. As explained earlier the theory of genesis and that of the origin of Varna system is differently described in various books. This implies that much use has been made of fancy. If the works had been based on facts there must have been affinity among them.

2. Not only there is absence of affinity but also there is abundance of inconsistencies and contradictions.

3. So much so that the authors of Puranas did not have complete information of the communal and racial heterogeneity among the people living around them. They regarded them as those boycotted by the Aryan society. The names of the human races contained in the later Sanskrit literature are just the other form of

those contained in the earlier works.

4. The extent of imagination can be well appreciated on reading that those authors brought into their imagination the seven continents and the oceans of wine, sugarcane juice, curds and fresh milk, side by side with genesis. They believed that the origin of the caste system can be imagined together with geographical description of measures and situations. They could not even think that in ages to follow man could be able to measure every inch of the earth and draw maps based on scientific surveys which would disprove their unbridled infancy.

The excavations of ancient cities have disproved the fanciful descriptions and far fetched conceits of the authors of mythological literature. Even the descriptions of towns are not quite convincing. These are exaggerated in as much as according to the earlier writings every citadel is said to have high defensive parapets, deep moats, broad streets, huge city gates, sky scrapers, crowded markets, pleasant parks, ponds etc. Such descriptive passages are frequent both in Sanskrit and Pali Text (see The cities in early historical India by A. Ghoseh P 35), which presents confusing situation. It is obvious that the literature does not convey a true description of the cities. This is corroborated by B.B. Lal (Ancient India vol. 10-11) who discovered in the excavations that the Hastinapur city of the great epic is only .25 x .50 sq. mile in area whereas it is said to have an expanse of 10 Yojanas in Bhavishya' Purana (Pritsarg parva 3-46). The later edicts also belong to the same category e.g. the Mandsore edict also describes the city of Daspura in the conventional form of literature (J.F. Fleet Corpus Inscription Indica Vol III(1888) PP81-82).

It is clear that the theories of origin of caste system explained in the Sanskrit literature are based on sheer fancy and are not even distantly related to facts.

References

1. CHI V.I-PP 82 and 99, Keith A.B.
2. Muller F. Max. Ancient Sanskrit Literature. PP 297-303.
3. Quoted by weber Albrecht in his book 'Indische Studien' II PP 112-113.
4. II-110-1, Bombay edition.
5. Muir J. 'Original Sanskrit text.' Vol. I, PP 182-183.
6. V.P. IV-1-6 to 12 and 17 to 19.
7. V.P. I-7-1 to 15.
8. Dutt N.K. also accepts this view see origin and growth of caste in India, PP 7-8.
9. Muir J.P- 238.
10. Senart Emile, "Caste in India" PP 136 and 144.
11. V.P. II-2-4 to 6.
12. V.P. Vol II P 110 by Wilson.
13. V.P. II-2-7
14. MBH VI-8-19 to 26.
15. V.P. Vol II- 3-1
16. V.P. II-3-8,9.
17. V.P. II-3-14 to 17.
18. Bhagwat Purana V-17-12
19. Colebrook H.T., "Miscellaneous essay", II, P 759.
20. V.P. IV-11-3.
21. V.P. II-4-1.
22. V.P. II-4-14.
23. V.P. II-4-15 to 17.
24. MBH VI-12-14, 15 (Gorakhpur edition).

CHAPTER X

Historical Origin Of Sudras

Dasa

According to D.D. Kosambi, the word 'Dasa' in ancient times meant 'donor'. In later literature, it meant slave, attendant or a servant. The scholars are of the view that the Dasa tribes were opposed to the Rigvedic Aryans but were gradually vanquished and then made to serve the Aryans. On this account, the meaning of the word Dasa changed from 'Donor' to slave, attendant or servant. In the Rigveda, the word 'Dasa' is repeatedly used for non-Aryans.

According to Manu Smriti (8-415) There are seven forms of Dasas-

DHVAJĀHRITO BHAKTADĀSO GRIHAJAḤ KRĪTADATTRIMAU I
PAITRIKĀ DANDADĀSASHCHA SAPTAITE DĀSAYONAYAḤ II

1. Dasa-won in the battlefield.
2. One who becomes a Dasa by virtue of his devotion.
3. Dasa-Son of a maid servant.
4. Dasa-Who has been purchased.
5. Dasa- obtained by donation.
6. Dasa-Who has been serving as such from the time of his ancestors.
7. Dasa-who has been made so by giving him some punishment.

In the previous chapter, it has been stated that the varnas are said to have been created by God. Similarly, in other religious books of Sanskrit literature, the stories about the origin of varnas not only differs from one another but are also some times contrary. It has been proved that these tales, which are the handiwork of Rishis, are based on unbridled fantasies rather than reality and are therefore not reliable. Such an origin is meaningless for a student who is desirous to conduct an impartial study of the history. He wants solid historical proofs which are not based on intellectual fantasies but on reality. Only archaeological, linguistic, ehnological and anthropological proofs can satisfy him from the scientific point of view.

Sir Childe[1] in his book "New light on the Most Ancient East" has expressed the view that 'There can be no doubt that in the developed society like Harappa there was such a gap in the economic levels that there must have existed various classes of society".

It is quite apparent that in the economically developed high society of the Indus Valley, the society must have been divided into classes, viz. soldiers, traders, artisans and farmers. In chapter seven it has been proved that the foremost objective of the war of Rigvedic Aryans was the assassination and plunder of wealth and property of non-Aryan 'Dasyus' and 'Dasas' of Indus Valley which means that the first target of the Rigvedic Aryans, as is but natural, would have been the professional soldiers, chiefs of the soldiers, rulers viz. the royal families and other rich traders. From the details given in the Rigveda, it seems that after victory, the non-Aryans must have been killed on a large scale.

Massacre of Dasyus and Dasas

According to Rigveda IV-16-13.. 50,000 Dasyus were killed
" IV-30-21...30,000 Dasyus were killed.
" IV-30-15...50,000 Dasyus were killed.
" VI-26-6....60,000 Dasyus were killed.
" VII-18-14...66,000 Dasyus were killed.
" VII-99-5...10,000 Dasyus were killed

Total 2,66,000.

It means that approximately two and half to three lakhs inhabitants of Indus Valley were killed. It may also be said that people in lakhs were killed.

Now, we make a rough estimate of the population of the regions of the entire Harappa civilization. S.R. Rao[2] has calculated the population of Lothal city in this way "The inhabitable area of Lothal city in stratum III was about 90,000 sq. metres in which there might have been 1600 houses. In this way, if we calculate at the rate of 6 persons per house, it becomes 1600 × 6 = 9600 or say 10,000 and if the hutments built outside the peripheral wall of the city are also taken into account, it may go up to 15000. This must be considered as a large population for the urban settlements of the third millennium B.C. The population of Harappa and Mohenjo-daro might have been a little more than twice that of Lothal, i.e. 35,000."

Shri J.M. Datta[3] has calculated the population of Mohenjo-daro and Harappa on the basis of the size of granary. According to him the population of Harappa was 37,000 and Mohenjo-daro 33,000.

Similarly, Basu[4] and others have calculated the population of these cities as:

Harappa = 37,155

Mohenjo-daro = 33,469

Until now, about 450-500 sites have been excavated in India, if we take into account the sites excavated in Pakistan and in the west of Pakistan (correct figures could not be received from Pakistan) to be 400, the total number of cities and towns goes upto 900 whereas even now the number of these sites and the area of the Indus Valley civilization is progressively increasing and in the north west, this limit has touched the Russian border. If we take the average population of these places to be 5000, the total population of these places comes to 900 × 5000 = 45,00,000. If the population of rural areas is also taken into account, the population of Indus country comes of one crore and even more then that.

On the other hand, the number of Aryan invaders, according to Sir Heine Geldren[5] must have been between fifty thousand and one lakh.

It is quite clear that the population of a vast country like the Indus Valley was hundred times more than that of the Aryan invaders. We have already shown on the basis of figures available from Rigveda that the Dasas and Dasyus were killed upto two and a half to three lakhs in number. After this we reach the conclusion that the widows and children of those killed were made Dasas or Servants in accordance with the Dasas low of Manu section one (taken captive in war) and their number might have been in lakhs. This means that the Rigvedic Aryans might have kept them in their houses in lakhs to get the domestic chores done. Instances are available in Rigveda and Atharav-veda, which are given below. The victor Aryans often made the 'Dasas' their captives and that is why this word appears in Rigveda (VII-86-7) two or three times as captive or kinkar and in the later vedic period this word has assumed general meanings.

In Rigveda, references have been made about the sale and purchase of Dasa, gifting them by Kshattriya to Rishis and doing jobs of cleaning and plastering the houses of Aryans by them. Some examples are given below:- R.V. VIII -56-3

SHATAM̃ ME GARDHBHĀNO SHATMŪRN ĀVATĪNĀMISHATAM̃ DĀSĀN: ATI SRIJAḤ II

- O, Indra donate me one hundred each of sheep, donkeys and Dasas.

R.V. I - 92-8

USATAMASHYĀM̃ YASHASAM̃ SUVĪRAM̃ DĀSAPRAVARGAM̃ AAYIMSHVABUDHYAM।
SUPPNSASĀ SRAVASĀ YĀ VIBHĀSI VĀJAPRASŪTĀ SUBHAGE BRIHANTAM̃ II

- O usha! you are lucky, please bestow me with beautiful sons, Dasas, horses with loads of glorious wealth, which are inspired by your action and power.

R.V.VI-27-8

DVAYĀN:AGNE RATHINO VINSHATIM̃ GĀ VADHŪMATO MAGHAVĀ MAHYAM̃ SAMRĀṬ।
ABHYĀVARTĪ CHĀYMĀNO DADĀTI DŪṆASHEYAM̃ DAKSHIṆĀ PĀRTHAYĀNĀM̃ II

- O Agni! (God of fire) Abhyavarti The son of a great donor and performer of Rajsuya Yajna, Chayamana-donate us twenty cows and chariots along with Dasis. No one can destroy this donation of King Abhyavarti of Prithu dynasty.

We have seen that repeated mention has been made in the above verses about the donation of 'Dasas' and'Dasis'.It shows that they (Aryans) had Dasas in large numbers and this is beyond doubt that they had not brought them along with them. These slaves might have been the widows and children of the soldiers killed in the war.

In Rigveda these Dasis have been referred to as Badhu (wife) at many places with which relation of husband could be maintained without performing any marriage ceremony. These were definitely the widows of the Dasyus and

Dasa killed in warfare. Since Aryans had come from far off places, they could not bring their ladies along with them in sufficient number and they considered it their insult to marry the black coloured, humilated, of low status women of the defeated people. But the satisfaction of natural feeling or the sexual desire was a necessity and in this way the above form of Dasis came into existence.

R.V. VIII - 19-36

- Trasdasu, the son of the most worshipped, efficient and patron of noble persons Purukutsa gave me fifty wives (Badhus)

R.V. VII-18-22

- O Agni! (god of fire), I come to the place of performing yajna appreciating the donation of two hundred cows and two chariots along with wives (Badhus) given by Sudasa, son of Pijwana and grandson of Dev Bhakta, and so I go to my home.

R.V. VIII-68-17

- I got six horses along with wives (Badhus) at the time of holy yajna performed by Indraut, the son of Atithigva.

R.V. I-126-3

- I have received ten chariots along with horses of the best breed along with best wives (Badhus) given by Swanam. Kakshiwan may receive sixty thousand cows at the beginning of the day.

Further after Rigveda mention of the existence of woman slaves (Dasis) is also found in the beginning portion of Atharvaveda. In this portion the woman slaves or the Dasis have been mentioned as plastering with mud and mixing dirty water with cow dung with wet hands.

A.V. XII-3-13

- When a crow surprisingly comes and makes his dwelling or the Dasi plasters with her (wet) hands, then the water and the pestle should be considered to be clean or sacred.

A.V. XII-4-9

- If the lady slave (Dasi) throws away the cow dung (Because it is an insult to the cow) the man cannot get emancipation from the sin and his face becomes ugly.

It clearly shows that they were engaged in doing domestic chores i.e. cleaning of utensils, cooking and general cleaning etc. which is done by servants.

Dasis of black colour

R.V. II-20-7

Indra, the killer of Vritra and the destroyer of the towns of enemies killed all the black coloured Dasis. He created land and water for the mankind. May Indra give encouragement to the appreciable task of yajman.

It is quite apparent that the black coloured widows of the 'Dasas' were kept by the Kshattariyas, whom they had acquired after victory in the war, who were demanded time and again by the suppliant Rishis from Indra in donation and some of the Kshattriya conquerors donated them to Purohits. The use of word 'Dasi' certainly proves that they were the wives of vanquished 'Dasas' or those who were killed in the battlefield and were not the actual wives of Aryans. The word 'Dasa' in its meanings as slaves has been used in Rigveda in its later portion and not in the earlier part.

Similarly in Brahadarnayakopnishad (VI-2-7) the father of Satvaketu in his own praise says---he has gold, cattle, horses, dasis and foodstuffs and clothes.

In Mahabharata (Calcutta edition II-33-52), it is described that hundreds of Dasis from Magadh were gifted away to Suta king Karna of Anga who were also adept in dancing and singing.

Likewise in Mahabharata king Shantnu of Kuru dynasty brings a Dhibari Dasi named Satyawati to his palace as a keep, who later gave birth to two sons Chitrangda and Vichitravirya.

Only non-Aryan Dasyus and Dasas were enslaved

In the details found in the Rigveda we find that war was fought not only between Aryans and non-Aryans but also between the Aryan-Aryan tribes. In Rigveda, a mention has been made of both types of enemies, the Dasyus and the Aryans. It is quite clear that both types of prisoners i.e. non-Aryan Dasyus and Aryans might have been taken captives. But after taking into consideration the human racial feelings it appears to be quite possible that in different ages the victorious Aryans might have given different treatment to the conquered Aryans and non-Aryans. This is further proved to be more correct from the fact as has been said in the foregoing pages that the Aryans were far less in number than the non-Aryans. They might have been haunted by the fear of their number being reduced or being deprived of their power.

N.K. Dutta[6] supports this view and says, "There might have been even Aryans slaves who were either taken captive in war, or who has lost their liberty by failing to repay debts or pledging their services to avoid starvation. But all these remained slaves for a limited period, and at all events, the lawful son of such an acquired slave became a freeman. Such must have been the traditional custom of the Aryans, and so no instance is recorded of a Brahman, Kshattriya or Vaishya slave being engaged in menial work, or of such a person becoming a Sudra because of his slavery. Kautilya lays down the rule clearly when he states,. 'It is no crime for Mlechchhas to sell or mortgage the life of their own offspring. But never shall an Arya be subjected to slavery. The offspring of a man who has sold himself to slavery shall be an Arya" (Arthasastra III. 13). Similar is the dictum of Manu (VIII.412): "A Brahman who, because he is powerful, out of greed makes initiated men of the twice-born castes against their will to do the work of slaves shall be fined by the king six hundred panas."

But the law is quite contrary for the non-Aryans in the same Shastras. They cannot get rid of slavery under any circumstances.

It is quite evident that the Aryans enslaved only the non-Aryans and not the Aryans. The Dasis, Badhus (wives) and black Dasis as mentioned in the Rigveda, were all non-Aryans and not Aryans.

In the later period, the offspring of these Dasis and their children became slaves from generation to generation according to the third dictum of Manu (The offspring of a slave is always a slave). "In this way, a separate large class of non-Aryans from others, came into being and the traditional work of brooming, cleaning utensils, washing clothes, cooking and cleaning and plastering of houses etc continued to be done from one generation to another generation. Aryans being the victors definitely considered them to be inferior and lower than themselves. When the Aryans created varna system these were the people who were called the Sudras, and were pushed to the fourth varna.

This view has been accepted by many scholars[7]. According to Taitreya Brahman (1-2-6-7) the Brahman caste originated from the gods (Aryans) and the Sudras from the Asuras and according to Taitreya. Brahman (III-2-3-9) the Sudras originated from nonetity.

According to Gautam Dharm Suttra X-69 the non-Aryans are Sudras.

Same thing happened in Egypt, Mesopotamia and Rome but in those countries the slaves were not tightened firmly in the chains of slavery for ever as was done in India. In the following chapter 11, this subject would be discussed in detail that, that kind of slavery was for a short span of time which under different circumstances came to an end by itself. It may be mentioned here that the credit for taking civilization of Egypt and Rome to the height of glory goes to those millions of slaves who were won in the battle-fields and who had worked very hard in a very miserable plight. The same thing happened in Mesopotamia but in a bit different situation. But contrary to this in India the advantage of slave-Sudras was derived in the form of spiritual progress in place of physical progress. A huge collection of Sanskrit holy books is the result of this progress.

In nutshell, it may be said that first of all the natives used to be annihilated-completely. There after, the policy was softened and instead of killing them, most of them were made slaves

In vedic hymns originally the word 'Dasa' has been first used for enemy and at a later stage it was used for a slave. In Rigveda, in the beginning, Female Dasis (wives of Dasas) have been mentioned repeatedly. It shows that first of all the ladies were made slaves, who were undoubtedly the widows and daughters of the non-Aryans who were killed in the battlefield (Vedic Index 1-357). Later on we find a reference to the male slaves. Certainly these males slaves were none else but the offspring of these 'Dasis'. In the earlier hymns of Rigveda, the word 'Dasa' has been used in place of word Sudra. Later on, the word Sudra has also been used in the context of a slave. According to Aitreya Brahman (VII-29), the offspring of Sudras might have been like others slaves who could be turned out or killed at will.

Origin of various castes from the Servile class

The convention of enslaving the persons vanquished in the battlefield by the conquerors has almost been in vogue in every time, nation and society. When the Britishers established their authority in India, even an ordinary English man used to keep an army of Indian servants in his house for service etc. Even today, separate and compulsory provision of servants' quarters is found in the bungalows constructed during the British regime. Cook, servant, barber, washerman, kahar (water carrier), gardener and watchman used to be amongst their servants. Similarly, a class of non-Aryans slaves used to do almost the same nature of jobs in the homes of vedic victor Aryans, who continued doing the same job from generation to generation. They used to do the work of a cook, servant, cleaning boy and kahar etc. and gradually their castes were based on these very names, which can easily be found in the present day society. Soods worked as the cooks, Kayasthas as domestic servants, Scavanger (Bhangi) did the cleaning and Kahar worked for cleaning utensils and the kitchen of the Aryans. Amongst the above castes, the first two i.e. the Soods and Kayasthas have merged with Dwijas and both of the them call themselves Kshattriyas. But it will be shown in following pages that these two castes did the aforesaid jobs for the Aryans in the ancient period. The remaining castes do the same jobs even today and are known as Sudras.

Sood

The question that now arises is that the castes engaged in all types of servile jobs are found in the country while there are no signs of any caste engaged in the task of cooking which is the most integral part of the household duties. We will prove it that this job was done by the Soods. In Sanskrit and Hindi the word Sood means a person who does the work of cooking. The antiquated name of kitchen is 'Soodshala'. As a verb the word 'Soodna' means to destroy, kill, murder or homicide, whereas the word 'Soodak' means a murderer. The word 'Sood' or 'Sudda' is the corrupt form of Sudra[8]. In addition to some Sanskrit books (Granths) the word 'Sood' has been used in place of 'Sudra' in Prakrit, Pali and in the Hindi literature of Bhakti (Devotion) period which has apparently been used for the one birth, non-Aryans. Sant Kabir and Guru Nanak Dev Ji also have used the word Suda in the Hindi literature during the Bhakti period:-

Guru Nanak Dev Ji

EK VŨND EK MALAMŪTTRA EK CHĀMA ARU GŪDĀ ।
EK JOTI SE SAVA HI JANAME KO BĀHMAN KO SŪDĀ ॥

Sant Kabir

TUMA KAT BĀHMAN, HAM KATA SŪDA ।
HUM KAT LOHŪ TUM KAT DŪDHA ॥

Similarly, in the Buddhist religious books (Granths) written in the Pali language, the word Sood, 'Sooda' or 'Soodda' has been used. Amongst them 'Dighanikaya'[9] is pre-eminent.

According to Buddha, the persons who were frightened and were of mean behaviour were called 'Suda'. Thus, the word Sood came into being (see Chapter 8). Even today, the word Sood is used in place of the word Sudra in the Punjabi language in the religious field.

It is now quite clear that the word 'Sood' is a corrupt form of the word 'Sudra'. And, this caste used to be called Sood in place of the Sudra in daily conversation during ancient times.

There are clear proofs to show in the ApastambDharma Suttra that the Sudras worked as cooks in the houses of the Kshattriya rulers, and priests (Purohits)[10].

Apt D.Suttra II -2-3-4

ĀRRYĀDHIṢṬHATĀ VĀ SHŪDRAḤ SANSKARTĀRAḤ SYUḤ I

It means that the Sudras who are under the authority of Aryans should take the jobs of cooking.

Some incident must have occurred as a result of which this class as a whole became the cause of hatred for the whole of the Aryan community who immediately prevented them doing the cooking work as a punishment. And, the Aryans had been left with no alternative but to entrust the Trusted Brahmans with the cooking work. In order to give respect to such cook, the practice of calling him 'Maharaj' might have been started. This practice is still in vogue. This incident might have occurred when the Aryans were still in Punjab and they had not yet put their feet on the plains of Ganga-Yamuna. This is the only plausible reason why this caste is found in North-west India only. Historical accounts reveal that in the past this caste lived in Sind, Rajasthan and Punjab. The incident and action might have been so hateful and fatal (which can be imagined from the meaning of the word 'Sudana' to exteriminate) on account of which the entire class of non-Aryans, which were prior to this called Dasa or Dasyus, was later called Sudra (Sud). Perhaps this was the decisive period during which the gap of hatred was widened between the Aryans and non-Aryans which could never be revived again. Possibly since then the mutual relation of messing in addition to marrying came to an end for ever.

According to Sir Denzil Ibbetson [11], "The people of this caste do government services and are petty traders. They indulge freely in meat and wine, and in habits, customs, and social position resemble very closely the Kayasthas. The tribe is apparently an ancient one, but I can obtain no definite information as to its origin. Various fanciful derivations of the tribal name are current, for the most part of an opprobrious nature. I attempted to make inquires from some leading Suds; but the result was the assembling of a Panchayat, the ransacking of the Sanskrit classics for proof of the Kshattriya origin, and a heated discussion in the journal of the

Anjuman".

At page 263 of this book the learned writer Ibbetson has called Kayasth caste as Sudra. This means that in his view this caste is also Sudra. When we look for the history of above tribe we find that this tribe lived in the Sind state of Punjab from pre historic period up to the Muslim invasion. Dr R.S. Sharma[12] puts forward his view with the support of few evidences from Mahabharata". In Mahabharata (VI-10-66-46 SHUDRA BHIRAYA DARDAH KASMISAH PASHU BHIHSAHA) Sudra tribe is said to have been living with the Abhira (Ahir) tribe. In the same description in one verse the word 'Peplada' has been replaced by 'Dasi'. It means as per author's view there is no difference between both the words and these words have been used for the above tribe in place of word Sudra... This tribe is one of those tribes which were vanquished by Nakula".

Mr Bhandarkar [13] while throwing light on the history of this caste has written - "Alexander must have had a confrontation during his return in the south of Sind province, with those persons who have been called `Sodagi' by Arrian and `Sodrai' by Diodorus. Scholars have identified Sodagi with Sodha Rajputs and Sodrai with Sudras. According to Mr J.W. McCrindle they may be called The remnants (Sudras) of earlier inhabitants who used to live here even before the arrival of the Aryans in India (Ancient India Vol.I, P 354). It can be clearly said that some people have read the word `Sodagi' as sodrai by mistake. The idea that Sood was the name of a tribe undoubtedly appears to be astonishing and a necessity of some more evidences is felt."

According to Vidhyadhar Mahajan[14] "There was a kingdom of Sudra dynasty in Sindh and while Hieuntsang visited India, a Sudra ruler laid down foundation of his kingdom in that region. Although Maharaja Harsha had included Sindh in his empire but after his death it became independent. The last Sudra king was `Sahasi', who was succeeded by Chuch, who was his Brahman Minister, who established his own kingdom. Chuch was succeeded by Chandra and Chandra was succeeded by King Dahir. This was the same king who faced the Araba invasion in Sindh in 712 A.D."

It is crystal clear from the above description that this tribe, which took birth in the Rigvedic period in Punjab, lived from this period up to the period of invasion of Muslims and remained in power from time to time.

As such the above statement of Bhandarkar has also confirmed all of my views mentioned above. Sudra was not a tribe but it was the same caste which is today known as 'Sood', In the eastern part of northern Sindh, Sudras and Abhiras had established their kingdom as a result of which these were known as 'Sudrabhirs' (see Chapter 15.)

Some books have been written on the origin of Sood caste, one of which was published in 1980 is 'Origin of sood-a critical Analysis' written by Shri Ram Rattan Sood. As has been the tendency, every caste has been claiming itself to be superior to others. Many of them have tried to call them Kshattriyas or Rajputs as has been done by Kayasthas and Marathas. A similar claim has been made in the above mentioned book also. In the end, the writer has tried to prove that the Soods are Kshattriyas.

The writer, Mr Ram Rattan Sood, after giving the details of views written earlier on this subject, has refuted them all. Some examples are given below:-

Salamat Rai in 'Mukul-Taarikhe Soodan' has tried to link this caste with the brave and famous Aryan Kshattriya king Sudasa of Rigveda who has strongly defeated a confederacy of ten kings on the bank of Parushni.

In 'Sood Yoga' Rulia Ram Kashyap has tried to link the word 'Sood' with the words of the same resemblance found in the Hymns of Rigveda. At one place, he has tried to relate this caste with 'Chandravansh' of Yadavas. After giving a detail of lineage of Chandravansha, he has tried to relate this caste with queen Sodha, the wife of king Moolraj second of Amarkot, who has committed 'jauhar' (self sacrifice) along with 2400 ladies after the Rajputs were defeated by Mughal army in 1258 A.D.

In the above book at page 131, this caste has been related to Sood, son of Rajput king Parmar.

Similarly, in another book entitled 'Sood Vansh ka Gauravshali Itihas' this caste has been related to Suryavanshi Ikshvaku king Sodasa whose grandson was Nal.

In 'Sood's History', it has been shown that the Soods were related to Raja Dahir of Sind (who was a Brahman) who was defeated in the battlefield by Kasim and gave his two daughters to Khalifa as a gift. But after refuting all these versions, the writer Ram Rattan Sood has at page 48-54 given the following three evidences in order to prove the Soods to be Kshattriyas:

1. It is not out of way to mention that worthy Lala Sawan Shah Sood of Dharamsala in 1874 or so called for a learned Brahman Shri Ramji Das of Kurukshetra and asked him to find out the origin of the Sood community. He was to be paid five hundred rupees if he succeeded in giving a conclusive result.

The Brahman made a search and after some time told Shri Sawan Shah Sood that Soods and Kshattriyas were the one and same caste. That Brahman told him a story that once upon a time there lived a king named DASIB CHATTARI He had two sons. One day Paras Ram (the Brahman who destroyed Kshattriyas of his time) caught hold of them and asked who they were? The first boy told him that he was a Khattri.(The word KHAT in Sanskrit means a place where grain is stored). Paras Ram thought that he was a trader of grains so he let him go. The other boy on enquiry said that he was a SOOD (in Sanskrit the word Sood means a cook) so he was also let off. The descendents of the former were called KHATTRI and of the latter were called SOODS.

2. In the second evidence the learned scholar has said that most of the Gotras of Soods have a commonality with the Kshattriya as well as Brahmans.

3. Thirdly he has said that they wear the sacred thread (Yagyopaweet) and take part in performing Yajnas. Sarswat Brahmans accept food served by them and the outlook of their face and their complexion is attractive.

The writer has proclaimed the Sood caste to be Kshattriya on this very basis but I refute this view:-

The story has been concocted by Ramji Das Brahman on the temptation of a huge sum of money in the same manner as Gaugbhat a Brahman of Banaras prepared a false lineage of Shivji's family to establish his relationship with the famous Sisodia dynasty of Rajputs just in order to prove him a Kshattriya. (see P-170). The Brahman has nowhere indicated as to from which original Sanskrit text or historical book the above story has been taken. The second thing pertains to the caste Khattri. The scholars [15] are of the view that in Punjab, the people pronounce the words 'Sh' and 'Ksh' as 'Kh' that is why the word Kshattri became Khattri, such as 'Shishya' becomes 'Sikh'.

2. The second evidence is the similarity between the Gotras of Soods and Kshattriyas. The writer has himself accepted that their Gotras are similar to the Gotras of Brahmans also. They can, therefore also claim to be Brahmans. In fact, the Gotras in the ancient era were named on the following grounds:

(a) According to tradition as preserved in the Mahabharata (Shanti, 196) the original Gotras were four in number, called after the names of Angira, Kasyapa, Vasista and Bhrigu. Later the Angira Gotra was split up into two, which were known by the names of the two grandsons of Angira, viz. Bharadvaja and Gautama. Bhrigu's name came to be substituted by that of his descendant Jamadgni. To these afterwards three new Gotras were added-Atri, Visvamitra, Agasta. Thus the number of Gotras rose to eight, as is mentioned by writers like Baudhayana and Manu. But the process of splitting-up and addition continued until the number has swelled to several scores. The registration of Gotras and Pravaras began at a time when the Brahman caste had become rigidly exclusive, and when the belief had become deep-rooted that all the Vedic Rishis belonged to the Brahman Varna and that none but Brahmans could claim descent from them. So naturally, the non-Brahmans could not have any Pravara of their own. Hence the dictum of Mitakshara following Asvalayna's Srauta Suttra that "a Kshattriya or a Vaishya at the time of sacrifice should recite the Pravara of his priest".

PAUROHITYĀN RĀJANYA VISHĀN PRAVRA ṆĪTE ITYĀSHVALĀYAN ITI MITĀKSHRĀ RĀJNYA VISHĀN PURAUHITGOTRAPRAVARAU VEDITTAVYO" (ITIRAGHUNANDANAH)

In the case, therefore, of the non-Brahmans, if we agree with the Brahman law-makers, there need not exist any blood relationship between two persons of the same Pravara and same Gotra. Therefore, the Gotra's names of all those Swarna castes were also given after the name of Brahman's Gotra. All other castes other than Maha Sudras, who were entitled to take part in the Yajnas, were also given the names of Brahman Gotras. This is the main reason for the similarity of Gotras[16].

As has been said earlier that Sood is considered to be one of the Swarn caste, and on this account it has the right to perform Yajna. Hence, the similarity amongst the Gotras of Brahmans, Kshattriyas and Soods is found.

(b) The Sudra servants who traditionally used to serve the Brahman or a Kshattriya family for many generations, also adopted the Gotra of that Brahman or Kshattriya family[17].

(c) Some castes adopted their Gotras from the names of cities or towns in which they had been living for quite a long period, i.e. from Kannauj to Kanaujia, Agra to Agarwal, Mathura to Mathur or Mathuria, Ahmedabad to Ahmedabadi and from Chambaner to Chambaneri.[18]

This is the main reason for which a similarity is found in the Gotras of different Aryan and non-Aryan castes. Therefore, the similarity of Gotras is meaningless. There appears to be another main reason (b) of similarity amongst the Gotras of Soods, Kshattriyas and Brahmans-the Sood cooks who served the Hindu Priests or the Kshattriya families in a traditional way from one generation to another generation, adopted the same Gotras which were the Gotras of Holy priests of Kshattriyas. In confirmation of this, I give below a comparative list showing the similarity of Gotras of Kahars (Kashyap) of Punjab which is a servile caste of Sudra varna, with those of Sood and Kshattriyas:

Kahar	Sood	Kshattariyas
Udhan	Uggal	Ugal
Kaliyan	Kariyal	-
Cheve	Chiv	Chiv
Jor	Jari	-
Jalandhari	Jalandhare	-
Jarpal	Janpal	-
Jhala	Jha!	Jhalla
Jhangre	Jhangri	Jhangri
Tandan	Tandan	Tandan
Tande	Tande	Dhode
Dodh	Dodan	Dodan
Dhut	Dhup	Dhupar
Vihal	Bahal	Bahal
Bansal	Basoil	Sol
Vagal	Valgan	Valgan

Mandlay	Mandal	Mand
Lamsray	Lamsay	-
Lunj	Ling	-
Sanotray	Salotray	Saylay

2. The next evidence is not so sound and it should not be treated as an irrefutable proof. In north India, the Brahmans take meals cooked by all Dwijas but contrary to this in south India the Brahmans do not take meals cooked by any non-Brahman. All the Swarn Jatis,may they be from the non-Aryan origin, take full part in the performance of Yajana or other religious ceremonies.

3. The third evidence pertains to the attractive face and fair complexion etc. A detailed description has been given on this subject on chapter 13 and 14. Here it would be quite sufficient to say that the castes which were born out of the servile class of the Aryans have the maximum possible admixture of Aryan blood. In the preceeding pages, we have discussed about non-Aryan 'Dasis' and wives of Rigvedic period. The Aryans could freely enjoy marital relations with these wives (Badhu) even without marriage. The main reason of their attractive face and fair complexion is admixture of Aryan blood to a great extent. This becomes more clear when we would discuss on the following pages that the scavanger Bhangi caste which has the lowest social status has fair complexion and also attractive features because of the admixture of the Aryan blood due to the same reason. From their good physique, height and other factors, we find him close to the Kshattriya varna.

Shri Ram Rattan Sood writes at page 68 of his book 'Origin of Soods a critical analysis' " Chauphari Rajputs in Ambota did not permit Soods to use band (bajas) in their marriage procession. Due to this there had been many clashes between Soods and Rajputs. Further I learnt that in a court of law it was decided some time in late nineteenth century that Soods should have a right to use bands in their marriage processions.

Lala Salamat Rai has also mentioned that Rajputs in some places did not allow Soods to take water from Bauris (water springs) and wells. A case was taken up in a court and decided in favour of Soods.

In this way, my above view is also strengthened that Soods were non-Aryans. Otherwise the Rajputs who are lower than Kshattriyas, in status should not have given such a treatment to the Sood Kshattriyas who are above them in terms of social status. There is a hearsay amongst the Soods that some time their ancestors used to live in Sind from where they came via Rajputana to settle down in punjab. In this way the Rajputs, the inhabitant of Rajputana know better about the racial affinities and its social status than Punjabis. It may be mentioned that even today the Soods are considered to be Sudras in Rajasthan.

In the end, Dr Fauja Singh, Director and Professor Department of History in the Punjabi University while appreciating the work of Mr Sood, writes in the preface of the above book "This effort cannot be considered to be successful until this fact is brought to light that why did they adopt other professions by giving up the profession of a Kshattriyas. How did this caste become Sood from Kshattriya varna?"

In this way, it is proved beyond doubt that the Sood caste was not Aryan Kshattriya but a cook in the service of Aryan people and was originally offspring of non-Aryan brave Kshattriyas of Indus valley country, who were founders of one of the oldest and greatest civilization of the world; who undoubtedly deserve to be called great. In this way this caste can be proud of their origin.

Kayastha

The offspring of the valiant men who were killed after their defeat in the war of Indus country were also related to the Kayastha class, who were kept as slaves by the Aryans in their houses. This was the same class which had worked as personal servants in the Houses of Aryan priests and Kshattriya kings. Famous anthropologist Sir Hirbert Hope Risley[19] gives his views about origin of Kayastha caste of Bengal "The servant- (Shagird Pesha) class of Bengal is a well known class whose origin is said to have taken place in the form of illegitimate progeny. Even today their number is increasing. There is a tradition in the high castes of Orissa and the Kayastha caste who came from Bengal, that they keep the ladies of very low caste Chasa and Bhandari in their houses as servants because there is no tradition of widow marriage among them. Progeny of these maid-servants is known as Shagird-pesha. Kayastha Shagird-Pesha (Professional servants) neither hold matrimonial relation with the Karana Shagird Pesha nor Rajput Shagird Pesha hold such relation with the Kayastha Shagird Pesha but they do marry the Karanas."

He further writes, "It is said that the word Shagird-Pesha is prescribed for the Kayastha descendants which is often called Sagar-Pesha, which means a domestic servant. Shagird-Pesha are also some times known as 'Gulam' (slaves), the word which is used for Sudras in east Bengal. Their family is also known by the name'Singh' or Dasa'."

It is quite clear that this caste might have been the servants of the Aryans during ancient time. Writing about the origin and social status of Kayastha caste, Shri Ram Prasad Chanda[20] says, "All the Kayasthas of Bengal were probably known as Karanas before the rise of Kulinism in Vanga and Southern Radha. In the accounts of castes given in the Brahmakhanda of the Brahmavaivarta Purana (Wilson's Indian castes, Vol.I pp 439-44) and the Brahaddharma Purana, the Karana occupies the place of the Kayasthas. The authors of both these accounts seem to disclose a familiarity with the caste system of Bengal and agree in assigning to the Karana the place of honour in their list of the mixed castes. The legend relating to the origin of these mixed castes is narrated in the Brahaddharma Purana, Uttarkhanda (chapter xiii). It is said that when Vena obtained the sovereignty of the earth he stopped the performance of sacrifices and other religious rites. The Brahmans then approached him and said, "O king, if religious rites are not performed and Vishnu is not worshipped, anarchy will follow and mixed castes will spring up from the illicit connection of men and women of different castes." The wicked king took the hint and compelled men and women of unequal castes to procreate mixed castes. When mixed castes of the first degree had been created, Vena compelled them again to create other mixed castes. The names of the so-called thirty six mixed castes as given in the Brahaddharma Purana, show how conversant the author was with the caste system of Bengal. I name them in the order in which they are mentioned in the text.

I. Twenty good mixed castes (uttama sankarah) having Srotriya Brahmans as their Purohitas-Karana[21] (Kayastha), Ambastha (vaidya), Gandha Vanik, Kamsakar (brazier), Sankhakara (shell dresser), Ugra, Rajaputra (Rajput), Kumbhakara (potter), Tantravaya (weaver), Karmakara (black smith), Dasa (Casi Kaivartta), Magadha, Gopa (Goala, milkman) Napita (Barber), Modaka (Mayra), Varjivi (Barui, grower of betel leaves), Suta, Malakara (gardener), Tambuli (seller of betel leaves), Taulika (seller of betel nuts, Tili traders.)

II. Twelve madhyama or intermediate mixed castes Taksan (wood cutter), Rajaka (washerman) Svarnakara (gold smith), Suvarnavanik, Abhira, Tailakaraka (oilpresser), Dhivara (fisherman), Saundika (wine seller), Nata, Savaka or Savara, Sekhara, Jalika (fisherman.)

III. Antyajas or outcastes-Malegrahi, Kudava, Candala, Veruda, Carmakara (Chamar), Ghattajivi (ferryman), Dolavahi, Malla."

Besides these thirty-six (really forty), the author names the Sakadvipi or Devala Brahamans and two other mixed castes Ganaka and Vadaka. From the body of Vena also sprung Mlechchha Pulinda, Pukkasa, Khasa, Yavana, Suhma Kamboja, Savara, and Khara. When the Rishi saw these castes born of sin they put Vena to death. Then they rubbed he arms of Vena and Prthu sprung up from them. Prthu restored religious rites, worshipped the Rishi and requested them to assign to the mixed castes their occupations and duties. The Brahmans asked the thirty-six mixed castes, also called Sudras, what calling each of them would adopt according to which they should also be named. "When all of them were thus addressed by the Brahmans versed in the sacred books, they began to speak, and Karana first (adau) spoke thus, we are ignorant out castes totally devoid of wisdom. Men like you are omniscient; please ordain for us what it fit. Then the Brahmans said addressing the King, "This is the Karana: let him always prosper. He possesses humility and is well behaved; he hath spoken well. He looks like one who is well versed in polity (nitijna) and he should do administrative work (rajakarya). He should worship the Brahmans and gods. This (karana) is a Sat-Sudra (good Sudra); there is no doubt about it. Reference for Brahmans, desire for worshipping gods, and good conduct, are the characteristics of a Sat Sudra. "The Karana then bowed his head before the Brahmans who added "Son, live on this earth, skilful in administrative work (rajakaryavisarada) and expert in writing (lipikarmavisarada)." This mythological tale (legend) is similar to other tales but this legend confirms my view that this is the caste which has the maximum admixture of Aryan blood and is certainly Sudra[22], the origin of which was related to the inhabitants of the Indus valley, made slaves due to their being defeated in the war. In the Ved Vyasa Smriti I-11, Kayasthas have been referred to as Sudras (see following pages under head Pani).

Ram Prasad Chanda[23] has given a story to prove that this caste used to be the servants of the Aryans as under:

"Among the non-Brahman castes of the Outer countries, five exogamous sub-sections of the Vangaja and the Daksinaradhiya Kayasthas of Bengal, viz., the Boses, Ghoses, Guhas, Mitras and Dattas, are said to be the descendants of five Sudra attendants who accompanied the five Brahman immigrants from Kanauj imported by Adisura. It is also said that the ancestors of the Boses, Ghoses, Guhas and Mitras when questioned by king Adisura, admitted that they were the servants of the Brahmans, but Purusottam Datta is said to have declared, "Sir, listen to me: Datta is not the servant of anybody; he has only accompanied; This is to be known about him". The king, offended at the arrogance shown by this speech, deprived him of his claim to the noble rank (kulinya). The social life of the Vangaja and Daksina Radhiya Kayasthas of Bengal is still guided by an unquestioned faith in this story."

Some scholars termed the above story to be baseless on the ground that in Kanauj from where the ancestors of the above mentioned Kayasthas had migrated, no Kayastha caste of such surnames are found. Secondly, this view is also disproved while we find out traces of these castes earlier to this event. In the region of Udra (Orissa) and Kosal a copper plate grants of the Soma Vanshi king Trikalinga of 11the century A.D. bears the names of officials whose titles are Ghosa, Datta and Natha Castes. But above myth is very famous in Bengal.

But Ram Prasad Chanda in order to prove that the above mentioned caste was certainly Sudra, further writes in the same book; "In fact two views are in vogue in Bengal-the pioneer of one view is Pt. Lal Muni Vidyanidhi who has written 'Sambandh Nirnaya'. He is of the belief that the Kayasthas originated from Sudras (Sambandh Nirnay, page 148-149). For this he accepts the Jatimala given in the Agnipuran as an evidence. According to Jatimala, Sudramati originated from the feet of Brahma. Sudramati gave birth to Hina and Hina in turn gave birth to Pradeep who gave birth to Kayastha. He had three sons Chitragupta, Chitrasen and Vichitra. Then Basu, Gosh, Guha, Mittra, Dutta, Karna, Mrityunjaya and Anukarna were born to Chittarsena. From amongst these brothers Karna gave birth to Naga, Natha and Dass and Mrityunjaya gave birth to Deva, Sena, Palita, Singh and many other (Sambandh Nirnaya p 102)."

Rev. M.A. Sherring [24] while accepting this view has said "According to Padma Purana the Kayasthas have been claimed to have originated from Brahma, like the other high castes, who is the first god of Hindus. Brahmanas accept this view but side by side they also say that they originated from the feet of Brahma, which is a part of our body commanding minimum respect from where all the Sudra castes had originated. Jatimala says that in fact the Kayasthas are Sudras; they are the offspring of a Brahman father and Sudra mother."

Further R.P. Chanda puts forward his view on this subjects. "The other school traces the Kayastha caste to Kshattriya origins and advise those among the Kayasthas who follow Sudra usages to adopt Kshattriya usages. The authorities relied on by this school are put in a nutshell in a vyavasthapatra or a paper containing the opinion of the leading Pandits of Benares issued in 1873 (The annual report of the Vanga desh Kayastha Sabha 2nd and 3rd year appendix A & B) In this paper extracts are given from the Padmapurana and the Skandhapurana, wherein we are told that the Kayasthas are the descendants of two Kshattriyas, Chitragupta and Candrasena, who were degraded to the rank of writers by two sages, Mandavya and Dalbhya, respectively. These texts cannot be regarded as mere modern fabrications, for they are quoted in a authoritative compilation, the Sudradharmatattva by Kalamakara, better known as Sudra-Kalamkara. But all these legends throw little or no light on the origin of the Kayasthas. The only basis of fact that may be discerned in them is the reflection of the opinion of the contemporaries of the writers regarding the place of the Kayastha caste in the Hindu society. The authors of the different legends probably had in view Kayasthas of different provinces and the author of the Jatimala evidently had in view the Kayastha caste of Bengal, for sub sections of which are said to have purchased the parent of Kulinism by declaring themselves as Sudra servants of Brahmans. But kulinism, which involved the admission of Sudra origin, was not recognised by two of the four sub-castes-the Uttara Radhiya and Varendra Kayasthas. These Kayasthas preferred to be known as members of the mixed karana caste than as pure-blood Sudras."

On the basis of the discussion given in the above mentioned traditions and tales it becomes quite clear that the Kayasthas belong to the non-Aryan Sudra caste. Because the people of this caste have been the personal servants of the kings and Rishis (their illegitimate progeny in some cases), they became Clerks, State Govt. employees, higher officers, secretaries, ministers etc. by taking advantage of their closeness, affection and sympathy and taking advantage of the same situation got themselves included in the Dwijas (of two birth)..But inspite of all this the Brahmans never accepted them as Aryans but Sudras. D.N. Majumdar [26] has justified these views in the following words:

"The Kayasthas in Bengal are more heterogeneous than the Kayasthas of northern India as they have been recruiting to their castes people who are ambitious to rise in the social scale. Neither are they conceded a very high social status by the Brahmans. For long they were regarded as Sudras, and had to fight their way up, by education and influence. The Kayasthas and Brahmans of Bengal constitute what is know as the Bhadralog class i.e. the lower middle and middle classes, but there are significant differences between the Kulin or, pure Kayasthas and the general run of the Kayastha caste."

Mr. Majumdar again writes in the same book at some other place [27]- "Brahmans may live in the east or the west but it is very difficult to find any difference among them. Different classes of Kayasthas do not seem to be belonging to the same ethnical group. Kayastha is possibly a cultural (professional) name and not a single ethnic group or one caste."

Here Majumdar means people of a single blood group or race when he speaks of caste. The very reason of this diversity of breed is the admixture of blood in various ethnic groups and proportions, which may be called different proportion of cross-breed. This confirms the basic concept of origin of this caste.

Rishi Yagyavalkya (I-92) has described the origin of this caste to the mating of Kshattirya with Sudra mother, but according to Manu-Samriti[28] by a Vaishya from the womb of a Sudra or Pritiloma who are called Sudras or backward castes.

The Cephalic measurement[29] of Kayasth caste is 72.6 and that of the Chamar is 72.8 which gives an indication of the similarity of the breeds of these two castes. We shall discuss about the nasal index and the blood group in Chapters 13 and 14.

Dr B.R. Ambedkar has highlighted the present day social status of the Kayasthas by giving details of some court cases in his book entitled, "Who were the Sudras?"[30]

"In the Calcutta High Court (Raj Kumar Lall versus Bissessur Dyal) case on the subject is to be found in I.L.R. 10 Cal. 688. The question raised in the case was whether the Kayasthas of Bihar were Kshattriyas or Sudras. The High Court decided that they were Sudras. The partisans of the Kayasthas took the position that the Kayasthas of Bihar were different from the Kayasthas of Bengal, the Upper Provinces and Banaras and that while those in the Upper Provinces and Banaras were Sudras, the Kayasthas of Bihar were Kshattriyas. The court refused to make this distinction and held that the Kayasthas of Bihar were also Sudras.

The third case is reported in (1916) 20 Cal. W.N. 901. Here the question raised was whether Kayasthas of Bengal were Kshattriyas or Sudras. The High Court of Calcutta held that they were Sudras. The case was taken to the Privy Council by way of appeal against the decision of the Calcutta High Court. The decision of the Privy Council is reported in (1926) 47 I.A. 140. The question whether the Bengali Kayasthas are Sudras or Kshattriyas was not decided upon by the Privy Council but was left open. In between 1916 and 1926 the Calcutta High Court gave two decisions which held that intermarriages between Kayasthas of Bengal and Tantis and Doms two of the low castes, were legal on the ground that both of them were sub-castes of Sudras.

These decisions which caused further deterioration in the position of the Kayasthas were followed by another which is reported in I.L.R. 6 Patna 506. In a most elaborate judgement extending over 47 pages, Mr. Justice Jwala Prasad went into every Purana and every Smriti in which there was a reference to the Kayasthas. He differed from the Calcutta High Court and held that the Kayasthas of Bihar were Kshattriyas"

The reason for such a decision was their political approach and nearness to judges. Nothing is left to prove that the Kayastha caste is not Sudra. Traditionally, they worked as personal servants of the Aryans, and even if they are poor, specially in Bengal they still do the same work. Undoubtedly, they are the offspring of the slaves won in the Indus valley battles.

Scavenger (Bhangi)

This caste is called as 'Dom' in Bengal, in Central India it is known as 'Chandala' or ' Bhangi' and in punjab it is called 'Chuhra' and their main task is to clean the streets and roads and to remove refuse or filth from the houses and is the lowest caste in the Brahman caste system. They are also the descendants of the unfotunate 'Dasas' and 'Dasis' of Indus valley who were kept by the Kshattriyas and priests in their houses for cleaning etc., after their victory in the war. This view has also been accepted by Ghurye[31]. Previously this class used to do the work of cleaning the kitchen and houses from inside and outside but when the population of Aryans increased, this class was split into two parts with the gradual and progressive steps of the civilization moved from jungle huts to rural and then to urban areas. Uptill now the Aryan kings, priests and prosperous persons used to go to the jungle as per tradition to answer the call of nature etc.. but now when the population of small and big towns increased it became impossible for them to go to jungle for this purpose. Specially it was not possible for the ladies of royal families and other rich people. Therefore, artificial laterines had to be constructed in the towns. Since then the above said class of society had to do this job of cleaning which was very much morbid and hateful and possibily they might have carried out this arduous responsibility with a great difficulty. But they were helpless slaves, they had to do this work. Now that they had started cleaning the streets, roads and lavatories, naturally not only the people of other three higher varnas began hating them but also their own people who did the cleaning of houses. This inferiority complex had not only kept them away from the general masses but actually raised a wall between the first and the second class of this caste, which means this class had been divided into two parts. One part which consisted of those persons who did the cleaning work inside the houses and were called 'Dheevar' or 'Kahar' and the others were known as 'Bhangi' or 'Dom'. This was the most unfortunate moment when in place of the introduction of a system of cleanliness like that of the Indus valley civilization such an inhuman system came into being, of which no example is found in any part of the world because the black slaves had the blood of the non-Aryans flowing in their veins, which was in no way related to the high caste Aryan conquerors.Therefore,those helpless and unfortunate persons were forced to do this inhuman and hateful work.On this account,this class of society came down to the lowest range of the social ladder.

There are anthropological evidences to prove this fact. Like all the other servile castes,they worked day and night and remained in their direct contact.That is why Aryan blood has penetrated into their veins to such a great extent. This is the only reason that inspite of being at the lowest range of the social ladder,half the physical Characteristics of this class are similiar to those of the Aryan Kshattriyas and half are similar to those of 'Chamars'[32].

D.N. Majumdar[33] writies : "The Dom,though they represent the lowest range of the social ladder,have probably a higher racial status than that ordinarly conceded to them.Risley has placed the Dom alongside the 'Dravadian'tribes, but on anthropometric and serological evidence,this is difficult to uphold.On the one hand the Doms approach the Kshattriya in stature, sitting height and other characters,on the other they show a close relation with Chamar. The Doms are not uniformly of dark complexion nor are their features always irregular. Leaving aside the large hybrid elements among them, which competent eyes would trace to the general laxity of their marital code,the average Dom of the U.P.,is certainly of lighter complexion and possesses occasionally a narrow and even fine nose. As it is not wholly true to say that the laxity of morals of the Dom women has resulted in a lot of illegitimacy and hybridization, it is equally a fact that the incidence of handsome and attractive features among the Dom women is a cause rather than merely a consequence of such miscegenation. Whatever be the cultural status of the Dom, their dissociation from the tribal groups and their affiliation to the Bhil and the criminal Bhantu and the Haburu is definite.It is just possible that the Dom's social disabilities have been imposed from outside."

The above mentioned views of Shri D.N. Majumdar justify my concept that this class is undoubtedly the descendants of the brave Kshattriyas of Sind country. The women and the children were made captives and kept in the houses as slaves after their massacre and defeat in the war and out of revenge they might have been compelled to do most hated menial jobs in their houses because they were the blood relatives of their bitterest enemies. The ladies not only did the cleaning work etc. in the houses but were also subjected to perform the funtcions of a wife (Badhu) as well without any marriage ceremony, as has been mentioned in the Rigveda. In this way, this is the only class in which the maximum Aryan blood is mixed.That is why some of their physical characteristics are similar to the Aryan Kshattriyas and their ladies are beautiful and capable of attracting others towards them. This quality is not found in any other low castes. Hence my view is more clear and authentic and refutes the view of D.N. Majumdar,who says. " The charateristics of the Kshattriyas have permeated with this class bacause of the characterlessness of their women". A question can be raised as to why this thing did not happen in the case of any other low caste? The following view put forward by Sir H.H Risley[34] has openly corroborated my view . He writes, "The Doms, among whom we find scavengers, vermin-eaters, executioners, basket-makers, musicians and professional burglars, probably represent the remnants of a Dravidian tribe crushed out of recognition by the invading Aryans and condemned to menial and degrading occupations." In this way the views of Mr. Risley also justify that the Doms were undoubtedly related to the ruling class of the Indus valley.

Mr. G.S. Ghurye[35] while writing about the origin of this caste, says :"There was a group separately recognised by Vasista, which was called Antyavasayin, which he declared was the progeny of a Vaishya female by a Sudra male. According to Manu, however, the Antyavasayin was of much more depraved origin, being the progeny of a Chandala male and a Nishada female. His work was confined to the cremation ground, and according to one commentator he was to be identified with the Chandala. It is not easy to explain away the absence of the listing of this group by other Dharma-writers and by Kautilya the administrator. Both Baudhayana and Vasista mention a degraded caste called Svapaka. Baudhayana once declares the group to have risen from the union of an Ambashtha male with a Brahman female".

According to the table given in VI-18 of Gautam Dharm Sutra, the Chandals are the progeny of a Sudra male and Brahman female.

In the early period, this caste used to live in the village alongwith Aryans but during the Manu period (x-51-52) this was made to live outside the village. Even today, their houses are located in the outskirts of the main village.

Similarly, as has been stated above, the Kahars also originated from this class of the Indus Valley, who are engaged traditionally in the service of the Aryans till now. Anthropological and physical statistics of this caste given on chapter XIII show that even after their division into two parts (Dom and Kahar), and there has constantly penetrated Aryan blood in later caste till today., they are closely related to each other. Ladies of both these castes are equally beautiful.

The Theory of Historical Origin of Caste System and Sudras

The most important sociological proof of the already detailed historical origin of the caste system and Sudras is the same prominant characteristic of caste system - the feeling of high and low social status, which originated on the same base. As such, the class which had won in the war, naturally started considering itself to be superior or higher than the other which was defeated and conversely the defeated class started to consider itself inferior to the victor class. It reveals that in the combat of two classes, victory confers higher social-status while defeat confers lower social status. This is the only reason that the Negrito, which is the aboriginal race of this country and the proto-Australoid who was possibly the first one to come to this country from the east Mediterranean region are present even today in mixed up condition in the form of scheduled tribes and the lowest castes in the society. This class is the under dog of social system. The scholars are of the view that the next race which came to this country from the mediterranean area was the Sumerian type which brought the Indus valley civilization to its glorious height.The blood of this race can be traced out among the artisan castes. These castes are considered as backward class or Sudras. As regards the social status, they are the next higher castes to the aforesaid class. The same blood flows in the veins of Dasa Baniks also. The reason for their acquiring a higher position than the artisan castes from the point of view of Nasal index and B blood group (see Chapter 13 & 14) is the inclusion of statistics of

Aryans vaishyas also in the above statistics. The third race which settled in this land after having migrated from outside were the Nordic Aryans who command the highest status in the society. This race now includes upper three varnas i.e. Brahman, Kshattriyas and Vaishyas. This class of society made rigid social and religious laws and made the caste system stable, and did not allow the races which came here later in due course, to rise above them. Those castes which came here later and settled here after defeating the previous Indian races, were called the Rajupts (Gurjars+Huns) and Jats (Kushan). Being invaders and conquerors these castes enjoyed high status inspite of the fact that the Brahmans had declared them as Sudra (Brahad Dharm Purana Uttar Khand Adhyaya XIII). Consequently they have been living in the society as Kshattiyas. Clear examples are of Gurjars and Jats, according to Bhavishya Purana VIII-27-28 they were declared to be Varna-Sankara and Mlechchhas but in the fact they are living like Kshattriyas in the society. It may be mentioned here that the same thing had happened in Egypt. When Egypt was conquered by the Greeks, latter possessed higher social status than the Egyptians. Subsequently Egypt was conquered by the Romans who in turn assumed the highest status and the Greeks were relegated to the middle class, while the Egyptians became the lowest. It becomes very clear that a high caste refers to a group of victorious people and low caste to a group of the defeated people. On this very basis, the social status of the invading classes became stable one after or one above the other. In this stratification we find the historical reason as a theory of origin of the caste system.

Artisan castes

Now, we take up another class i.e. the artisan class about whom there are clear archaeological evidences to show that they were the original inhabitants of Indus Valley.

A table of artisan castes is given in Amarkosha (II-10-5-10) as to who are included in the Sudras-garland makers washermen, potters, brick workers, weavers, tailors, painters, weapon manufacturers, leather workers, brass workers, shell workers, gold smiths, carpenters, dancers, singers and drummers etc.

It has been described in the first chapter that the Indus valley civilization was an artisan's civilization and the above mentioned artisan castes originally lived in Sind country. There were towns like Lothal and Chanhudaro where artisans used to live and these towns were modern like Industrial towns.

Potters

Some historians have satirically called the pre-historic period as the period of potters history which is otherwise a reality. In order to know the history of pre-historic period we recognise the ancient by the pot-sherds or the pottery unearthed by the archaeologists and name those civilizations on the basis of the same pottery such as Grey Ware culture, Black and Red Ware culture, Painted Grey Ware culture etc. Similarly, for the identification of the Indus Valley or Harappan culture, there is a particular type of pottery which is called Burnished Painted red ware culture.

Although potter;s wheel was first of all discovered in Mesopotamia but the examples of pottery found in the Harappan assemblage are unique and there is no' parallel to it found in those days. We are now to cite the proofs to show that the ancestors' of modern potter were residents of Indus Valley cities. S.R. Rao in his famous book "Lothal and the Indus Civilization"[36], gives the details of a residence of a potter discovered from the Mohenjo-daro," A special type of a house has been found from there, which has a small courtyard in front of the entrance and which connects with a larger courtyard through a passage. Near the passage there is a small room having a well and adjoins a pucca toilet. The larger courtyard measures 9.22 sq. metres which is connected by a small passage with the room having a well. It is very surprising to note that the baked earthen pipe which is surrounded by the brick work merges with the outer drain passing under the room and carries the courtyard water to the main drain constructed in the street. A similar pipe is fixed from up to downward in the wall of the room situated in the east of the courtyard which brings down the dirty water of the upper storey. The upper storey was connected with the floor through a stair case constructed in the courtyard. Another outstanding feature of this house is a small room or cell which is made of round corners in the L shaped verandah."

It is quite clear that potter of those days is a Sudra in the present society, who not only enjoyed a high status in the society but also a high standard of living. He lived a very comfortable, prosperous and luxurious life.

Mr Mackay was one of them who undertook the excavation work of Indus Valley cities. he has given the description of what he has himself seen about the potters and their rich art in his book entitled,"Early Indus Civilization:[37]:

"The people of the Indus Valley had a large variety of pottery, both decorated and plain. Practically all the ornamented wares are coated with an opaque, red slip, upon which various designs and motifs are painted with a thick black pigment. The clay used for both the plain and painted pottery appears to have come from the adjacent river and was tempered with sand, generally containing a large percentage of mica, or lime in the form of fine particles, though quite large grains of this material were sometimes included. The pottery made in Mohenjo-daro differs very little in shape and mode of decoration from that of Harappa, and only in a comparatively few cases would it be possible to say definitely in which city a jar was made.

The regular striations inside practically every vessel show that they must, almost without exception, have been shaped on the potter's wheel. To judge from the customs prevailing in a village near Mohenjo-daro today, it seems likely that the men performed this process, while the women gave the finishing touches to the pottery and also painted the designs. Although, being made of wood, no potter's wheels have yet been found, the kilns in which the pots were baked have survived; they are round structures between six and seven feet in diameter, with a perforated floor upon which the vessels were laid. A wood fire was kindled in a space below this floor, fed from outside, and the smoke was carried away through a hole in the domed roof-though no kiln is sufficiently well preserved to retain this upper portion. The heating was well controlled, for most of the pottery is efficiently fired; a few over-baked vessels have come to light, but these had retained their shape sufficiently to be put into use.

The slip used for a great part of the painted ware is red ochre, a substance which may have come from somewhere in the country or from Hormuz in the Persian Gulf, which at the present day exports an excellent variety of this material to India. After a jar had been shaped on the wheel, the ochre was painted thickly over it, and when dry was carefully polished with a piece of bone or a pebble. This process resulted, after firing, in a beautiful, highly burnished vessel, which in first-class work has the sheen, colour and appearance of red chinese lacquer."

Even today the potters living in villages adjacent to Mohenjo-daro make such coloured pots and their wheel, which is the modern one, is operated by foot where as previously it was operated with hand with the help of a rod by placing it in the hole of the wheel, as is the practice amongst the potters in most parts of India. Even today the pots are baked in an open ground by covering them with fire wood and cow-dung cakes, but it is interesting to note that very fine type of kilns existed in the Indus civilization era. Thus, it becomes apparent that the potter who lived 4-5 thousand years ago was much advanced than the present day potter. How surprising it is.

Painting and polishing of pots

Mr. Mackay[38] writes on the above mentioned subject at next page of the said book:-

"The designs several of which also occur on the pottery of other ancient countries, although some are peculiar to the Indus Valley, were painted on this red surface with a brush before firing, the material used being a thick, black or purplish-black, paint made from manganiferous haematite. The most popular design is composed of a series of intersecting circles, a pattern which does not appear on the wares of any other ancient civilization. Such designs have been painted on a long jar. Another design which seems to be more popular, is a tree along which other designs have also been painted. Another design resembles with comb. There are other designs of the sun also, but these are beyond identification."

The above mentioned archaeological evidences are sufficient to prove that the potters existed in the Indus Valley country.

Copper smith (Brasier)

Iron had not been discovered as yet in the Indus Valley and no traces of iron has come to notice yet. Only copper and brass was used. Brass was prepared by mixing tin in copper. In this way, untensils of brass and copper for domestic use, implements and weapons for war were manufactured by the copper smith in those days. Mackay[39] gives a detailed description of this craft:

"There was evidently no scarcity of copper and bronze in the Indus cities round about 2500 B.C. for the latter has been found even at the lowest levels of Mohenjo-daro, where one specimen contained as much as 22.2 percent of tin. Frankfort and Woolley have also noticed that tin was frequently used as an alloy to toughen copper in Sumer at a period contemporary with the Indus civilization.

It is difficult to say where the metal-workers of the Indus Valley obtained their tin, for although it is to be found in several places in India, such as Burma, the Bombay Presidency, Bihar and Orisas, it is uncertain what sources were available in ancient times. It is a moot point whether the tin used by the early Sumerians and the Harappa people came from the same place, but the writer considers that this in all probability, was not the case.

With regard to the copper used by the ancient inhabitants of the Indus Valley, supplies of this metal may have come from Rajputana or Baluchistan. Desch has shown, however, that the copper and bronze of the ancient Indus cities, like that of the Sumerians contains as appreciable amount of nickel, and as Peake has suggested that a possible source of the Sumerians' copper was Oman, where old working have been found in which the ore is of this type, it has been suggested that this district of Arabia also supplied the Indian cities. The presence of nickel has, however, also been detected in the copper from the old, but still worked, mines of Chota Nagpur in India, and it is perhaps safer to assume for the present that the copper used at Mohenjo-daro and Harappa did not come from abroad.

The use of tin to alloy copper has the effect of hardening the later and also facilitates casting, but too much tin makes a brittle product. As a rule 9 to 12 percent of tin suffices for ordinary purposes, but in some of the bronze from Mohenjo-daro over 26 percent has been found. It would seem that the metal workers of the city, like the early Sumerians, either used no fixed proportion of tin to copper or obtained their bronze ready mixed from sources over which they had no control.

The finding of a considerable amount of copper ore in a brick-lined pit at Mohenjo-daro proves that this metal was smelted there, although no furnaces have been discovered in which it could have been reduced. A very simple method would have been to heat the ore mixed with charcoal in a hole in the ground by means of a blast. The shape of several copper ingots from the city, one of which weights two and a half pounds, suggests that this was done, and that the metal when molten ran through a channel into an even, semi-circular depression in the ground; a projection on one side of some of these ingots shows how the moulds were filled. The flat upper surfaces of all the ingots are very puckered owing to unequal cooling.

No trace has been found of soldering in the copper or bronze work, although this process was employed on gold and silver. Rivets were generally used to join the two first-named metals, but in one instance a handle was fastened to bronze cover with a rivet, which was then made more secure by running a little molten metal over it.

With the exception of three very plain silver vessels, all the metal utensils yet discovered are made of copper or bronze, the majority of these being extremely simple in shape and in many cases following the forms of the pottery. They were either beaten out of sheet metal or were cast. It was not the custom to engrave these metal vessels in any way, and the only fluting occurs on a censer whose edge is also ornamented with indentations. Some of the jars with very narrow bases had the latter made separately and then lapped on, but in no case does an edge appear to have been turned over to stiffen the rim. With the exception of certain frying—pans no metal utensil has yet been found with a handle or spout."

In addition to the metal utensils found so far other things i.e. knives, daggers blades axes, saws for sowing the wood, hammers, blades of spears, arrow heads and swords etc have also been excavated, in the manufacture of which the metal workers of Indus Valley have given a unique example of their efficiency and ability.

Bronze statues have also been found which include a cart and an animal. A statue of buffalo and a dancing girl has also been found which speak of high technology of casting. For the purpose of casting, the same method might have been adopted which is called the wax process. Such technique was known to Sumerians and the Egyptians since the early ages[40].

Copper Chariot :

Another interesting thing found is a small two wheeled chariot with a pointed canopy. A charioteer is sitting in the front having a bun-shaped hairdo. This toy-chariot is possibly the oldest example of the wheeled vehicle of the world.

Kedar Nath Shastri[41] gives a detailed description of a big findings of metallic material goods-"Copper and bronze were used for manufacturing weapons, utensils, ornaments and many other things used for domestic purposes. The most remarkable find was a copper cauldron which was covered with a lid made of the same metal, More than one hundred copper Weapons, tools, ornaments had been placed in it. It has been excavated from mound F of Harappa, trench No. 2 at a depth of 5 feet 9 inches. The following items were found in it : 21 axes, spear heads, daggers for flaying, head of a club, lances, two double edged axes, 11 daggers, arrow heads, small daggers, two saws, ten chisels and the ornaments included a bracelet, half-moon shaped tops for threading and making garlands and one bowl, balancing bar of a scale and writing pen etc."

Gold Smith

The men and women have been donning beautiful ornaments since the rise of civilization till today. Specially the beautiful ladies have always loved the ornaments. The jwellers have been meeting their demands since the early ages. Even the Indus Valley society cannot be an exception to this.

Mr. Rao[42] while throwing light on this subject writes:

"The Harappans, both men and women, decorated themselves with a large variety of ornaments produced from every conceivable material ranging from precious metals and gemstones to bone and baked clay.

Hoards of jewellery recovered from below the house-floors at Mohenjo-daro and Lothal include necklaces of gold and semi-precious stones, copper bracelets and beads, gold ear-rings and head-ornaments, faience pendants and buttons, and beads of steatite and gemstones".

Similarly the ornaments which were worn by the women folk round the neck included Hansli, necklace and bracelet. The necklaces were made of gold, silver, copper, stone, faience, conchshell, ivory beads etc. Beads made of gomeid, green emerald, Agait, Lal varda, Plaza etc. were worth seeing. Most of these stones were brought from different regions of India, and Afghanistan and Baluchistan where mines of these stones are found even today.

Other ornaments of ladies included conical flowers, pendant, an ornament for the forehead, ear ornaments, clips, bangles, arm ornaments, ear and nose rings, girdle and anklets[43].

Mackay writes,[44] "Gold might have been procured from India itself, whereas silver must have been procured from the mines situated in Afghanistan. This metal has not been found in sufficient quantity in the Indus Valley cities as compared to gold and copper. Electrum also might have been procured from within India."

The scholars are of the view that the goldsmiths of the Indus country used the same technique for casting the ornaments, which the Indian gold smiths have been using traditionally. The furnance which could be lifted easily was made by breaking the half lower portion of earthen pitcher, the bottom of which is the mouth of the pitcher and which is filled with earth, one lighting lamp and a long metallic blow pipe.

Mr. Mackay[45] gives details about the jewellery found from the excavations of Indus Valley cities- "The ornaments of the type which have been mentioned above have been found mostly from Mohenjo-daro and Harappa and they were kept in the pots made of copper, silver and brass to keep them secure and these were found burried beneath the pavements of the houses. The most interesting achievement has been made by Rai Bahadur Daya Ram Sahni, who unearthed at Mohenjo-daro a number of necklaces and fine hard stone beads, some of which were contained in a silver jar and others lying loose in the soil. It was possible to see, moreover, that this jar had once been wrapped in a cotton cloth, for the patina that formed on the jar preserved some of the material. Dikshit also unearthed at Mohenjo-daro, a small silver vase containing some very fine necklaces, various silver and gold objects, including fillets, and fragments of scrap metal. At another place a very elaborate girdle was found in a large copper bowl, on top of which a copper dish had been placed to serve as a cover. At Harappa, Vats made a notable find of ornaments some resembling the jewellery of Mohenjo-daro and others quite unlike it in design. This last hoard was discovered in a bed of hard earth..

The fine girdle mentioned above deserves a detailed description. It consists of six rows of barrel-cylinder translucent, red carnelian beads, each bead being about five inches long and separated from the one following by spherical bronze beads and a bronze spacer pierced with six holes for the strings. The girdle, which is about three feet four inches long, has at each end a flattened hemispherical terminal of bronze, originally gilded, and through these terminals the strings were carried and fastened. Some of the female figurines wear girdles of this type, the beads and spacers being represented by strips of clay. The holes in the carnelian beads are as well polished as the outer surface, and it must have required great skill to bore such hard stone. Each bead had been drilled from both ends, in many cases with such accuracy that the holes meet exactly in the centre- - - - Several statues unearthed at Mohenjo-daro show as we have seen, that, as in Sumer, fillets or head bands were worn round the forehead. Quite a number of these have been found with the other jewellery, coiled into rolls to save space, and in many cases still retaining their flexibility. These fillets are usually thin ribbons of gold, a little under half an inch in width, and sometimes as much as sixteen inches long. The ends are rounded and pierced with a small hole to enable them to be tied together. As a rule, the fillets are severely plain, but specimens are known with holes bored along one edge to enable ornaments to be suspended from them, and in one case a device was indented at both ends of the band. Fillets ornamented in a similar way, either with a row of dots or with figure of animals, are well known in early times in sumer.

Small metal cones are worn to-day on the top of the head by women in the Punjab, and ornaments of this kind have been found among the hoards of jewellery unearthed at Mohenjo-daro and Harappa. These cones, which average 2.45 inches in height and two inches in diameter, are of gold, silver, copper, and faience, and have a loop soldered inside the tip, through which a lock of hair must have been passed to keep the ornament in place. Certain hollow hemispherical or cone-shaped objects, made of two, three, or even four pieces of shell carefully fitted together, seem to have served the same purpose. Several of the female figurines wear similar head ornaments.

The presence of ear-rings on some of the figurines shows that they were sometimes worn, but actual specimens are very rare, owing perhaps to the fact that a ring which pierces the ear-lobe is of all ornaments the most difficult to lose."

From the above, it is quite clear that such a great and beautiful work of artistic skill must have been done by a traditional and proficient artist and there would be no exaggeration if we call them the ancestors of the goldsmith.

Carpenter

The scholars are of the opinion that there was plenty of wood in the Indus Valley. The wood was used in the potter's kilns and in the factories for making fire, in addition to its use for baking the bricks. Wood was also used for constructing houses and for making other instruments for domestic use. Though no remains there of have been left today, i.e. after four thousand years, even then evidences are there to prove the above mentioned fact,

Mr. Mackay[46] writes,"In some of the larger houses, however, deep recesses have been found in the walls, and these, in all probability, were once fitted with wooden shelves. Chests of wood must also have been used for storage purposes; to them probably belonged the numerous piece of shell inlay that have been found. Fasteners of bone and shell attest the use of boxes, and we can safely say that beds and stools were also ordinary articles of furniture; a stool appears on one of the seals. Some of them had legs carved in the shape of a bull's foot, after the manner of ancient Egypt, but nothing very definite can be said on the subject of furniture as not a single article has survived."

He further writes,[47] "One of the most interesting tools unearthed is a bronze saw, sixteen and a half inches long, which once had a broad wooden handle; three rivet-holes indicate where it was attached to the blade. The astonishing thing about this saw is that the toothed edge is undulated in order to prevent its binding in a cut, in contrast to the modern method of setting each tooth separately to achieve the same end. Saws with the teeth set in any way whatever have hitherto been unknown before the time of the Romans, and it is extremely interesting to find so much earlier a specimen, and one, moreover, in such a good state of preservation."

Similarly, Chisels have been found in large number having sharp edges on both sides. Manufacture of boats must have been the main work of the carpenters. It is said that in addition to the wheeled-vehicles, the ploughs and all other agricultural implements used to be made of wood. The potter's wheel was also made of wood. Mr. Mackay[48] gives an account of tools & implements found from the sites, "Several defective castings that have been found show that the blades fresh from the mould were of the same shape as the finished articles, except for their rough surfaces, so that the metal must have been tempered and consolidated mainly with a hammer; even a bronze blade with a small amount of tin could be so hardened in this way that it equalled mild steel, some of the blade-axes are of considerable size, and one, eleven inches in length, weights four pounds three ounces. It cannot be assumed that these were used in war, as there is no evidence that their inhabitants were ever seriously threatened by outside enemies until the last phases of the existence of the Indus cities; but they could have been used in working wood, in the chase, and perhaps against dacoits, like the little battle-axe so often carried by the country man of Upper Sind"

These findings throw light on the fact that these tools must have been used by a carpenter during those times.

Large scale evidences have come to light about the trade relations of Mesopotamia with Indus Valley by sea route. Miss Jacquetta Hawkes[49] writes "What goods were carried in the single masted Indus boats? perhaps rare woods were exported (there is also a mention of Meluha Table), also such luxuries as cornelian, pearls, ivory and probably pet monkeys." From the above evidences we can easily reach conclusion that the expert and efficient carpenters of the Indus Valley not only manufactured furniture for the requirements in the country itself but also exported the surplus to other countries for sale. The manufacturers of such a beautiful and large scale furniture were definitely the ancestors of the present day carpenter. According to Satpath Brahman I-1-3-12 the mere touch of a Texan (carpenter) can render the performance of Yajna, impure, this means he was a non-Aryan Sudra.

WEAVER

Cotton was the main crop of Indus Valley and it was exported to other countries. In Mesopotamia, the Indian cotton was known as 'Sindhu' and in Greece it was known as 'Sindan. Both these words denote' Sindhu', which means the product of Indus Valley. Goats and sheeps were found in large numbers in this country which clearly shows that the craftsmen of Indus Valley also weaved beautiful cloths to wear[50]. This fact has also been established from the objects and designs carved on the seals and statues found during excavations of the cities of Indus Valley that the inhabitants of Indus Valley used to wear different types of clothes which were manufactured by weavers. They did not only manufacture the clothes for their own use, but also exported the same to other countries. Muslin cloth made in Indus Valley was exported to Sumer, Akad and Babylon and it was also known by the name of 'Sindhu'. So many evidences of this fact have been found from the excavation of the cities of the said civilization. Mr. Mackay[51] puts forward some evidences,"Cotton was used as textile in Mohenjo-daro and presumably over the whole area inhabited by the Harappan people. As markings on the robe of one of the Statues seem to indicate embroidery, it is probable that this handicraft was commonly practised. The period being much too early for printed cotton cloth of the type made in Sind today. Needles of copper and bronze, some times, with pierced eyes sometimes with eyes formed by looping over the top of the needle itself, are well known though in comparison with modern specimens they appear too clumsy to have been used on closely woven material. A set of three gold needles, the largest two inches long, found with a hoard of jwellery by Dikshit may have been employed in a special kind of embroidery. They all have cylindrical handles which terminate in a sharp point containing the eye. Two of these needles seem to have been held frequently between the teeth, to judge from the marks on the handles."

Mr. Mackay [52] further writes: "In addition to the mother goddess of power (Durga) a figure which is engraved on a seal is seen wearing a skirt which is longer from behind and shorter in the front side. The tradition of wearing such like clothes is in vogue till today among the women of South India and it shows that this tradition emerged from Harappa. The women of Harappa used to wear such clothes and this tradition has lived upto this period.

It is difficult to deduce anything concerning the costume worn by men from the male figurines or from the heroes and deities portrayed on the seal-amulets; the former are invariably nude, while the latter wear only a thin band round the loins. From the few statues which have been found, none of which is perfect, it seems that a robe, with or without embroidery, was worn over the left shoulder and under the right arm. One statue wears such a garment extending well below the knees and another, a seated figure, is dressed in a long skirt secured round the waist by a running cord. The figure of a man on a sherd found at Harappa might be wearing breeches or, alternatively, a close-clinging dhoti.

Another figure has worn a gown. This gown covers only the arms, not the chest and does not fall below the skirt. It might perhaps be used during the winter. It gives us pleasure when we see a piece of cloth wrapped round the handle of razor".

Textile workers needed spindle-whorls, spools, bobbins and loom-weights some of which were made of baked clay and others of wood. Two types of terra-cotta spindlewhorls, one of an arecanut shape with circular concave base and narrow top and the other a disc of plano-convex section, both having a hole in the centre are found at Lothal, A few other discs having two marginal holes were used for fixing a split spindle. Terra-cotta discs with a third hole had a bottom-pin to facilitate quick movement of the whorl, Marginally perforated terra-cotta discs or wheel like objects served the purpose of spools which were held together by sticks. It may be noted here that the Bharwars, a semi-nomadic cattle rearing tribe who call themselves Maharashtrian Yadavas used both type of spindles for spinning wool[53].

Clear evidences are available that, cotton cloth was manufactured and used in the Indus Valley but no signs are available to show that linen and woollen clothes were also manufactured in the Valley. But such type of clothes were definitely manufactured in Sumer during that period and perhaps those clothes must have been brought from there by the traders like other goods.

It can definitely be said on the basis of the above evidences that it was only the skilled weaver during those times who used to export fine quality of muslin to other countries after meeting their own demand to whom we can call the ancestors of the present day weaver.

DYERS: Mr. Wheeler while traced a shop of dyers in Mohenjo-daro observes, "Of another kind is a building fronting upon one of the main streets 'first street', in Mohenjo-daro. Its outside dimensions are 87 X 64.5 feet, but within that considerable framework are included not only residential quarters round the courtyard but also towards the street industrial or commercial premises of some note; in particular, three rooms neatly paved with bricks on edge, one room with five conical pits or holes sunk in the floor and lined with wedge-shaped bricks, apparently to hold the pointed bases of large jars. In corner of room is a well and nearby is the usual brick stair-case. The premises may have been a public restaurant, but it is alternatively possible that the implied jars were rather, dyeing vats. A half figure of stone found from Mohenjo-daro is wearing dyed and printed cloth and a shawl".[54]

It can easily be presumed that in the Indus Valley also lived the ancestors of the present day dyer who were called the craftsmen or artisans who used to make the clothes of the general public more attractive by dyeing them in various colours.

Ivory workers

M. Wheeler while Tracing ivory workers from two heaps of skeletons found from Mohenjo-daro, observes :

"Two heaps of skeletons have been unearthed in the D.K. area of Mohenjo-daro which were lying close to each other and have been mentioned in chapter 2. Among them five were children. It appears that they were hurriedly thrown away at a low lying place and covered with earth. Mackay is of the view that these skeletons were the remains of a family out of which some were ivory workers. Two full size tusks have also been found along with the remains of the family, who at the time of invasion might have tried to flee with their valuable belongings but were caught and killed by the invaders, one skeleton has undoubtedly: worn a bangle of Indus type".[55]

Ivory pins and combs have also been found. A fine double-toothed comb of ivory, decorated on both faces with a series of incised, concentric circles was found close by the skull of a young girl. It possibly belongs to a girl who may have decorated her hair with it.[56]

Ivory was actually worked at Mohenjo-daro, for not only have a couple of tusks come to light but several half-sawn, blocks have been unearthed.[57] Craftsmen used to make useful and beautiful articles of daily use such as hair pins, combs, scales, handles for holding wooden boxes etc.

Mason

Superiority of the craftsmanship of the Harappan civilization is well known. Multi-storeyed pucca houses and sewerage system coming up to the modern standards is a clear proof of the efficiency of the masons of Harappa. They constructed the corbel type of arch for covering the drains and other places. They had no knowledge of constructing the modern type of arches. The plumb, needed by masons for brick laying were generally made of terra-cotta. Many of carrot shaped plumbs have been found at Lothal. Another type of plumb bob made of shell appears to have been used at Mohenjo-daro[58].

For the purpose of brick laying the masons used mud plaster or mortar and the technique used for this work was the same as is in vogue in India today and is known as the'English technique i.e. the joint of the upper bricks always come in the middle of the lower brick. A mixture of earth and lime was also used in place of mud morter. No plastering of any kind was traced on the walls. The walls have often been found without any such plaster. Resin and gypsum was used in order to check leakage of water (in bathrooms and rooms). In the drains plastering was done with lime and gypsum[59]. Use of tiles in rooms and bathrooms have come to light in the excavation of Kalibanga.

According to S.R.Rao the great progress made by the Harappans in the field of engineering can be termed as a remarkable contribution to the human civilization. According to some scholars, the evidences, which have come to light in respect of the high technique of engineering for the sewerage system in the Indus Valley, are not found in any other civilization during that period.

It must have been the proficient craftsman-the mason to do the brick laying work based on such a high technique in that period. which can be termed beyond any doubt as the ancestor of the present day mason. Even today, a caste named Khati is found in Haryana which performs all the jobs connected with the building construction. The same man does the brick-laying, wood work and the work of a black smith.

Agri (Stone workers)

It is said that where the Mesopotamians used unbaked-and baked bricks and Indus Valley inhabitants used baked bricks for the construction of huge buildings, the Egyptians used stones for construction of Pyramids. Stone has nowhere been used in the construction of buildings in the Indus Valley. Stone has been used in plenty for making tools, domestic implements and statues. Domestic implements include large grinding stone, stone pestle and hand operated grinding mill, which may have been the requirement of the house wives at that time. The domestic knife made of a very fine quality but the stone craftsman of Lothal made a unique contribution to the mankind by inventing a big sized revolving grinding mill, which requires a little effort to operate and flour in large quantity could be ground. This grinding mill consisted of two big grinding stones[60].

Mr. Mackay[61] writes, "Stone vessels are remarkably scarce, and very few have been found undamaged. The majority are shallow bowls, which are simple in shape, clumsy in workmanship and carved out of the softer stones. such as alabaster, sandstone, limestone, or slate. A few more complex pieces, nearly all of which are alabaster, imitate the pottery, but their interiors are so badly bored that they cannot have been of much use. A flat-based Tumbler, a little over four inches in height, which was found with a hoard of copper and bronze, is made of the very rare, jade-green crystalline stone called fuchsite a material at the present time to be found no nearer to Mohenjo-daro than Mysore.... Other figures made of slightly harder stones, like alabaster and limestone, are not quite so well finished, though they show more artistic merit, three of the best preserved statue heads from Mohenjo-daro being quite as fine as anything of the same date from Mesopotamia, although falling much below the standard of the Egyptian statuary of the old Kingdom".

In India, the use of stone for building construction started from the Maurya period. Even today stone is used in the construction of buildings but we can conclude from the above evidences that the stone worker (craftsman) did exist during that period who possibly also carved statues along with domestic implements.

Bead makers

We have explained in the first chapter that[62] the work of making beads was done mainly in the two major industrial towns of the Indus Valley, i.e.Lothal and Chanhudaro. In Lothal big bead making workshops consisting of 6-7 rooms have been unearthed, in which there were separate godowns for storing raw and finished beads. These beads were used for making valuable ornaments and garlands etc.' These beads were made of gold, silver and precious stones. These stones were probably procured from South India. Mr. Mackay[63] as observed, gives an account how beads were manufactured; "When the nature of the stone permitted, the bead was first flaked longitudinally into shape and subsequently rubbed smooth with a hone. The final shaping may have been done on some such instrument as a Lathe, but, though it might be supposed that the presence of the hole would have facilitated this process, the actual boring was, as a matter of fact, done last of all. Unfinished beads of later date found in other parts of India also show that the boring was left until the end. Probably glazing was done on the beads by placing them in furnaces before boring.

Beads 4-5 inches long have also been found, which are very beautiful and polished from inside and outside. It may have been very difficult at that time to make a hole in those long beads made of hard stone. Tools for making holes in such type of beads have been found from a bead making workshop in Chanhudaro. Experts have experimented to see as to how much time would have been taken and what method used for boring a hole in an ordinary type of bead with those tools. After having a look at these beads, it appears that great care had been taken to polish them from within and it speaks of the best specimen of art of that period."

A number of beads of beautiful workmanship were found scattered loose in the ground around one of the hoards of jewellery at Mohenjo-daro. These beads are in a variety of materials and, though not unusual in shape, are in polish and regularity quite equal to anything that has been found at any ancient site. Great care had been taken when cutting them to get their natural veinings in as regular a position as possible, a task which called for considerable skill on the part of the lapidary. To enhance the beauty of some of these variegated stones, especially of those with natural veinings, they were sometimes capped at each end with gold, a custom which also prevailed in Sumer.

By cementing two or more different stones together, beads were sometimes made up to simulate well marked, or perhaps more valuable specimens. A barrel-shaped bead of this nature, although only 0.49 inch long, was made up of no less than five alternate segments of red carnelian and white or blue chalcedony; it was so carefully constructed that its compound character might never have been detected if it had not fallen to pieces in the copper canister in which it was found. Another bead, made to imitate an onyx, had two faces, one of shell and the other of pink limestone.This is an example of the best craftsmanship of that period.

Fisherman

A large number of fishing hooks have been found from the items unearthed during excavations. The most remarkable painted sherds from Harappa show scenes with human figures. One shows a fisherman carrying two nets suspended from pole across shoulders, with a fish and what is probably a turtle near his feet which rest on a cross-hatched band, presumably the river by which he is walking[64]. Undoubtedly, he may have been the ancestor of the present day fisherman.

Barber

Mr. Wheeler[65]giving details about the things found from the excavations writes "Some small, blades made of metal having cutting edges on both sides and corners bent towards backside and cloth is wrapped on one of them, was undoubtedly a blade of a barber which was used by him for cutting moustaches, beard and hair. Such type of blades have been found in large numbers from the cities of the Indus Valley, from which the scholars have derived a conclusion that probably both the men and women got their hair cut".

Mackay has also given details about some of such other findings- "At least four types of blades were traced which were used by Harappans, most of which have sharp edges on both sides, One of which is L shaped. There is another one of third type whose blades are bent backward at the corners. The fourth type of blades, which are a few in number, is a long one and made of a very thin edge and has one round corner".

The half figure of stone, wearing an embroidered and dyed shawl, looks like a Sumerian priest and its moustaches have been cut in a Sumerian style. It shows that the hair was cut in that period also and this job might have been done by a professional barber as is done today. It is very difficult to cut self hair from the beard,moustaches and head with such type of blades. Similarly, in view of the large population of urban areas it can easily be said that this class of society must have been doing the job as is done today and who can be named as the ancestor of the present day barber.

In this way, it can be proved that oilmen (Teli). sailors, gardeners, shepherds etc castes existed in Indus country who also did farming and worked as landless labourers in addition to their own traditional professions.

In some cases the brick floors of the bathrooms had been polished by the friction of bare feet, while in others they show a deep red deposit, which may have been caused by perspisation or by the use of oil to prevent the skin from cracking-a custom prevalent in India at the present day. Marks of oil have been found on the floors of bathrooms in the cities of Indus Valley[66].

Possibly such type of oil was used in the lamps at night for making light. It is also quite clear that oil in such a large quantity was produced by a professional oilmen (Teli) as is done today. The Indus Valley people mostly carried on their business through the rivers by means of boats. The existence of a vast port like

Lothal proves that the business was not done only through the rivers but also through sea routes with Babylonia and Mesopotamia. It may have been the professional sailor to sail the boats through long rivers and to far off places through the sea, who was beyond doubt, an ancestor of the present day sailor.

The scholars are of the view that the houses were decorated with green plants, flowers and the creeper plants. This work might have been done by the gardener during those times. hence the existence of the ancestor of gardener cannot be denied[67]. The existence of milch cattle like buffaloes, goats and sheeps shows that the cattle wealth may have been in plenty in the Indus Valley and there must have lived shepherds and milkmen to graze the cattle, In Lothal, such evidences have been found that a particular type of spindle used for spinning is till used by 'Bharwars', a semi-nomadic cattle rearing tribe who call themselves the Maharashtrian Yadavas about whom we have discussed earlier in this chapter.

In this way, this view becomes much established that almost all the artisan castes included in the Sudras existed in the Indus Valley before the arrival of Aryans in India who included these non-Aryans into the fourth varna of their varna system being their enemies. In fact, it appears that the first class i.e. the servile class was included in the caste system by force whereas the other class i.e. the artisan class was only declared to be included in the caste system that they are also Sudras being the non-Aryans. But their professions were not changed and they continued working as usual.

Famous scholar D.N. Majumdar[68] also holds the views of Rai Bahadur Sharat Chandra while supporting the above views,"The Hindu caste system was rather the outcome of the interaction between the Indo-Aryan Varna system, on the one hand, and the tribal system of the pre-Dravidian and the occupation class-system of the Dravidian, on the other."

Now we shall discuss that section of the Sudra class who are different from the castes given above and who are directly or indirectly connected with the agriculture, i.e. Kunjre, Mali, Saini, Kurmi etc. These castes were also agriculturists or agriculture labourers before the arrival of Aryans in India and who were in reality the backbone of the vast production of Indus country. Supporting this view, D.D.Kosambi[69] writes-"A village must be located near a greater city like Harappa which to meet the demands of the urbanites in respect of the foodstuffs and can produce foodgrains in plenty. In fact the city is the main residence of administrative power, other producers live in adjoining villages". The anthropological and genetics statistics of present agriculture castes have a similarity to the non-Aryan Dravidians and other Sudras (see Chapter 13 & 14).

Now we take up the trader class which has repeatedly been mentioned as 'Pani' in Rigveda and who formed the basis of indigenous and foreign trade in Indus.

Pani (Banik)

Pani was a particular class of the non-Aryans who were wealthy traders.

They were faithless and greedy and were unable to face Indra in the battlefield. Such references have been repeated about the 'Panis' in Rigveda. Dialogues between the Panis and Kukur goddess Sarma (Mother Goddess of Lake) has appeared in the later but famous hymns of Rigveda, who was sent by the militant leader, of the Aryans and God Indra. It does not seem to be an ordinary dialogue but a detailed historical incident. From the dialogue it appears that the Panis had stolen the cattle of Indra and hid them somewhere. Goddess Sarma requested them to return the cattle to the Aryan, followers of Indra, but the Panis rejected her request. Thereafter, the Goddess Sarma threatened them to be ready to face the consequences. This may have led to the invasion of Indra against the Panis at a later stage. Rigvedic verses in connection with the above references are as under:-

Miser Pani R.V. V-34-7

SAMĪ PA ṈERAJATI BHOJANAM̃ MUŚE VIDĀSHUŚE BHAJATI SŪNARAM̃ BASU I DURGE CHAND DHRIYATE VISHVĀ Ā PURU JANO YO ASYA TAVIŚĪ MACHUKRUDHAT II

-Indra goes forward to plunder the foodgrains of the miser, Panis and gives wealthy things to the donors and who earns the wrath of Indra's strength, he imprisons all those persons in a fort.

Miser and usurer Pani

Rig VIII-66-10

KADŪ MAHĪRADHRA ŚTĀ ASYA TAVIŚĪḤ KADU VRITRAGHNO ASTRITAM I INDRO VISHVĀN BEKANĀṮ ĀN: AHARDRASHA UT KRITVĀ PARṆĪN: RABHI II

-When was the great strength of Indra not worth finishing the enemies? When the Indra's enemy Vratra has been saved from his violence. This Indra dominates all the usurer and miser Panis with his good deeds.

Miser Wolf Pani

RV VI-51-14

GRĀVĀṆAḤ SOM NOHI KAM̃ SAKH:TVANĀY VĀVA SHUḤ I JAHĪNYA TRIṆAM̃ PAṆIM̃ VRIKO HIŚḤ" II

-O (Som) god of peace! our people even those who have a stony heart keep friendship with faithful people. You shouid punish the unmannered and eater Pani. Because he is a wolf and he can be equated with a wolf in society.

MRIDHRAVACH USURER DASYU PANI

R.V. VII-6-3

NYAKRATŪN GRATHINO MRIDHRAVĀCHAḤ PAṆĪ: RISHRADDHĀN: AVRADHĀN: AYAGYĀN' I PRAPRA TĀN DASYŪN: RGNIRVI VĀYA PŪRVA SHCHAKĀRĀPARĀN: AYAJYŪN" II

God fire undoubtedly finishes all those Dasyus who do not do righteous deeds, speak a language which cannot be understood, who are unfaithful usurers Pani, who are to be degraded, who are unfaithful usurers Pani, who are to be degraded, who do not practise sacrifice. Chief Agni degrade those who do not practise sacrifice and do not give them high position.

Merchant Pani

Similarly yaskacharya has described Panis to be merchants or Baniks-(NIRUKTA VI-26-27 PARNIRNARNI GBHASI)

Conversation of Pani and Sarma

R.V.X.-X-108-1 to 11

O Sarma ! for which purpose have you come here? This place is far off. One who comes here can not look back. How many nights have you spent to be able to reach this place? How could you cross the deep water of the river? What thing do you want to have from us (1) O Panis ! I have come to you as a messenger of God Indra. I want to have the cow wealth which you have collected here. I got scared of the water on my way to this place but I was protected by the water itself and that is how I was able to cross it. (2)

O Sarma ! how does Indra look like, on behalf of whom you have come here as a messenger? What is the type of his army? What is the extent of his power? That Indra should come to us, we are prepared to make friendship with him. He can take away our cows.(3)

O Panis ! the Indra, as a messenger of whom I have come here, is invincible. He is capable of defeating all. The rivers having unlimited quantity of water cannot create any obstacle in his way. he is capable of killing you all.(4)

O Sarma! you have come to this far off place from the heavens, so we will give you all the cows which you wish to have otherwise who can give the cows without a war. We are also equipped with sharp armaments.(5)

O Panis! your statement is not such as should be made by the brave. You are not clear minded persons. Your body may not be pierced by the arrows of Indra. This passage (way) of yours may not be attacked by gods? If you do not give cows, you would be inviting troubles and Brahaspati would put you in trouble.(6)

O Sarma! we are protected by the mountains (forts). We are prosperous with cow, horses and other luxurious goods. Our brave men deputed for security can protect this place very well. Your arrival to this place where we have kept our cows is useless.(7)

Angrisas and Ayasya Rishis will come to this place after having acquired the power of energetic Soma, He will take away all of your cows. At that time your pride will have a fall.(8)

O sarma! you have come here at the instance of fear stricken gods, but we regard you as our sister and give you away a part of our cow wealth. Now you should not go back from here.(9)

O Panis! I do not know the tale of brother and sister. Indra and Angrisas know it very well that they have sent me here to take away your cows after giving me full protection. I have been able to come here under their protection, therefore, you should go to a far off place from here.(10)

O Panis! go to some distant place from here. May the cows, which are suffering at your hands, take shelter at a religious place after coming out of this mountain (fort). The drinker of Soma, mountain like strong Rishis, Soma, Brahaspati and all other-learned people know well about these hidden cows.(11)

From the above Rigvedic descriptions it becomes quite clear that the Pani people were Banik, non-Aryans Dasa traders, who were misers and usurers and were like wolves in the society whose main objective was to collect wealth by all fair and foul means. The scholars are of the view that the Panis had stolen the cows of Aryans. Sarma, the messenger of Indra had probably come to them with the request of returning those cows. From the conversation, it is quite apparent that possibly the failure of above talk would lead to the war between non-Aryan Panis and the Aryan Indra and Brahaspati warriors. As a result thereof, Indra killed the panis and destroyed their cities.

R.V. VI-20-4

SHATAIRAPA DRANPAṈAYA INDRĀTRA DASHOṈAYE KAVAYE'RKASĀTAU I

-O Indra! Panis fled away from the battlefield along with hundreds of soldiers with the fear of your supporters who were prepared to give lot of wealth.

Similarly, an account of the defeat of Panis is also given in the following verses:

R.V. I-11-5

TVAM̐ VALASYA GOMATO'PĀVARADRIO VILAM'
TVĀM̐ DEVĀ ABIBHYUŚAS TUJYA MĀNĀS ĀVIŚUḤ"

-O Indra! you opened the gate of the fort of Bal Asura, who stole the cows and there upon the aggrieved gods (Aryans) came to you and took shelter.

Since the Panis opposed to the worship of Indra, they were called by the Rigvedic Aryans as Asuras or Dasyus. The name of their god was 'Bal' who represented one form of Sun-god and came to be identified as Vratra who had stolen the cows of gods and opposed them[70].

It is quite apparent now that the only cause of the above mentioned war was that the god of Panis', 'Bal' Asura had stolen the cows of Indra (Aryans). The cows were not set free even after a request was made by Sarma, and this led to war and Indra forcibly opened the gate of the fort and got the cows released after defeating the Panis.

Now, the question arises as to who were the Panis and what is their later history. D.D. Kosambi[71] throws some light on this subject in these words : "Panis do not seem to be Aryans but this word survived in the later Indian civilization. Today's traders 'Banias' acquired this name from the Sanskrit 'Banik', which might have been derived from the word 'Pani'. In Sanskrit 'Pana' is a coin. The whole of the trading goods are Panya (Panini IV-4-51).In India the ancient standard form of weight of coin was undoubtedly Harappan. From this it appears that some Harappans escaped the avarice of Aryans so that old traditional business and trade etc could survive."

Shri Avinash Chandra[72] Dass giving his views, has written, "In Rigveda there is a mention of rich pretentious Panis at many places. It is quite clear that the Indus Valley civilization was a civilization of the traders and they used to sell their goods upto Mesopotamia, Egypt and Babylonia. The immense wealth of the Panis has repeatedly been mentioned in Rigveda. Excavations of the old cities have revealed that the inhabitants of Harappa.i.e. the Baniks and rulers were a very rich class "

From the above views expressed by scholars it becomes quite evident that the Pani was none else than the trading class of the Indus Valley who travelled to far off countries of the world by sea for carrying on trade. According to the Baudhayan Dharam Suttra I-1-24, the Brahmans (Aryans) who travelled by sea, were treated as out caste on account of this being denied by the Shastras i.e. the above Panis travelled by sea because of their being non-Aryans and this very class of people later used to be called Panik (Pani), then Banik, who were the ancestors of today's traders the Banias. As given on footnote (no. 71) of foregone pages that in pali language'P' is replaced by 'V'.

A reference has already been made in the first chapter about foreign trade of the traders of Indus Valley. Now we will give here a detailed account there of after A.C. Dass[73]- "A written evidence has been found dating back to 2450 B.C. pertaining to the reign of the Natse, the king of Lagash and the ships of Dilman had brought wood for him from foreign countries. After about one and a half century, during the times of Sargon the great of Sumer, the boats of 'Dilman', Magan and Meluka had stayed in his newly constructed capital. About 150 years later, the famous god fearing king Gudiya of Lagash says, that the wood was brought by ships from Dilman, Magan, Meluka and 'Guti'. A mention has been found in the Akad literature about the arrival of a caravan from Dilman during the second millennium B.C. There are different views about the geographical situation of these places, most of the scholars are of the view that Dilman was an ancient name of Bahrein. Magan was located in Baluch Makran (now in Pakistan) from where traces of copper mines have been found. Similarly, Meluka was the name of Sind province of India. According to some scholars, western shore of South India was known as Meluka and the area located between the gulf Bahrein to Cambay was known as Dilman where the Indus civilization had spread.

Indians had their own locality in Babul. From the clay tablets used for keeping accounts, found from the bunglow of Murush of Nippur we come to know that bunglow was used as a trade centre with Indians (Journal of Royal Asiatic Society 1917, p 237). Some Greek terms came into being from the Tamil words as a result of these business relations, such as from Arsi (Rice), Orija, Karur (Cinnamon), Corprain, Injiwar (dried ginger), Triniveses, and Pippi (Pipal).

pepeti.

The backbone of trade was Dilman. There was a class of businessmen who worked with the name of 'Alik Dilman' and had a monopoly over trade. These traders brought cloth, scented oil, leather and wool from Tirgis in ships and in return carried Ivory, precious shining stones, beads, cloth, precious wood and wooden articles from Indus valley.

The above mentioned Panis, the Indian traders who carried on trade in western countries at a later stage shifted to Malabar coast from Sapta Sindhu through western coast of Gujarat as a result of the invasions of Aryans. From there they moved to the banks of Tigris and Euphratis by sea route. There, they spread their civilization. From there they went to Phoenicia (Lebanon) on the eastern coast of mediterranean sea by land route. There, they set up their colonies in the islands of mediterranean sea and in the north of Africa. They used to get the articles manufactured by the captured or bought slaves and carried on their trade in the southern Europe. So much so that they carried on their trade up to Britain and Scandinavia by sea route and spread their civilization. In this way, the civilization spread from east to the western countries during ancient times as in the modern times the western countries engaged in trade, have spread the civilization in the east. Till some time ago from now festivals of God Bal or Balder (of panis) used to be celebrated in Scandinavia. A heap of wood was set on fire on the top of a hill and the people living in the surrounding areas would collect, sing, dance, rejoice and make noise on this occasion. Baltic sea, Belt, Belteberg, Baleshangen and Balestronden have been named after the name of God Bal."

The scholars are of the veiw[74] that the word Punik originated from Panik and from Punik the word Finish and from Finish came into being the word Finix and after this word the country Phoenicia was named. These people were perfect in ship building, fond of sea travel, greedy for wealth and worshipped the house hold diety Bal. The statue of their diety always held a fire receptacle in its hands. At the time of national distress, hundreds of children were sacrificed in that fire. Similarly, the enemies captured during war were also burnt in that fire. At one time they had a colony in the southern part of Iran or in the eastern part or in the southern sea coast of Arab. Similarly, they had their last colony in Carthage in the north of Phoenicia, which was destroyed by Romans after a number of wars. These wars were known as Punic wars. People living on the coast of Mediterranean sea learnt shipping and trading from them. They also gained the knowledge of astrology, mathematics and such art of writing which was based on phonetic in place of the pictorial script. Their alphabet had 22 letters, which were based on the ancient scripts of Egypt and Mesopotamia. The Greek letters and many other writing systems developed under the influence of this script which also includes the Devnagri writings system.

According to A.C.Dass[75] these Phoenicians retained a multifarious form of Rigvedic cosmogony and were nature worshippers like the Aryans of Sapta Sindh.

Their principal deities being Bal, the sun god and Uranus or Varuna. This god Bal or Bala is also mentioned in the Rigveda and identified with sun. the Rbhus whom Sayan identifies with solar rays, were the sons of Bal or Baal (RV IV-33, 34, 35, 36 and 37).

Fire was also called a son of Bal. The Panis of Sapta Sindhu under the leadership of Brabu of their cruel practices, one may be mentioned here, viz. the practice of human sacrifice on the occasion of any extraordinary ceremony, an unusual number of victims were sacrificed.Human sacrifice was also part of the established ritual and every year a youthful victim was chosen by lot. Infants were burnt alive and the most acceptable of all sacrifices was that of an only child. The image of saturn was made of brass, the out stretched hands were hollowed so as to receive the body of the child which slid thence to a fiery receptacle below. Mothers brought their infants in their arm and quieted them by their caresses till the moment they were thrown into the flames, since any manifestation of reluctance would have rendered the sacrifice infructuous. It is a strange dispensation of God that both in olden and modern times the selfish and greedy merchants should have been related for the spread of a particular civilization in other lands. As the European merchants have paved the way for the spread of western culture in eastern lands, so did the Panis also keep on spreading the culture of the east in western countries in ancient times."

Brief history

After Rigveda the Panis reappear as the backbone of trade in India during the period from 600 B.C. to 300 B.C. D.D. Kosambi[76] giving details cited below:

"The monarchical empire of Magadha can be described as the first biggest empire in India. The biggest source of income of this empire was the vast mines of various metals located therein. Its capital was Rajgiri, whose detailed description is given in Chapter 12. Probably the coins came into use before the end of the seventh century if judged from the coins found.

The eastern standard of weight for silver coins was the karshapana of 5.5 grams weight in Magadha, while the solitary Kosalan hoard known is of 3/4-karshapana standard. The weight goes back to the Indus valley culture, which had in fact, produced accurately cut stone weights of just this magnitude. Taxilan currency belonged to a foreign weight standard just above 11 grams, which would approximate to the Indian rupee in historic times. The karshapana was of 32 units weight, whereas the frontier coin, shaped like a bent bar, was 100. Originally the coins were issued as silver blanks by the traders themselves, and the weights checked regularly by their guilds during the period of circulation. The checking was shown by tiny marks punched on one side, which guaranteed weight and purity to all who knew the code of guild marks. These punch marks extended beyond the Uttarapatha into Afghanistan and Iran; sometimes they are found even on a few Achaemenid darics, presumably such as had circulated in Gandhara. Some of the punch marks themselves derived from Indus characters, probably from the descendants of the Panis whom we have named and noted in passing. The other side of the silver piece was originally blank at the time of issue. By the sixth century the kings has stepped in to put their own issuing marks on the coins, on the side that had once remained blank. This was a regular system of four marks for Kosala and five for Magadha and the rest. Because of the marks, we can distinguish between dynasties and say approximately how many kings there were in each, but giving the individual king's name is still not simple, and generally remains a matter of conjecture. Violent changes of dynasty are revealed by counterstruck coins; the new king restruck coins of the displaced ruler found in the treasury with his own marks before issuing them again for circulation".

As per Buddhist Jataka story or discourse 'Vaveru' No. 339 they have been found trading in Babylon where a mention has been made that one crow could be sold for 100 karshapana and a pea cock for 1000 karshapana. According to story No.1, Appanak, no. 2 Vanupath, No. 90 Aktajju, these Panis who were generally called Sarthvaha used to travel daily on various Indian trade routes in a big carvan of 500-500 vehicles, braving inconveniences and difficulties of dangerous beasts, thieves and decoits of vast forests and deserts.

Highlighting the emergence of the above trade caravans, D.D. Kosambi[77] again writes:

"More important than ordinary tribesmen were the traders, generally called Sarthavaha (caravaneers) or Vaidehikas. The later name means 'men of the Videha tribe'. Though all traders no longer belonged to any one tribe or Janapada and the Videha tribe had vanished, the nomenclature shows the origin of the profession as with a particular tribal guild. The groups of merchant-caravaneers extended in a long chain from Taxila to the very end of Magadha. The bolder went beyond any known Janapada limits, especially on the Deccan route. The trade was no longer of the primitive type confined to 'trade friends', unless perhaps with some of the forest savages who might still retain the institution."

It is quite clear that the Panis of Indus valley who were once uprooted, had again established and stabilised the economy of India after about one thousand years. Business and trading classes had formed guilds having joint capital. Possibly this may be the main reason of the progress and prosperity of this period and at a later stage of Magadha regime especially during the Maurya period. The credit of making India golden sparrow can be given to this class.

R.K. Mookerji [78] thorws light on the highly developed condition of trade and industry of Gupta period in these words; "The outstanding fact of the economy of those (Guptas) times is the organisation of industry or handicrafts under guilds called Srenis. Their corporate character is brought out by the seals which were issued by them. The abundance of seals found at only one city like Vaishali shows to what extent these guilds played their part in the economic life of the country. These Vaishali (Basarh) seals bring to light the guilds (Nigamas) of bankers (Sreshthis), traders (Sarthavahas) and Artisans (Kulikas). Some times these guilds federated themselves into a larger corporation, as in the legend 'Sreshthis-kulika-Nigama' i.e. the corporation of bankers and artisans. There are again many seals testifying to the corporation formed by the federation of the three guilds of Bankers, Traders and Artisans. One seal also has the legend 'Prathama-kulika' showing that he was the President of the Guild of Artisans. As Dr. T. Bloch, who discovered these Vaishali seals points out: it looks as if during these days, something like a modern chamber of commerce existed in upper India at some big trading centre, perhaps at Patliputtra (Archaeological Survey, Annual report 1903-04, p 104). It will be apparent from these numerous seals that Vaishali in those days was a very flourishing centre of trade, banking and business."

R.K. Mookerji further writes in the same book, "The Damodar copper plates pertaining to the period of kumar Gupta I (414-455 A.D.) also give details of Sarthavaha (chief of the guild of merchants) and Prathama Kulika (Chief of the guild of Artisans)."[79]

The Gupta empire extended its limits to Bay of Bengal on one side and the Arabian sea on the other side and that is why the foreign trade along with the local trade flourished. Cloth, seeds, medicines, coconut, ivory, pearls and gems were exported to foreign countries from India and gold, silver, copper, lead, silk and horses were imported. Trade activities were carried on with European countries from the Bharoach, Cambay and Khambat ports in the west and with Ceylon, Java, Sumatra and China from the Tamraliptaka port. We do establish this fact on the basis of mere supposition that trade with foreign countries was carried on but solid evidences have been found that the Roman coins pertaining to the earlier centuries of Christ have been found in the upper portion of Gangetic basin mainly in the Prayag province. Main trade routes in the country connected Patliputtra, Bharoach, Tamraliptaka, Peshawar, Prayag, Vidisha, Ujjain etc with each other and big caravans of the merchants' guilds used to travel on those routes.

Banik Sudra

It has been mentioned in the foregone pages that the Aryans pushed all the non-Aryans to the fourth Varna of the society and started calling them Sudras and they were made to serve them and do other arduous and cumbersome work done by an artisan, this job was, prior to this done by the Aryan Vaishyas (common man). Now the Vish had kept with them the trade, agriculture and animal husbandry. But the trade was already done by the Panis in the Indus Valley and they were very proficient in this profession, therefore, it became very difficult to differentiate between the 'Panis' and the 'Vish' on the basis of castes and division of work, even though they had declared the Panis as Sudras on account of their being non-Aryans[80]. As a result of the above mentioned difficulty the Panis gradually started mixing up and dealing with the 'Vish'. Because the Panis had unlimited wealth, which the Aryan priests needed every time for the performance of Yajna etc., so they started respecting the Panis. In fact, Panis had started giving donations to the Aryan priests in the Rigvedic period itself and the priests started praising and speaking high of the Panis and in this way the relations of both the classes gradually started becoming cordial. There are some evidences to this effect in the Rigveda-

R.V. VI-45-31

-Among Panis Brabu has been held in highest esteem and he is superior like the banks of Ganges.

R.V. VI-45-33

We always praise and appreciate Brabu who donates one thousand cows.

It is quite clear that some Pani Dasas had deserved favours of the greedy Aryan rishis by giving them donations etc and certainly escaped the wrath (invasion) of the brave Aryan Kshattriyas. This was the basic reason that they were partially included in Dwijas as of the Aryans social set up or they had intruded into it in later period.

Some verses of Yajurveda say that Vaishyas and Sudras have emerged from one class,i.e. Vaishyas and Sudras were non-Aryan Dravidians[81]. Here Vaishyas represent Baniks.

Similarly, it has been clearly written in Satpath Brahman[82] that those who are neither Kshattriyas nor priests (Purohits) are incomplete.

It is also sufficiently clear that the Sudras were not allowed to participate in the performance of Ashavmegha and Rajsuya political Yajna. At the end of the vedic period, they were undoubtedly expelled out of the religious life. The Vaishyas were also given the treatment meted out to the Sudras in many cases and they were deprived of so many rights.

It has been very clearly laid down in some of the codes of conduct that a Vaishya can become the husband of a Sudra lady and vice-versa[83]. The main reason for framing such rules was that there was social equality in the Indus Valley and there were mutual messing and marrying relations in them, which were also prevalent amongst the Panis who had mixed up with the Vaishya caste. The Rishis who made laws did not think it to be improper and made the law as such.

In this way, the Vaishyas suffered a lot more than the Kshattriyas at the hands of Brahmans in accordance with the provisions made in the Manu Smriti. Since the Vaishyas are said to have born from the thigh of Brahma, they were, therefore, declared to be equal to Sudras by Manu.(V-132)

ŪRDHVA NĀBHERYĀNI KHĀNI TĀNI MEDHYĀ NISARVASHUḤ I

YĀNYADHA STĀNYA MEDHYĀNI DEHĀCHCHAIVA MALĀSH CHYUTĀ II

In our body all the pores, above the navel are pure and those below it are impure-because the Vaishyas are born from a part below the navel, they are of low status (impure).

It has been given in chapter 12 that the Brahmans had full freedom to perpetrate atrocities on the Sudras.

According to Manu XI-11 and 12 if a Brahman who is performing a Yajna, failed to complete the same due to scarcity of money, if the king is religious, then the Brahman performing the Yajna, has the right to bring the necessary things from the house of a Vaishya who does not perform a holy Yajna of sacrificing of many cattles and is without a Soma Yajna. If he does not give such things on demand the Brahman can bring the things by force even by stealing. The religious king should not punish him in such a case.

It has been mentioned by Manu (VIII-277) that in case the Vaishya and Sudra abuse each other, the Vaishyas should be given punishment of first grade and Sudra of medium.

In Manu VIII-418 it has been stated that it is the duty of the king to compel the Vaishya and Sudra to do their duties otherwise the whole set up of the society (world) would be shattered.

Similarly, according to Maitriyani code IV-2-7 the Vaishya and the Sudras can be exploited by snatching their cattle such as cows etc.

It is evident that during the time of Manu also, the Vanik class who had started intruding into the Vaishya had to face the disgraceful laws and treatment as meted out to the Sudras in place of being respected like the Kshattriya. This is the main reason why after being fed up with such type of behaviour by the Aryans they had started embracing equality based Jain religion.

It appears that there was still a clear distinction between the Aryan Vaishya and the non-Aryan Vaniks up to the Gupta period whereas there was no specific distinction between the Vaniks and Sudras and their duties were also alike. The business (trade) of sale and purchase done by the present day Vaniks was also done by the Sudras viz. the Vanik class was still considered to be Sudra. This possibly went on for a long time. According to sherring (see following pages) this went on upto the period of muslim invasions.

Markandeya Puran 25-7,8

DĀNAM̃ YAJNOAPA SHUSHRŪ ŚĀDVIJĀTĪNAM̃ TRIDHĀMAYĀ I
VYĀKHYĀTAḤ SHŪDRA DHARMO APIJĪ VIKĀKĀRU KARMAJĀ II (7)
TAD VAD DVIJĀTI SHUSHRŪ ŚĀPOŚAṆAM̃ KRIYA VIKRAYEḤ I
VARṆADHARMĀ ISTVAME PROKTĀḤ SRŪYANTĀN̄ CHĀSRAMĀSRA YAḤ II (8)

The Sudras are to do three duties i.e. to give donations, to perform Yajnas and to serve three other Varnas their means of livelihood are the service of Brahman, rearing of cattle and sale and purchase of things. I have said about the duties of the varnas.

Vishnu Purana III-8-32

DVIJĀTI SANSRIRTA KARMA TĀDARTHYA TEN PUŚṆAM I
KRIYA VIKRIYA JAIRVĀPI DHANAIḤ KĀRUD BHAVEN VĀ II

The Sudras should work according to the objective of the Dwijatis, this is their livelihood. Apart from this they should earn their livelihood by sale purchase of articles and artisan jobs.

Vedvyas Smriti I-11

BAṈIKA, KIRĀTA, KĀYASTHA, MĀLĀKĀR KUṮUMBINAḤ I
ETE CHANYE CHA BAHABAḤ SHŪDRĀ BHINNA SVAKARMABHIḤ II

Banik, Kiraat, Kayasthas and Mali (gardener) are all related to Sudras and are distinct by their duties.

A list of 36 Varna-Sankara or hybrid castes has been given in Brahad-Dharam-Puran (Uttrakhand chapter XIII) in which the names of Gandha vanik (in which M.K. Gandhi was born) and Swarna Vanik castes have been given. Here both these castes have been said to be Varna-Sankar, i.e. Sudra (see origin of Kayastha).

The muslim historian Alberuni, a contemporary of famous muslim invader Mehmud Ghaznavi (997-1030 A.D) had travelled North-Western India. He writes in his famous book "Albaruni Ka Bharat' (Adarsha Hindi Pustkalya, Malviya Nagar, Allahabad, 1967) at page 87 about the social status of the Banik class "Among the lower caste people after the Sudras are the Antajya, who do various type of servile jobs. They are not included in any particular varna but they are considered to be particular professional or artisans. They comprise eight castes and leaving aside Banias, Mochis (cobbler) and Julahas (weavers) all these castes freely establish mutual messing and marital relations, because other people do not accept to deal with them. These eight castes are:Dhuniya, Mochi, Madari, basket and shield maker, sailors, fishermen, Aheriyas (hunters) and the weavers (julaha). These people live near but outside the village and towns where people of four varna reside."

It is quite clear that about one thousand years ago from now and approximately upto the period of Muslim invasions the Banik class (non-Aryans) was considered to be Sudra. This caste partially intruded into Dwijas during the political and social upheaval as a result of the Muslim invasions. The following view of M.A. Sherring[84] also corroborate this-

"Sudras and Vaishya castes are related to those tribes which had entered India much before the Rigvedic period and gradually settled in different parts of the country. The view that the Vaishyas first of all belonged to rural areas, is a matter of controversy. If they belonged to the rural areas, then who were the Sudras? were they ancient Dasas and slaves? some were aboriginals and some were not? There is no need of entering into any controversy over this. The reality is that the Vaishyas are hardly, the farmers while the Sudras have taken their place which was previously occupied by them. Similarly, they have inter mixed so much during the social and political upheaval, at present taking place in the country that it is very difficult to raise a wall of identification amongst them and it can hardly be said as to who is pure Vaishya and who is Sudra. Though the Vaishyas had been a separate caste for a long time but now no caste can give a satisfactory answer about their caste. In some matters the history of their traditions and customs can be traced upto a few hundred years ago, in most of the cases we cannot go beyond the period of Muslim invasions. Lack of proof regarding ancient history of any caste necessarily cannot be accepted as evidence. Even then it is not impossible that some Vaishya (Aryan) castes with some what admixture maintain their relationships with previous Vaishya castes (Banik) and are maintaining their caste traditions very strictly".

It has been said in the beginning that the Aryan Vaishyas had kept some profession with them, the main amongst them being agriculture, cattle rearing (Animal husbandry) and trade. It means that the present day Vaishyas have an element of those Aryans who did not give up the above professions. Some of them are still called Vaishya (Vish) by way of their separate sub-caste or Gottra. The other non-Aryan class is called 'Dasa' who were related to to the Indus Valley civilization and they have been called in the Rigveda as 'Dasa'. In order to elaborate the above fact, the famous sociologist G.S.Ghurye[85] while giving evidence, writes:

"The Visha and Dasa divisions are so far integrated units that there are a number of charity trusts for each separately. Thus Dasa Disawal, Dasa Gomathia, Dasa Gujjar Banik, Dasa Lad, Dasa Modh Adalji, Dasa Modh Mandaliya Dasa Porwad, Dasa Shrimali and Dasa Zarola Banik are all represented in the Directory of Charity Trusts of Charity Commissioner of Maharashtra mentioned above. Among these the Dasa Shrimali claim at least sixteen such trusts in the Directory (see pp 301-3, 881, 954, 966, 973 etc.). Among one section, that of the Shrimali Banias, instead of the lowest subdivision being called 'Pancha' is known as 'Ladva' (Desai P 103). And difference of nomenclature is accompanied by difference in social treatment. The Visha and Dasas of the Shrimali, though they do not intermarry, interdine but neither of them interdines with the Ladva. More or less, similar is the case with the Panchas of the Oswals, who call the section alternatively Leta (Desai, P 78)."

He[86] further writes: "I shall close this brief account of evidence of fission forming sub-castes with the interesting illustration recorded in a Privy Council case of over a century-and-a half ago and that too among the so-called function caste of traders and merchants. Some commatte-Vaishyas of Orissa filed a suit against a Brahman organisation which had declined to give them professional services of Vedic ritual, concluding that the so-called Vaishyas had been practising Sudras customs for two thousand years. Inter alia it came out that the adoption of the so-called Sudra customs had led to three divisions or sub-castes in the group, Byri Comaties, Borkka Comaties and Nogaram Comaties (Moores' Indian Appeals (1836-72) with complete digest, by Hari Rao, Vol. III, PP 226-41)" Even today in most of the eastern states Baniks are included among the Sudra Varna.

In the Aggarwal Itihas Chintnika[87] it has been written, by giving a reference of Satyaketu Vidyalankar that Aggarwals have two divisions i.e. Nag Vanshi and Raj Vanshi. In the context of Aggarsena, two names of Nagas have been mentioned i.e. Vasuki and Kumud. Nagas lived in Khandava forest which was located at a distance of about one hundred miles from Agroha (p 12). Once upon a time a king named Kumud came to earth along with his Madhvi daughter, Indra was attracted by her and he demanded the girl from Nagraj but Nagraj married his daughter to Aggarsen. The same Madhvi girl is the mother of all the Aggarwals (P 27).

Mahalaxmi was pleased with Maharaj Aggarsen and asked him to go to Kolhapur at that very moment where the Swayambar ceremony was being performed of the daughters of Mahidhar, the incarnation of Nagraj and marry them. He did so (P 28). Eighteen sons of Aggarsen married the daughters of Nagraj (p 38-39), and after their names, the eighteen sub castes[88] (Gotras) of Aggarwals were named (P 13) (see P-263 the Nagas have been termed as non-Aryans).

The description given by the writer (Satyaketu Vidyalankar) in his book 'History of the Vaish Aggarwala' about the branches of the hierarchy of Aggarsen, shows the names of Kansa, Jarasandh and Shishupal of the Mahabharta period. He writes,"The King Jarasandh of Magadha belonged to the dynasty of Karamchand, the third son of Aggarsen and king Chandragupta of the Gupta dynasty belonged to the fourth son Manipal (see PP 278-297 both have been proved to be non-Aryan kings)... and king Shishupal was from the dynasty of the eighth son Vasudeva (P 43). The Nagavanshis abandoned the vedic religion and embraced Buddhism (P.47). The king Divakar embraced Jainism (P 48) (It is well known that both of these religions were embraced by non-Aryans).

Even today a picture of Nag is depicted on the doors of the houses of Aggarwals in many districts and there is a custom of decorating lock of hair of the girl at the time of her marriage, like the hood of a cobra (Page 27). The Marwari and eastern Aggarwals all are Nagvanshi (P 46).

It is quite apparent that most of the classes of Aggarwals are definitely related to the non-Aryan Dravidian and Alpine races or Nagas. Even today they can very easily be identified physically in the markets of North India. They have black complexion, somewhat ugly face and plumb nose (pletyrrhines) distinct from the Vaishya Aryans, who have established their monopoly over business (now in the industry too) in the country. The tradition of writing the word 'Dasa' after their names is still in vogue. A majority of them can be found very easily at the places where the Indus Valley civilization flourished more. Who does not know about the popularity of Sindhi, Marwari and Gujrati Baniks? I am of the view that the deities (gods) whose names end with the word 'Bal' (as Bahubal), and which are worshipped by jain Baniks in south or west India, are related to 'Baal' the god of Panis as referred to in Rigveda. (See PP 229-31)

It can, therefore, be said that a major portion of the Baniks belong to Dassa class and the number of Vaishyas among them is very low. Jain Baniks belong to the Dasa class. World famous jews businessmen are the off shoots of the same Dasa Panis, who went to the western countries from India and spread the Indian civilization there, as in the modern times the western traders have spread the western civilization in the east. The business jurisdiction of the Jews has today extended all over to the Western world and the U.S.A, of whom not only the Baniks and Sudras of India but the whole country can be proud of.

In chapter two. it has been said that the credit of bringing the Indus Valley civilization to the extreme limits of progress goes to that class of people who had come from the region of mediterranean and Sumer and settled here. The Sumerian civlilization consisted of artisans and traders. It can, therefore, be said that the artisan class and trader class of the Indus Valley civilization, was that class of people who settled here at a later stage and who would definitely have become rulers after winning the Australoids in the war. At least the Assyrians (alpine), who were famous traders, reached here in the mature Harappan period and came into power. The above view is also confirmed by those Rigvedic descriptions in which it has been said that the Aryans, the followers of Indra, fought a war with Panis, in which the Panis were defeated and they fled away. This means that these were the Panis, who were the rulers of Indus Valley. It is quite clear that the present day Baniks are the descendants of those great people who were the ruling class of the Indus Valley civilization.

In brief it can be said that the present day servile class, and the Baniks and artisans classes are the descendants of that class of Indus Valley who was very rich and was the ruling class. The castes engaged in agriculture are possibly the descendants of the agriculturists of the Indus valley. All these castes approximately comprise more than 90 percent of the total population of the country and are engaged in the entire production of the nation.

References

1. Ibid. P 175.
2. Rao S.R. Lothal and the Indus civilization. PP 151-152.
3. Cited by Fuchs Stephen in his work, "The Aboriginal Tribes of India", P 12. Footnote.
4. 'Human Skeleton from Harappa'. ASIC (1963) P 10.
5. Cited by Fuchs Stephen. Ibid P 21.
6. Dutta, N.K, 'Origin and Growth of Castes in India.' P 53.
7. (a) Ghurye, G.S. 'Caste and Races in India' PP 172-173.
   (b) Bhandarkar D.R. 'Some aspects of Ancient Indian Culture', P 10.
   (c) Dutt, N.K. " P.P.18-19.
   (d) Dasa, A.C. "Rigvedic Culture", P 130.
   (e) Kane, P.V. "History of Dharm Shastra", II (1) P 33.
8. Fick Richard' The Social Organisation in North-East India in Budha's time', P 314. Translated by S. Maitra.
9. (a) The dighanikaya PP 74-75 (III Pathika Vagga) edited by B.J. Kashyap 1958, published by Pali Publication Board, Bihar Government.
   (b) David Rhys, "Dialogues of the Budha", P 90 and 91 Part III (D III-95) translated from Digha Nikaya by T.W. & C.A.F.
10. Dutt, N.K. has Supported this view. P 152.
11. "Punjab castes", P 246.
12. Sharma, R.S. 'Sudras in Ancient India' PP 32-34.
13. Bhandarkar, D.R. P 10.
14. Mahajan Vidyadhar 'History of India' P 14.
15. (a) Risley H.H. 'The people of India'P 113.
    (b) Majumdar D.N. 'Races and culture of India' P 70.
    (c) According to later research work Khattries are the off Shoots of later Iranian invaders.
16. (a) Dutt N.K. PP 68-69.
    (b) Hutton J.H. "Caste in India" PP 51-70.
    (c) Vishwanathan S.V. "Racial synthesis in Hindu culture", P 168.
17. *Note:* In West-north India, most of Gotras of Washerman (Dhobi.) caste are similar to those of the Rajputs, i.e. Chauhan, Pawar, Andwar, Sisodia, Tomar, Arabariya, Bahmaniwal and Solanki etc. The reason for this similarity is quite clear, the families who used to serve the Rajput families from generation to generation in a traditional way.

adopted their Gotras. Even today the castes Nai or Dhobi working in the backward block of Army Regiments (Jat or Rajput) claim themselves to be related to the said Regiments.

18. Hutton, J.H. P 181.

19. Census report of India 1901, Vol. 1.P. 524.

20. The Indo Aryan races, 1C 194 to 196.

21. According to Manu (X-22) from Vrattra Kshattriya in to a Svarna woman will be Jhalla, Malla, Lichchhavi, Nat, Karna, Khasa and Dravida. All above castes are non-Aryans.

22. Ibbetson Denzil P 263.

23. Ibid 1C 185.

24. "Hindu Tribes and Castes" P 305 (Tribuner and Co. London)1872.

25. After Chanda R.P. 1C 193.

26. Majumdar, D.N. PP 315-316.

27. Ibid P 70.

28. Dutt N.K. P 5.

29. Risley HH. P 400.

30. Ibid PP 185-87.

31. Ghurye, G.S.P 320.

32. After Ghurye G.S.P 173-174.

33. After Majumdar, PP 69-70.

34. Risley, H.H. P. 138.

35. Ghurye, G.S.Vol. 11.P 310.

36. Ibid page 21.

37. Ibid P 108.

38. Ibid P 109.

39. Ibid PP 93-95.

40. After Mackay, PP 95-107.

41. Sindhu Ghati Sabhyata Ka Adi Kendra 'Harappa' P 186.

42. After Rao S.R. P 102.

43. After Shastri Kedar Nath P 177.

44. After Mackay, E. P 82.

45. After Mackay, PP 81-87.

46. After Mackay E. P 30.

47. Ibid P 97.

48. After. Mackay. P 96.

49. "The first great civilization" P 270.

50. After Shastri, Kedar Nath P 180.

51. After Mackay E. P P 131-132.

52. After Mackay, E. P P 77-79.

53.. After Rao SR P 107.

54. Wheeler, M."The Indus Civilization." Vol. 1, P 51.

55. After Wheeler, M. P. 130.

56. After Mackay, E. P.90.

57. After Mackay, E. P. 131.

58. Rao, S.R. P107.

59. After Shastri Kedar Nath P 168.

60. After Rao, S.R. P. 105.

61. After Mackay, PP 122-123.

62. Rao, S.R.PP 68-70.

63. After Mackay, E. PP 83-86.

64. Piggott, Stuart "Pre historic India" P 193.

65. Ibid P 77.

66. After Mackay E. P 32.

67. After Rao, S.R. P 190.

68. Ibid P 300.

69. "The culture and civilization of ancient India" P 54.

70. Dass, A.C.'Rigvedic India', P 187.

71. After Kosambi DD p 80. and Dass A.C. PP 175-176.
The word 'Pani' is of Sanskrit origin to which the suffic 'K' is added. Whereas the word 'Vanik' is from Pali languge. In Pali language 'P' becomes 'V' because a few words of Sanskrit language change into Pali language like this k into g, t into 'th' or d, p into V, ch into J and d into t (Bharat Singh Upadhyaya, Pali Sahitya Ka Itihas P 21).

72. Dass, A.C. PP 188-191.

73. After Dass.A.C. PP 180-190.

74. (a) Reo Vishweshwar Nath, "Rigved par ek Itihasik drishti" P 238-239.
(b) Louis Finkelstein, 'The Jews their history, culture and religion' Vol. I, PP 4-7.

75. Dass, A.C. PP 186-197.

76. Ibid PP 120-132

77. Ibid P 24.

78. Mookerjee, R.K, 'The Gupta empire', (Bombay 1959) PP 148-149.

79. Mookerjee R.K. P 80.

80. Nesfield, 'Caste system' P 11.

81. (a) Maitriyani Samhita II - 8-6.
    (b) Kathaka Samhita XVII-5.
    (c) Tait Sam.IV - 3-10-2.

82. VI-6-3-12,13.

83. Satp Brah XIII-2-9-8. Tait Brah III-9-7-3

84. Sherring Rev M.A. "Hindu Tribes and Caste" P 242 London (1872)

85. Ghurye, G.S. P 207.

86. After Ghurye, G.S. P. 210.

87. Aggarwal Itihas Chintnika, Ram Prasad Saraf Aggarsen Smriti Bhavan, 30A, Kalakar Street, Calcutta.

88. Gangal,Tayal, Mangal, Bhandal, Nagal, Kuchchhal, Jindal, Bindal, Mittal, Goyal, Bansal, Kansal, Singal.

CHAPTER XI

Sociological Theories Regarding Origin Of Caste System & Sudras and Their Comparison With Historical Origin

Hindu scoeity is divided into groups each of which is termed "Caste". As it is said it is not an easy task to define "Caste" because all the castes do not have a common origin particularly when the caste system has developed gradually and in this way it is not the result of an arbitrary division or a contract but it is the result of evolution.

Different theories

There are numerous theories of the origin of caste system, each different from the other. Infact the sociologists are not agreed on any one common theory. Rather we may say that as to the origin of caste system where there are eight sociologists, there are nine opinions.

Mr Senart holds that the caste system originated quite early among the Aryans and has an economic basis. According to him the Varna and caste system existed with all its merits and demerits even before the advent of the Aryans. This view is supported by 'Zend Avesta' which tells that the Persian Aryans were also divided into three Varnas of Atharvas, Rathaesthas and Vastriya fshuyants corresponding exactly to the three classes of Brahamans, Kshattriyas and Vaishyas of India. The Atharvas were priests, Rathaesthas were charioteers, Vastriya Fshuyants were peasants and Huitis belonged to the artisan class. The only difference is that of the fourth Varna which comprised of artisan in Persia and Sudras in India. This difference is not so significant as it appears to be. The reason is that even in India the jobs of artisans were entrusted to the Sudras. In Rome there were Gens and Curia castes, in Greece were family, Phratria Phyle and in India were family (Parivar), Gotra and caste. In Rome, children born of heterogeneous parents (belonging to different castes) had a lower social status as compared with the aristocratic class of patricians. The Indian tradition of adoption of Husband's Gotra at the time of marriage was prevalent in Rome also.

According to N.K. Dütt caste system grew as a result of the strict laws of Manu. That is to say the laws formulated by the Brahmans and Kshattriyas were the leading factors of origin of castes system but as we shall see later these laws did not give birth to caste system but undoubtedly these supported its growth and rigidity.

Hockart says that caste system grew out of religious customs and traditions. According to him, for performing religious rites the people were divided into four classes based on white, red, yellow and dark complexions.

Slotter believes that before the Aryans came to Indian the Dravidians had among themselves classes based on crafts. In southern India caste system is prevalent in the islands separated from the sub continent and in the western Ghats. Thus slotter has corroborated my view partially.

We will see later on, on discussion that none of the above theories is complete in itself. however, some of them throw partial light.

Nesfield traces the origin of caste system to professional work. He believes that the caste system developed in the same way as agriculture and industry. Every caste occupies the same social status as is warranted by its profession[1].

Thus, there are two classes among the artisan and professional workers. One belongs to the pre-metal age (this is of lower strata), the other is concerned with the development of metallic industries and this is superior. In this way, they are classified into hunters, fishermen, herdsmen, land tillers, labourers, traders and the servile classes.[2]

Every class or a group of the class is associated with some or the other stage of industrial development. This is not the case with India only but this is a universal fact. The high or low social status allocated to any caste is based on whether the work carried on by that class is associated with the backward era or developmental era of human progress. Seen in this way the rise and fall in industrial progress and natural history is concerned with the origin of castes.

Apparently Nesfield's view is correct but on a deeper scrutiny it does not have the reality which it claims. In northern India even today many higher castes are engaged in agriculture though this stage is only next to hunting. Some scholars give the earliest place to Brahman caste which holds the highest status in society. The other castes were based on this model and came into existence at a later stage only.

Origin of Brahmanhood and Brahman

Now we shall have a comparative study of some theories of prominent sociologists with the theory of historical (discussed on P-211) origin of the caste system and Sudras . We shall first of all take up the view of Prof. Roth[3] who put forward the theory of origin of Brahmanhood and Brahman based on the views of Dr Haug cited below:

"Dr Haug derives the word Brahmana from Brahman (neuter), which originally meant "a sacred song , prayer".as an effusion of devotional feeling . Brahma was the "sacred element " in the sacrifice, and siginified "the soul of nature, the productive power ". The Brahmanic sacrifices had production as their object , and embraced some rites which were intended to furnish the sacrificer with a new spiritual body wherewith he might ascend to heaven , and others calculated to provide him with cattle and offspring .The symol of this Brahma, or productive power,which must always be present at the sacrifice , was a bunch of Kusa grass, generally called Veda (a word alternating with Brahma), which at the sacrifice ,was passed from one priest to another , and given to the sacificer and his wife . The corresponding sybmol of twigs used by the Parsis was called in Zend 'Baresma', which Dr Haug considers to have been originally the same as Brahma. As it was essential to the success of these sacrifices it has always embraced in itself the highest spiritual acquisition of the nation."

Prof. Roth [4] further puts his own view regarding the origin of the word Brahma-"This word has a great significance.... The original signification of the word Brahma, as we easily discover it in the Vedic Hymns,is that of prayer,not praise or thanksgiving , but that invocation which ,with the force of the will directed to God , seeks to draw him to itself , and to receive satisfaction from him... From this oldest sense and form of Brahma(neuter) was formed the masculine noun Brahma, which was the designation of those who pronounced the prayers, or performed the sacred ceremonies,and in nearly all passages of the Rig-veda in which it was thought that this word must refer to the Brahmanical castes ,this more extented sense must be substituted for other more limited one... From this sense of the word Brahma,nothing was more natural than to convert this offerer of prayer into a particular description of sacrificial priest, as soon as the ritual began to be fixed, the funtions which were before united in a single persons, who both prayed to the gods and sacrificed to them ,became separated, and a priesthood interposed itself between man and God."

Then further on, after quoting R.V iv. 50, 4 ff,[5] Prof. Roth continues:"In this manner here and in many places of the liturgical and legal books, the 'promise of every blessing is attached to the maintenance of a priest by the king . In as much as he supports and honours the priest, the latter ensures to him the favour of the gods. So it was that the caste of the Brahman arose and attained to power and consideration : first, they were only the single domestic priests of the kings;then the dignity became hereditary in certain families; finally a union, occasioned by similarity of interests, of these families in one larger community was effected; and all this in reciprocal action with the progress made in other respects by theological doctrine and religious worship .Still the extension of the power which fell into the hands of this priestly caste would not be perfectly comprehensible from this explanation alone. The relation of spiritual superiority in which the priests came to stand to the kings was aided by other historical movement".

Professor Roth then proceeds:"When - at a period more recent than the majority of the hymns of the Rig-veda- the Vedic people, driven by some political shock, advanced from their abodes in the Punjab further and further to the south , drove the aborigines into the hills, and took possession of the broad tract of country lying between the Ganges,the Jumna and the Vindhya range ,the time had arrived when the distribution of power , the relation of king and priest, could become transformed in the most rapid and comprehensive manner. Principalities separated in such various ways , such a division into tribes as had existed in the Punjab were no longer possible here , where nature had created a wide and continuous tract with scarcely any natural boundaries to dissever one part from another . Most of those petty princes who had descended from the north with their tribes must here of necessity disappear, their tribe beccome dissolved, and contests arise for the supreme dominion. This era is perhaps portrayed to us in the principal subject of the Mahabharata, the contest between the descendants of Pandu and Kuru. In this stage of disturbance and complication, power naturally fell into the hands of those who did not directly possess any authority,the priestly races and their leaders,who had hitherto stood rather in the position of followers of the kings, but now rose to a higher rank. It may easily be supposed that they and their families, already honoured as the confidential followers of the princes , would frequently be able to strike a decisive storke to which the king would owe his success.If we take further into account the intellectual and moral influence which this class possessed in virtue of the prerogative conceded to, or usurped by, them, and the religious feeling of the people , it is not difficult to comprehend how in such a period of transition powerful communities should arise among the domestic priests of petty kings and their families , should attain to the highest importance in every department of life ,and should grow into caste."

In order to render the probability of this theory still more apparent professor Roth goes on to indicate the relation of the other castes to the Brahmans,"The position which the three superior classes occupied in the developed Brahmanical system was one of gradation, as they differed only in the exent of their religious and civil prerogatives, the Kshattriya being in some respects less favoured than the Brahman, and theVaishya than the Kshattriya. With the Sudras, on the other hand, the case was quite different. They were not admitted to sacrifice, to the study of the Vedas, or to investiture with the sacred cord. From this Professor Roth concludes that the three highest castes stood in a closer connection with each other, whether of descent, or of culture, than any of them did to the fourth. The Indian body politic, moreover, was complete without the Sudras. The Brahman and Kshattriya were the rulers, while the Vaishyas formed the mass of the people. The fact of the latter not being originally a separate community is confirmed by the employment assigned to them, as well as by their name Vaishya derived from the word vis, a word which in the Veda designates the general community, especially considered as the possessor of the pure Aryan worship and culture, in contradiction to all barbarian races. Out of this community the priesthood arose in the manner above described, while the Kshattriyas were the nobility, descended in the main from the kings of the earlier ages. The fourth Varna, the Sudras, consisted according to prof. Roth, of a race subdued by the Brahmanical conquerors, whether that race may have been a branch of the Aryan stock which immigrated at an earlier period into India, or an autochthonous Indian tribe."

Dr Roth in his above description has explained the birth of Brahmanhood and its evolution. He has informed that the period of its birth was indefinite but its evolution took place in Rigvedic and later Rigvedic period. This view he supports by a reference to the Zend Avesta, in which he finds evidence of a division of the followers of Ahura Mazda into the three classes of Atharvas, Rathaesthas, and

Vastriya fshuyants which he regards as corresponding exactly to the Brahmans, Kshattriyas, and Vaishyas of India. The Atharvas, or priests in particular formed a class or even a caste; they had secrets which they were prohibited from divulging; they were the spiritual guides of their nation, and none but the son of a priest could become a priest-a rule which the Parsis still maintain. From these facts, Dr Haug deduces the conclusion that the nation of which both the Indo-Aryans and the Perso-Aryans originally formed a part had been divided into three classes even before the separation of the Indians from the Iranians.

Regarding the birth of fourth varna, Prof. Roth has given the same view which has been put up in the theory of Historical birth in the previous chapter. The only difference is that he has mentioned that those Aryans who were defeated were also included in the Sudras which is not correct at all. Such a view has already been disproved on P-195. It can be further explained that only Dasyus and Dasas were enslaved and not Aryans. If enslaved, that would have been for a very short period or temporarily.

Views of G.S. Ghurye

Ghurye's theory is very close to the theory of 'Historical origin of caste system in India'. He compares likewise social systems took worth and evolved in different colonies of Aryans in detail[6]:

"The people, who are known here and elsewhere as Indo-Aryans and whose earliest literary records have furnished us with information about the institution of caste and class, belong linguistically to the larger family of people designed either as Indo-Europeans or as Indo-Germans. They comprised the Celts, the Anglo-saxons and the Teutons, the Romans, and the Iranians among others. The Spanish and the Portuguese too belong to the same family. In prehistoric times about 5000 B.C., the ancestors of all these peoples seem to have occupied one fairly defined region and to have been in close cultural contact with one another. When for some reason they dispersed from their centre of characterization, various groups started in different directions and had varying adventures. Their separate language diverged yet retained sufficient common structure and content to enable the 19th and 20th century philologists to group them together and reconstruct the primitive speech which must have been the stock-in-trade of their ancestors in their centre of characterisation. One of the branches of these peoples which reached India about 2500 B.C. (now 1700-1500 B.C.) with the kind of religion represented in the early Vedic religion is called the Indo-Aryans.

As shown above their favourite word for certain groups and others of people was 'varna', 'colour'. Thus they spoke of the 'Dasa varna', 'Dasa colour' or more properly the Dasa people. Iranian literature, though in the bulk very much later than the Vedas, has preserved the significant information that the Iranians spoke of the people, whom they found in occupation of certain areas which later they captured, as 'Daha'. Iranian 'Daha' is the exact equivalent of Vedic 'Dasa', making allowance for the linguistic values of the sounds of the last syllable. Like the

Vedic Aryans they spoke of themselves as 'Arya' or 'Airya' whose identify with the Sanskrit word 'Arya' need not be pointed out. The 'Daha' are the predatory tribes of Turan, where before their bifurcation and further dispersal the ancestors of the Vedic Indian and Iranians lived together as one community, designating themselves by the term 'Arya'. Though 'Daha' means enemies or robbers, their nationality is suspected to be Iranian. The Vedic Indians might well have applied the term to their enemies in India, the native population of the punjab.... Just as the Vedic Aryans came across, in India, a civilized people, those perhaps who have left the traces of their culture in the mounds of Harappa in the Punjab and at Mohenjo-daro in Sindh, the Greeks were confronted in their land of choice with the higher Aegean civilization........ Some eight or ten centuries passed after the Greeks were face to face and in close contact with another civilization of much greater antiquity, stability and width, when they established a colony at Naukratis in Egypt. It is well known that after Alexander's death when his vast empire was parcelled out among the various claimants, Egypt fell to the lot of Ptolemy. The social history of Ptolemaic Egypt in general and that of the cities like Naukratis and the newer Alexandria is instructive. Pride and exclusive spirit, which are so patent in the early Vedic literature, were exhibited by the Greeks even in their dealings with the Egyptians........... They treated the Egyptians as a subject people being themselves the conquerors. In spite of their appreciation of the high antiquity of the civilization of the Egyptians they showed themselves as the heirs and representatives of a higher one......... In the cities of Alexandria, Naukratis, etc., they seem to have segregated the populations. And marriages between them were not permitted. Even Greek males could not marry Egyptian females. But in the country, where there was no such bar, the Greek and Macedonian soldiers and ordinary settlers had no horror of intermarriage with Egyptian women. The Egyptians on their part had realised that in order to get on with the victors and rulers it was necessary for them not only to learn Greek but also to dress and behave like the Greeks. From this double process ensued a fairly continual mixture of blood. The racial difference too began to grow less and less, so that large numbers of people in Egypt, who later on called themselves Greeks were in reality mainly Egyptian in blood, refined or diluted by a slight admixture of the blood from Greek males. The distinction between the higher stratum of Greeks and the lower stratum of Egyptian did not cease, Yet if the Ptolemaic rule had continued longer and had not been cut short by the incursion of the proud Romans, the difference between the Greek and the Egyptian might have gradually faded away. Edwyn Bevan who opines thus also informs his readers that the rule of the Romans further depressed the condition of the Egyptians, who thenceforward came third in rank and thus almost represented the castaway." G.S.Ghurye further opines that on the other hand conditions in India were different. Here the natives were of dark complexion as compared with the fair complexioned (Red) Aryans. This difference of colour became a wall between them. Secondly, the Aryans also did not adopt the characteristics of the life of the natives.

There existed strong hostility between them. Inspite of all this the Aryans took the native women for entertainment and luxury. But the Aryan women always tried to keep the native males at an arm's length because of her feeling of divine right of superiority. A comparative study of the social history of the European branch of Aryans, the Romans, is very helpful in understanding the sociological development of the Indian society. Roman society was divided into two parts (1) Patrician aristocrats and (2) Plebeian commoners. The patrician aristocrats comprised of a privileged class. They had a high sense of superiority. The condition of the Plebeian commoners was just the reverse and this discrimination was based on birth. Even Cicero the philosopher of that period had also talked of the racial superiority while those with stoic indifference to pleasure and pain were making efforts to arouse sentiments of fraternity. But this state of affairs could not last long owing to the following causes:

The aristocratic class which lived in urban areas became smaller because of their mutual political warfare and massacre and frequent infertility.By the end of democracy the number of slaves had become so high that the aristocrats found themselves in a tangle. In this way they lost their influence on the other class.

Secondly, the Roman religion which did not command much influence remained free from the conservation of rituals and customs. But in India things were quite different. The Indians by nature did not favour any alterations in their religion. It was the above described flow in the Roman religion which paved the way for the victory of Christianity over them.

A majority of the slaves were Greeks or Hellenized Orientals like the Egyptians, the Assyrians, the Jews of the Latins and the western barbarous people. Physically they were not different from the Romans but among them some were of fine appearance, some were educated while the jews and the Assyrians were expert in trade and business. The slavery of the able and handsome persons was itself a big hurdle.

The fifth group of the Aryans consisted of celt and Anglo-saxons were different from the Romans in many aspects. They developed their original traits more or less according to the Indian system. Their civilization remained based on the original principles for a fairly long period. Drud the high priest of the celts had acquired great power and even formulated laws which were similar to Brahmanism. The European conquerors after the sixteenth century also declared their superiority wherever they founded their colonies. They isulted the natives and degraded them. Of course by this time they had accepted the freedom principle of Christianity which condemned the feelings of social superiority and arrogance and preached universal brother hood of man. They accepted the woman of the people subjugated by them as their wives but they did not allow the women of their own class to become the wives of the natives.

Exactly the same treatment was meted out in the Gangetic valley by the Vedic people to the aboriginals. When they came to India they consisted of three varnas or classes. In other words they were already divided into three sections. Intermarriages were not encouraged, though there was not strict bar against them. The first step taken by them in this direction was to segregate the Sudras from worship and rituals who mostly belonged to the aboriginals. So much so that their entry in the Yagyashala was banned which became the important reason of strengthening the caste system. Similarly they banned marriages with Sudra women. A Sudra marrying a Brahman woman was considered the greatest social sin. The Sudra class as a matter of fact grew out of the section of aboriginals and who had admitted the mastery of the Aryans over them. According to the Sanskrit literature there were only three classes in the beginning. The fourth varna was born out of reaction. In this way the hostility between the Aryans and the Dasas described in the Vedas, was in the Brahmanic classification, transformed into the twice born and the single birth. Thus the later Brahmanic writers gave the name Sudra to the Dasas.

The idea of maintaining the purity of blood took birth when the Aryans came into contact with the natives of the Indo Gangetic plain. This fact is worth noting that the great scholar Patanjali wrote in 150 B.C.-"The Brahmans were of a fair complexion, pale brown hair which was their natural feature while the non Brahmans were of dark complexion (Vyakaran Mahabhashya Suttra 2-2-6)." According to Dr. Ghurye, "caste system in India is Brahmani child of the Aryan civilization who was brought up in the plain of Ganges and Yamuna and then migrated to the other parts of the country." The chief characteristic regarding the origin of caste system is borne out by the word Varna which means colour. The use of word 'caste' is of a later origin which is a class membership of which is based on birth the literal meaning of the word Jati (caste) is 'born into'. This word has not been much used as a synonym for 'varna' by the ancient writers.

Further, Dr. Ghurye puts forth his views on pages 176 to 179 of his book as follows:

"As an important constituent of the Brahmanic culture in connection with the sacrificial ritual the Aryan notions of ceremonial purity took on an exaggerated aspect. Not only the correct wording and pronunciation of the sacred formulae but also the strictest adherence to the minutest details of the ritual procedure were essential for the proper performance of rites. Distinctions began to be made between things pure and things impure. Whatever was unclean was of course impure. And with the change of outlook on the animal world even some of the formerly honourable occupations came to be looked upon as degrading. How fastidious the Brahmanic ideal of ceremonial purity had come to be by the time of the Suttras is best illustrated by the meticulous rules laid down in them for purification and for general conduct.

The Brahmans, partly out of their honest desire to preserve the purity of Vedic ritual, partly being the victims of their own ideas of ceremonial purity, and partly also owing to their consciousness of superiority over the aborigines, first enacted rules for the guidance of their own members, which were intended to prevent the possibility of the Sudra in any way lowering their moral standard and introducing their low blood.

It is because[7] the Brahmans put restrictions on the acceptance of food and drink from the Sudras during the second stage of the development of their culture that we find that in Northern India generally there is some leniency shown by them towards some of the higher castes, while in Southern India such an attitude and practice is considered a great sacrilege. As the taboo was laid against the Sudras and as the Brahman most probably continued to treat the other two castes as almost his own equals in this matter..................When the pioneers of Brahmanic culture progressed into southern India with restrictions against food and water from the Sudra as one of the items of their tradition, as they had none of the other castes-the Kshattriya and the Vaishya-to whom they were accustomed, to think of in their new regions, they applied their rules against the Sudras to all the indigenous population of the Southern countries. And the seed fell on a very congenial soil...... This is why the restrictions on food and drink are so rigorous in South India, where, as I said, the Brahman does not accept food or water at the hands of anyone but a Brahman.

With the progressive assimilation of the Vaishyas with the Sudras the Brahmans enacted rules to keep their group free from admixture with them by assigning different status to the issue of the union of a Brahman male and a Vaishya female. And with the march of time and particularly after the overthrow of Buddhism they stopped taking food at the hands of the Vaishyas. Owing to the peculiar position of the Kshsttriyas, the king having belonged to that group, in theory at least the Brahmans did not prohibit food being taken at their hands. Yet they tried to preserve their racial purity by treating the offspring of a Brahman male and a Kshattriya female as belonging to a separate group.......... This social pattern set for themselves by the most respected class in society, could not fail to be imitated with fervid enthusiasm by all manner of groups that would claim respectability. Thus it must have been that the original restrictions on intermarriage and regulations about the acceptance of food, which contemplated only four classes in society,came to be the characteristics of each and every well-marked group.

Group solidarity and group prestige would soon assert themselves against marrying on unequal terms :the lower group would refuse to marry their females to the males of the higher classes only to create a new group giving itself superior airs .It was bound to close up its ranks and be endogamous.

With functional differentiation in society there came into being separate occupational groups with more or less distinct interests .We have noticed it as a widespread feature of ancient and medieval society that the occupation of each group tends to become customarily hereditary among its members .Only the Brahmans reserved as their monopoly the occupation of a priest .No doubt they were in the beginning inspired by the laudable motive of preserving the all-important sacred lore. But later on they looked upon their priestcraft as their monopolistic activity and rigorously kept it up,while the traditional occupations of the other two castes were progressively encroached upon by other castes. There is also a natural inclination for each occupational group, as we have already noticed,to be habitually endogamous. Both these tendencies became rules: the former more less nebulou, and the latter very rigid, after the pattern of the Brahmans. Occupations thus became endogamous groups .

The attitude of respect for details that was first fostered in connection with ritual became the prevailing attitude in social behaviour .Adherence to detail of social and customary etiquette became the distinguishing mark of membership of a group . Distinction in any detail tended to be translated into separateness of membership and hence of a group.

The lack of rigid unitary control of the State, the unwillingness of the rulers to enforce a uniform standard of law and custom, their readiness to recognise the varying customs of different groups as valid, and their usual practice of allowing things somehow to adjust themselves helped the fissiparous tendency of groups and fostered the spirit of solidarity and community feeling in every group.

Both these circumstances conspired to encourage the formation of small groups based on petty distinctions.

Special rights for the higher classes and disabilities on the lower ones was almost a universal feature of the class society : and the Brahmanic theory of four Varnas with their rights and disabilities does not call for any special explanation only the practice of untouchablility is peculiar to the Hindu system. It is clear from the above discussion that the idea of untouchablity and unapproachablity arose out of the ideas of ceremonial purity, first applied to the aboriginal Sudras in connection with the sacrificial ritual and expanded and extended to other groups because of the theoretical impurity of certain occupations."

We may sum up the views of Ghurye as follows:-

1. Just as all the branches of the nordic Aryans ,Persians,Greeks and Romans defeated aboriginals,made them slaves and humiliated them and Anglo Saxons and Celts developed Brahmanism (Drud) they behaved in the similar way in India. They defeated the natives ,made them their slaves, meted out to them insulting treatment and developed Brahmanism. They were also divided into three varnas before their coming to India.

2. Indo-Aryans segregated the Sudras from Yajna and worship which ultimately became the main factor in the growth of caste system.

3. Purity of the holy ritual of Yajana which again paved the way for the growth of caste-system and untouchability.

4. The colour bar was raised as a strong barrier to protect racial purity.

The first factor of Ghurye simply bears out the theory of historical birth explained in 10th chapter. Like other colonies the Aryans here also defeated the natives in wars and made them their slaves . Ultimately declaring them as Sudras and pushed them into fourth varna consisting of non-Aryans . But the strangest thing that happened in India was that whereas slavery in other colonies gradually lost its hold and finally disappeared, here it came to be rooted permanently. The main cause responsible for this was the writing of scriptures by the Aryans which on one hand urged the Aryans to destroy their enemies the non-Aryans, defeat them, destroy their business to weaken their being and snatch their virtues while on the other it also called out to them to augment their own power, strengthen their defence, rob the non-Aryans and rise in prosperity (see chapter 7). Once again this literature was declared to be of divine origin and it grew as more and more writings were added to it so that gradually this established the intellectual victory of the Aryans over the non-Aryans. Of course the great Roman philosopher Cicero following this path preached superiority of birth but these views could not stand long before the philosophy of the thinkers preaching the equality of man. Finally, the Christian principles of fraternity rendered them utterly meanigless and human slavery was wiped out of Europe.

The great Buddhist and Jain religious thinkers launched such views in India which spread like wild fire not only throughout the country but also in Tibet, China, Japan, Burma, Indonesia, Ceylon, Afghanistan and Central Asia and is still existing there. But in India, as a result of a Brahmanical conspiracy that light also gradually vanished after the decline of the Mauryan dynasty. Towards the decline of the Gupta empire caste system got established again firmly and this time the newly raised walls of colour and caste discrimination were thicker, higher and impenetrable than earlier one. The main factor behind this was the inspiration by the Vedic literature and other literature of later date. As already denoted the miracle of this literature was something extraordinary to that which is generally thought to be. Because their literature was further declared to be of divine origin hence nobody could dare go against it or commit hearsay. This sacred literature further declared caste system to be of divine origin, which demanded blind faith for all. This impulse being consistently fed not only glorified the institution of caste system but also made it strong and stable.

Now let us take up the remaining three factors. The second factor relates to the segregation of the Sudras from the vedic rituals like Yajna and worship, the third one relates to the sanctity of the Yajnas and the fourth is the maintenance of racial purity. These factors only evolved the system. Actual caste system came into existence when the white coloured Aryans invaded the black coloured natives and enslaved them. It gave two results (i) the victor suffered with proud of winning war or superior complexity, while the other defeated suffered with humiliation of defeat and inferior complexity, (ii) There existed an unending enmity among both, the master and slave group which created a high wall between them. Such a situation can be termed as birth of caste or varna system. As a matter of fact other causes such as sanctity of the Yajna, segregation of Sudras from the rituals like Yajna and maintenance of racial purity added to its evolution and strength.

This view is also supported by Mr. V.M. Apte[8]-'Rigveda contains mention of three Varnas-the Brahmans, the Kshattriyas and the Vaishyas. The fact that there is no mention of the fourth Varna does not imply at all that the fourth Varna did not exist. Of course if there is any variation in social classification between the beginning and the ending dates of Rigveda, it is because the fourth Varna was included at a later stage, while after the war and social upheavals, the natives Dasyus and Dasas were also included in the Aryan social system".

It means that most of the castes of one birth and the Dwij (twice born) castes were in existence separately in the beginning of the Rigvedic period also.

The above detailed discussion can be summarised thus-In all the Aryan colonies, the natives were made slaves, they were put to humiliation but there this in human state of affairs died out gradually. But in India it became deep rooted and its bitterness was enhanced when the inhuman institution of untouchability grew out of it and which has no parallel in the world. This was due to three causes:-

1. **Colour discrimination :** The Aryans were of fair complexion (rosy) while the natives were of dark complexion. As a result of this difference, intermarriages were not possible.

2. **Sanctity of Yajnas :** This gave birth to the feelings of pure and impure, sanctified and defiled beings. Those activities, which were considered virtuous earlier, now became to be considered as vicious. Those who were engaged in defiled occupations, began to be hated, which as a main factor paved the way for untouchability. Similarly, the Aryans deprived the Sudra cooks of their occupation out of danger of food purity.

3. Writing of such literature as described the caste system being of divine origin demanded blind faith from all. This impulse, being consistently fed, not only glorified the institution of caste system, but also made it strong and stable. Secondly, since caste system was said to be of divine origin, nobody could go against it or commit hearsay. Such conditions were never present in other colonies.

Because of the causes explained above the Tree of caste system fully blossomed and became a parasite creeper while in other colonies it got dried up and finally fell.

References

1. Nesfield "Caste system," P 9.

2. Nesfield Ibid. P 88.

3. The origin of Brahmanism, P. 7, cited by Muir J. in original Sanskrit text P. 293.

4. 'Brahma and the Brahmin', Journal of the German Oriental Society. Vol. I, Prof. R.Roth cited by Muir J. P. 290-293.

5. R.V. IV-50-4.7

BRIHASPATIḤ PRATHAMAṀ YĀJAMĀNĀ MAHO JYOTIŚAḤ PARAME VYOMAN I
SAPTĀSYASTUVIJĀTO RAVAṆA VISAPTA RASHMI RADHAMATTA MĀNSI II (4)
SAINDRĀJĀ PRATIJANYĀNI VISHVĀ SHUŚMEṆ TASTHĀVABHIVĪRYEṆ I BRIHASPATI
YAḤ SUBHARATAṀ VIBHARTI VALGŪYATI VANDATE PŪRVABHĀJAM II (7)

Brahaspati, who has knowledge of Mantras, first time appeared in the solar system, than with seven verses (Chhandas) on his lips (mouth) staying in the sky, he destroyed the darkness with his shine. (4) king, who protect the Brahaspati well and give 'Havya' and invate, bowing down with due respect, he neutralize the power of his enemies with his own power.(7)

6. Ghurye, G.S. "Caste and races in India" PP 163-180.

7. It is strange to note that the brilliant scholar has given only one sole reason i.e. ceremonial purity, for imposing restriction on acceptance of food and drink from the Sudra. I have given another reason in chapter X as to how the ban was imposed on the profession of cooking by the Suds (Sudras). This was perhaps original source of any of such idea. The ceremonial purity may have helped in its evolution later. However, the scholars have to be very cautious before taking any final decision on the subject.

8. Apte V.M. "were Caste formulated in the age of Rigveda?" BDCRI Vol. II, No. 1 & 2, P 35.

CHAPTER XII

Later Brief History Of Harappans (1100 B.C. to 500 A.D.)

Exodus of Harappan refugees to South

After their decisive defeat and having been chased out by the Nordic Aryan invaders, the non-Aryan Harappans moved towards the South-east. A large group of those Harappans moved towards far South along the sea shore via modern Gujarat and permanently settled there. We have read in the previous chapters that after the devastation of Lothal that had been completed upto 1600 B.C., many people continued living there even much longer after that. Life flourished even after that in the towns south of Lothal. After reaching the South, they constructed urban localities in Maski and Brahmagiri on the Indus pattern. Mr. D.N. Majumdar[1] has given a description of the findings excavated at Maski in his book' Races and Culture of India'. He writes:

"The pre-historic finds at Maski, Mysore and other Centres in peninsular India tell the cultural history of the Deccan during the last 3000 years or more. At least three layers of cultures are represented at Maski as evidenced from the pot burials and artifacts discovered in association. Yazdani dates the funeral pottery, polished stone implements and chert flakes to about 1000 B.C. or even earlier. The beads and chank articles and some of the terra-cotta figurines, he thinks date from 500-300 B.C., while the seal impressions and ornamental pottery and some terra-cotta figures date from 700-500 B.C. Maski must have been an important cultural centre in pre-historic as well as in proto-historic times. It was at any rate a great centre for bead and chank industries. The raw materials for the various industries found at Maski, particularly shell and bead, must have been brought from distant places, even from as far as Persia, showing a maritime trade between Maski and the Arabian Sea coast, also with the Mediterranean belt, which was under the control of the Carthagians, Romans and Arabs. Egyptian influence through trade and association must have penetrated into India and even the Far East, while bronze, cereals, tamed animals and many other culture elements of Europe including religious cults are traceable to the Near East. Traces of gold working also have been discovered in Maski and the gold dust found on the sandy bank of the Maski river must have tempted immigrants from far and near to work the industry and build up an urban culture superimposing on indigenous moorings.

Similarly, such type of culture has been excavated by the Archaeological Survey of India at Brahmagiri in Mysore."

During that period, south India had become the main centre of trade than north India. S.V.Vishwanathan[2] while throwing light on this, writes :

"The traditional fame of South India as the seat of the precious metals and gems seems to have been carried down to the time of the Arthasastra, where we read that with the exception of blankets, skins and horses, other articles of merchandise, such as conchshells, diamonds, precious stones, pearls, and gold are available in plenty in the South.

The South Indian Dravidians were a great maritime people in antiquity. It is no wonder, being surrounded by the sea on three sides, that they should have developed the arts of ship building and sea-borne commerce. In the Manimekalai, one of the most ancient pieces of literature of the Tamils, there are a good number of original words denoting the sea : Kadal, Paravai, Punari, Arkali, and Munnir. The waves of the sea were known to the Tamils as ola. The only word in the Rig-veda which has been interpreted to contain a reference to the sea is Samudra. The word oda meaning a boat is an original term, and there are words which denote a ship in Sangam literature, e.g. Kalam, Marakalam, Mitavai and kappal, which are independent of outside influences; while in Rig-Vedic literature we have only Nau, Durona and Plava to denote a boat, sometimes with many oars. What we have in earliest Tamil literature is certainly reminiscent of the life that was led by the Dravidians of South India in much earlier times."

It is quite clear that they carried that great tradition of the Indus Valley to the south and it flourished there. Even today we find the best examples of architecture of ancient India in the southern-India. Other arts also developed there.

In the beginning, the mountain range of Vindhya had become the natural boundary of Aryans, but in due course the Aryan missionaries and colonizers gradually moved to the south. According to a saying Agast Muni (son of Pulasta) had gone to South and lived there with the Dravidians and established good relations with them, spread Aryan culture there and in this way paved the way for the arrival of Aryans in South. Only after that the Aryan Kshattriyas set up colonies there.

Escape of Indus refugees to the east

Many groups of the non-Aryan refugees fled towards the east under the pressure of the Aryan invaders and settled in the plains of Ganga-Yamuna. There are clear cut archaeological evidences of their migration to that region. The traditional history of the Mundas[3] discloses the migration of these aboriginal people apparently under the pressure of the Aryan invaders. But the fact remains that they had not abandoned the Indus Valley completely. They were no doubt deprived of their independence by the predominance of the foreign Aryans but still all of them did not adopt all the traits of Aryan civilization, traditions and customs. The remains of the non-Aryans are found even today throughout India. These have been traced out in north India at Brahui on the North Western border, Mahar (Mar or Mahar) on the South-western border, Pariyah, Bhar, Palar, Malar. Malla and Gond in the South and the Santhal in the east.

In fact, the remains of these non-Aryan castes and tribes can be found in each and every part of the country. Apart from the Dravidian and Munda languages spoken by them, their main mark of identification was the tradition of totemism called Alla in Hindi language. On the other hand, there was tradition of Gotras in Aryan tribes and castes.

It is not surprising therefore to find that if some castes or tribes or a group of families living together accept an animal or a plant as their totem, it is called the totem of that caste or class viz. monkey, bear, fish, serpent, dear, eagle, tortoise, pea-cock, duck and many plants etc.

The characteristics of totemism may be summarized thus : killing certain animals or eating there of is Tabooed in some clans. Some tribes bear sign there of. The Totem animal when it dies, is ceremonially mourned and buried as a member of the clan concerned. The skins of animals which are the totems of clans are donned by the totemic group on specified solemn occasions. Many totemic groups paint their persons with the picture of the totemic animal and take the picture as their coat of arms or even tattoo it on their bodies. The totem animal, if dangerous, is propitiated in the belief that it will spare the members of the totemic clan. If the totem plant or animal is edible, the members may eat it on ceremonial occasions or after offering their excuses to the animal. The clan recognizes mystic ties with the animal species and believes that the animal will foretell the future, protect and warn the members of tribe. The assumptions with regard to totemism are that totem organisation is universal. J.F. Maclenon was the first to understand the significance of Totemism as a primitive social institution[4].

Majumdar[5] gives an account of totemistic tribes as follows: "According to Ethnographic Survey of India, the Santhals have more than 100 totemistic clans, Hos have more than 50, Mundas 64 and Bhils 24. Many castes in Orissa the Kurmi, the Kumhar, the Bhumia, who have advanced in culture in recent years are named after the serpant, pumpkin, jackal and other totems. The Katkaris of Bombay, the Gond tribe of M.P. and of Rajasthan also have clannames after the fauna and flora of their habitat. The Dhelki Kharias, a major section of the Kharias of Chota Nagpur plateau, are divided into eight totemic clans. viz. Soren (rock or stone), Muru (tortoise), Samad (deer), Barliha (a variety of fruit), Gharhad (bird), Hansda (the eel), Mail (dirt) and Topna (kind of bird). These names show how a totem may be an animal, plant or often material object or parts thereof.

Some Indian Tribes are divided into three, four or more phratries and some of the clans in a Phratry may have an animal or plant name. The Dauris of Bengal (Bankura District) are a depressed caste and they own four major divisions, Mala, Dhala, Sekhoria and Mana. Some investigators take them as geographical divisions. The Malas are from 'Malla bhumi', the Dhalas are from Dhalbhum and the Mana from Manbhum. Each of these phratries is a closed and endogamous group and contains 5-20 exogamous clans. Totemic traces are noticed in their reverence for the striped hereon and the dog, and in their taboo of horse-dung, but most of the clans have little to do with animals or plants.

The Bagdis, Mahisyas and Koras of Bengal have animal clan names, but no totemic beliefs as are met with among other totemic tribes. The Kora, originally from Chota Nagpur and most probably belonging to the Munda stock, venerate tortoise, duck, fish, egg, etc. but they are not organized on a totemic basis".

We find in historical period that there were many totemic ruling families of non-Aryan blood, such as Mallas, Nagas, Mauryas, Lichchhivis, Gonds, Bhars etc.

Malla

Mr. Gustab oppert[6] highlighting the Malla tribe, writes:

"Another branch of the Mallas came into collision with Alexander the Great, while he was progressing towards the south along the Valley of the Indus. In the fight which ensued during his attack on their city he was, as is well known, severely wounded. This happened not far from the present Multan, which word I assure to denote Mallasthana, the place of the Mallas, not Mulasthana, as has been assumed hitherto. In fact Sir Alexander Burnes states in his 'Travels into Bokhara' (Vol. III, P 114) that "Mooltan is styled `Malli than', or `Mali tharun` the place of the Malli, to this day"................. According to holy books of Buddha religion, Buddha, the great reformer of India, preferred to die among the Mallas in Kusinagara. The citizens, when they heard of the arrival of the dying saint, met him sorrowfully, and among the last acts of Buddha was that he appointed the Malla Subhadra as an Arhat. In those parts which had for their capital the cities of Kusavati or Kusinarā (Kusinagara in Nepal according to Smith, or near Kasia according to Wilson and Cunningham) and Pava modern village Padaraona or Fazilpur) The Royal family belonged to the Ikshvaku family or the solar race, while Manu (X-22) makes them degraded Kshattriyas (Viratyas)."

In Mahabharta "Malla Nation" and in Ramyana `Malla land' has been mentioned many a times. The above mentioned Malla Kingdom was one of the 16 Janpadas in north India during the Buddha period.

One section of the Mallas lived in Bengal. Even today their descendants are found there and are known as Mallas. Malda district was named after them. Though their number there is very low, a large number of them live in the mountains of Rajmahal, which are known as Malla Paharia today.

Bhar or Mar

There is also a mention of Bhars in Ramayana along with Rama and his sons but after that all of a sudden we find them missing from the historical scene and they reappeared suddenly before the Muslim invasion. At that time, they were the actual owners of a vast area of land. In fact, the Bhars once ruled a large part of India, which extended from Awadh in the West of Bihar in the east and also extended upto Chhota Nagpur, Bundelkhand, and in the South upto the coastal area. Their name resembles with the names of many places even today such as Bihar, Bahraich (Bharaich), Vara, Bhadoi, Varagaon, Barabanki, Varhavara and

Varvan in Audh and Bareily, Barhan, Bahar (Bharhar) in north west province and var, Varavar, Baradhi and Varhia in Bihar and Barva, in Chota Nagpur etc.[7]

Corroborating the above view Sir Henery M. Elliot[8], writes," The entire area from Gorakhpur to Bundelkhand and Sagar and Badohi in Banaras, the entire division which was previously known as Bhardai, was under the control of Bhars. A number of old forts made of stone, dams, under ground caves which are found in Gorakhpur, Azamgarh, Jaunpur and Mirzapur are called Bhardih. 'Var' in Awadh was built by a Bhar king whereas the name of Barabanki is said to be related to another king Jas. According to a hearsay the Shivling on the top of Varapara hill near Gaya was established by a Bhar king, whose battle with Lord Krishna is still remembered by the people. Varharara sub-division is still inhabited by the early Bhars." Mr. Sherring[9]puts forth his view in the same context". A hearsay is popular even today among the inhabitants of Azamgarh district that during the time of Rama, who ruled Ayodhya, their country was adjacent to Ayodhya and it was ruled by King Bhar and demons. Bhar King has left behind so many vast forts made of mud, the remains of which can be found even today in Harvanshpura, and Unchagaon near Azamgarh and in Ghasi, the Kuwar and Meghai rivers were connected by a canal called Asurain. This work is said to have been done by the early inhabitants. The Hari Dam in Amin Nagar in the Nizamabad sub-division is said to have been constructed by them".

Apparently, the Bhars lived in Indus Valley. They were driven away by the Aryan invasions and thereafter they came to this area and established their power. Same type of dams, as referred to in Rigveda(Vratra) and canals, one example of which has been found in Lothal, were constructed by them here for irrigation purposes. They also reclaimed the land from forests, irrigated it, grew good crops, constructed forts and built many cities on the pattern that existed in the Indus Valley. But when the Aryans reached that place also as a result of some historical incident, they were again driven away or were made slaves by the Aryans.

Many Rajputs have Bhar blood in their veins and Dr. Francis Buchonan wants so far as to state that the Parihara Rajputs of Shahbad descended from the Bhars (Report in Montgomery Martin's Vol. II P 463)[10]

According to modern research work, all the regions from Bareilly to Allahabad and up to Gorakhpur in the east, was under the domination of Bhar kings before the advent of Muslims in this area. According to R.S. Rawat and K.K. Rawat of Barabanki modern passi caste and classes are the descendants of Bhars and Rajbhars. According to Lucknow Gazetteer of British period part XXXVII P.P.137-138, king Trilok chand was king of Bahraich. Similarly Suhaldev of Gonda is said to be of the same origin. He gave a stiff resistance to a famous Muslim chief Saiyed Satar Masud'Gazi' at the bank of river Kauriyala in 1034 A.D. and finally killed him after giving a defeat. According to other sources Bharpassi king Suhaldev ruled upto the end of 11th century A.D. Gorakhpur, Basti, Bahraich, Gonda and Sitapur Janpada were part of his kingdom.

There is a very interesting story of his war with Turkish chief Masud Gazi. Gazi Launched an attack at Bahraich in 1034 A.D. But Suhaldev offered a very stiff resistance in return. So, Gazi put some cows in front of his soldiers to save himself from defeat. However, on the next day king Suhaldev answered in the same coin and put some pigs before his own troops Ultimately the king dragged the Muslim chief to the nearby forest where he had a hand to hand fight with him and killed him with his sword near the lake Chitaura where his dead body was buried later by his soldiers (weekly Apanna Abhiyan Dated -1-6-91 Kanpur)

Mar or Mahar

Western part of India was under the dominion of Mahar tribes before advent of foreigners in this region, Gustav Oppert puts forth his views:

"Mahars or Mhars, whom I recognised as the people who had given their name to Maharashtra. But it was not to that country alone that the Mahars were confined, for they have always been occupants of Rajputana. The provinces which now go by the name of Mhairwara (Ajmer) and Marwar (Jodhpur) are their ancient home. "The Mair or Mera is" according to Colonel Tod, "the mountaineer of Rajpootana, and the country he "inhabits is styled Mairwara or the region of hills". These hillmen by and by populated the plain and are also found there (see Annals and Antiquities of Rajasthan by Lieutenant-Colonel James Tod. Vol. 1, 680-The name of Marwar is generally connected with Sanskrit maru, desert, mountain, rock I believe this derivation to be wrong, though it gives a pretty good explanation of the diversified nature of the country, which is hilly in one part and arid in the other). They remained masters of the soil until they were ousted later on by victorious invaders. As chiefs and Warriors, like other aboriginal tribes, they have a claim to be called Rajputs, for the name of Rajput or Rajaputra confers only a social, and not an ethnological distinction. The term Rajput is generally applied to an Aryan Kshattriya, though everybody knows that the victors intermarried freely with the vanquished non-Aryans, who were never totally annihilated, and that the Mars and other non-Aryan tribes claim relationship with the Rajputs.

No real ethnological difference between a Mar (Mhar, Mahar) and Mhair (Mer) has been found to exist. It has been previously mentioned that, according to Colonel Dalton, Mar or Mala is a very uncertain name applied to or assumed by different people in different parts of India, but it may be that there is some affinity between all the tribes who bear it"[11]. It may be mentioned here, that father of Indian constitution Dr. B.R. Ambedkar was born in a Mahar family.

Naga

It is well known[12] that before the victory of Scythians, the Nagas used to live in the Avanti region it is very difficult to say as to who were these Nagas. According to G.A. Grierson, they may have been the ancestors of the non-Aryan inhabitants of Hunza-Nagar, whose language Barusaski has not been identified as belonging to any known family of speech. In later times, the nagas spread through the whole of North India and settled in Madhya Pradesh and Maharashtra where a city nagpur, under this name, still exists.

Nagas were a totemistic tribe worshipping serpants. Some seals and seal impressions found from Indus Valley cities, bear the marks of snakes. In one seal, there are two serpants standing on left and right side of deity having buffalow head and hands bent on knees, who is sitting on a wooden stool. Similarly, on another seal there is a snake resting its hood on a wooden stool protecting a nearby tree or devdrum. In another seal, a snake is standing behind a bull, which is being attacked by a bull fighter man from front side with a spear in his hand[13]. In all the above seals or seal impressions, serpant appears to be a protector deity. This is a clear proof of Nag totemistic traditions in the Indus Valley civilization. This means a part of Indus Valley people were Naga worshipper or nagas.

Perhaps this tradition came to Indus Valley from assyria or elam. There are few verses in Athravaveda which draw our attention towards this fact (see PP 64-65)[14].

A.V. V-13-6 to 8 and 10.

ASITASYA TAIMĀTASYA BABHRIRAPODAKASYACH I SĀTRĀSĀ HASYĀHAM MANYOKHĀ JYĀNMIV DHANVANO VIMUN CHĀTI RATHO IVA 11 (6)

ALIGĪCHA VILIGĪ VA PITĀ CHAMĀTĀ CHA I VIDMA VAH SARVATU BANDHVARASĀḤ KIMKARIṆYATH II (7)

URUGULĀYĀ DUHITĀ JĀTĀ DĀSYASIKANYĀ I

PRAT Ṅ KAM VAṬRUŚOṆAḤ SARVĀSĀMARAM AM VIŚAM II (8)

TĀBUVAM NA TĀBUVAM TETVAMASI TĀBUVAM I

TĀBUVENĀRASAM VIŚAM II(10)

The meaning of above Verses is as under: I release(thee) from the fury of the black serpent, the Taimato, the brown serpent, the poison that is not fluid, the all conquering, as the bow-string (is loosened) from the bow, as chariots (from horses)..(6)

Both Aligi and Vilgi, both father and mother we know your kin everywhere. Deprived of your strength what will ye do?...(7)

The daughter of Urugula, the evil one born with the black of all those who have run to their hiding place the poison is devoid of force.(8)

Tabuvam (or) not Tabuvam, thou (o! serpent) are not Tabuvam through Tabuvam Thy poison is bereft of force...(10)

These Verses are apparently for making the poison of snake bite ineffective, which are enchanted by Ojhas or snake-Charmers.

Mr. Tilak[15] has given his view based upon the view of Sir Blumfield that the words Taimato, Aligi, Viligi, Urugala and Tabuvam are non-vedic and Akkadian.

Dr. Burnett has discovered from the record of Sumer (Assyrian deptt.) of 3000 B.C. where names Aligi and Viligi were the names of father and son in a dynastic list (this list has been published in Cambridge History of India, Vol. I also). Dr. Bhagwatsaran Upadhyaya has to his credit the discovery of the above secret of immense value[16].

It is to be noted that above list of names of kings discovered from Ur and names of serpents mentioned in above verses of Atharvveda are one and the same. This gives hints to the fact that perhaps above dynasty of Ur had tradition of Nag totemism. Where from this tradition reached India with the arrival of round headed Assyrian Alpines, who had settled in Indus Valley before advent of Aryan tribes (PP 60 and 65).

Later History of Nagas

Before the settlement of Kurus in Hastinapur this land was under the rule of Naga kings. According to Mahabharta we find traces of these Nagas in north west India. It would appear that there were at least two branches of the Naga tribe. The northern and the Southern. Those in the north had perhaps originally established themselves at Takshila. The chief of them was Vasuki. They killed Parikshat, and his son Janmejaya is said to have performed a serpent sacrifice. This only illustrates that Janmejaya avenged the death of his father and in a war that ensued, the Nagas were defeated and destroyed.

This event shows that after the extermination of Aryan Kshattriyas in the Mahabharta war, non-Aryan Nagas tried best to regain their power lost by their ancestors in combat with Aryan Kshattriyas.

In historic period, we trace these Nagas again in Magadha region, perhaps they were dragged from north and established their power in Magadha. The Sisunaga dynasty of Magadha was related to these Nagas. According to Puranas this dynasty was founded by a king named Sisunaga. He was succeeded by the Kakavarna, Kshemadharman and Kshemjit, Bimbisara, Ajatsatru, Darsaka, Udaya or Udasin Nandi-Vardhan and Mahanandin. According to the Matsya Purana, these Sisunagas ruled for 360 years. Their capital was Rajgiri. Detailed description there of is given in later pages.

At a later period, according to Puranas, Naga rulers flourished at Vidisha, Kantipuri, Mathura and Padmavati. After a lot of discussion, Dr. K.P.Jaiswal gave the following chronology of the Nagas of Vidisha[17].

(1) Sesha Naga(110-90 B.C.) (2) Bhogin (90-80 B.C.) (3)Ramachandra (80-50 B.C.) (4) Dharma_Varman (50-40 B.C.) (5) Vangara (40-31 B.C.) (6)Bhutanandi (20-10 B.C.) (7) Sisunandi (10 B.C. to 25 A.D.)(8) Yasah Nandi (25-30 A.D.) (9) Purusha Datta (10) Uttama Datta (11) Kama Datta (12) Bhava Datta(13) Siva Nandi or Siva Datta

These Nagas ruled for a period of about 200 years from about 100 B.C. to 78 A.D.

Nava Naga

According to K.P.Jayaswal Nava Naga was founder of the Nava Naga dynasty whose official title was'Bhar Sivas'. He was contemporary of Vasudeva the Kushana ruler and he ruled from about 140 A.D. to 170 A.D. He ruled in U.P. His coins were issued from Kosambi. By his coinage he was also connected with Padmavati and Vidisha and with Virsena on the other hand.

Virasena

In about 175-180 A.D. we find a Naga king named Virsena establishing his power in Mathura.

Bhava Naga

Bhava Naga ruled for 30 years from about 210 to 245 A.D., Trava Naga ruled from about 245 to 250 A.D., Barhina Naga ruled for 7 years from about 250 to 260 A.D. Charaja Naga ruled for 30 years from about 290 to 315 A.D., Bhava Naga was a contemporary of Parvarsena who was a contemporary of Samudra Gupta.

It is apparent from the above account that previously these Naga lived in north west and later on they spread in other parts. The northern Nagas fall into four groups (1) Naga Bodo (Northern), comprising the Kachcha and the Kabui (2) Western Naga including Angamis, Kezomas, Rengmas and Semas (3) Central Nagas chief of whom are AO's and Lhotas (4) Eastern Nagas, known as Naga Kuki and cheif Tribes being Mao and Tangkhul.

It has already been mentioned that the Naga dynasty ruled for quite a long time. The queen of Chander Gupta second, named Kuber Nag was the daughter of this family. It was a very civilizated tribe which got built so many Buddha statues and stupas. Many of the Nagas embraced Buddhism. This tribe was pioneer in architecture, dance and playing on instruments. Their ladies were very beautiful and often attired themselves with beautiful flowers.

Pulinada

The statement of the Puranas, Pulinda-Vindyamulika, shows that the Pulindas lived on the Vindhya region. They belonged to the Proto-Australoid stock. In the Mahabharata they are condemned as low and barbarous. The capital of the Pulindas (Pulinda-nagara) probably lay to the south east of Dasarna i.e. the Vidisha or the Bhilsa region (Raychaudhuri). This shows that the aborigines lived within the jurisdiction of the Haihaya-Yadavas.[18]

Tamraliptaka

The Tamraliptakas form a part of the Suhmas living in the present Tamluk region of Midnapur. It was an international port and possibly with the purpose of trade, people from different regions settled here. B.C. Law thinks that it was a colony of the Tamils. We may note in this connection that the Koras of Midnapore, whom Risley thinks of Dravidian origin but S.C. Ray of Oraon origin, speak a dialect of Dravidian language.

Regarding the racial composition of Bengalees of the early days we may note the following observations of T.C. Raychaudhuri: "We have seen that there is a faint trace of pre-Dravidian or Nisadic element among the Bagdis and Namasudras."[19]

Similarly, the Angas of Bhagalpur area of Bihar and Bangas of Bengal, Kalingas of Orissa were the kingdoms of Australoid tribes who occupied a prominent position among the Janpadas of ancient times. The battle of Ashoka with Kalinga people is very famous.

Later Vedic period from 1100 B.C. to 600 B.C.

Atharvaveda

Before establishing the period of composition of Atharvaveda first of all we take up the period of the composition of the Rigveda. N.K. Dutt[20] accepts this period to be 2000-1400 B.C.. According to Keith[21], a treaty between the Hittites and Mittani kings was reached in 1400 B.C. The language,of writings being similar to the language of Rigveda, the period of the composition of Rigveda is accepted as the same.

In chapter eight, we have already discussed that the caste system emerged out of two races i.e. Aryans and non-Aryans and this system went on developing gradually.

The famous Purushu Shukta of Rigveda in which first of all four varnas have been mentioned, is said to have been composed at a later date. According to Keith[22], the period of the later part of the composition of Rigveda is between 1000 B.C. to 800 B.C. This means that the four varna system had developed during this period.

First of all, we take up the Atharvaveda of later vedic period. In this period also the Aryan and non-Aryan forms of varna system developed. Following examples corroborate this fact.

In A. Veda IV-20-4-8, the suppliant expresses his desire to be able to see the Aryans and the Sudras with the help of herbs so that he may catch hold of the magician.

A. Veda XIX-6, make me a darling of both the Aryans and the non-Arayans.

A. Veda V-11-3. The priest claims that nobody can disturb the routine of life which he has made, neither the Arya nor a Dasa.

In A, Veda IV-20-4, the word Arya has been used for the three higher Varnas and word Dasa has been used for Sudra.

In A. Veda V-22-7,8 the suppliant prays to the Takman fever that he should attack Sudra, a lady of bad character and also should attack Mujanwat, Vahilka and Mahavarsha.

In the above four hymns, the words Aryan and non-Aryan (Sudra) have been used for two classes Dwij and of one birth. The later verse expresses ill will of the Aryan invoker towards the Sudra. It becomes quite clear that during the later period of Rigveda the wall which was raised between the Aryans and the non-Aryans i.e. the Dwij and the Sudras had grown up-very clearly and there was a considerable increase in the ill will towards the Sudra. The Aryan priests (suppliants) had started praying even the natural distresses like the painful fevers etc. that they should attack the Sudras and give them unbearable pain and destroy them.

The main region where the Vedas were composed, is considered to be Punjab. This means, the Vedas were composed at the time when the Aryans were still in Punjab. After that they proceeded further and settled in the area falling between Saraswati and Yamuna rivers, which was called Kurukshetra and this very region used to be known as the sacred place of Aryans. The area upto Ganges across the river Yamuna was known as Kuru-Panchala region and it became the main region of the composition of Shraut suttras and the Brahmans at a later stage. According to Keith, some of these suttras were composed in Madhya-desha and this period is considered to be 1000 B.C. to 600 B.C. [23] (Kane accepts the period of the composition of Brahmanas to be the period before 1000 B.C.)[24]. Maxmuller also accepts the period of composition of Brahmanas to be before Budha i.e. before 600 B.C.

According to Keith and Belvakar[25] Panchvimsh Brahmana is the earliest creation. According to Keith thereafter Taittireya Brahmana, according to Belvakar Aitreya Brahmana (from I to V) were composed. Satpath Brahmana is considered to be a later composition. Keith and Belvakar have given these compositions the following order in accordance with their time:

	Keith		**Belvakar**
1.	Panch Vimsha Brahmana	1.	Panch Vimsha Brahmana
2.	Taittireya Brahmana	2.	Aitreya Brahmana (I to V)
3.	Aitreya Brahmana	3.	Taittireya Brahmana

4.	Satpath Brahmana	4.	Aitreya Brahmana (VI to VIII)
5.	Gemini Brahmana	5.	Satpath Brahmana
6.	Kaushitki Brahmana	6.	Gemini Brahmana
7.	Shankhayan Brahmana	7.	Gopath Brahmana
		8.	Samhitop Brahmana
		9.	Devtadhyaya Brahmana
		10.	Arsheya Brahmana

Among the Shraut Suttras, the Apastamb was composed earliest of all [26] and the Baudhayan is of later date.

The dates of the principal Shraut Suttras viz. those of Apastamba, Ashwalayan, Baudhayana, Katyayana, Samkhyayana, Latyayana, Satyasadha and Grihasuttra Ashwalayan, Apastamba etç. have been fixed between 800 B.C. to 400 B.C. The Dharam Suttra of Gautam, Baudhayan, Vasista and Apastamba have been placed between the 600 B.C. to 400 B.C. [27]

According to Mait Samh (code) IV-2-7, 10 - the Sudra had cattle, which the high caste people could snatch from them at the time of Yajna.

According to Tait Samh (VII-1-1) no Sudra can participate in the Yajna but he can do so after washing the feet of religious Brahmana. This means that the importance of washing the feet of religious Brahman is equal to participating in Yajna.

According to Satp Bra (IV-1-1-10), the Brahmans participating in the Yajna should not talk to any Sudra.

Panch Vimsha Brahmana (VI-1-11): The Sudra originated without a God and Yajnas but they own a large number of cattle.

Apparently, the origin of Sudras has been described to be without God (Aryans) viz. they were non-Aryans who had nothing to do with the Yajna. They were not allowed to participate in the Yajna. But according to Maittriyani Samhita (code) the cattle could be taken away forcibly from the Sudras for the Yajna i.e. they could be made economically weaker by force.

Gemini Brahmana 1-68-69

"SŪDRO ANUSTUPACHANDĀ VESMĀPATI DEVĀS I
TASMĀDU PĀDĀVANE JYENĀIVĀ JIJIVIPĀTI"

The Sudra had originated from the feet of Prajapati, were without Gods and therefore, the master of houses (Brahmans) is his God and he should therefore earn his livelihood by washing his feet.

It has already been proved by giving examples from Rigveda and Atharvaveda (see P-194) that the Aryan Kshattriyas had made many of the non-Aryans, who were defeated in the battlefield, their slaves who were later on called Sudras. In order to please their Brahman priests, the Kshattriyas had gifted many of the Sudra slaves to them. It is quite clear from the above hymn that these very Sudra slaves used to work as servants in the houses of Brahman priests during that period. This verse corroborates the system devised in the vedic period. This hymn completely fills up the gap of Rigvedic period and the period when Gemini was composed.

Now we take up the intention shown in these lines : it means that because the Sudras originated without the Gods (Aryans) so Brahmans are their Gods and it is the sacred duty of the Sudras to serve them viz. the Sudras have nothing to do with the worship of Gods of heaven. Their Gods are the visible Brahmans of this world. The Sudras will get the same reward (heaven etc.) by serving the Brahmans which the Brahmans get by performing Yajna or by worshipping the gods.

In Brahadarnyakopanishada VI-2-7 Aruni, the father of Swaitketu, while praising himself says that he has gold, cattle, wealth, horses, slave women (Dasis) and clothes.

It is quite clear that the Brahmans had made not only laws for enslaving the Sudras but it was a reality also. The Dasis (slave women) were at their service. Moreover, those Dasis were like a part of their property. It was a matter of great pride for the master. It is also proved here that the tradition which started in the Rigvedic period for keeping Sudra women as slaves in the houses remained in vogue in later times also.

According to Taitt Bra (III-2-3-9) the Sudras are not eligible for giving a gift pertaining to Yajna. Again, Katyayana Shraut Suttra (VII-105) says that only Brahman kshattriya and Vaishya can participate in Samyajna. Baudhayana Shraut. Suttra XXIV-31. Taittreya Brahman iii-2-3 and 10 and Maitrayani Samhita (code) (VI-1-3) says that no Sudra milk any cow be meant for Agnihotra. From the above examples, it is clear that the Brahman Rishis first of all ousted the Sudras from participation in Yajnas in the name of their holiness and in due course usted them from their personal life also. Later on, the Kshattriyas and Vaishyas also started copying them (Brahmans) and in this way the infectious disease of keeping the Sudras away viz. the 'Untouchability' gradually spread in the society and all corners of the country. All persons started hating the Sudras. The people not only started taboos regarding eating, drinking, having company with them but also were afraid of becoming impure even from their shadows. This was the main reason of this social malady. In this way, the walls of casteism had become stronger that endure even upto this age.

Although the period of the composition of Ramayana is considered to be 300 B.C. and that of Mahabharata between 400 B.C. and 400 A.D.[28] and if these are historic incidents in reality, the period of these events is considered to be earlier than 600 B.C. Therefore. it would be necessary to consider some of the incidents from both of the epics. The principal incident in Ramayana which is mentioned in the Uttar Kand is the murder of Sudras Rishi Shambook by Rama. Shambook Rishi stopped his traditional job and started doing the job fixed for

Brahmans, viz., he started meditation. The Brahmans came to know of this unholy task and consequent upon a particular incident this information was conveyed to Ram Chander Ji and it was also informed that the divine wrath like the unusual incidents of the death of the son of a Brahman before the eyes of his parents in his Ram Rajya will come to an end only when the Sudras stop doing the jobs fixed for Brahmans. As a result of this Ram Chander ji entrusted the administration of his kingdom to his brothers and himself set out for the search of such a sinful Sudra. After a thorough search, he found a Rishi in a dense forest who had hung himself upside down on the branch of a very big tree in meditation. On enquiry, it was found that he was the same Sudra Rishi Shambook who was doing the sinful act and who was a big blot on the white sheet of his Ram Rajya. Lord Rama immediately took his arrow and beheaded him. The gods were happy and started showering flowers from the heaven. He had put an end to a great sin in his Ram Rajya.

One thing becomes quite clear from this incident that upto this period not only the castewise tasks prescribed in the religious books were got enforced in letter and spirit very rigidly but the punishment for their violation was death which had been accepted and enforced by an idealist king himself. In this way, not only the walls of casteism had became stronger but it had also become quite impossible to change the task fixed for every caste.

It would also be proper to mention an incident from Mahabharta: Krishna Dvipayan and a slave women (Sudra) gave birth to a son named Vidur. Though Vidur was the son of an Aryan Kshattriya but he remained a Sudra for all the time because his mother was a Sudra slave woman. This has been mentioned in the epic time and again. He and his descendants could never become Aryans (Kshattriyas). The Brahmanical laws had become so rigid that even if Krishna Dvipayan wanted that his son born of Sudra slave woman may become Kshattriya that was impossible. While his other sons born to Kshattraini were Kshattriya. It is quite clear that even the sovereign Kshattriya kings could not break those walls of division not to speak of common men.

Pre-Mauryan period (600 B.C. to 300 B.C.)

By this period the Aryans had possibly settled up to Magadha in Bihar and in the south up to the hills of Madhya Pradesh. This period is called the period of Suttras when in addition to Grah Suttras and Dharam Suttras the Asht-Adhyayi or Paninis' Vyakaran was composed during this period. According to Kane[29] the period of their composition is from 600 B.C. to 300 B.C. (N.K. Dutta accepts this period from 800 B.C. to 300 B.C.). Sraut Suttras contain method and manners of Yajnas. The Dharam Suttras contain religious customs and rituals whereas Griha Suttras contain rules and regulations pertaining to domestic life. Gautam Dharam Suttra is said to be the oldest one. The land where it was composed is known as Arya vrata. At the end of this very period, the Buddhist religious books in Pali language were also written out of which Dirgha-Nikaya, Majhim Nikaya and

Vinay Pitka are the prominent ones. According to Apastamb Dharam Suttra (1-1-1-6,7), the duty of the Sudra is to serve other three castes. This is the only source of their freedom.

It appears that new duties of the Sudras to serve other varnas had not been prescribed here and only the duties of the early Sudras of servile class have been mentioned.

Apt. D.S. 1-9-27-11 Black castes (Sudras) are opposed to and against the Brahmans.

Apparently the present day like estrangement between two classes was also present during that period. It appears that the Sudras had not yet forgotten their glory of Indus Valley civilization age.

Apt. D.S. 11-10-27-15 If the Sudra vies with the Brahman, he should be whipped.

In Apt. D.S. 11-10-26-15, it has been said that a Sudra who lives by washing the feet of the Brahmans, should not be taxed in any way. Here the washing of feet of the Brahman indicates service with loyalty. Here the kings have been asked to exempt the Sudras from state taxes so that they may be kept engaged in the service of the Brahmans by giving them the allurement of exemption from taxes. From this we can very easily reach the conclusion that upto this period no land or any other form of property was left with the Sudras. If they had any land they would definitely not have been exempted from the payment of taxes in this way. Gautam D.S. X-51 to 59-Sudras should live in a humble way and speak the truth, wash the feet of Brahmans, do service to them and take whatever is given to them by the Brahmans, i.e. old clothes, umbrella, carpet and left over foodstuff etc.

Gaut D.S. X-62 means that the Sudra can make his both ends meet by doing the job of an artisan with the help of tools. Here the composer has referred to those artisan jobs details of which have been given in Chapter 10th, viz. the jobs which the people of Indus valley had been doing since the early ages, such as weavers, copper smith, blacksmiths, potters, goldsmiths and leather workers etc. Here it cannot be said whether the Sudras were permitted to do these jobs in this period.

Ban on Education (Study)

Apt. D. Sut. 1-3-9-6 and 15 and Gaut D.S. XVI-19- Sudras and Chandals should not be caused to hear Ved Mantras. Gaut. D. Sut XII-4, 26- The Sudra deliberately hears the Veda, melted lead should be poured into his ears. If he recites Ved Mantras, his tongue should be chopped off. If he learns Ved Mantras, his body should be cut into two pieces. The Sudra should not learn about the conspiracies (See Chapter 7) hatched against them in the Ved Mantras (Rigveda IV-28-4), that is why there was a complete ban on the hearing and learning of Ved Mantras by the Sudras and the punishment for its violation was death, which is in itself a clear cut evidence. Possibly this was the main reason that the Sudras were not allowed to participate in the Yajna, where Vedic hymns were recited. This later on became the base of caste system and untouchability. Gautam Samhita XX-The teacher who teaches the Sudra will be born as a Sudra in the next life.

According the Majhim Nikaya (1-429), it was mandatory for an archer to declare whether he was a Brahman, Kshattriya, Vaishya or a Sudra.

According to Dirgha Nikaya (1-193), Lord Buddha often used to say during his communications that people expect wise man to tell whether the woman, he loves, is either a Brahman, a Kshattriya, a Vaishya or a Sudra.

These examples clearly show that a man was given respect in accordance with his caste. If he is a Brahman, he was seated on a raised seat. He was served food etc. according to his status. if he was a Kshattriya, he was given respect less than that given to a Brahman and if he was a Vaishya, he was given even lesser respect. In case he was a Sudra, he was shown no respect. In every aspect of life, as on today, distinction was made in the dealings i.e. differential salutation, intimate relationship, eating and drinking and speech etc. had started. It seems that after reaching this stage the caste system had entered into every aspect of human life. The Sudras used to be treated like animals and the walls of casteism became more and more stronger.

In the book entitled, Angutara Nikaya[30] of the Buddhist literature, a mention of 16 famous Kingdoms has been made which were called Maha Janapada. Possibly these were the foremost states to appear on the scene of Indian history about which the historians have got believable evidences. It is a matter of inquisitiveness that a majority of these states. were the kingdoms of Non-Aryan kings. These states were the following :-

1. **Kashi**

2. **Kosal-** During Budhha's period its capital was Sravasti and prior to that the Saket and Ayodhya.

3. **Anga-** It was located to the east of Magadha (near Bhagalpur) Champa was its capital.

4. **Magadha-** It was in the region of modern Patna and Gaya district. Its capital was Giribrija. Its famous kings before Budha were Brahadratha and his son Jarasandha.

5. **Vajji-** It was a federal kingdom of 8 tribes, of which Videh, Lichchhavi, and Janatrika were the main. It had Vaishali as its capital. In this state the common people resembled the mongols like the Lichchhavis while the upper class people were a mixture of Nordic[31] and broad headed people.

6. **Malla-** Its area was in the mountain slope to the north of Vajji. Its capital was in Kusinara and Pava.

7. **Cheti or Chedi-** It comprised of modern Bundelkhand area near Yamuna. Its capital was Suktimati Nagar.

8. **Vats-** Its capital was in Kosambi which was built by king Nichachhu

after Hastinapur was washed away in floods. Buddha's contemporary king was Udayan.

9. **Kuru-** Its area was round about Delhi. Major cities were Indraprastha and Hastinapur. The political value of Kurus was equal to nil.

10. **Panchal-** Its area was modern Ruhelkhand and middle of Doaba. Its capitals were Ahichhattra and Kampila.

11. **Matsya-** Its area was to the west of Yamuna and south of Kurus, its capital was Virat Nagar (Virat in Jaipur).

12. **Sursen-** It was a Yadava Kingdom of Mathura.

13. **Asaka-** Its area was near Godavari and capital was Potali.

14. **Avanti-** It comprised western Malwa area and its capital was Ujjain.

15. **Gandhara-** Its area was in east of Afganistan and its capital was in Taxila.

16. **Kamboj-** Its region was in north west India and Dwarika and Rajpur were their main cities.

In the following paras we will give a detailed account of Lichchhavi, Vajji, Kosala and Maghadha Kingdoms because these were certainly the Kingdoms governed by non-Aryan kings.

Lichchhavi: There are many forms of Lichchhavi, Lechchhavi, Lechchhaha, and Nichchhavi.

The word Lichchhavi is often found in the Pali books. The Lichchhavi form is found in the Kautilya Arthshastra. The Banga commentator Kullook Bhatta has written the word Nichchhavi. In the fifteenth century there was similarity in the words, 'N' and 'L' of Banga alphabet hence the word 'Ni' was read in place of word 'Li'. On the seals of Chandra Gupta first, the word Lichchhavya [32] is found which is used as plural.

In the context of the similarity of old system of justice of Vaishali and the system of Justice in Modern Lhasa, we can say that the Tibetians learnt all these traditions and their religion from the Lichchhavis, who conquered Nepal in the middle age and settled there and proceeded further and conquered Tibet and also settled there. We know very little about the Tibetian civilization pertaining to the ancient Budha period. we learn this from the Lichchhavi traditions found from the Tibet and Pali literature.

Manu (X-22) says that Jhalla, Malla, Lichchhavi, Nat, Karan and Dravids originated from Rajanya Vratya*

---

*Highlighting Vratya, Vasudev Sharan Aggarwal (Panini Kalin Bharat P 95) writes- 'Vratyas were the people who made their livelihood by resorting to looting etc. and had settled on the borders of Aryavrat since ancient times. They were called Vratya. During the time of panini, these persons were considered to be outside the caste system of Hindu society the Brahman, Kshattriya and Vaishya. Vratyas were considered to be alike Sudras. He further writes at page 453 Vratyas were like those fighting castes who had a confrontations with the Aryans and who made their livelihood by looting etc. In Mahabharata the inhabitants of Dardabhisar and Darda Janpada have been called Vratya (Dronaparav 93/44) The particular word 'Vraten Jeevit Vrataen' has been proved. (5/2/21). Here Vratya means Utsedh or looting etc.

It is clear that the Vratyas were originally Sudras out of the Aryan society, who lived by looting etc. who had lost their original land in confrontation with the Aryans and started living out of borders of Aryavarta.

The Indian people particularly the Brahmans do not consider foreigners even as Vratyas.

We know that Nabhag and his descendants were declared Vaishya because Nabhag had married a Vaishya girl in defiance of the orders of Rishis, though the girl had Kshattriya blood flowing in her veins. She did not reveal her identification at the time of marriage but when her husband tried to hand over the throne to his son Bhalnandan then the Vaishya girl revealed her identity as to how she belonged to the Kshattriya dynasty. His son Bhalnandan also could not be considered as Kshattriya because he was considered to be degraded being the son of a Vaishya. Therefore, from the beginning of the Vaishali kingdom, some kings of this dynasty were considered to be degraded or Vratya in the eyes of the Brahmans and their descendants used to be known as Vratya Kshattriyas. But Lichchhavi people were the prominent leaders of non-Brahman society, Jains and Buddhists.

Relation of Lichchhavis with Mongols

The horrible custom of exposing [33] the dead bodies to be devoured by the wild animals was common to Vaishali and Tibet when the Baudhisattya (Gautam) was at Vaishali, he is said to have observed a cemetery under a clumps of trees and to have questioned the Rishis who explained:

"In that place the corpses of men are exposed to be devoured by the birds (Vultures) and there also they collected and piled up the white bones of dead persons as you perceive. They cremate dead bodies there also and preserve the bones in heaps. They hang the dead bodies also from the trees, some were buried there also which have been slain or put to death by their relatives, dread lest they should come to life again, whilst others are left there upon the ground so that they may return if possible to their former homes". Whatever idea or belief may have been but it certainly proves that the ancient inhabitants of Vaishali disposed off their dead sometimes by exposure, sometimes by cremation and sometimes by burial. The tradition is supported by the discoveries made at prehistoric cemeteries in other parts of India, which disclose various methods of disposing off the dead. Similar tradition was in vogue in Tibet during the ancient period and it is in this way proved that the people of Vaishali were Mongols.

Vajji

These Lichchhavis[34] possibly may be the Richchhas of the epics and Puranas who were often mountainous and lived in the valleys of Nepal and Tibet. The word Lichchha is a corrupt form of Richchha (totemism). The people of this dynasty used to be called 'Lichchhai' or 'Lichchhavi'. word Richchha also means a bear or a star. During the ancient times this word was also used for a ferocious animal like lion. Lion denotes power, that is why the Lichchhavis selected the lion as the sign on their flag, which was also adopted by the Sisunagas and Guptas in due course. Lanka (Ceylon) was also named after the name of 'Singh' (Vijay Singh) as Sinhal. In ancient times, during the reign of King Trinbindu the people of Vaishali had made Ceylon their colony. Even Lord Mahavira, who was born in Lichchhavi family, also adopted Lion (Singh) as his insignia. This proves that Vajjis are from the dynasty of 'Richchha'. In the plot the Lichchhavis have been described to be quarrelsome. But the corrupt name of Varjin may be 'Varji', and not 'Vriji'. The form which is often found. They are called Varjin or Vajji possibly for the reason that they decorated their hair in a special style. The hair of a lion are beautiful and curly. May be that the Vajji people decorated their hair in that manner. It may be mentioned that the Vajji people were nomade cow herders whose totemism was Richchha or Kesari, their description has been given in Ramayana. Lichchhavis were certainly non Aryans[35].

Kosal and Magadha Kingdoms

The sixteen Janpadas of seventh century B.C. or possibly one century earlier as a result of their mutual war fares, were amalgamated and had left only four major Janpadas by the end of the sixth century or the fifth century B.C, out of which two powerful tribal oligarchical Janpadas were Lichchhavi or Vajji (nomade cow herders) and malla. Both of these tribes had a tribal administration board or committee, which was very famous for justice and equality and had a whole time military service. Both these Janapadas had Kosal kingdom in north-west and Magadh kingdom in south-east and both had monarchical systems of government and had tribal Janapadas like other Janapadas. Kosal was the oldest and the most powerful state of the 6th century B.C.

According to Kosombi," The sixth-century kings of Magadha and Kosala met most of the requirements. Both were of low birth, without tribe or tribal assembly to restrain them. The principal king of Magadha was Bimbisara, who ruled from 543-44 B.C. to 492-91 B.C. The Magadhan Bimbisara's lineage is not given in pali records, but the Sanskrit Puranas ascribe him to the Sisunaga line. Certainly, the royal house and dynasty ended as Sisunagas about ten generations later. The termination Naga for the name would be impossible in Vedic usage; here it should indicate aboriginal blood, or at least aboriginal culture. The Brahman records speak of the dynasty with contempt as the lowest of Kshattriyas, Kshatra-bandhu, which means at any rate that they paid scant attention to Vedic customs, except an occasional Yajna for victory. Indeed, the most prominent pre-Buddhist shrine at Rajgiri (Maniar Math) was dedicated to some Naga Cults and maintained its character through the centuries till the place was deserted. Bimbisara of Magadha had the special epithest Seniya, with an army. This indicates that he was the earliest king to have a regular standing army unconnected with any tribe.

The Kosalan Pasenadi claimed descent from King Ikshvaku of Vedic fame; but the claim was not admitted in his own time and place. When he asked for a Sakyan girl in marriage, the demand embarrassed the Sakyans, though he held powers of life and death over them and they, too, claimed descent from the same King Ikshvaku. Ultimately, they cheated the monarch by sending the lovely Vasabha-khattiya, daughter of Mahanama Sakya by a slave woman Nagamunda. The mother's name again shows aboriginal birth. The deceit was later exposed, but the son of this union, Vidudabha, remained heir-apparent. Pasenadi's chief queen Mallika was daughter of a flower gardener, hence technically of low caste; but even the eastern caste system was not very rigid at the time, except for some Brahmans.

Pasenadi went a step beyond Bimbisara in creating a new office of commander-in-chief, Senapati, for his son and heir, who is always referred to as Vidudabha-senapati. No Senapati (Lord of the army) is known before him. The king had, like the earlier tribal chiefs, personally to lead and manage the army. However, the Malla Bandhula had virtually held supreme command over the Kosalan army and was treacherously murdered at Pasenadi's orders under suspicion of wanting to usurp royal power. This was an error of judgement, especially as Bandhula's nephew Digha Karayana was allowed to retain the senior ministerial office. This minister was undoubtedly the master of state craft referred to as Dirgha (long) Carayana in Sanskrit (Not only is such change of pronunciation attested in other cases e.g. Asoka's queen Kaluvaki for Caruvaci, but the Kashmirian Kṣhemendra actually gives the name as Carayana in his Buddhist narrative poem Avadanakalpalata). For the time being, however, neither Kosala nor Maghadha provoked a war. Both kings were of relatively unaggressive temperament; both patronised the new religious philosophers with pleasure. They are reported as being close friends and admirers of the Buddha, but also as generous supports of all major sects of the time, including a few Vedic Brahmans. There was even a marriage alliance, for Pasenadi's sister was Bimbisara's chief queen and some accounts make his daughter wife to Bimbisara's son. However, both armies were in constant action against forest savages and perhaps small Aryan tribes ; both kings performed costly Yajnas for victory in battle. That they gave away entire villages in priestly fee has been mentioned. Vivid descriptions remain of the misery and dismay of the peasantry when innumerable beasts were requisitioned - without payment, of course- for the royal fire sacrifices. Thus, the leading kings were not yet entirely free of the Vedic malpractices which no longer suited the new class society.

The first step towards the inevitable conflict was taken by Ajatasatru, son of Bimbisara. This prince, undoubtedly with some unreported theoretician of statecraft behind him, imprisoned his own father and eventually had the aged ...

good-natured Bimbisara starved to death in the dungeon. Even so the Buddhists, though shuddering at the parricide, admit that Ajatasatru was a just and able ruler; we have noted that he appears as a philosopher-king in a major Upanishad. Pasenadi's reaction was to rescind the gift of a village in the Kasi Janapada which had formed part of his sister's dowry. This was too valuable to be surrendered, a bridgehead for Magadha across the river from which both the Ganges and a branch trade route could be blockaded. The Magadhan hold upon the Janapada was retained in a series of battles, all won by Ajatasatru. The Kosalan side was not slow in countermoves. The Chief Minister, Digha-Karayana, handed over the royal insignia in his keeping to Vidudabha, who already controlled the army and was promptly installed as king. The aged Pasenadi, deserted by all except one servant woman, fled for refuge to his nephew. The gates of Rajgiri were closed for the night when the royal fugitive arrived; before they opened the next morning. Pasenadi had died of exhaustion outside the walls of the Magadhan capital. Ajatasatru gave a sumptuous funeral to his uncle's corpse and had a claim therefore to the throne of Kosala."

The lineage of Magadha kings is on the one hand available in the Puranans and on the other it is available in the articles of sinhal, but the two differ from each other.

In Puranas	**In Sinhal articles**[36]
1. Sisunaga	1. Bimbisara (in 543 B.C. he was enthroned at the age of 15)
2. Kak Varna	2. Ajatshatru
3. Kshem Dharman	3. Udayan or Udayadhra
4. Kshemjit	4. Anurudha
5. Bimbasara	5. Munda
6. Ajatshatru	6. Naga Dasak
7. Darshak	7. Sisunaga
8. Udain	8. Kalashok
9. Nandi Vardhana	9. Thereafter ten kings but the main was Nandi Vardhana
10. Mahanandin	

Affinity of Indus Valley Culture in the captial Girvrija (Rajgiri) of Jarasandha and Bimbisara

Rajgriha was the capital of non-Aryan famous king of Mahabharata Jarasandha who had, after his son-in-law Kansa was killed, fought a battle with Krishna. Rajgriha had other names Girivrija, Vrahadrathpur, Kusagrapur and Magadhpur. This vast city and fort was located in the middle of five mountains name Bainbhara, Pandav (Vipulgiri), Vipulaya (Ratnagiri), Girdharkut (Udaigiri), and Rishigiri (Sonagiri).[37]

The city of Rajagriha was laid after the principles of fairly advanced town-planning. It was surrounded by a 10 feet high and 16 feet thick boundary wall of uneven block of stone, each block about four feet long. The wall connected the crests of all the five adjoining hills encircling the valley for a length of about thirty miles. Above the wall (rampart) was raised a superstructure of smaller stones or bricks. Solid rectangular bastions of the same material about 50'x 40' in plan, strengthened the wall at irregular intervals. Stairs and ramps were built in the thickness of the wall, along its inner face, in order to give access to the top which accommodated soldiers for defensive purposes. Helmet, breast-plate, armour, hand guard and thigh guard made of iron and bronze as well as bow, arrow, sword, shield, axe and lance, etc. equipped the soldiers in defending the city.

The wall all round had 32 large and 64 small gates. More important gates contained very heavy doors of stone slabs. The slabs were joined together by strong iron clamps both vertically and horizontally. Other gates had lighter doors of stone or of wood strengthened by metal plates. The larger gates were spanned by lotus-petal shaped, strong arches flanked by tall Watch-Towers of statley proportion. The smaller gates were supported by thick stone lintels over Corbels. Several Watch-Towers are yet to be seen adjoining the hills. One of them, situated at a place 250 feet above the bed of the Banaganga rivulet is known as 'Jarasandha-ka-Baithak'. The Baithak was composed of huge undressed stones piled one upon the other and is now seen about 50 feet square and 28 feet high. This Baithak and the fort of Rajgriha, according to Fergusan, are the specimens of the first archietcture after the Indus Valley culture, in which stone and burnt bricks have been used.

According to Chatterjee Girivrija has been mentioned in Ramayana and during the Mahabharata period it was administered by Jarasandha and Vrahadratha. The period of the splendour and prosperity of Girivraja was the period of Bimbisara (519-491 B.C.). The city of Rajagriha was constructed after (Just like the cities of Indus Valley) the principles of advanced town planning. There were streets made of beautiful stone. Water supply and drainage were regulated in an efficient manner. The drains along the roads and streets were covered with big slabs of stone. Main holes were provided for cleaning purposes at small distances. The court was constructed on a high basement having many high stone pillars. Underneath the kings' palace, there were apartments with fountains. There were high water tanks made of stone, which provided water to the swimming pools and baths for the royal family. The female apartments had beautiful gardens with different types of flowers. There was a zoo for the members of the royal family, which had enclosures for lions and other animals and cages for birds. The palace had a theatre, an Akasakaksha (sky parlour). The stucco-plastered walls of the parlour were so highly polished as to reflect the image of the queen Maha Kaushala Devi. In the palace, there was a chamber for the summer season called 'Samundra-grih' in which lotus flowers of various types bloomed. There were10-12 storeyed beautiful houses inside and outside the royal palace.

The city had beautiful markets. There were rest houses for staying merchants coming from outside.

The striking remains of 'Manihar Math', associated with the 'Mani Naga' of pre-historic significance, have been found in an excavation in the heart of the ancient city of Rajagriha. It is said that the royal treasure of some mythical king was stored in a well adjoining the 'Math' and the Naga king 'Manikara Naga' was enshrined there in order to guard the same. There is a tradition that the 32 queens of King Srenika (Bimbisara) used to take their morning bath and worship the same god. This serpent worship is a clear cut proof to the fact that kings of Magadha were non-Aryans[38]. Mr. Chatterjee[39] writes further : "In the 4th century B.C. Avanti (Malwa) with its capital Ujjayini formed an integral part of the Magadha empire. It was situated on the highway of the latter's commercial enterprise with Egypt and Babylon through Broach and Surparaka i.e. Sopara (near Bombay), while Magadha's communication with the outer world by land-route passed through Gandhara.

It is believed that through Gandhara and Malwa, Magadha had connection with the earlier pre-Vedic civilization of the Indus valley extending from Sind to the Punjab. Excavations at Pataliputra, Rajagriha and elsewhere in Magadha of the old have very seldom exposed any antiquity which can distinctly be termed Vedic, Buddhistic or Jain. On the other hand, the finds include a large number of terracotta female figurines, male terrocotta and demoniac figurines and animal models. The figurines suggest that the cult of sakti with the worship of Siva and Sakti (Matrika) prevailed in Magadha also in the same way as those among the finds of Mohenjo-Daro and Harappa indicate. Even though certain minor figures and female deities like Diti, Aditi (Ambika) and Prithvi of the Vedic pantheon have been unearthed in the excavations of Magadha. It has been proved conclusively that non-Vedic pre-Aryan elements, descendants of the primitive people of the Palaeolithic and the Neolithic Ages, abounded in and dominated that remote age of Magadha. Animism and Saktism controlled the bulk of the Magadhis as they did with the people of the Indus Valley 5000 years age. Every hill, every river, every tree, every household and individual had protective deities (Araksa Devata). The Mahabharata mentions about two Naga, Mani Naga and Svastika, in Girivrja. The Manihar Math, excavated by the Archaeological Department, is said to be the shrine of the same Mani Naga in the heart of Rajagriha. But its architecture indicates later construction. The Yaksha of Shiva protected Sitavana."

Now it can explicitly be said that for quite a long time Magadha remained under the rule of non-Aryans and the Vedic Brahman culture was kept at an arm's length there. They were the descendants of the great people of the Indus valley, who had overthrown the Brahman authority and had established their complete authority, who have repeatedly been referred to as demons (Rakshas) in the epics and a feeling of terrible enmity has been expressed against them. Here, there are two points which come up before us - The Indus valley people who overthrew the Brahmanic authority of Aryans and challenged them time and again and the successfully clashed with them, are referred to as Rakshasas (demons) in the Brahman granths and secondly those who accepted their authority and surrendered to them, were included in the fourth varna and declared Sudras and were made their slaves to serve them.

Nanda dynasty

Mahapadam was the first king of this dynasty. Puranas say that this king ruled for 28 years but on the other hand the Sinhalook writing put the entire period of rule by this dynasty to be 22 years. The rule came to an end in 322-21 B.C. According to Puranas the first king of the Nand dynasty was Mahapadam or Mahapadampati, the word which means - owner of limitless or boundless army. According to the Mahabodhi Bansa the name of the king was Uggarsain, according to the Puranas, he was the son of the last king of the preceding dynasty and was born of a Sudra woman. On the other hand, the Jain religious books have described him as the son of a barber born of a Ganika. Curtious (Crindle's Invasion of India P 220) has written that in fact his father was a barber who used to make both ends meet in one way or the other with his meagre income but he became the favourite of the queen on account of his attractive personality and became the confident of the king due to the influence of the queen but later on he deceived the king and brutally murdered him and gained control over the entire authority on the pretext of patron of the princess and later murdered the princess also and became a king himself. The present kings are his descendants.

The slain king about whom Curtious has mentioned seems to be Kakvarna Kalashok and according to Buddhist traditions his sons who were nine or ten in number were deprived of all authority by Uggarsain Nand. This royal family had boundless army and huge wealth about whom all the books have made a mention. According to classical authors the last king of the Nand dynasty had 20 thousand cavaliers, two lakhs infantry, two thousand four-horse chariots and about three thousand elephants which were kept deployed for the protection at all the entry points of the country. Diodorus and Plutarch (Crindle's Invasion of India, p 222-23) had put the number of elephants to be 4 and 6 thousand. Plutarch has put the strength of the army of the kingdom in the Ganges plain to be 20 thousand horses, two lakhs infantry, eight thousand chariots and 6 thousand elephants.

Shastri Shri Neelkanth[40] draws a picture of the wealth of Nanda dynasty and says : "The number of successor princes of the first Nanda king is available as 8. It is said that out of them the eighth prince (Dhan Nand) was addicted to amass wealth and he had wealth worth 800 million (80 koti). He had got dug a rock at the bottom of river Ganges in order to conceal his wealth. He again amassed wealth by imposing tax on animal hides, gum, trees and also stones and concealed that wealth in the same manner. This detail has been taken from the commentry on the Sinhal writings and it can be considered to be historical to some extent.

The famous Chinese traveller Hieun-tsang of the seventh century has described about 5 treasures of king Nanda which consisted of seven types of valuable jewels (Vetter's II p 296). In this way it is proved from many sources that the royal family of Maha Padam Nanda had vast wealth, boundless armed forces with the help of which Maha Padam Nanda made armed victories in the north, west, south and east and almost all the Kshattriya kings of that time were destroyed by him. That is why he has been termed as 'Sarv Kshattra hantak' or the second Parshurama in the Puranas, who destroyed all the Kshattriyas. The kingdoms conquered by him are Ikshvaku, Kuru, Panchala, Kashi, Sursena, Mithila, Kalinga, Ashmak and Haihaya etc. etc. In this way, the 'Nandas' established the first vast and omnipotent kingdom in the history of India which no one dared to challenge. No evidence is available about the expansion of the boundaries of Magadha state. According to some historians this kingdom consisted of valley of Ghaggar-Haksh in the north, Godavri river and Kalinga in the south, Anga in the east and some part of Rajasthan in the west."

According to the compiler of Brahad Katha, in the reign of Nanda, Saraswati and Laxmi both blessed Patliputra which means that Patliputra had become the home for both the education and material prosperity. Varsh, Upvarsh, Panini, Katyayan, Varruchi, Vyadi and Udbhatta were the scholars of this period.

According to some grammarians, the kings of this dynasty stabilised the scales for measure and weight (Nand pakramni Manani). According to rock inscriptions of elephant caves, Mahapadamanada got the canals dug for irrigation purposes. The achievements made by the great kings of Kosala and Magadha on the historical screen are as follows :

1. Bimbasar first of all set up regular and permanent army in the history of India.

2. Pasenadi first of all created the office of Commander prior to this the duty of a commander was performed by the kings themselves.

3. Well organised economic system on the pattern of Indus valley was set up during this very period. Commercial and Artisan's guilds came up. The coins were first of all circulated bearing punch marks of the Indus valley alphabet. The units of coins and weights were based on the units of Indus valley (see chapter 10 Pani).

4. A vast state exchequer was set up first of all in the history of India, a powerful army was organised, an empire having vast area was first of all set up. The biggest city like Patliputra was set up during that period. The memory of vast long walls and forts of the cities of the Indus valley is freshened when we come to know about the 30 mile long wall around Rajgiri. This great progress resulted in to that the kingdom became the home of education (Saraswati) and prosperity (Lakshmi).

But inspite of all this, the Brahman writers have nowhere said anything in their praise. Neelkanth Shastri writes - It is very surprising that no book pertaining to that period gives any account of the lineage of Nanda only because that was a royal family of non-Aryan Sudras. Had there been any Kshattriya Aryan king like

Nanda, another Mahabharata or Ramayana would certainly have been written in his praise.

The Brahmans and Kshattriyas have always displayed hatred towards them by calling them Sudras, so much so even Porus could not help saying these words to Alexander that Nanda was a low caste born king and his father was a barber. Although the circumstances, their hard labour, courage, fore-sightedness and wisdom made them the emperors yet the Brahmanical law did not make them a Kshattriya from a Sudra.

Sudhakar Chattopadhyaya[41] has rightly written, "Thus we find that in the historical period the Sudras produced a large number of royal dynasties in India, though, according to the strict varna system royalty was the privilege of the Kshattriya class. In the background of the varna system these royal Sudras should be regarded as belonging to the rank of the Kshattriyas, though in the jati mirror they remained Sudras for ever."

This meant that with the change of occupation the varna can be changed and not the jati (caste). It gave rise to such a strict marriage code that a powerful king like Pasenadi could not marry a Sakya Kshattriya girl, who were under his dominion and he was deceitfully married to Vasabh-Khattiya, a daughter of maid-servant Nagamunda. It is quite clear that the walls of caste system had by this time become so stronger and deep rooted that an all powerful king also could not break them.

Maurya period (300 B.C. to 200 B.C.)

Arthshastra of Kautilya is considered to be the principal work of this period. Kane accepts the period of this creation to be from 300 B.C. to 100 B.C. Kautilya and Vishnugupta were the other names of the Brahman Chief Minister Chankya of Chandra Gupta. Some scholars are of the view that Arthshastra was composed at a later stage. This composition contains sources to augment the income of the state exchequer.

Arthshastra II-I

Independent Sudra agriculturists have been mentioned here. Perhaps this tolerance has been shown for the reason that Maurya belonged to a low birth dynasty.

According to Arthshastra III-18, if a low caste's man abuses a high caste man, then he should be given the maximum punishment.

Arthshastra-III-19 : The part of body of Sudra with which he beats a Brahman, should be chopped off.

Arthshastra - IV-13 : If a Kshattriya depraves an insecure Brahman lady, he should be punished for the highest insult, the property of the Vaishya should be forefeited, and if the Sudra does so, he should be burnt alive by wrapping him in a carpet.

It is quite apparent that there were laws of very hard punishment even for the petty offences committed by the Sudras. In comparison with this the Aryans were awarded minor punishments. Not only this, there was a law to enslave the Sudras under all circumstances and contrary to this the Aryans were not allowed to be enslaved.

Arthshastra-III-13 : The Aryans captured in war cannot be made slaves.

It seems that during this period also the walls of casteism were becoming firm and very strong day by day although the emperors of this period belonged to a low caste.

Chandra Gupta Maurya a Sudra emperor

On one side when the Aryans were making all efforts from head to foot for the publicity and expansion of Brahmanism, and caste system, on the other hand coming into power of the non-Aryan Nanda and Maurya was such an unusual incident under those circumstances which possibly did the maximum harm to Brahmanism. It is very much surprising that we do not find any trace of Nanda lineage (dynasty) in any sacred text of that period. There is one clear reason for this that if any such description existed in any text, it was expunged therefrom in due course or the whole creation was destroyed. Patanjali composed the epic 'Maha Nanda' which has been mentioned in the first three Verses of the epic 'Krishna Charit', written by Maharaja Samudra Gupta. But remains confined only to a mention of the above epic uptil today (Sanskrit Sahitya Ka Itihas, page 14, Raj Vansh Sahai Hira).

The above mentioned views have been corroborated by Kosambi[42] also.

A. A. Macdonell[43] also throws light on this subject : "Indeed oral tradition offered a better guarantee for the preservation of the original text than the repeated copying of manuscripts. Thus the hymns of the oldest sacred text, the Rigveda, have been preserved entirely unchanged for 3000 years, whereas later works dating from a period when writings was widely used for literary purposes, have been so much changed, that it has in many cases been critically impossible to restore such texts to their original form".

V.A. Smith[44] has given a fine example of the changes made in the books based on historical facts,as such, "The Nandas were well known as better enemies of Brahmans and that is why the period of their rule was excluded from the historical chronology by the 12th century poet Chandra, who used the Ananda (without Nanda) Vikram Samvat, from which 90 years of Nanda's reign were excluded. In this way, the period of Ananda Vikram Samvat was prescribed to be ordinary Samvat minus 90 years." It is clear that where the non-Aryan royal dynasties were removed from the history by the conspiracies of Brahmans, tempering with the records of historical facts of such royal families cannot be ruled out.

Keeping in view the above facts we must discuss the social origin of Chandra Gupta, the founder of Maurya empire. Most of the historians have tried to prove that he belonged to an ordinary poor family (may be an Aryan) or a Kshattriya family. However, there are clear evidences that Chandra Gupta belonged to a non-Aryan Sudra family.

Sources of origin of Mauryas

The sources about the origin of Chandra Gupta can be divided into two parts :

1. Foreign
2. Indian

The foreign can be divided into four parts -

1. Greek
2. Chinese
3. Sinhalook
4. Burmese

The Indian sources can be divided into the following five parts -

1. Puranas and commentators
2. Buddhist literature
3. Jain literature
4. Mudra-Rakshasa play
5. Kashmiri writings

Foreign sources

Writings of Magasthenes of Greece are principal amongst the foreign sources. The original articles which were written by Magasthenes are not available today, but the later writers have quoted him in their writings. They are Strabo, Diodorus, Pliny, Arrian, Plutarch (Life of Alexander), Justin and Curtius.

1. Curtius: The views of Curtius have been expressed in the foregoing pages in which Porus told Alexander that the modern king (Emperor Nanda) was originally not only an ordinary man but also of a very mean nature. In fact his father was a barber, who had impressed the queen with his handsomeness and as a result there of he established close relationship with the king. At one occasion he deceptively murdered the king and later on became the patron of the princess and deceitfully himself became the king. Later he also murdered the princess.

2. Diodorus : Porus had told Alexander that the king of Gangaridai (Nanda) was a man of low character, who commands no respect in the society because he was considered to be the son of a barber.

3. Plutarch : Androkotus (Chandra Gupta) had himself met Alexander when he was a young boy and had informed him that he (Alexander) can very easily establish his authority over the whole of the country because the then king was being looked down upon because of his low birth.

4. Justin- India after the death of Alexander who with the power of its yoke had shaked the neck, had died. Chandra Gupta was a leader who got it liberated from the paws of Greek power. He was born in very pitiable circumstances, whom a fearful man had led to the royal throne. He had disappointed Nandras (Alexander) with his misbehaviour, who ordered his murder but he hurriedly fled away. :Smith (page 123) has derived the meaning of Nandras as Nanda.

Radhakumud Mookerji [45] has given his own views about the above four quotations that in the first two only the origin of king Nanda has been described. In the fourth citation Justin has described the origin of Chandra Gupta as pitiable and not low. But according to Plutarch the remarks by Chandra Gupta himself that origin of Nanda was low, proves that he himself belonged to a high caste.

Such a view has also been given by certain other scholars also but this author is not prepared to accept it because Diodorus has given the name of the leader who met Alexander as Phegus and Arian says his name was Phegela[46]. By the name Phegelas, Justin has derived the meaning 'Bhagela', one who runs away[47]. Therefore, it is not proper to accept the name of that leader Sandrokotes as Chandra Gupta. The word Phegela or Phegu appears to be a Sanskrit word. Bhagla, which was the name of a royal family of Kshattriya caste has been mentioned in Ganpatha[48].

Another reason can also be given for this Suppose what ever Plutarch has said is correct, that Phegela was none else but Chandra Gupta or Chandra Gupta had met him. As there was a bitter enmity of Chanakya with Nanda kings, similarly Chandra Gupta had more enmity with that family. Not only a conspiracy was hatched against him to deprive him of the kingship, because he was the son of king from maid servant (Dasi), attempts were also made to kill him. It is said that when he fell into the clutches of Chanakya, he was an innocent child of 7-8 years whom Chanakya provoked against his father Nanda throughout his life and called him mean, born of a low caste, which changed his way of thinking. It is quite evident from the history of the world that the greed for power has caused the murders of thousands of fathers and brothers and in the similar madness if Chandra Gupta has termed Nanda as mean and of low birth then it would not be a strange thing. It is quite clear that the above logic of the scholars is not so strong as to reach a conclusion easily. It seems that the Greek writer must have made the basis of his writings, the stories, concocted by the Brahmans during those days.

Indian sources

According to Kashmiri texts there were two Nandas (1) Purva Nanda stated to be the father of Chandra Gupta (whereas his father is named as Nanda in the Mudrarakshasha): (ii) Yoga Nanda, father of Harigupta (R.K. Mookerji, P 13). The following conclusion can be derived from the Puranas : (1) that the Nanda kings were base-born, and had inaugurated unrighteous and unlawful Sudra rule which the Sastras do not approve, (2) that it remained for a militant Brahman, the redoubtable Kautilya, as the custodian and upholder of Dharma, to rid the country of its usurpation by Sudra rulers and restore it to the lawful rule of the Kshattriyas, and (3) that, after accomplishing this mission of his life by uprooting the race of Nandas, Kautilya chose Chandragupta for the throne to which he was consecrated by the performance of the ceremony of abhisheka or anoinment prescribed for royalty. R.K. Mookerji[49] is of the view "The formal anointment of Chandragupta to sovereignty by an orthodox Brahman of unbending strictness, a master of the Sastras and an uncompromising champion of Dharma, like Kautilya, is a positive proof that the man of his choice must have been one of noble lineage, a Kshattriya who was eligible for kingship."

But This view of Mookerji is not acceptable due to following reasons that the writer should have made a thorough study of all the incidents before reaching this conclusion. Chanakya or Kautilya was appointed the president of that royal institution of the Nandas who respectfully used to give food and donation to the Brahmans. It is quite clear that in those circumstances Chanakya had no malice against Nanda being a Sudra king, otherwise he would neither have become the president of the royal institution nor accepted the donation and remuneration by yielding to the authority of King Nanda. In fact Chanakya had become the bitter enemy of Nanda family when king Nanda insulted him for his physical ugliness and under those circumstances Chanakya selected Chandra Gupta to take the revenge. Because there could be no other bitterest enemy of Nanda other than Chandra Gupta, when conspiracies were being hatched for murdering him or depriving him of royal authority. Chanakya was in need of any such terrible and bitter enemy to take revenge and there was no question of a Sudra or non Sudra. It is evident from the above facts that Chanakya had no grudge or feelings against Nandas of being Sudra and such a feeling has never been shown anywhere else.

S.R. Goyal[50] has also expressed identical views, that Magadha has always produced unorthodox (Asanatani) emperors. Here the word Kshattriya means a professional soldier which can also be a non-Aryan.

It appears that writings which contained historical facts of that period declaring Maurya family as Sudra have been wiped out. This view has already been given with evidences in this chapter. In addition to it, the worthlessness of Brahman Puranas have already been proved in chapter IX whose meaningless and absurd utterings and uncontrolled imagination have been used for the achievement of objectives. Therefore, this thing is not proved here that Chandra Gupta was not Sudra or he was not from a low caste.

Buddhist Literature: In Buddhist literature it has been said that 'Nandeen' belonged to an unknown caste. These books have stated that Chandra Gupta belonged to the Maurya family (dynasty) of the Shakya royal family, the same Shakya family, which gave birth to Buddha. It is said that the king Hewas of the Maurya family lost his life also along with his rule. His queen who was pregnant at that time, along with her brother, went to Patliputra to seek help and protection from her relative, Nandas. There Chandra Gupta was born and he ascended the throne of the Last Nanda,[51].

In fact the Jain Granthas have tried to show every great emperor as belonging to the Jain religion and the Buddhist literature has gone ten steps ahead of the Jain literature in this regard and almost every king of that period has been claimed to be Buddhist king or that Lord Buddha had himself met him and the king gave him a most cordial and affectionate treatment. It appears to be a work of imagination to claim that the great king of that period also belonged to the same dynasty to which Lord Buddha belonged. But it is worth noting that here too the mother queen of Chandra Gupta has been said to be belonging to Nanda family.

Jain literature: According to Jain literature, Chandra Gupta was born to the daughter of a villager who looked after the royal peacocks.

Maurya from Mura

Mookerji [52] gives his views on term Maurya derived from the word Mura "The theory of the base birth of Chandra Gupta Maurya was first suggested by the derivation which a commentator was at pains to find for the epithet Maurya as applied to Chandra Gupta by the Puranas. The commentator on the Purana text takes Maurya to be the son of Mura who was one of the wives of king Nanda. Heavens save us from commentators who supplement texts by facts of their own creation. The commentator here makes the astounding statement that Chandragupta was a son of the Nanda king against the silence of all the Puranas on the subject. Such a fact completely militates, against the context of the references which the Puranas make to Chandragupta, as already indicated. It may be noted that if there is any sort of connexion between preceding and succeeding dynasty, the Puranas as a rule do not omit to mention it. For instance, in the case of the Sisunaga dynasty which was succeeded by that of the Nandas, it has been clearly stated that of the ten Sisunaga kings, the ninth was Nandivardhana, and the tenth was his son named Mahanandin, and that, "as son of Mahanandin by a Sudra woman will be born a king, Mahapadma (Nanda) who will exterminate all Kshattriyas, Thereafter, kings will be of Sudra origin (Vishnu Purana IV-24-21). If this history had repeated itself in the case of the Mauryas, and if the first Maurya king were also related to the preceding Nanda king in the same way as the Nanda king was related to the preceding Sisunaga king that history could not have been omitted by the Puranas. It is nothing but a pure and simple invention of the commentator to explain grammatically the formation Maurya from Mura. But he is as innocent of grammar as of any concern for truth. It is impossible to derive by any grammar Maurya as a direct formation from Mura. The derivative from Mura is Maureya. The term Maurya can be derived only from the masculine Mura which is mentioned as the name of Gottra in a Ganapatha to Panini's Suttra (IV I,151). It is strange that the derivation of the term has not been traced by this track. The commentator was more interested in finding a mother than in grammar. The only redeeming feature of the commentator is that not merely is he innocent of grammar and history : he is also innocent of any libel against Chandra Gupta. For he has not stated that Mura, the supposed mother of Chandra Gupta was a Sudra woman or a courtesan of the Nanda king. He is severely silent about her caste, while he describes Mura as lawfully wedded wife of the king. Thus even this commentator of the Purana cannot be held responsible for the theory of Chandra Gupta's low origin."

Undoubtedly, this is more than sufficient to say that, keeping in view laws given in 'Hindu Law Books', no man of high caste can be a rearer of royal pea cocks.

Mudrarakshasa

Now take up Mudrarakshasa. In this play Chandra Gupta has been said to be Kula-hina. In this very drama Chandra Gupta has been said to be the son of Ṇandas, whom all the Scholars regard as Sudra. (II-4)

IṢṬĀTMAJAḤ SAPADI SANVAYA EVA DEVAḤ SHĀRDALAYOT MIVA VAM̃ PARIPUṢYA NAṢṬAḤ,

TAS YAIDHA BUDDHI VISHIKHENA NADYI MARMA, VARMĪBHA VEDYAD INA DAIVAMADRA SHYAMĀNAM (4)

(Meaning)-Rakshasa (says) In case our own destiny, which is against our progress, is not prepared to save him, then it is certain that I would shatter the most vulnerable point of Chandra Gupta with my arrows of sagacity, who was reared like the cub of a wolf and in turn he destroyed, the son lover emperor Nanda and his dynasty (commentator-Satyavrata Singh).

IV-8(Meaning) It is possible that Amatya Rakshasa might have come to the side of Chandra Gupta because of his devotion to the Nanda family and for the protection of his friend thinking that he too belonged to the Nanda family, and Chandra Gupta would embrace him after thinking that he is also Amatya of his forefathers.

Similarly there is a conversation in II-3 and IV-13 which proves that Chandra Gupta was the progeny of Nandas.

But most of the scholars have not accepted this view for they consider the play to be composed at a later date. But V.A. Smith[53] opposing this view writes : "The play Mudrarakshasa gives a very interesting and detailed account of revolution. Scholars used to believe that the play dated from the seventh century...But Hillebrandt, speyer and Tawney affirm it to be much older and certainly earlier to the Panchtantara and Bharatrihari who died in 651 A.D. It is suggested that the play may have been composed in the time of Chandra Gupta II about A.D. 400."

In fact this drama (II-2) gives a detailed account of the celebration of the Kaumudi-mahotsava, a festival which used to be celebrated with great fervour during the early Gupta period. From the description of political manoeuvers given finely, it appears that the composer Vishakhadutta himself may have been a seasoned politician and the political situation during his times must have been such. This period can certainly be the period of Chandra Gupta II, whose stories about political manoeuvers are still very popular in the society. It may be noted that the composer Vishakhadutta, in his short introduction has claimed his father and grand father to be related to some royal family. Some scholars, regard the period of composition of the drama to be earlier than this. Quite possible that the composer may have used imagination to some extent. But by that time the epic 'Mahananda' composed by Patanjali, whose mention has been made in the earliest three verses of the epic 'Krishna charita' (see this chapter's P-284) composed by emperor Samudra Gupta (father of Chandra Gupta II), had not been destroyed in which there may have been a detailed account of the Nanda royal family. Under such circumstances, there remains little chances for imagination when during the time of Vishakhadutta, there was an epic containing the full details about the royal family of Nanda and their end. Atleast there remains no necessity of tempering with the historical facts. Thus we will have to believe that the historical facts given in it are really historical. In fact most of the religious books of Sanskrit only were tampered with during the Gupta period and later on, and only literary books escaped this change. Mudrarakshasa is also one such work.

It is worth noting that some Puranas also accept the above view given in the Mudrarakshasa Chandra Gupta Maurya has been described the progeny of Mahapadam Nanda in Matsaya Purana. In Vayu Purana the Mauryas have been said to be the kings of the Nanda dynasty.

Thus on the basis of Mudrarakshasa, we can conclude that Chandra Gupta Maurya was definitely non-Aryan Sudra King and this is also certain that he belonged to the Nanda dynasty. Other evidences can also be cited to prove it :

A view has already been expressed in Chapter VIII that this fact is more or less certain that the Indian have always been worrying about the-lunacy of caste system and have always been attracted from lower social status to the higher social status and whenever there was occasion every non-Aryan claimed himself to be a Kshattriya or Rajput, but contrary to this no Aryan Kshattriya or a Brahman claimed himself to be a non-Aryan Sudra. It can be concluded from this that whenever there was a controversy about the caste of a particular person or about a particular caste that certainly may have been a non-Aryan Sudra. As an example we can take up the well known controversy of Chhatarpati Shivaji, which has already been mentioned in Chapter VIII. The same thing has happened with Chandra Gupta Maurya also. It is quite strange to note that the every non-Aryan prince has been said to be the son of a Sudra wife (Dasi) of a king, though the king himself may have been a non-Aryan Sudra. Mahapadamnanda has also been said to be the son of a Sudra wife, whereas Sisunagas themselves were non-Aryans. The same thing has been said about Chandra Gupta Maurya that he was from a Sudra wife named Mura of king Nanda. Similar is the case of king Asoka. According to a story given in Divyavadanam (26-Panshupradanam) he was the son of Bindusar from a Barber woman. At the same time he has been said to be the progeny of Nandas. It can be said that all the kings of Magadha were non-Aryans, also the Maurya family. Its name, as there was a tradition of totemism amongst the non-Aryans, was placed after the name of a bird peacock (Mor, Moriya in Pali language) as Maurya (totemism)[54].

In this way, it turns the table of all the above controversy and is proved as a conclusive evidence. Above evidence gets the support of archaeological findings that Asoka got this emblem marked on all the monuments. The Asoka pillar at Nandangarh has been found to bear at its bottom below the surface of the ground the figure of a peacock, while the same figure is repeated in several sculptures on the Great Stupa at Sanchi, which are associated with Asoka on the basis of the stories of his life which these sculptures translate into stone. Both Foucher and Sir John Marshall agree with Grunwedel who was the first to suggest that this representation of the peacock was due to the fact that the peacock was the dynastic emblem of the Mauryas.

Buddhist and Jain literature also support this view of totemism. This fact is clearly proved that the Maurya family was definitely a family of the native non-Aryan blood who belonged to the barber caste[55]. This fact was either ignored in the Brahman compositions of that period or expunged in due course[56].

This fact is also proved on the basis that the top ranking arrangement of administration, urban administrative organisations, organisation of army in a new scientific way, which were made by Chandra Gupta is not found during that age or thereafter of any other Kshattriya Aryan king. This view has been corroborated by Stuart Piggott[57] in the following words:

"The Dark Ages of India in the second half of the first millennium B.C. are suddenly illuminated, round about 300 B.C., by light from the West. Megasthenes a Greek at the court of the first of the great Sovereigns of the Mauryan dynasty, Chandra Gupta Maurya, wrote an objective account of the civilization in which he found himself which has survived in fragments. He presents a picture of a regime which had established control over a large part of Northern India at least: fully literate, urban, highly organised, and ruling from an impressive citadel within a great walled town at Pataliputra on the Ganges. The state is held together by a powerful army, with a war office divided into six departments, dealing respectively with cavalry, infantry, light mobile armour (chariots), heavy armour (elephants), quarter masters stores and maintenance of war engines, and finally liaison with the naval forces. No less elaborately organised is the civil service, which has a ministry of agriculture and public works controlling road construction, irrigation canals, mines, forests, land taxes, and big-game hunting. The city council, subdivided like the war office into six departments, deals with industry, weights and measures, registration of births and deaths, control of state shops, collection of sales tax, and the supervision of the affairs of foreign visitors. There is surely something very familiar in this starting picture of an authoritarian regime, with its power so large a tract of India, the control of manufacturers, and of weights and measures; the elaborate city civilization, with its centralized government. The picture we can reconstruct from the evidence of the Harappa civilization is, after all not so dissimilar. The Mauryan empire may be the result of indigenous evolution of the Aryan tradition, from the humble beginnings in the log cabins of the West to this sophisticated bureaucratic state a thousand years later, but can we ignore altogether the other more ancient, urban tradition of India which the Aryans found? Chandra Gupta Maurya was not a foreigner, no invader such as Babur coming in from the north-west to impose his will on the Indian people, but a product of a long tradition with in India itself, he must have based his rule on long-established Custom, in which was blended the ancient civic tradition of Harappa, with its bureaucracy and mercantile organisation and the more barbarous but invigorating Aryan warrior caste which could make the state strong against its enemies and implant something to offset the fatal tendency to stagnation and decay that had been Harappa's downfall.

Perhaps it would be too much to say that Chandra Gupta Maurya and his dynasty were the ghosts of the Harappa Empire sitting crowned on the ruins thereof, or to claim, in Toynbee's phrase, that the Harappa kingdom was 'apparented' to that of the Mauryas."

From the above facts it becomes quite clear that definitely the rulers of the Maurya Royal dynasty were the great sons of Harappan non-Aryan (Sudras) who once again got an opportunity to rule and took the country out of the ditch and carried it to the skies. But conspiracies continued to be hatched constantly for their destruction. At last as a result of a Brahmanical conspiracy the last emperor of this dynasty Brahadratha was murdered by his own Brahman chief of army Pushyamittra Shunga.

But it is very surprising to note that the great emperors like Chandra Gupta Maurya and Asoka have been insulted by calling them Kula-Hina, Sudra and the son of a barber woman. It is proved beyond doubt that by this time the walls of casteism had become so strong that they had become impenetrable even by the great and powerful emperors like Chandra Gupta and Asoka and as a result of this they had to submit to the Brahmanical set up. They pursued the policy of tolerance by pleasing the Brahmans after giving them donations. But whenever they got an opportunity they made the Jain (Chandra Gupta) and the Buddhist religions (Asoka) as their state religion which were fully opposed to the Brahmanical system as a result of which the Brahmanical set up was destroyed in the society . But in the end this royal family had to inflict a defeat at their hands.

Post-Mauryan period (200 B.C. to 100 A.D.)

We get the maximum information about this period from the Manu Smriti[58]. Manu has named the India of this period as 'Brahamvrata'. This was the period when the star of the Sudra rule of the Maurya's and of Buddhist and Jain religion had gone into the grip of adversity after being in ascendance all of a sudden. Then the Brahman Shunga kings massacred the Buddhists to their hearts' content and the foundation of the Hindu and Brahman rule again became stronger. This was the period when the most famous book of the Hindu code 'Manusmriti' was composed by Mahamuni Manu in which the most stringent laws were framed against the Sudras as a result of which they lost their freedom which they had during the Mauryan empire. They were gripped in the most strong chains of slavery. See the following example-it has been said in Manu Smriti viii-418 that it is the duty of the king to compel the Vaishyas and Sudras to perform their duties otherwise the structure of the whole world will stagger.

Economic code (laws)

Manu X-129-Sudra should not be allowed to amass wealth otherwise he will harm the Brahman.

Manu VIII-417-The Brahman can have the wealth of his Sudra slave with full confidence because he (Sudra) has no right to property.

Manu XI-14-If a Kshattriya is dying of hunger then he cannot take the money of a Brahman but he can take the money of a Dasyu.

Manu VIII-142-The rate of monthly interest should be charged according to Varna i.e. from the Brahman, Kshattriya, Vaishya and Sudra, two, three, four and five per cent, respectively.

Manu VIII-179-The man with whom money is to be deposited, should be an Aryan.

These are the laws (codes) as a result of which the Sudras became most poor. Inspite of the fact that they had been toiling and working very hard constantly they did not get anything as remuneration except left over food stuffs and used clothes. They were barred from becoming owners of land and property because of the fear that they may not become prosperous and equal to them in status etc. This is the only historical reason why in modern age the government is compelled to provide reservation for all Sudras in government services.

Their duty to serve the Brahmans only

Manu X-123 and IX-334-The service of the Brahman is propitious religion of Sudra. Anything else done by him is useless.

Manu VIII-413-Sudra may have been purchased or not, his duty is to serve. He has been created for the service of Brahman.

Manu VIII-414-Even if the master terminates the services of a Sudra, he cannot be relieved of his duties, because this is natural.

Manu X-122-Sudra should serve the Brahmans in order to attain a seat in the heavens or for prosperity in both the worlds. His birth is successful only if he says that he is the servant of such and such Brahman.

The meaning of the second sloka is very clear that God created the Sudras only for service of the Brahmans i.e. the God itself made the law for the Sudras to serve-the Brahmans. According to the last sloka they can find pleasure in the two worlds by serving the Brahman. No need to speak that who will deny to do the duty from the core of his heart in the performance of which one finds so much pleasure and who will revolt against the law (code) which has been enacted by the almighty God. Here Manu has used the third section of his code (see P-191) according to which any body can be made or compelled to become a slave by making him a devotee or showing him the fear of God. This is a unique example of human cleverness of making others one's devotees or slaves we do not find any other example of this type in the world. History bears witness to the fact that in Rome, Egypt and Mesopotamia force had always been used to enslave a particular group or community or persons. In Rome in acncient age the slaves(serfs)were kept chained in hand cuffs and shackles and they were made to work with hoe in the fields in the same position like animal. But here the hand cuffs and shackles which were used for man were invisible and so strong that it seems very difficult to cut them even today after 2-3 thousand years. It can confidently be said that the theory of incarnation was also a part of the same chain (technique). Even today the entire country is devotee of Lord Rama. Not to think of raising a finger against any of his wrong deeds (murder of Shambook and cutting the nose of Sharupnakha) every one (also the non-Aryan Sudras) bows his head on hearing his name. All the historians have in one voice said that this was the spiritual victory of Aryans over the non-Aryans. It is possible that some scholars having colonialistic views may brand my views as exposure or a naked protest of Hindu philosophy and criticise me but the basis of this fact is scientific, just, logical and nothing else but a hard fact.

Entitled to eat only left over food and wear worn out clothes

Manu X-125: Sudras should be given left over food stuffs, old worn out clothes and bedding. Those articles which human beings throw away after use or which become useless, should be given to the Sudras. If this is called the ideal religion (moral) then I fail to understand what should be called as immoral.

Value of life less than even the animals and birds

Manu XI-131: when one has to do penance after killing a cat, mongoose, magpie, frog, dog, ignana, quil, crow, one should do the same penace which is prescribed for killing a Sudra.

Punishment for scurrilous words

Manu VIII-268: If the Brahman uses scurrilous words for a Kshattriya, he should be fined 50 Panas, if uses such words for Vaishya, he should be fined 25 Panas and if he says such words to a Sudra he should be fined 12 Panas. Manu VIII-267- Contrary to this if a Kshattriya says scurrilous words to a Brahman, he should be fined 100 panas and 150 panas if a Vaishya does this. If a Sudra uses scurrilous words to a Brahman he should be fined 200 panas and given physical punishment.

Manu III-271-If a Sudra speaks ill of a Brahman out of enmity, a ten finger long iron nail should be heated and put into his mouth.

Manu VIII-270-If a Sudra speaks unseemly to a Brahman, Kshattriya and Vaishva his tongue be got chopped off because his origin is from a low-caste.

Manu VIII-272-If a Sudra recites religious sermons to a Brahman out of pride, the king should pour boiling oil into his mouth and ears.

Manu VIII-279-The limb of the body with which the Sudra hurts a high caste person, the same limb should be got cut, this is the order of Manu.

Manu VIII-280-If a Sudra has raised his hand or taken a stick to strike at the Brahman, his hand should be got cut and if he strikes with his leg in anger, his feet should be got cut.

Manu VIII-283-If a Sudra out of pride catches hold of a lock of hair on the top of the head (choti). feet, beard, Naar or testicles of a Brahman the king should chop off both of his hands.

Code for doing Sexual intercourse with an Aryan woman

Manu VIII-359-If a Sudra touches the untouchable parts of the body of a Brahman woman, then he should be killed.

Manu VIII-366- If a low-caste man cohabits with a high-caste girl he is liable to be killed. If he is of the same caste, then the father of girl can get him released.

Manu VIII-374- If a Sudra cohabits with a Brahman, Kshattriya or Vaishya woman who is not secure at the hands of her manfolk, the king should get his penis cut and take away all his wealth and if a Sudra cohabits with a woman of these castes who is secure in her house, the king should take away all his wealth and award him capital punishment. Similarly, according to VIII-273 and IX-224, if he tries to change his caste he should be fined 200 panas and death punishment.

It is very well clear from the above that Manu had prevented the mixture of blood by enacting such rigid laws (code). This is the reason that today even after two thousand years the scientists have been able to divide the blood of these two groups into two separate groups 'A' and 'B'. If these codes (laws) had not been framed,the scholars would not have been successful in dividing the Aryan and non-Aryan blood separate (see chapter 14).

The above mentioned examples clearly show that although the duty of the Sudras was to serve the high caste people (Brahmans) with profound devotion and sincerity,they had no rights except that they should wear the worn out clothes and eat left-over food by their Aryan masters. They were not allowed to make money or property, to read and write and change their caste. The punishment for the defiance of these was death sentence or exile.

In this way,the Brahman intellectuals deprived him of all the human rights by hatching a conspiracy against him and they had reduced him to the position of an animal in the form of a human being and as such had enslaved the great sons of Indus valley for ever in the guise of Varna system.

In view of the above codes of Manu , it can be said that during that period the caste system had strengthened its roots very deep and particularly the Sudras had been encircled in so high walls of caste-system that it had become completely impossible for them to come out of them.

Pre-gupta and Gupta period : Period of the composition of smrities (100 A.D.to 500 A.D; Period of changes)

This was the period when the Puranas were rewritten in order to stregthen the caste system from all aspects and these were tampered with. According to Kane[59] Vishnu,Narad,Brahaspati and Katyayan Smriti were composed during this very period and Yagyavalkya is the principal amongst them because its area falls in Northern India. Possibly the area of its composition is Mithila[60]. Later on the religious laws were very rigidly enforced in this very area because the number of tribes and low-castes,the converts of the above tribes was higher around this area and it was utterly necessary to keep the Aryan blood pure from these castes.

According to E.W.Hopkins[61], the Shanti Parva and Anushasan Parva of Mahabharata were also added to this book during this period. Those chapters of Vishnu, Markandeya and Bhavishya Puranas, in which the duties of Varnas have been detailed, appear to be of the Gupta period.

According to Markandeya (25-7-8) and Vishnu Purana III-8-32 the duty of the Sudra is to serve other castes (Varnas).

According to Shanti Parva 60-27 of Mahabharata, Prajapati has created Sudra as the slave of other three castes. (Varnas).

It may be noted that prior to this, the Sudras have been described as the servants of Brahmans only but the authors of this period declared him the servant of the three Varnas, i.e. the whole society.

According to Anushasana Parva (S.E.) 97-29, the Sudras are meant for doing hard work with hands and feet, viz. they are servants or labourers.

Shanti Parva 60-29 the people of the three Varnas should keep the Sudras as attendants or servants.

Vishnu Purana III-8-33-The principal duties of a Sudra are submissiveness, cleaning of latrines or disposal of excrement, loyalty, Yajna without mantras, Asteya-satsang and protection of Brahman.

From the above instances it is very much clear that during this period the Sudras had been bound to firm bonds of those arduous and dirty occupations, the clear glimpse of which we can have in today's life also-he is engaged in the service of the three high Varnas, he is a servant who does the hard work, serves everyone with devotion and carries everyone's excrement over his head.

It has been mentioned in Anushasana Parva(208-33) if there are no Sudras, there would be no body to work.

In this way, all the works required hard work and services were entrusted to the Sudras by this period. Gradually the codes (laws) used to be enforced so stringently that even today their influence does not appear to diminish. Even today we get some news items to read in the newspapers that if a high caste man himself tries to do some work involving hard work (even ploughing of his own land) in Bihar and eastern Uttar Pradesh, he is excommunicated from the community. It is universally known that in some parts of the country even today a high caste man would accept dying of hunger than doing a work entrusted to Sudras or involving hard labour. This is the major reason of poverty, hunger, backwardness and bad luck of the nation. Everyone knows that hard work is the key to success & prosperity but since it is contrary to the religious code, the nation is not prepared to accept it.

It is ordained in Shanti Parva (60-32-33) that the Sudras should use the umbrella, turban, beddings, sheets, shoes, fans and worn out clothes used by high caste people.

The Sudras were given only the above mentioned rights in return for their devoted service and hard labour. Here there is a repetition of Manu Smriti X-125 in which a rule was framed for the Sudras to eat the left over foodstuffs and wear only worn out clothes. These traditions are still in vogue in the society. The poor fellow collects the left over food after a feast, in his utensils to eat later days together. Similarly, when the clothes of a high-caste person are torn to pieces, he gives the same to a Sudra to wear the same. He is, in this way, obliged by his master. This is not an imagination of a poet, but a hard fact which can be seen with one's eyes. Evidently, the caste system in that period had been moulded in such a pattern, whose image can be seen in the present day society as well.

Gupta Emperors non-Aryan Sudras

Before discussing the caste-etc of the Gupta emperors, it would be necessary to know the political and social conditions prevailing in Magadha before the Guptas came to power. The scholars are of the view that before the beginning of that period the Lichchhavis ruled in Magadha for a short period. Before them the foreigners Murundas (Kushanas) ruled there for more than 200 years who left deep influence on the political and social life.

The capital of Kushana empire was Pushap Pur (Modern Peshawar) and they deputed Kshatrap Vanaspar to rule over Patliputra, who was related to the Murunda royal family. This royal family was an ardent follower of the Buddhaist religion and terribly opposed to Sanatan Dharma. Patliputra (Magadh) remained under the rule of the descendants of Mahakshatrapa Vanaspar for a longer period even after Ganga-Yamuna Valley got independence from the Kushana rule. There were 13 kings of this dynasty who ruled Patliputra. We get following information about Vishwaphani from various Puranas. According to Bhagwat Purana (XII-1-36-37) the king of Magadh would be Vishvaphurti. He would be called Puranjaya the second in addition to the earlier Puranjaya. He would convert the high castes like Brahman etc. to Pulinda, Yadu, Madra, Mlechchha castes. He would be so wicked that he would protect the Sudras and destroy the Brahmans, Kshattriyas and Vaishyas and will up root the Kshattriyas with his wisdom and force. According to Vayu Purana (VI-236-237) he will protect Kaivartas, Panchakas, Pulindas and

Brahmans. According to Vishnu Purana (IV-24-61,62) the king of Magadha named Vishwaphatik will introduce other castes and give kingdom to Kaivartas, Pulindas and Brahmans.

Evidently Vishwaphani finished the high caste Kshattriya kings and made the low-caste people like Kaivaratas, Panchakas, Pulinds and Thanvas etc. political chiefs and created a new ruling class out of the Sudras. He also patronised the Brahmans along with the Sudras. It is very much clear that during this period, on one side where the Sudras made some progress, the Brahmans also made the roots of Hindu religion strong taking shelter and power on the other. It appears that the Murunda kings were opposed to the Hindu religions but they continued to hit the Kshattriyas in place of Brahmans (actual root)out of misunderstanding.

Now we take up the origin of the biggest royal family of the Guptas of that period. In fact, the origin of this royal family is also very controversial because the Guptas have nowhere written in any of their writings about their caste and sub caste etc. Whereas the daughter of Chandra Gupta II and the queen of Vakataka king Rudrasen II, Prabhavati has mentioned her sub caste as 'Dharna' on copper plate of Poona[62]. Now because the sub caste of her husband was VishnuVridha we can conclude from this that Dharna was the sub caste of her father, i.e. the Gupta royal family. S.R.Goyal[63] has put forward the views of Dasharath Sharma, "According to Skanda Purana (Brahma Kanda 35-37), Brahmans of Dharna sub caste lived in Dharmaranya in the Mirzapur region. It proves that the Guptas, who belonged to eastern Uttar Pradesh, were Brahmans. But Mr. Sharma has shown a little belief in the view expressed by Jaiswal that the Guptas were related to the Jats of Punjab (Dharni is the Sub caste of a Jat family in Amritsar District). Now he believes that either the Guptas were Kshattriya or Vaishya because they had possibly accepted the Brahmans of Dharna sub caste as their Guru (Family priest) and as per Tradition they adopted their sub caste also. But this is only a view and nothing more than that."

In the play 'Malvikaginimitra', composed by Kalidasa, the great poet of Sanskrit language, the queen of the king Agnimitra of the Shunga dynasty has been mentioned as 'Dharini'. At the same place her brother Virsen has been said to be belonging to a low caste (Varna varo- Bhrata) who was appointed a incharge (Kiledar) of a fort located on the borders of the Shunga empire on the banks of Mandakani (Narmada). From the Prabhavati's writings of the copper plate of Poona, it is proved that during the ancient times, there was a tradition of separately identifying the various queens of a harem by calling them by their parental Gottra. So it is quite evident that 'Dharana' was the Gottra of a Sudra family. Similarly, the various theories based on the interpretation of the word 'Gupta' do not appear to be very convincing. This word reminded Allan of Chandra Gupta Maurya, who, according to the learned scholar, "Was certainly of low caste origin, as his name would imply, and it is very possible that the history of the rise of the founder of the Gupta dynasty closely resembles that of the great Maurya" (catalogue of the coins of the Gupta Dynasty and Sasanka king of Gauda in British-museums by

John Allan London 1914 P XVI). It has also been maintained that according to the Vaishya Purana, the names ending in Gupta are characteristic of the Vaisya caste, so, the imperial Guptas must have belonged to this social order, but in ancient India despite the injunction of the Vishnu Puranas, the name Gupta had no specific caste association.

Satyaketu Vidyalankar (Aggarwal Jati Ka Prachin Itihas) is of the view that Dharan is also a sub-caste of a popular caste of Vaishya Aggarwal caste which has also been accepted by Altekar, Ayyangar, V.V. Mirashi. In this way, it can be said that the emperor Gupta may have been related to the Vaishyas. But some scholars say that during the ancient period the word Gupta was followed by a number of persons of various castes i.e. a Bodhi mendicant Upgupta, Chandra Gupta Maurya and his Brahman minister Vishnu Gupta. It is, therefore, not necessary that the Gupta royal family were belonging to the Vaishyas caste only on this account.

I think the discussion based on the word 'Gupta' seems to be useless, when we find that the use of this word after the names of the emperors of this royal family is not indicative of the caste. This was the name of the first king of this royal family, which has been fully described in the copper plate[64] of Poona in respect of Prabhavati, which was accepted as the additional name of the family during the regime of Chandra Gupta I.

In the play 'Kaumudimahotsava', which has been described in the following pages Chandrasen (Chandra Gupta) has been mentioned as Karaskara[65]. Vayu Purana (78/23) says the Karaskaras, as the residents of Kalinga and country to the north of Sindhu, are devoid of Asharam Dharma, which means the Karaskaras were non-Aryan Sudras. The Bodhayan Kama Suttra corroborates this fact. V.S. Dahiya[66] is of the view that Karaskara is the name of a province and not of a caste. Here the learned writer forgets the fact that in ancient days the provinces and regions were named after the names of the principal tribes. This was a well established tradition in the aboriginal tribes of India. i.e.Magadha, Anga, Banga, Kalinga, Videha etc.

Marriage relations

Some scholars have indicated the relationship of Guptas in the Brahman Royal families, viz. Prabhavati Gupta, the daughter of Chandra Gupta II was married to Rudrasen II, who was a Brahman. But one thing is to be noted that during that period there was a tradition of the Anulom marriage (marriage of a man of a higher caste with a woman of lower caste) and not the reverse of it. The marriage of Prabhavati was also an Anuloma marriage. The marriage relations of Guptas with Lichchhavis who were certainly non-Aryans, can be said Anuloma. It may be noted that the queen of Chandra Gupta I was from Lichchhavi family and the mother of Prabhavati, the queen of Chandra Gupta II, was Kuber Naga. Therefore, these Anuloma marriages also do not prove that the Gupta were related to Brahmans, Kshattriyas and Vaishyas.

Magadha-a non-vedic empire from the very beginning

Now we take an ordinary look on the past history of Magadha before reaching a conclusion on this subject. It may be noted that the non-Aryans had established their authority over Magadha from the very beginning-Jarasandha Sisunaga family, Nanda family and Maurya emperors were definitely the non-Aryan rulers. Mr. S.R.Goyal[67] gives his version on the above subject as follows:

"Now we should take up the question of the area association of the Brahmanical revival, for, generally speaking, one would except to find that the dynasty which became the spearhead of this movement was produced by the region which was its greatest stronghold. Viewed from this angle, Magadha, which was traditionally a heterodox area, would appear to be the least likely region. Vedic culture penetrated here quite late and failed to make any deep impression on it. That is why in the later Vedic and post-Vedic periods it was the centre of the Vratya culture. (The name Magadha first appears in the Atharva-veda (V. 22.14) where fever is wished away to Gandharis, Mujavats, Angas and Magadhas. In the Vratya book of the Atharva-Samhita (XV.ii.5), the Vratya is brought into very special relation to the Pumpsbali (harlot) and the Magadha.) This was the region where the Brahmans could associate with the Vratyas,the Rajanya could admit the Sudra girl to a harem, the Vaishya and even the Yavana could be promoted to gubernatorial office, hereditary rulers of aristocratic lineage could be expelled to make room for the offspring of a nagara-Sobhini (Prostitute) and the royal throne of kings was not beyond the reach of a barber (Political history of Ancient India, H.C. Raychowdhuri, 1953,P. 189). It explains why this region repeatedly produced arch enemies of the Kshattriyas-Jarasandha of epic legend, Sarvakshatrantaka Mahapadma, the notorious founder of the Nanda dynasty and Visvaphani who tried to establish barbarians and fishermen etc. in place of the old Kshattriya order. Here, it may be noted that these kings were interested not in the extermination of their contemporary kings; they wanted to uproot the Kshattriya order as such something which was totally against the Chaturvarna system on which the Aryan society was based.

The heterodox character of Magadha was accentuated by the rise and popularity of Buddhism, Jainism and Ajivikism. The rulers of the Maurya dynasty proved themselves great patrons of these faiths. (Chandra Gupta Maurya became champion of Jainism and Asoka Patronized Buddhism.) It was one of the causes due to which, during the Brahmanical revival of the Sunga age, the centre of political power had to shift to Vidisa. Even after the decline of the Kushanas. Magadha continued to be ruled by the Murundas who, according to the data at our disposal, were the patrons of either Buddhism or Jainism. And after the fall of the Murundas, the Vratya Lichchhavis, the traditional champion of Buddhism, became its rulers. In these circumstances, the dynasty which assumed the leadership of the Brahmanical renaissance could have hardly originated in Magadha".

Now we will have to discuss the problem of the origin of the Guptas in view of this idea.

Now we give here the views of V.G.Gokhaley[68] for solving the enigma about the origin of Guptas after having the views of various scholars about words Gupta Dharana and Karaskara, which certainly carry us to a definite conclusion. He writes:- "What was the social background of this Gupta family? The question is beset with considerable difficulty. The Gupta inscriptions do not refer to their caste and it is left to Prabhavati Gupta, the daughter of Chandra Gupta II, to mention the fact that their Gotra was Dharana....... It has also been suggested that this Dharana Gotra may be taken as an indication of the fact that the early Guptas were related to Dharini, the chief queen consort of Agnimitra Shunga. (Ray Choudhury P 443). such conjuctures are no doubt interesting but do not encourage acceptance based as they are on rather doubtful evidence. The fact, however, remains that the silence of the Guptas about their Gotra is not only intriguing but also seems to be deliberate......... It has been stated that the Guptas were comparatively speaking, people of low birth who raised themselves to a higher social status by their political greatness and that they themselves nowhere disclosed their origin or caste status as if they have purposely concealed it. (K.P.Jayasawal`History of India P 114). But such adjectives as `low' or `high' are unsatisfactory as indicators of precise social status. Perhaps the key to our understanding of the social origin of the Imperial Guptas may be found in the marriage of Chandra Gupta I with the Lichchhavi princess, Kumaradevi. This marriage was an event of great significance for the early history of the Gupta dynasty. It is prominently referred to in the Allahabad Pillar Inscription and in subsequent epigraphs Samudra Gupta is proudly described as the son of the daughter of the Lichchhavis. The political significance of this marriage will be seen presently. what did it mean in social terms?

The clan of the Lichchhavis figures very prominently in the annals of early Buddhism. They are invariably described as Kshattriyas. Buddhaghosa, the celebrated Pali commentator has the following story to tell about the origin of the tribe of the Lichchhavis. "It came to pass that the Chief queen of the king of Banaras was with child. when her time came, she was delivered, not of a child, but a lump of flesh, of the colour of Lac and of Bandhu and Jivaka flowers. Fearing the displeasure of the king if he should hear of this, the queen put the lump of flesh into a casket marked with the royal seal and placed it in the flowing waters of the Ganges. However, a certain god, wishing to provide for its safety, wrote with a piece of cinnabar on a slip of gold the words,"the child of the chief queen of the king of Banaras", tied it to the casket and replaced it in the river. The casket was discovered by an ascetic, and taken by him to his hermitage, where he cared for the lump of flesh. After the lapse of some time, the lump broke up into two pieces of flesh, which gradually assumed shape, till finally one of them became a boy resplendent like gold, and the other a girl. Whatever entered the stomach of these two infants looked as if put into a vessel of precious transparent stone (Mani) so that they seemed to have no skin (nicchavi). Others said: the two were attached to each other by their skin (Linacchavi) as if they had been sewn together, so that these infants came to be designated Lichchhavis. (B.C. Low, "Tribes in Ancient India P 299). This is obviously a fanciful interpretation of the two variant forms of the name Nichchhavi and Lichchhavi-whose precise meaning Buddha ghosa does not seem to know, but the significant point in the narrative comes. Further on when we are told that on coming of age the boy and the girl were married to each other and from this brother and sister union sprang the race of the Lichchhavis. In this connection we may refer to the remarkable similarity in the stories connected with the origin of the Sakyas and the Lichchhavis since both these groups are described as progenies of brother and sister Unions (Sumangalavilasini I P 258). The Laws of Manu (X-22) describes the Lichchhavis as Vratyas, clearly implying thereby that they were outside the pale of the Brahmanical civilization (Manav Dharamashastra X-20-22). It is true that like the Sakyas the Lichchhavis are also described as Kshattriyas but the term Kshattriya in this context may be taken to mean representative of political power rather than a specific caste in the Brahmanical hierarchy (Richard Fick "Social organisation in north east India in Buddhas' time-translated by Maitra, P 81). The Lichchhavis were one of the most prominent of the republican tribes of ancient India and had such pride of race that their laws forbade the marriage of a Lichchhavi girl with an outsider (Chakravorty 'Origin of the Lichchhavis of Vaishali', Indian Historical quarterly, P 58). This law must have had the most rigorous implementation when it came to the marriage of a daughter of a leading oligarchic family like that of Kumaradevi, the mother of Samudra Gupta. It may, then, be assumed that such a marriage would indicate that the Guptas must have been, both ethnically and culturally very close to the Lichchhavis and like the Lichchhavis (According to Smith Lichchhavis were non-Aryan Mongoloids, Indian antiquary 1903, P 233), were originally, members of a non-Brahmanical milieu and were recent entrants to the Brahmanical hierarchy. This is indicated by their enthusiasm for the performance of the Vedic sacrifices and Sanskrit religious literature and their role in the ushering of the Brahmanical religion which is a characteristic of the culture of the Gupta age [69]. Caste and Gotra, therefore, become somewhat irrelevant as indices of social origins and status......... The Allahabad Pillar Inscription mentions three very significant facts about Chandra Gupta I. The first is that he is described as Maharajadhiraja instead of the simple Maharaja, a title used for his two predecessors. This seems to be deliberate and must be taken to mean his higher political status. Whether this elevated status accrued to him was because of some fresh conquests and consequent enlargement of his dominions or was a result of his marriage with the Lichchhavi princess Kumaradevi we do not know. The second and perhaps the most important event of his carrier was his marriage. This marriage had a clear political significance since it is constantly referred to in Gupta records. It is probable that at the time of this marriage the Lichchhavis were the masters of Patliputra[70] and that as a consequence of this marriage the Gupta and Lichchhavi territories were united to build the foundations of the future Gupta empire. This marriage was commemorated by the Gupta with the issue of a set of new coins (medallions?) bearing the figures of Chandra Gupta and Kumaradevi on one side and the legend of the Lichchhavis on the other [71]. The Gupta Kingdom which comprised parts of north and west Bengal and parts of north Bihar and north Uttar Pradesh must have been held by the Lichchhavis. This union, then, brought to Chandra Gupta important political influence and marked the beginning of the political advent of the Gupta on the political scene of northern India.

Chandra Gupta I is also credited with the foundation of the Gupta Era. It is generally held that the initial year of this era may be placed in 319-320 A.D. though there are divergent opinion on this. (Fleet P 130 for the 320 A.D. date: Mr. G. Pai places the initial year of the Era in 272-273 A.D. Journal of Indian History, XI, P 188; D.N. Mukerji equates it with the Vikrama Era of 58 B.C. on astronomical evidence. I.H.Q. VIII PP 85-92; see also J.J.H. XVI, P 132, where Mr. Sundarraman equates it with 284-285 A.D.)

The adoption or initiation of the Era must have marked some important event which may either have been the coronation of Chandra Gupta I or his marriage with Kumaradevi which may or may not have preceded his coronation. The coronation of Chandra Gupta I could not have been that all important event which his marriage certainly was. And if there is some strength in the argument that the Guptas possibly adopted the Lichchhavi Era as their own and called it the Gupta Era then the marriage of Chandra Gupta with Kumaradevi must certainly claim as the important event for the starting of the Era. In this context we may refer to the insistence with which Samudra Gupta is described as the son of the daughter of the Lichchhavis and not the grandson of Guptas......... There has been considerable controversy about the identification of Chandra Gupta I with the king Chandra of the Mehrauli Pillar Inscription. This Chandra is an illusive personality and attempts have been made to identify him with persons as far removed from each other in time as Chandra Gupta Maurya, Chandra Gupta I and Chandra Gupta II as also Chandravarman of Pushkarna. (Seth H.C. in J.J.H., XVI PP 117-123, for identification with Chandra Gupta Maurya; Basak, R.G. for Chandra Gupta I in History of North-Eastern India, P 16; for Chandra Gupta II Dasarath Sharma in J.J.H., PP 14-15; also Jayaswal in Annals of the Bhandarkar Oriental Institute, XVIII, P 31; for identification with Chandravarman of Pushkarana see M.M. Harprasad Shastri in I.A., XII, PP 215-219. Without going into the details of the controversy it seems most plausible to hold that the description of the exploits of the Chandra of the Mehrauli Pillar are applicable more to the known facts of the life of Chandra Gupta II than that of his grandfather. The play Kaumudimahotsava has the figure of a Chandra in its plot and this has been taken to mean it was Chandra Gupta I. On the strength of this, a detailed reconstruction of some events in his life is attempted. It is pointed out that "at the time of the rise of Chandra, called by the original name of Chandasena[72] in the Kaumudimahotsava, the king of Magadha at Patliputra was Sundaravarman, ruling from his palace called Su-Gana...King Sundaravarman was an old man, having a child of a few years of age yet in the charge of nurse. Chandra or Chandasena had been adopted as his son by the king of Magadha, evidently before the birth of the young prince. Chandra regarded himself as the heir, being the elder, though a Kritaka son. He entered into a marriage alliance with the Lichchhavis who are described as the enemy of the Magadha dynasty in the same playKaumudimahotsava. The Lichchhavis with a large army and Chandra laid a siege to Patliputra. A battle was fought in which the old king Sundaravarman died. The young prince Kalyanavarman was carried away to the Kishkindha Hills by the faithful ministers...Chandra having his caste against him and being somewhat a Usurper, was disliked by the Magadhas of his day. Particularly as he failed to adapt himself to the traditional Hindu way of government. He showed a hostile, repressive attitude to the people of Magadha. The Kaumudimahotsava records that Chandrasena had put leading citizens into prison. The people of Magadha looked down upon him as something like a particide. Chandra Gupta I had thus several elements against him. A cry was raised that he was not a Kshattriya, he had practically killed his aged adaptive father on the battle field, he had called in the aid of the hereditary enemies of Magadha -the Lichchhavis, he had married a lady who was neither a Magadhan nor a Brahmanical Hindu. Finally Chandrasena was ousted and killed (K.P.Jaiswal 'History of India' PP 113-118). (According to play he was killed when he had gone to quell a revolt by Sabras-a tribe). Due to the tragic description of the hero of the play, Chandrasen, is not considered to be Chandra Gupta I because it is not in consistence with the reality and this play is also not accepted as a historical incidence".

But R.K. Mookerji[73] has a quite different view he writes : "From the evidence gathered from the coins, this Chandrasen himself was Chandra Gupta I as according to the inscriptions also Samudragupta has called himself a maternal grandson of the Lichchhavis...These coins (which were found in Burdwan, Gaya and Ayodhya) portray the marriage, some showing the husband offering with right hand a ring to his wife. They also bear the legends, Chandra or Chandra Gupta on obverse, and Kumaradevi or Sri Kumaradevi on reverse, and on left: while on reverse, and on right, there is the significant legend, Lichchhavayah, the Lichchhavis as a people to whom belonged the princess, and the Gupta Empire as its foundation owed so much."

So it is quite evident that Chandra, Chandrasen and Chandra Gupta were different forms of the same name. As was in the case of Chandra Gupta II whose mention has been made in the preceding pages. It is quite clear that as has been mentioned in the play that the Lichchhavi dynasty helped Chandra Gupta ascend the throne of Magadha with their power. Mookerji again writes on the same pages: "Another suggestion in support of the historical value of the play is that the Kota-Kula mentioned in the Allahabad Pillar Inscription may be taken to be Magadha Kula of the play and that Kota-Kulaja of the inscription is no other than Kalyanavarman whose defeat by Samudra Gupta must have been recorded in certain missing syllables of line 13 of the inscription, while the inscription definitely tells that Samudra Gupta defeated Nagasena, King of Mathura, who was the brother-in-law of Kalyanavarman in the play. Nagasena is taken to be the son of

King Kirtisena of Mathura, the father-in-law of Kalyanavarman."

Experts are of the view that the writer had to write this play in haste (very short time) in order to stage it on the occasion of the Kaumudimahotsava because it is not so well fabricated like the play Mudrarakshasa and there are also some inconsistencies in it. In fact, this play is a love story of the prince Kalyanavarman and Kirtimati, daughter of the Yadav king Kirtisen of Mathura, which is connected with the above historic context and which reached its climax on the occasion of the Kaumudi festival (A festival of the spring season in the ancient era) when the prince and the princess get married. This was the occasion when the writer had to compose (write) this play in a hurry or due to limited time to be played at this occasion. This was the time when Chandrasen (Chandra Gupta I) the king of Magadha had to go to the frontiers of Magadha to quell the revolt of the Sabra tribe which was excited by the former Prime Minister MantraGupta of Sundaravarman (According to the play he (king) was killed in that confrontation). The Citizen's Assembly (Nagrik samiti), which was already annoyed with Chandrasen for being a patricide and a Sudra, restored prince Kalyanvarman to the throne.

If we take a close look at the developments, it appears that the Citizen's Assembly (Nagar Samiti) and the writer of the play had made up their mind or they had imagined that Chandrasena had died in the above battle. It seems that he may have been defeated in the battle but he might not have died and might have hidden himself at some place to save his life. In fact neither the celebration of the above festival and the composition of the end of the play and staging the play nor the restoration of throne to Prince Kalyanvarman seem to be proper without the imagination or contemplating the death of Chandrasena.

In the end, we can say that the scholars may say whatever they want, but this play fills the gap which exists between the declaration of Chandra Gupta I as Maharajadhiraj against his all Maharaja-predecessors and the repetition of the name of Lichchhavi dynasty on the coins and inscriptions of the Gupta emperors. If the historians had not found the above mentioned description of the play, the reason would have been under cover of great mist why the Gupta emperors gave so much importance to the Lichchhavi family.

This view is also corroborated by the views expressed by Dr. Bhupesh Chandra and Kumari Savita[74] Datta. They have proved Guptas to be Sudra on the basis of the above play. According to them, the hero of the play Chandrasena himself is Chandra Gupta I. The learned lady writer has said Chandrasenas (see foregone pages of this chapter) to be a Karaskar. Vayu Purana (78/23) says, Karaskaras, the residents of Kalinga and north Sind, are devoid of Ashrama Dharma i.e. They were non-Aryan people. According to Bodhayana Kamasuttra, Dr. Jayaswal considers the Karaskar caste to be Sudra. In this very play a person (Chandrasen) of a low caste is said to be ineligible to become a king. There is also a description of the marital relations between Chandrasena and the Lichchhavis and the Lichchhavis have been said to be Mlechchhas in this very play.

It is very much clear that Chandrasena and Chandra Gupta I were two names of the same person whose caste was Karaskar, who according to Bodhayana Kamasuttra and Vayupurana was a Sudra caste. According to copper plates of Poona, his sub caste was Dharna, which has been said to be Sudra in the play Malvikagnimitra. Therefore, the view put forward by Gokhaley is proved to be true on the basis of the evidences that Gupta emperors were certainly nomade cow herders non-Aryan Sudra like the Lichchhavis. It seems that Guptas had penetrated into the ruling class during the Shunga and Murunda period, whom the Murunda royal family gave preference over the Kshattriyas because they were Sudra. According to Sudhakar Chattopadhyaya[75] possibly, Srigupta and Ghatotchaka were not sovereign kings but they were chiefs (Maharaja) of the provinces of the Murunda empire. The Chinese traveller Hieuntsang had heard in 672 A.D. that king Srigupta had got constructed a Buddhist monastery in the Mrigashikha forest for the Chinese travellers and had given 24 Villages to the monastery for the expenses. It is quite clear that Srigupta was a protector and follower of Buddhism.

It is a point to be noted that Brahmanism prospered much during the Gupta period; the first reason was the protection and shelter of Brahmana by the Murundas and the second was the marriage of Kumaradevi with Chandra Gupta I and the birth of princes Samudra Gupta. Possibly Chandra Gupta embraced Hinduism in view of the circumstances prevailing at that time and prince Samudra Gupta got his early education on the pattern of Hinduism. Now the question arises as to what were those circumstances. It seems that Brahmanism had started consolidating its position during this period in Magadha and it was actively progressing in this region. As is clear from the Kaumudimahotasava incidents that Chandra Gupta I had realised in the first stage of his life that it would not be possible for him to run the administration without submitting to Brahmanism and pleasing Brahmans. It is not merely a thought but a reality. In the preceding pages it has been mentioned that this was the period when the stringent codes (laws) of casteism and caste system were made and such codes were also added to the books composed in the past.

According to B.G. Gokhaley[76] Gupta Kings pursued the policy of compromising with the Brahmanism instead of opposing it." Due to this reason Guptas performed a number of Yajna gave donations etc. to the Brahmans and encouraged the Sanskrit literature.

In addition to this, they did so many other things simply on one side to please them and on the other to suppresss their voice, as to how they could not dare to call them of low birth.

Needless to say that the most powerful and sovereign emperors of that period had to bow down before the power of Brahmanism,then what to speak of a common man. The main source of power of Brahmanism was their powerful organisation and strong means of publicity (as is to day from Shankracharya to Mahamandleswar and from Mahamandleswar to Mandlewsar and from

Mandleswar to the priest of temple of town and street and even small village) who had direct access to every person and who had established their authority by brain washing them, established a complete empire in all respects. Before the miracle of theories of Atma-Parmatma,Lok-Parlok and Swarg-Nark everyone became blind to such an extent that even the uttermost lie or falsehood became the truth and only truth. Under these circumstances, if a king was declared by them to be a non-Aryan Sudra, then, even a common man turned against him.

If we go through the religious and social codes (laws) made against the Sudra and the political incidents right from the period of Rigveda till todate, we find that the four varna system, the foundation of which was laid during the period of compesition of the tenth mandala of Rigveda, the walls thereof went on growing high and stronger gradually with the passage of time by the epic period and the Buddhist period. These walls again started raising with a highspeed during the Manu's period after a pause during the Maurya period due to the expansion of Buddhism and Jainism, After a little pause during the Kushana period these started raising vehemently and changed into a sky scraper by the end of the Gupta period. In one enclosure out of the four (Varna) the great people of the Indus Valley were enclosed after enslavement, giving them the name Sudra and even after that the Hindu Kings strictly following the codes of Manu made this wall more stronger. This wall became so stronger that even today these people are encircled by it as usual. Any Sudra may he become the richest man of the country, the President or the Prime Minister of the country, will remain a Sudra. Even after the right to equality of the democracy, they are practically being grinded in the two mill stones of the social codes of Manu and are still the loyal servants of the three higher varnas. I mean to say that the social set up which had come up by the end of the Gupta period, exists as usual since then.

References

1. Ibid P 29.
2. "Racial Synthesis in Hindu Culture." P 62.
3. Vishwa Nathan, S.V. P 75.
4. Majumdar, D.N.'Races and culture of India'. PP 345-46.
5. Majumdar, D.N. Ibid P 347.
6. Oppert Gustab,'The Original Inhabitant of India', P 20.
7. Oppert Gustab, 39.
8. 'Supplement Glossary of Indian terms', Vol. I, PP 33-34.
9. Sherring, M.A. "The Hindu tribes and caste." PP 353. London Trubner & Co., 1872.
10. Oppert Gustab, P 45.
11. Oppert Gustab, Ibid. PP 47-48.
12. Vishwanathan S.V. PP 77-78.
13. Shastri Kedarnath,"Sindhu Sabhyata Ka Adi Kendra Harappa", P 132.
14. Upadhayaya Dr. Bhagvat Saran, "Bhartiya Samaj Ka Etihasik Visleshan" PP 44-45.
15. Mentioned by Upadhyaya Dr. Bhagvat Saran. PP 44-45.
16. Mentioned by Avantika Prasad Marmat in his book'Ved Kalin Nag Jation Ki Khoj'. PP 6-7.
17. After Mahajan V.D. Ancient India PP 320-23. 1960. S. Chand & Co., Delhi.
18. Chattopadhyaya Sudhakar,"Racial Affinities of early North Indian Tribes", P 90.
19. After Chattopadhyaya Sudhakar, P 77.
20. Dutt, N.K. "Aryanistation of India", P 55.
21. Keith A.B. CHI Vol.I. P 98.
22. Keith, CHI. VoL I. PP 99-100.
23. JRASGBI (1908) PP 387-388.
24. SBE Vol I. Introduction P-LXVII.
25. (a) Keith AB "Harvard Oriental Series," XXV PP 44-45.
    (b) Belvakar and Ranade "History of Indian Philosophy" PP 36-37 (The Creative period).
26. Keith AB- XVIII P.XLI and XLII.
27. (a) Majumdar, R.C. 'The Vedic Age'. P 477.
    (b) Kane P.V. 'History of Dharam Shastra' II, Part I.P xi.

28. Hopkins, E.W. CHI, P 230.

29. (a) Kane, II, part I, P xi.

(b) Period of creation of Ashtadhyayi Vayakaran of Panini has been described by Mecdonell to be 4th, 5th century B.C. A.A. Mecdowell, 'India's past P. 52. According to Harvard series XVIII, P. XLI before 300 B.C.

30. Ibid, I-213, IV-252, 256,260.

31. (a) Chattopadhyaya S. P 80.

(b) Smith V.A.-IA (1903) P 233.

32. Trived Dr. Dev Sahai, Prag-Maurya Vihar, P 42.

33. Smith, V.A. I.A. Vol; 32 (1903), P 233-234.

34. Dr. Trived Dev Sahai. P 45.

35. Kosambi, D.D.'The Culture and Civilization of Ancient India'. PP 120-132.

36. I.A. Vol. 32, 1903, P 229.

37. Chatterjee S.C."Magadha Architecture and Culture", PP 3-22.

38. Slotter Gilbert "The Dravidian element in Indian Culture", PP 55-56.

39. Chatterji. Siris Chandra. P 23.

40. Shastri Neelkanth, "Nand-Maurya-Yugin Itihas", P 16.

41. Ibid P 115.

42. "Prachin Bharat Ki Sanskriti Aur Sabhayata" P 125 (Hindi).

43. India's Past. P 54.

44. "The Early History of India", P 44. foot note.

45. "Chandra Gupta Maurya and his time", PP 6-7.

46. M.C.Crindle, "The Invasion of India by Alexander the Great". P 281.

47. Smith, V.A. P.42.

48. Chaudhari Hem Chander Ray,"Political History of Ancient India", P 240.

49. Ibid PP 8-9.

50. History of Imperial Gupta. P 67.

51. Waddell, L.A.,' Report on excavation at Patliputra." P 61.

52. Mookerji, R.K. ibid. p 10

53. Ibid p 45.

54. R.K. Mookerji. p 15.

55. (a) Chandra Gupta Maurya was the low born son of Mura and founder of Maurya Empire. The Cambridge History of India Vol.I. P 199.

(b) Chandra Gupta Maurya according to learned school was certainly of low caste.. Catalogue of coins of the Gupta Dynasty and Saṣanka

King of Gauda (in British Museum) by Johan Allan London 1914 Introduction P. XVI cited by S.R. Goyal in his book "A History of Imperial Gupta". p 75.

(c) Chandra Gupta Maurya seems to have been an illegimate scion of the Nanda dynasty of Magadha-Ashoka' p 13, V.A. Smith.

56. Kosambi is of the view that alteration was made in the Puranas only, but I think that every word of literature which was against the vest interest of the Brahamans was expunged. Ibid (Hindi ed) p 125.

57. "Prehistoric India" pp 287-288.

58. According to Kane, Manu smriti was composed during the period from 200 B.C. to 100 A.D.

59. Kane gives the following dates for Smities-Vishnu (100-300 A.D.), Yagyavalkya (100-300 A.D.), Narda (100-400 A.D.) Brahaspati (300-500 A.D.), Katyayana (400-600 A.D.) "History of Dharam Shastra" II. Part I, P xi.

60. C.F. CHI. Vol. I, p 279.

61. "The Great Epic of India," pp 397-98.

62. (a) EI XV, pp 42-43.

(b) Kalidasa in his play 'Malvikagani Mittra' has denoted that queen of Agni Mittra Sunga was from Dharini gottra Dr Jaiwal- JBORS IV 1918, PP 258-59

63. "A history of the Imperial Gupta" pp 74-75

64. EI XV P 43.

65. MR (Nov. 1929), P 409, F. It has been suggested that the Guptas were of the Karaskar origin.

66. "Jats, the ancient rulers." P 194.

67. Ibid PP 66-68.

68. Samudra Gupta. pp 25-32.

69. According to Daniel ed Wright (History of Nepal-Calcutta 1966, PP 72-73), as we get information from the inscription of Allahabad of emperor Samudra Gupta that Nepal was a part of their empire. Even after the end of this empire in Magadha, some Gupta kings ruled Nepal. In the history of Nepal these Gupta rulers are called cowherders or Goalas. They are also called Ahir. It is evident from this that Gupta rulers were originally cow herders or farmers like Lichchhavis.

70. We also get clear cut evidences from the inscription of Lichchhavi king Jaidev II of Nepal that Lichchhavis were ruling the Magadha in first century A.D. According to which his ancestors were born in Patliputra in first century A.D Probably since than Lichchhavis

would have been in power in Magadha (Mookerjee R.K. The Gupta Empire, P 8).

71. Such a unity was not alone in coins. Even Guptas had adopted the symbol of flag of Lichchhavis.

72. Pravarsen the son of Prabhavati has given in his writings of three grants name of father of Prabhavati Dev Gupta which was another name of Chandra Gupta II. In the inscription of Sanchi his name is given Dev Raj. EI XV P 42. This is clear from this that Gupta kings were having their different names.

73. Ibid pp 14-15.

74. "Gupta Kalin Bharat." P 25.

75. "Early history of north India-Calcuatta" (1958, P 141.)

76. Samudra Gupta. P 36.

CHAPTER XIII

Anthropological Proofs

It has already been established in Chapter X that towards the end of the Rigvedic period, the Aryans had founded society based on four Varnas out of which one Varna comprised of the Sudras who, the natives of the Indus valley, were given this name and put in segregation and practically enslaved. These offsprings of the Indus valley people had to suffer increasing tyranny of the rigorous socio-religious rules. They could not break those chains of slavery until 500 A.D. and even after that are not free even till today. They, in this way, comprise the lowest stratum of society and are quite separate from the Aryans both by Varna and racially. Obviously, even after 3500 years, there can still be drawn a line of racial separation between the Aryan castes and non-Aryan Sudras. The purpose of this chapter is to prove this fact on the basis of anthropology. Anthropology is a perfect science related to physical shape and appearance, i.e., appearance of head, nose and other exterior parts of body.

Before starting discussion on this subsject, it is essential to understand definition of the term 'race'[1] . "A race is a biological inbred group possessing a distinctive combination of physical traits that tend to continue from generation to generation using the term in a biological sense a race is a group united in blood or heredity."

In the second chapter it has been proved that the population of the Indus valley with some exceptions, comprised of Australoids and Sumerian type people. In order to understand properly the biological and ethnological analysis, it is necessary to know the difference between two classes. Some scholars are of the opinion that both the races on account of their living together for thousands of years,have got intermixed to such an extent that it is hard to distinguish one from the other. But in my opinion, there was difference in between them even in tribal form during the days of Indus valley civilization, Rigvedic period and it is continuing even today. The trading class or vaniks, the artisan castes and servile castes which are included in the Sudras have mostly the blood of Mediterranean type of people with a blend of Alpines in their veins, while the rest all other castes are Australoids. The causes of such classification have already been explained in length in chapter II,IV and X that the Australoids were the earlier immigrants of this region. Later on, came the Sumerians who were better civilized, skilful craftsmen and traders who were followed by the Alpines and became ruler one after the other. The chapter X also contains mention of the fact that there took place a massacre of the rulers, soldiers and the rich sections of the Indus valley. The widows and the orphaned children of these very people were made slaves by the Aryans, who gave birth to the servile castes. It has also been explained there that the vaniks and artisan classes and the servile classes have mostly the Sumerian blood flowing in their veins, while Vaniks have a admixture of alpine race also[2].

In the opinion of Stephen Fuchs [3], racially the Dravidian speaking tribes who had migrated toward central India and further north may belong to the so called Proto-Australoid or Veddids as Guha and Eickstedt call them.

Let us now take up the points of dissimilarity between these two races. Risley has given the name of Dravidian to both; Huxley applies this name to Australoids only but Guha has classified both into Australoids and Sumerians. This has been dealt with elaborately in chapter II.

In fact, it is a hard task to locate any solid dissimilarity between the two except that of language. A.B. Saran has tried to prove intimate relations between the two. He[4] writes: " Munda (Australoid) and Oron (Dravidian or Sumerian) tribes have difference of language only, but their civilization is most probably one and the same, the economic methods are similar and they have been residing together in the Chhota Nagpur since ancient period. Among the tribes of Chhota Nagpur, alongwith the similarity of races and civilization, their style of sitting mode of living, behaviour and habits of drinking Honaria (wine extracted from rice), methods of trading and marketing, similar type of games and sports and their way of playing, similar peculiarities of character and immorality, same type of ritualistic customs and festivals and most probably, ambitions and objects of life are also the same."

It is clear that except for language there is no other glaring difference between the two. As a matter of fact, both seem to be the branches of one and the same race and the difference of language can be attributed to any other factor.

The aboriginal tribes[5] of India are listed below:-

Tribes, speaking Munda language:- Santhal, Munda, Ho, Kharia, Savar, Gadav, Virja, Virheer, Korku, Mahli, Kharvar, Bhumij, Kol, Asur, Juang, Korva, Chairo, Turi.

Tribes, speaking Dravidian languages: Panyan, Korusva, Eskala, Yarana, Bodaga, Rodo, Chenchu, Kora, Oran, Mala, Kui, Khond or Gond, Pariah, Mudia, Bhatra, Parja, Kolom.*

Mongolian type: Naga, Khasi, Garo, Mikir, Mizo, Daphla, Lepcha, Angami Naga, Konyak Naga and Toda alone are of Nordic type[6].

Now, we have to see how are the Indus valley people, who have been termed Australoid and Sumerians by ethnologists while both have been termed Dravidian by Risley, related to Sudras ethnologically:-

According to the renowned ethnologist Mr. H.H. Risley[7] all the parts of human body are affected by the climate, mode of living and food. But the head form and the nasal shape remain unaffected. Therefore, in order to identify a human race the ethnologists examine the cranial and the nasal shape.

Risley's cephalic index: To meausre the head, first of all we measure the length from the centre of the fore-head to backside. This is the length of the head.

* Note: Guha has termed Bhils as Australoid. Huddon and Risley recogni: them Dravidian and Majumdar. Dravidian Negrito language Hindi They have been mentioned as Pulinda, Nishad in Sanskrit literature.

Then from a little above the ears we measure the middle part of the head. This gives us the breadth. The percentage of ratio is obtained by the help of the formula given below:

$$\frac{\text{Breadth}}{\text{Length}} \times 100 = \text{percentage of ratio or cephalic index}$$

The length of the head is taken to be 100 and accordingly the breadth is worked out. This is the percentage of head or cephalic index. The heads measuring cephalic index as 80 or above are called brachy cephalic. Between 75 and 80, these are called Meso or Mesati cephalic. The long headed having cephalic index of less than 75 per cent are termed Dolicho-cephalic.

Cephalic measurement in India

Except for the Mongols, the people of India are mainly Dolicho cephalic. The inhabitants of the Himalayan region are Brachy cephalic. The residents of Punjab, Rajasthan, and U.P are Dolicho cephalic. As we proceed eastward we meet Brachy cephalic people. The Brahmans and the Kayasthas are the broadest headed or the most brachy cephalic.

Nasal index: The nasal index is worked in the way similar to the cephalic index i.e.

$$\frac{\text{Width}}{\text{Length}} \times 100 = \text{Nasal Index.}$$

If the nose of a person is as long as wide, as is the case with Dravidians, we suppose the index to be 100 or 100%. This measurement is divided into three parts. A thin and beautiful nose having nasal index of less than 70 is called Leptorrhine. The wide nose measuring above 85% is termed Pletyrrhine. The medium nose has nasal index between 70 and 85 and is called Mesorrhine.

The wide nose is a marked physical feature of the Dravidian and Negritos and by the correct data of nasal index we can clearly distinguish the two races. The Aryan and Alpine races are famous for their long and beautiful nose. Where different races are mixed up they can be individually identified with the help of the nasal indexes and we can determine the extent of mixture. That is Why the ethnologist have accepted the nasal index as a tool of explanation of the caste system and racial identification.

We are giving below tables showing the cephalic and the nasal indexes of various Indian castes and tribes after H.H. Rishey[8].

TableI

Sr No	Caste or tribe	Cephalic Index	Nasal index
1.	Aryans of Punajab and Baluchistan	72.4 to 74.4	66.9 to 75.2
2.	Scythian- Dravidian (Gujarat and Maharashtra)	76.9 to79.7	72.0 to 81.9
3.	Aryan Dravidian (U.P. and Bihar)	72.0 to 76.8	73.0 to 86.0
4.	Dravidian (M.P. and South India)	71.0 to 76.6	73.1 to 95.1

Table II (H.H. Risley) [9]

According to social order from higher to lower class.

S.No.	Castes/tribe	Language	Region	Cephalic index	Nasal index
1.	Brahman	Eastern Hindi	U.P.	73.1	74.6
2.	Kshattriya	,,	,,	73.0	77.7
3.	Kayastha	W.Hindi	,,	72.6	74.8
4.	Bania	E. Hindi	,,	71.3	79.6
5.	Kahar	Bihari	Bihar	76.1	79.7
6.	Koli	E. Hindi	U.P.	72.1	83.6
7.	Carpenters	,,	,,	71.8	80.8
8.	Black Smith	,,	U.P.	72.8	82.4
9.	Chamar	Bihari	Bihar	76.0	82.8
10.	Passi	E. Hindi	U.P.	72.6	85.4
11.	Kachhi	,,	,,	72.1	82.9
12.	Chamar	,,	,,	72.8	86.0
13.	Dom	,,	,,	74.8	83.0

Note: The causes of similarity between the data of Kayastha with the upper castes have been explained in Chapter X. P-207

Table III : Arya Dravid (After 'Majumdar and Census Report of U.P. 1941)

S.No.	Caste/tribe	Length	Cephalic index	Nasal index	Facial index	Sitting stature
1	Brahman	165.70	72.89	72.16	87.74	52.25
2.	Agaria	167.47	73.31	72.81	87.89	50.17
3.	Kshattriya	163.33	72.12	68.08	89.72	50.36
4.	Muslim	162.45	72.16	71.23	88.97	50.37
5.	Bhil	162.92	75.62	77.54	85.62	-
6.	Dom	166.53	73.69	75.98	90.76	50.55
7.	Kurmi	161.35	72.97	73.90	87.99	51.70
8.	Tharu	163.33	72.33	76.22	88.43	51.17
9.	Chamar	161.88	72.92	75.41	86.80	49.66
10.	Tribes					
	Non-Aryan	160.69	72.69	80.80	87.08	49.97

(H.H. Risley APPENDIX III)

Table IV Scytho-Dravidian

S.No.		Cephalic index	Nasal index
1.	Mahar (Pune)	77.00	81.9
2.	Maratha (Pune)	78.3	80.1
3.	Baniya (Ahmedabad)	79.3	75.7
4.	Nagar Brahman	79.7	73.1
5.	Prabhu (Sitara)	79.9	75.8
6.	Deshasth Brahman (Sitara)	76.9	79.3

Table V-Aryan

		Cephalic Index	Nasal Index	Height
1.	Gujjar	72.4	66.9	1703
2.	Arora	72.6	71.2	1658
3.	Sikh Jat	72.7	68.8	1716
4.	Meo	73.0	75.5	1690
5.	Chuhra	73.4	75.2	1666
6.	Khattri	74.0	73.1	1662

Table VI. Mongolo Dravidian (from Risley)

S.No.	Castes/tribes	Language	Region	Cephalic (%)	Nasal (%)
1.	Brahman	Bengali	W. Bengal	78.2	71.9
2.	Kayastha	"	"	78.2	70.3
3.	Chandal	"	E. Bengal	78.01	73.9
4.	Kewat	"	"	77.3	82.3
5.	Mochi (cobblers)	"	"	77.6	74.9

Table VII. Dravidian castes and tribes (Risley)

S.No.	Castes/tribes	Language	Region	Cephalic (%)	Nasal (%)
1.	Pulaiyan	Malyalam	Travancore	76.3	79.3
2.	Parian (Pariah)	Tamil	Madras	73.6	80.0
3.	Irala	-	Chingleput	73.1	80.9
4.	Mukkuvan	Malayalam	Malabar	75.1	81.0
5.	Kanikar	-	Tranvancore	73.4	84.6
6.	Malavedar	-	-	72.4	84.9
7.	Malsar	Tamil	Coimbatore	74.5	87.2
8.	Yeruva	Kanarese	Coorg	73.6	89.6
9.	Kadia	Tamil	Anai Malai Hill	72.9	89.8
10.	Panyar	Malayalam	Malabar	74.0	95.1

Table VIII. Munda speaking Tribes (Risley)

S.No.	Castes/tribes	Language	Region	Cephalic (%)	Nasal (%)
1.	Virhor	Kharia	Ranchi	76.5	85.2
2.	Bhumij	Bhumij	Manbhumi	75.0	86.5
3.	Chero	Bihari	Lohardaga	72.4	87.3
4.	Kharia	Kharia	"	74.5	88.5
5.	Santhal	Santhali	Santhal Pargana	76.1	88.8
6.	Kharavar	Bihari	Lohardaga	75.5	89.7
7.	Munda	Mundari	"	74.5	89.9
8.	Korva	Koravari	"	74.4	92.5
9.	Asur	Asur or Agaria	"	74.0	95.9

After scanning the above tables, it can be said that the nasal index of the Dravidian tribes is the maximum whether they are the Arya-Dravidians of U.P. or Scytho-Dravidian of Western Coast or Mongolo+Dravidians of Bengal. The tribes having lowest social status or Sudras come next. It is obvious that the cause of the highest nasal index among the Sudras castes is that these castes are related to Dravidian tribes or they have descended from Dravidian tribes.

In the following graph are shown, from left to right castes in the order of highest to the lowest social status. On the left side, the Brahman have the highest social status and on the right we find Dom the lowest caste.

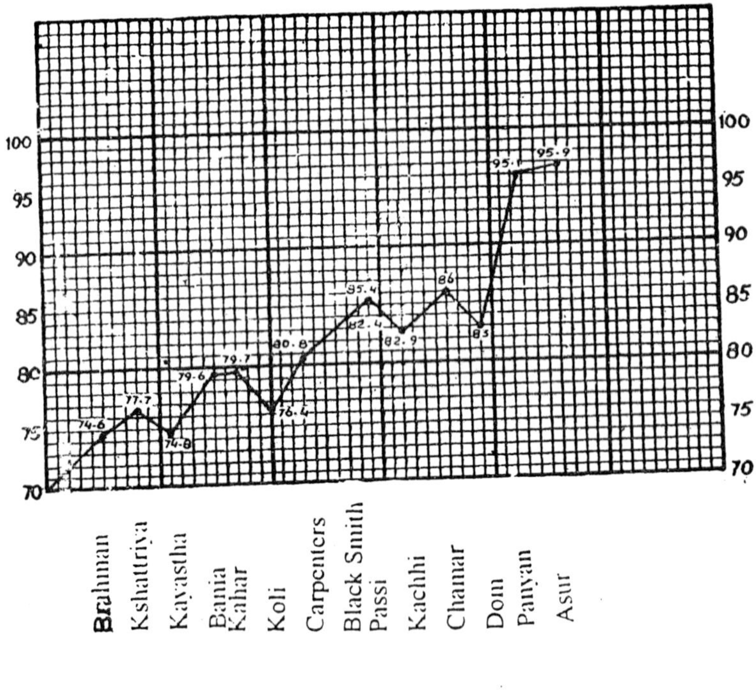

3. Graph showing the Nasal Index of various castes and tribes in the Sequence of social states from higher to lower class

After Doms, there are the non-Aryan tribes Paniyan and Asur (see Table VII & VIII). From the table, it is clear that although the Dom is the lowest caste in the Brahmanic Social order yet their nose (83.00) is more sharpened or beautiful than that of the chamars (86.00) although the chamars occupy a higher position than him in the social order. However, in Table V the nasal index of the same group (Chuhra) is 75.2 and the length is greater than any other except Brahman. Its reason has been mentioned in detail in Chapter X. (PP-209-210)

From the above tables, it appears that the natives of India wherever they may be are Sudras who occupy a lower status in the social order while the Aryans occupy a higher position wherever the invaders are in majority,there is a large number of high castes. The Aryan race is in Majority in the north. In the west in Gujarat and Maharashtra, the Scythian castes are in Majority and the higher castes have Scythian blood in their veins. On the other hand, if we go to Bengal i.e. eastward we find there Mongol and Aryan races is higher castes. There the round headed higher castes have Mongol and Aryan blood in their veins and the lower castes have the Australoid blood. Mr Risley has also presented similar views (see P-22). In this regard, Risley [10] writes further ahead: "It may be said that broad nose is noted in Chhota Nagpur where the Dravidian tribes and castes are in Majority. Beautiful and high nose is clearly found in the Punjab and Baluchistan where the Aryans are in Majority and between these two parts in the middle we find medium nose. The nose is high where the Aryans are in majority and low where they are in minority. Sometimes there is considerable variation in the index whereas among some people it is 122 and 53. The index of the Malpaharia and Dravidian tribe of Bengal is 94.5 while in the Punjab the index of Gurjar nomade cow herders is 66.9 and that of the Sikhs 68.8 and that of Bengal Brahman and Kayasthas it is 70.4. In other words among the Dravidian type people as is the case with the Mal Paharias the nose is wide like that of the Negroes while among the Aryans the nasal index is 68 as has been found by the Topenard. The nasal index of the Parsis who are Aryans is 69.4. The most interesting fact as is apparent from the graph is that there is close affinity between the nasal index and social status of the castes. If we prepare a table based on the average nasal index of some castes in Bengal. Bihar, U.P and Madras, we shall find that the caste possessing the most beautiful nose will be at the top as regards social status and the caste having the ugliest wide nose will be at the lowest level of society and so at the bottom in the table. We shall also find that the data in the table from top to bottom will be exactly in the same order whatever is the social order acceptable to the society. In this way, the tribes which have not been admitted so far to the Brahmanical caste system such as Kol, Korva and Munda will be at the bottom in the table. Next to them are rat eater Mushahara and the Chamar the leather tanner community then the fisherman Vorivind and kewat will occupy a slightly higher place. Then come the milkmen or cow herders, kurmi farmers and certain other communities, Brahmans accept water from whose hands, occupy still a higher place. From them we proceed to the trading khattri caste than Babham the landlords who occupy the highest status. In this way in the areas where Dravidian blood is prolific it will not be contradictory to formulate this order of classification that the social status of a particular class is inversely proportionate to its everage nasal index i.e. the greater the average width of the nose, the lower will be its social status. In other words, the lower social status is directly related to the Dravidian blood and the nasal index. It does not mean that we can arrive at only these two lines of thought viz. the social status and the physical features are inter related and exhibit each other, but J.F. Mc Lennan has gone further so as to say that in so called intermarriages there is an utter fusion of different races, the high and the low, and we can find out correctly the extent of this fusion with the aid of nasal index. To some extent this part of the nasal index becomes the basis of the index of the secret interrelations. In this way on the basis of some beautiful noses we can know the names of some clusters of village, classes and regions. Similarly, this is a key to the names of certain castes and tribes."

In Rigveda again and again the non-Aryan Dasas of the Indus valley have been described as Anasas or those with small noses so much so that many Dasa leaders like Vritra etc. have been addressed as Anasas. (See P-42)

From the above mentioned views of Sir Herbert Hope Risley the fact becomes clear that the higher nasal index is directly related to the Dravidian tribes and the low castes that is to say the low Sudra castes have intermixture of the Dravidian blood. The greater the fusion the lower is the social status. This has been elaborated and firmly proved in the chapter II that the majority of the Indus valley people comprised of the Dravadians. Therefore, this fact is also proved that the Sudras of the present day are the descendants of the Indus valley people. This is a proof based on science and rational thinking.

References

1. Kraeber, 'Anthropology' (New York, 1948) Chapter 'Living Races' mentioned by Rao, S.R. P 156.
2. This view has been accepted by Majumdar in his book 'Races and Culture of India', P 316.
3. Fuchs Stephen, ' Aboriginal tribes of India; P 34.
4. Saran, A.B. 'Tribal Studies'. P 69 (1978 ed.)
5. After Stephen Fuchs and Saran, A.B.
6. Bhomic K.L. 'Tribal India'. P 9.
7. Risley, H. H. 'The people of India', PP 26-28.
8. Ibid p 37-47.
9. After Risley, P 400.
10. After Risley, H. H. PP 28-29.

CHAPTER XIV

Biological (Genetic) Proofs

It is highly surprising to note that despite the fact that the two races (Aryans and non-Aryans Dravidian Sudras) have been living together for about three and a half thousand years in the same region, still the blood of the two can be separately identified. Its cause is strictly adherance to the system of marriage within the caste or endogamy. Violation of this rule was considered a great curse or a stigma. It was such a sin that could shatter to pieces the social system. In addition, there were very hard rules regarding caste system. For example, caste was to be decided by birth, eating habits and the attitude of living separately. According to the ideal institution of marriage among the Aryans, it was essential that the marriage must be settled within the same caste or group. Breaking of these rules was heavily penalised such as excommunication, amputation of limbs (G. Dh. Sutra XII-2 Manu VIII-374). Capital punishment (G. Dh. Sutra XII-3, Manu VIII- 350 and VIII-366), exile and seizure of movable and immovable property which has been mentioned in detail on P-295. In the earlier ages, it was a royal privilege and a question of king's prestige not to allow hybrid children. A king who uphold this rule was hailed as ideal and deeply religious. That is why not much intermixture of blood has taken place between the Aryans and the non-Aryans. That is why even after passage of so much time the blood of the two races can be clearly distinguished even today.

In U.P. [1] blood specimens of 21 men were tested and it was observed that different races can be identified on the basis of blood test. It has been found that there is definitely much difference between the blood of the high castes and that of the tribal people or low caste people.

Two specimens of blood, one each from one race was mixed up and the blood of the other groups was kept separately according to their social status. It was found that the blood of high castes and the blood of the tribals got separated. Encouraged by the above experiment, the experts started to undertake more and more experiments. Recently, Blood analysis was carried out on the basis of castes and tribes and it was observed that frequency of A blood group goes on decreasing as we move toward the lower strata while B group is more prominent among the lower castes, which is conspicuous by its absence among certain tribes in India. Both Macfarlane and Majumdar hold that owing to being hybridization among themselves B group is higher in lower castes. This distinction concerning blood was obvious. The scholars wondered why this distinction of blood had been persisting despite the together living of thousand of years. Its cause was ultimately admitted to be the one which has been explained above and has been accepted by the scholars unanimously.

What is Genetics?

According to Majumdar[2], scientists working on lines similar to the cephalic and nasal index technique also developed the technique of blood group analysis. Like the head and nose the gene blood cell and tissue, are immune to the effects of weather, diet, mode of living, environment etc. Therefore, in order to understand the racial differences the scientists examine the genes present in the human body. Genes are present not only in every cell of the body but are also mixed in the sputum, urine and serum and are hereditary. These genes can be classified into four categories which are called 1, 2, 3, 4 or O, A, B, and AB.

The complexion of human skin, the nature of hairgrowth (form) blue, black or grey colour of the eyes can be attributed to certain genes.

In order to find these blood groups in the human body their relative frequencies are worked out. The formula of calculating this relative frequency is given below:-

$$R = \sqrt{O}$$
$$P = \sqrt{O} + A - \sqrt{O}$$
$$q = \sqrt{O} + \sqrt{B} - O$$

where, $A = P, B = q, O = R$

Besides human being, these blood groups are found in Gorillas (A and B), Chimpanzee, Gibbons and Anthropoid Apes (A and O) also. This bears out the fact that these blood groups might have been present in a man and his allied beings millions of years ago. If there exists any difference of blood groups among the Aryans and the non-Aryans, it can be traced back to very olden times.

If we examine the graph and the tables carefully we shall find[3] that A group is largely found in the higher classes, with a decrease in the social status among other castes the frequency of A group also goes on diminishing. In a Brahman it is maximum i.e. 29.6, in a Khattri 24, in a Kshattriya 21.75. In this way it goes on diminishing in the farmer Kurmi and is the lowest in the chamars i.e. 18.67 who comes at the lowest level of social strata. In the graph A line of blood group goes on bending opposite to the B line. It is clear that the A group blood is directly associated with the Aryan class.

While presenting interesting facts about Blood Group A, Mr. Majumdar writes on P 92-93 of his book, 'The most dominating feature in the fair European races is the prominance of Blood Group A. AB group was born in some tribes of Asia and the centre of A group's origin is some where in Europe (In Europe A is 30, B 5 and O 65)'. It means 'A' flood group came India from some European or Eurosian belt, which is the peculiarity of Aryan race. Hence Aryan race came from above region. This is proved scientifically. This is most significant.

It has been found that throughout Europe from east to west and north to south the Aryan race is in majority. The Indo Aryan races came to India from South Russia in 1700-1500 B.C. approx. and brought along with them 'A' group of blood also which is clearly present among the higher castes of the Aryans even today, European Aryans also went from the same land and settled in all the countries of Europe & carried 'A' group of blood with them.

Table IX. Percentage of Group 'B' (from Majumdar)

S.No.	Caste	Blood (%)	Author
1.	Hindus	41.2	Hirsfield
2.	Southern Hindus	31.6	Bais and Verhoef
3.	U.P Hindus	37.2	Malone and Lahiri
4.	Pathans	30.0	Malone and Lahiri
5.	Marathas	34.0	Correia
6.	Jats	37.2	Malone and Lahiri
7.	Santhals, Mundas and Oraons	36.8	Malone and Lahiri
8.	Bengal Depressed Caste	42.7	Macfarlane
9.	Bengal Muslims	40.0	Macfarlane
10.	Chamars (U.P.)	39.3	Majumdar
11.	Bhatus (U.P.)	39.8	Majumdar
12.	Karwals (U.P.)	40.6	Majumdar
13.	Doms (U.P.)	39.7	Majumdar
14.	Tharus	37.5	Majumdar
15.	Todas	38.0	Pandit
16.	Muslims	33.7	Majumdar

Table X. Percentage group B among tribes (from Majumdar)

S.No.	Tribe	Blood (%)	Author
1.	Bantus	19.2	Pyper (1930)
2.	American Negros	20.0	Snyder
3.	Inhabitants of Solomon Island	16.8	Howells (1933)
4.	Papuans	13.2	Bijlmer (1933)
5.	Fiji	9.4	Howells (1933)
6.	Samoa	13.7	Nigg
7.	Pre-Dravidian Tribes of Madras	9.0	Macfarlane
8.	Paniyans of Madras	7.6	Aiyappan
9.	Angami Nagas	11.5	Mittra
10.	Konyak Nagas	10.2	Br, Ass. Res. Com. on Blood Groups
11.	Khonds (M.P.)	10.8	majumdar
12.	Australian Aborigines	8.05	Tebutt and MacConnell
13.	Korwa (U.P.)	20.4	Majumdar

Table XI. Percentage distribution of A B O blood in the Castes and Tribes of U.P.*

Sr. No.	Caste	(n)	Extent of blood groups (%) O	A	B	AB
1.	Kayastha	(111)	36.04	19.82	32.43	11.71
2.	Khattri	(125)	32.00	24.00	33.60	10.40
3.	Chamar	(150)	36.67	18.67	39.33	5.33
4.	dom	(179)	32.96	22.90	39.67	4.47
5.	Dom (Hills)	(125)	36.00	20.00	33.60	10.40
6.	Tharu	(240)	27.08	17.08	37.50	18.33
7.	Bhatu	(113)	27.43	24.78	39.82	7.96
8.	Karwal	(155)	25.81	22.58	40.64	10.97
9.	Korwa	(147)	31.97	35.37	20.41	12.25
10.	Muslim	(326)	34.05	23.01	33.74	9.20
11.	Shia	(106)	35.85	25.47	33.96	4.72
12.	Sunni	(220)	32.73	21.36	36.82	9.09
13.	I.T. College Students (Girls)	(202)	34.65	21.78	38.61	4.95
14.	Khasa	(246)	30.49	30.08	28.05	11.38
15.	Khasa (Artisan)	(108)	25.00	24.07	40.74	10.19
16.	Kshattriya	(415)	30.84	26.75	32.77	9.64
17.	Brahman (Basti)	(203)	31.53	29.06	31.53	7.88
18.	Brahman (Luncknow students)	(816)	27.96	29.57	35.48	6.99
19.	Kurmi (children)	(107)	34.58	19.63	34.58	11.21
20.	Lucknow University students	(582)	32.65	22.34	36.77	8.25
21.	Bhoksa	(144)	30.55	19.44	36.11	13.89

*U.P. Anthropometric and Serological Survey, Census Operations, 1941. (After Majumdar P. 111)

Table XII Percentage of A and B Blood Groups, among castes and tribes, based on social status (From Majumdar)

Castes and tribes according to social status		B	A
1.	Brahman	31.53	29.6
2.	Khattri	33.60	24.00
3.	Kshattriya	33.60	21.75
4.	Kayastha	32.43	19.82
5.	Kurmi	34.58	19.63
6.	Khasa Craftsman	40.74	24.7
7.	Chamar	39.33	18.67
8.	Dom	39.67	22.90
9.	Toda	38.00	—
10.	Bengal Depressed class	42.7	—
11.	Santhal, Munda	36.8	—
12.	Karwal	40.64	22.58
13.	Korva (U.P.)	20.41	—

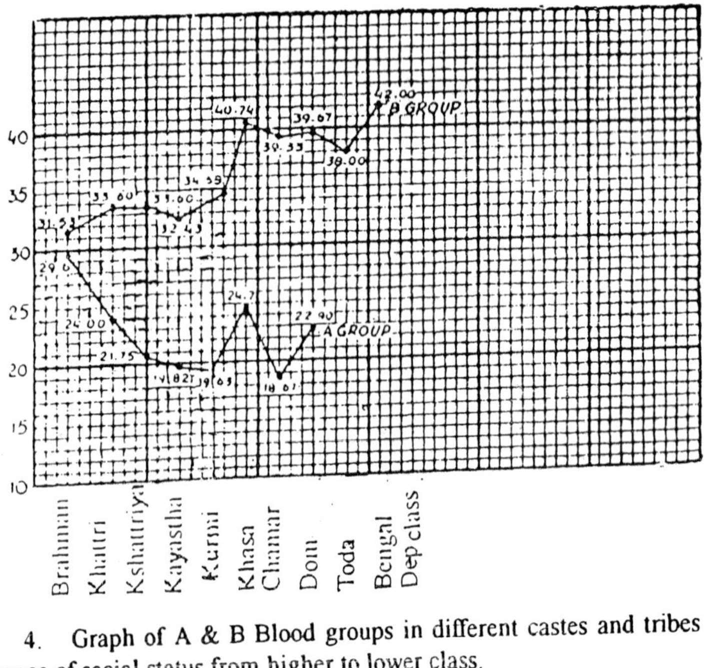

4. Graph of A & B Blood groups in different castes and tribes in the sequence of social status from higher to lower class.

Now we proceed to B group. If we study closely the tables and the graph, we find opposed to A group the B graph curve extends along the low castes in the opposite direction, Obviously, the prominancy of blood group B is amongst those Australoid and Sudra Castes whose social status is lowest. In the Brahman caste the lowest frequency is 31.53, Khattri and Kshattriya came next with 33.60, then in artisan Khasa it raises steeply to 40.74. In chamars it is 39.33. It increases to 39.67 in Doms and finally in the Dravidian castes (tribes) of Bengal it is 42.1

It is clear that the frequency of blood group B varies directly with the Dravidian tribes and Sudra castes.

D.N.Majumdar further writes expressing his views on the presence of blood group B largely among the lower castes (PP 101-102), "From the comparison of the blood groups data available yet, it appears that the B concentration is most marked among those social groups which have passed from the tribal to caste status or those which are known to be hybrid castes. The depressed castes in Bengal show a high B concentration, so do the criminal tribes of northern India. The Paniyans (Aiyappan), the Naga tribes, Angami and Konyak, the Bhils, all exhibit a lower percentage of B. But as soon as we include in our survey those tribes who are known to be mixed or those who from the nature of their occupation or otherwise allow inter-tribal marriages and extra-marital relationship with neighbouring tribes and castes, the percentage of B suddenly increases."

In my view, the cause of prominence of group B among Sudra castes is the hybrid descendants of the Australoids and the Sumerians to which the Aryans are not a Party. Among the high castes of Hindus, hybridity is maximum in the Kayasthas but they have only 32.43% of B group blood. There were inter caste marriages among the Kshattriyas also but their group B is 33.60% On the other hand, in the Sudra castes the lowest caste is Chamars which have a majority of Australoid and Sumerian blood and only these two tribes have joined this caste in maximum number. This caste has a increased value of B 39.67. Similarly, there is example of depressed classes (castes) of Bengal which have come up most probably from the Proto-Austroloid tribes. These castes have highest value of B 42.7. It is clear that the reason of presence of higher value of B among the low castes is hybridization between Australoids and Sumerians or Dravidian type of tribes and castes.

To establish the above view more strongly more proofs can be produced. In this regard, Majumdar (P 107) further writes -

1- In Central India low frequencies of B are found. Most of the Maratha groups reported by Dr Karve and also the Bhils of the border areas have smaller percentage of B.

2- The proto-Australoid groups of South India have higher values of B.

3- Maha Gujarat. comprising Gujarat, Cutch and Kathiawar, has groups with higher percentage of B than those of Central India.

4- Most of the U.P. groups have high values of B but not the highest as suggested by Dr Karve. This range extends to the groups of cis-Himalayan region. The tribal population of Mirzapur district in U.P. has a somewhat lower percentage of B gene.

5- Orissa, and Bengal present a very interesting picture. The anomalous position occupied by the Asuras with very low percentage of B gene has been explained by Dr Sarkar. The rest of the Munda speaking groups of Bengal and Orissa have high percentage of B gene. Pods and Mahishyas of Bengal have similar percentages.

6- The Assam tribes like the Nagas, Lushais, Konyaks have very low percentage of B. We can explain away this only when more data from Burma are available. If the preponderance of B is found in Burma then this low percentage of B in Assam may be due to the isolation of the groups from the rest.

When we take a survey of above regions, one thing becomes more clear. That these are the regions according to Risley, which are densely populated by the Dravidians or Proto Austroloid races. Risley has clearly mentioned this in his account of classification of different races in India (See chapter II P-22). South India is the region which has the highest density of Dravidian races. In Maha Gujarat, there is intermixture of Scythians among high castes and Dravidian among low castes, and castes of middle social status have fusion of both of them. In Uttar Pradesh among the higher castes are Aryans, in low castes are Dravidians and in the middle castes there is fusion of both. In Bengal among higher castes are Aryans and Mongoloids, in low castes are Dravidians and in middle castes there is fusion of all the three. Higher the density of Dravidian races, the greater will be the extent of group B. Obviously, the extent and degree of percentage of B group is because of the predominance of Dravidian castes in the region. Therefore, it can be easily concluded that the high degree of B group is directly associated with Dravidian race. Undoubtedly which may be attributed to intermarriages among them. This view has been confirmed by macferlane also. Among a few Dravidians and Mongoloids tribes of Assam if the degree of B group is very low, this can be attributed to some other unknown factors, which should be the subject of research for the scholars. This can also be attributed to the segregation of these tribes from their own race for a very long time in the remote past or strict law of endogamy particularly in any one group can also be one of the reason but we have no knowledge of it so far.

Mr. D.N. Majumdar further writes on Page 101 of his book, "Macfarlane made careful study of the distribution of the B element in the Indian population. She thinks that B has been in India for millennia and may have originated there in the ancestors of the lower castes of the north-east where the highest concentrations are found, whence it has diffused into the higher castes. As the amount of O and B are found to vary inversely, she thinks that there may be genes for O in these low caste people with a relatively high mutation rate for B."

It appears that B group must have been present among the lower castes millenniums years ago. Undoubtedly much earlier when the Nordic Aryans with predominance of 'A' group had captured this region in about 1700-1500 B.C. and settled down here. They married the 'B' group Indian women or raped them; (see chapter 10 PP 193-94) then there might have occurred interblending of 'A' group. This can be again understood from the views of Wyman and Boyd quoted by Majumdar (page 101). According to them "It would require 7,45,000 years for the genes A and B to attain their present frequencies". Gates has proved with the aid of Fisher, that "If the rate of mutation from O to A were one in 1,00,000 then without any intervening of selection there would be 10 per cent of A in the population after 2,50,000 years". The present frequency would require so high a mutation rate that many consider it improbable. While some, however, still believe that "There are periods during which particular mutations occur at a greatly increased rate".

Macfarlane (Majumdar P104) observes on the basis of large number of investigations, "In the few instances where there were data from two related communities in one locality (except in Cochin) the lower caste or that which probably contains more 'Dravidian' admixture shows a high frequency for B, We should put the 'Dravidian' out of this statement, replacing it by 'proto-Australoid' or 'pre-Dravidian'. If this be true, it is necessary to collect data from groups living in the same locality."

The fact is crystal clear that the high intensity of 'B' group is directly associated with low castes non-Aryans and Dravidian and Australoids. Among the low Sudra castes, the degree of 'B' group is high because they have Australoid and Sumerian blood flowing in their veins that is why they are the direct descendants of the Australoids and Sumerians (Dravidian) whose relation with the Indus valley people has been established in chapter 2, whose skeleton remains have been excavated from the last strata of Mohenjo-daro and cemetery R 37 of Harappa, who were the founders of that great civilization. This is to say that the founders of Indus valley civilization were the ancestors of Sudras.

If we cast a glance at the subject matter of anthropology and genetics and their conclusions, we shall find three things are inseparably integrated - lower level of social status, high nasal index and high frequency of 'B' group blood. Gilbert Slotter has added a fourth factor also. viz. average, black complextion. He[4] writes - "In sanskrit language the original name of caste is varna (colour). The social status of different castes descends according to blackness of their average colour*". If on a base line of castes in the sequence of social status from higher to

*Note - If opposed to the above conclusion, there are sporadic colour variations, it may be due to two causes :-

First the legal and illegal fusion of Arya blood. Second - their own blood being pure. It is because as has been said in chapter 2, the original home of both the Australoids and the Sumerians was the coastal region of the Mediterranean which explains their complexion being fair. On coming to India, there was fusion of the blood with the Negrito blood which led to changes in the complexion. Those who have so far protected the purity of blood are of fair complexion even today.

lower, graphs of average colour, nasal index and B blood group frequency are drawn separately, we will find them surprisingly to be parallel to one another. How clear this scientific proof is'. This proves the truth of the historical origin of the caste system. This truth is also corroborated by the principle of historical origin of the Śudras. Width of the nose is directly associated with the Indus valley people, which is again evident from Rigvedic description, where aboriginals are repeatedly called Anasas or flat nosed. Similarly, the relation of 'B' blood group frequency is also confirmed as they were Dravidian type of people. In Rigveda the original inhabitants of Indus valley or Dasyus or Dasas are repeatedly called of black colour. In this way, complexion statistics also fit well with the features of the Harappans. All these proofs are scientific. So, this fact is also proved scientifically that the Sudras of today, who are leading a life of slavery, are the off-shoots of Indus valley people, who were the founders of the one of the most ancient and great civilizations of the world. Not only the Sudras but the whole nation can feel proud of them.

References

1. Majumdar, D.N. "Races and culture of India". PP 96-97.
2. Majumdar, D.N. PP 86-87.
3. Majumdar, D.N. PP 92-107.
4. Slotter Gilbert, 'The Dravidian elements in Indian culture: P 22.

CHAPTER XV

Views Of The Scholars On The Historical Origin Of The Sudras And Their Refutation

It has been mentioned in the preface that Dr R.S. Sharma in his book "Sudras in Ancient India" and S.R. Rao in "Lothal and the Indus Civilization" have expressed contradictory views about the historical origin of the Sudras. This publication would remain incomplete without refuting their views. So I express the same here.

Dr. R.S. Sharma

Dr. Sharma Professor of the Department of History in the Delhi University, has in his book "Sudras in Ancient India" termed the Dayus as non-Aryan and the Dasas as Aryans. In the end, he has concluded that these Dasas ultimately became Sudras. This view expressed by the learned scholar contradicts the historical origin of Sudras as given in Chapter X P-211 of this book, in which it has been proved that the Nordic Aryan invaders enslaved the non-Aryan Dasyus and Dasas who were inhabitants of the Indus Valley and these were the persons who became Sudras in due course. These views given by Dr Sharma require to be repudiated. Dr. Sharma while proving the Dasas as Aryans writes[1], "Who were the Dasas? They have been generally confused with the Dasyus. But the absence of the word Dasa-hatya (Slaughter of the Dasas), in contrast to Dasyu hatya (Slaughter of the Dasyus) as auxiliaries in the inter-tribal wars of the Aryans, the absence of their description as Apa-vrate, Anya-vrata, etc., the mention of Dasa visas (clan) at three places (II-11-4, IV-28-4, VI-25-2) and above all their identification with the Iranian Dahai, a Scythian tribes, sharply distinguishes the Dasas from the Dasyus, who seem to have had hardly anything in common with the Aryans. On the contrary, the Dasas were probably an advance guard of mixed Indo-Aryan peoples who came to India at the time when Kassites appeared in Babylonia (C. 1750 B.C.) This can be linked up with the archaeological hypothesis which assumes either a continuous movement or two main movements of peoples from Northern Persia towards India and places the first movement fairly soon after 2000 B.C. It is perhaps this which accounts for the Aryan policy of conciliation toward them and easy assimilation into Aryan fold of their chiefs such as Devadasa, Balbhoota and Toruksa. It is because of this that the Dasas appear as frequent allies of the Aryans in their inter-tribal conflicts. Thus, it would appear that the name Dasa in the sense of slave was derived not from the non-Aryan inhabitants of Indian but from a people allied to the Indo-Aryans. In the later period of the Rigveda the term Dasa may have been employed indiscriminately not only to cover the survivors of the original Indo-European Dasas but also pre-Aryan people such as Dasyus and Raksasas,and also those sections of the Aryans who were impoverished or reduced to subjection on account of internal conflicts within their ranks".

The above views of Dr Sharma have been supported by S.R. Rao[2] in his book 'Lothal and the Indus Civilization'.

The above views given by the scholars clearly indicate that the first batch of Aryans who came to India immediately after 2000 B.C. was 'Dasas' (Aryans) whereas Dasyus were non-Aryans. But this ideological propounding cannot be accepted on the following grounds:-

1. The Dasyus and Dasas have been repeatedly referred to as the owners of the cities having forts and ramparts but such a reference has no where been found in Rigveda where the alleged leaders of Dasas like Sudas, Balbhoota and Truksha may have been referred to as the owners of forts and cities. Such references are certainly found when the forts of non-Aryans were conquered by Indra and handed over to Sudas or Sudas himself conquered those forts. This clearly shows that Dasyus and Dasas were close to each other but supposed leaders of Dasas were different.

2. Prof. Sharma has derived the meaning of the word Dasa as of Aryans and the word Dasyus as indigenous non Aryan, but there are instances in Rigveda where these words were used as synonymous or having equal meanings. Rigveda 1-103-3

SAJĀTŪBHARBHĀ SRADDA DHĀNAH OJAḤ PURO VIBHINDANNA CHARAD VI DĀSĪḤ/
VIDVĀN VAJRIN DASYAVE HETIMASYĀ ĀRYĀ SAHO VARDHAYĀ-DYVMṆAMINDRA11

Indra, who wears the thunderbolt and has faith in power moves about, by destroying the cities of Dasas, O learned and thunderbolt wearer Indra ! you throw arms on these Dasyus and increase the power and honour of the Aryans.

3. If the Dasas were Aryans then why the whole of Rigveda is full of malice against them whereas feelings of friendships have been expressed towards their so called leader Sudas etc. why?

4. In all the three hymns given above by Dr Sharma the word Vish denotes both the Aryans and non-Aryans i.e. the common men of the subjects, which fact has been accepted by all the scholars. In IV-28-4 and IV-25-2 the meaning of word Dasa Visha has been given by the Sanskrit scholar Shri Pad Damodar Sat Balekar as a non-Aryan common man, apparently the word vish has not been used here in that sense in which Dr sharma has expressed.

5. As has already been said on PP 151-52 that Sudas was an Aryan Kshattriya king because he did not have his own forts which was a major quality of being a Dasa or Dasyu. There are so many instances where the word Dasa or Dasyus are suffixed to the name of Aryans. In rigveda IV-42-9 the name of the son of Aryan Purukuts was Tridasyu who was a Rajrishi who has composed 42 sukta of fourth mandal of Rigveda. Similarly, the name of the son of the wife Itra of a Rishi was Mahi Dasa as mentioned in the preface of Aitreya Brahman written by Sayana. Aitreya Brahman has called him Mahidasa Aitreya. Thus, it is not necessary that a person is certainly a non-Aryan if his name is suffixed by the

word Dasyu of Dasa. On the other hand on P-238 it has already been proved with reference to the Banik non-Aryan Caste that one class of Vaishyas is till today called Dasas, about which it has been proved that they were from the later wave to enter India, who were related to the Sumerians well known for trade and industry. It appears that these people have been called Dasas in Rigveda. It is to be noted that round headed alpine Assyrians, reached here during mature Harappan age. They were efficient traders and have been called Asura from term Assyria. These people have been recognised as Yadus etc.(See Chapter 10) It seems that a part of them also had joined above Banik class. They were racially different from the nordic Aryans and are included among the non-Aryan Sudras in present day society also- They spoke a language Suraseni termed as Mlechchha in Bhavishya Purnana.

Dr. Sharma, while giving some examples from Mahabharata writes at Page 32-34 of the same book-"In Mahabharata (VI-10-66-46 SUDRABHIRAYA DARDAH KASMISAH PASHUBHIH SAHA) the Sudra people have been said to be living with the Abhira (Ahir) caste people. At the same place in another article the word 'Dasi' has been used in place of the word Paipalada which means that there is no difference between the two words according to the writer and these words have been used for the above tribe in place of Sudras.

In Mahabharata the word Sudra has been repeatedly used with Abhira. This story tells the difference between Sudra family and the class and this word has been used with Kshattriya, Vaishya, Abhira, Darda, Tukhara etc. tribes. This name also comes with the tribes conquered by Nakul. It appears that the Sudras came to limelight as a tribe at the time of Mahabharata battle. Thereafter, they spread in the whole of Punjab. By the repeated mention with the Abhira tribe, it appears that it was an old tribe.

Now the question arises whether the Sudras were Aryans or a tribe which existed before the Aryans ? The scholars do not have one view over this question. First of all it was thought that the Sudras were a Batch of Aryans who came first. But later on it was thought to be a tribe (Fick) which lived prior to the Aryans.

It is astonishing to note that the word Sudra has always been used with the Abhiras who used to speak an Aryan language Abhiri. Prior to this the word Sudra has never come with the people who lived prior to the Aryans, such as Dravidians, Pulinadas and Savaras etc. They always lived in North-western India which became the main habitation region of the Aryans. Abhiras and Sudras lived near Saraswati."

On the basis of the above proofs the learned writer has come to the following conclusions:-

1. Because the name of Sudras has been mentioned repeatedly with the Abhiras in Mahabharata, therefore the Sudras must have some racial connection with the Abhiras.

2. Because the Abhiras used to speak an Aryan language Abhiri, therefore,

the Abhiras were Aryans. When Abhiras were the Aryans then the Sudras also must be Aryans.

For consideration, These points scan be divided into two parts- the first part relates to the language. If the Abhiras spoke an Aryan language, Abhiri can they be accepted as Aryans on this very basis? The second part is whether the Abhiras were Aryans?

Here first of all the first part is taken up. It often happens that a particular class of society is first related to the mother tongue, secondly to the state language or the official language. If both the languages are the same, then no problem arises. If the offical language is different, then one has to learn the official language also to get benefits from the government or for official work. And in case the circumstances press hard then one has to adopt the official language. In India during Muslim period because Arabic, Persian or Urdu were the languages of ruling class the entire work was done in these languages, literature was also written in these languages. Public functions, poetic symposiums (Mushairas) private and Govt. functions may have been conducted in the official languages. Thus these languages got good publicity. Even today after passage of hundreds of years the effect of these languages can be seem on different dialects throughout the country. Not to speak of this. the Urdu language is much extensively spoken in the region of erstwhile state of Hyderabad which is surrounded by the Dravidian languages of south. The English language started commanding an overbearing influence when British rule was established in India. Though the British rule came to an end about 48 years ago, yet its influence is not going to end. The Dravidian tribes who have been living in north India since ancient time, have gradually forgotten their own languages and adopted the languages spoken and written by the ruling class(Aryans). Today these languages have become their mother tongues. Even today some tribes of Bihar are gradually adopting Hindi language. It is clear that the human race does not have any relation with any particular language.

Corroborating this view. Dr P. Giles[3] writes, "In the Island of Britain many persons of Welsh blood, many persons of Irish Celtic and Scottish Celtic origin speak English. It is many centuries since it was observed that Normans and English who had settled in Ireland had learned to speak the Irish language and had become more Irish than the Irish themselves. It is well known that by descent the Bulgarians are of Asiatic origin and of an entirely different stock from the Slavs, a branch of whose language is now their mother tongue." It is, therefore, clear that it is impossible, without historical evidence. race of any class of people, cannot be established on the basis of their language.

It is quite clear that the view put forth by Dr Sharma that Abhiras were Aryan because they spoke an Aryan languages.is baseless. Some Scythian tribes of Central Asia even today not only speak Indo-European languages but the physical characteristics of many of them resemble those of the Aryans. but they cannot be accepted as Aryans. The people of Nordic race are the only Aryans (See PP-126-27)

This is not proved that the Abhiras who spoke an Aryan language, were Aryans, therefore, the Sudra tribe having relations with them also cannot be accepted as Aryans.

Now we take up the second part, to see as to what the historical origin of the Abhiras was and to which human race they are related.

Vasudev Sharan Aggarwal (Panini Kalni Bharat Varsh P 95) while throwing light on the word "Shudrabhir" writes-

'Katyayan (4/1/4) has referred to 'Mahashudra' caste. According to Kashika this was the name for Abhira caste. They had high status than the Sudras and therefore, they were called 'Mahashudra' (high status Sudras) Patanjali has mentioned the example of the word 'Shudrabhiram (TYADADINI SARVERNITYAM 1/2/72 and 6). This composite word has two parts. The first Sudra is for Sudra varna and second Abhira stands for particular type of Sudra. In the north-east region of Sindh there was a large kingdom of Abhiras and attached to it another Kingdom of Sudras that is why this compound word name 'Sudrabhiras' has come into existence.'

Ram Prasad Chanda[4] writes on this subject- "The Saurastras classed as men of mixed origin by Baudhayana, and the Abhiras, called Mlechchhas in the Mahabharata (XVI.7.63), became dominant in western India after the fall of the Yadavas. In the Harivamsa (94, 5161) the Yadava Kingdom called Anarta is described as 'mostly inhabited by the Abhiras (Abhira-prayamanusam)" The Anarta country and its inhabitants were called Surastras or Saurastras, probably after the Rattas (Rastras) akin to the Rastikas of Asoka's rock edicts, now represented by the Maharastras or Marathas. These Saurastras and Abhira from whom the Gujaratis of our day have evidently sprung, were Aryan in speech and belonged to the Indo-Afghan stock. The monotheistic religion that Krsna-Vasudeva taught to the men of his own clan was handed on by the Satvatas (Yadavas) to the Saurastras and the Abhiras, who gave it the un-Vedic turn. Vasudeva, his brother Samkarsana, his son Pradyumna, and his grandson Aniruddha were probably defied by these Outlanders who lay outside the pale of Vedism."

It is clear that the Abhiras were Afghani type of people who were not Aryans and were called Mlechchha. It may be noted that the word Mlechchha is a corrupt form of the word Mulekha[5]. Possibly the Sumerians called the inhabitants of the Indus Valley as Mulekhas in the ancient times, who were undoubtedly non-Aryan Sudras. Such evidences have been found on the basis of which it can be said that the inhabitants of Lothal had relations with an Ahir nomadic tribe named 'Bharvar[6] of the present day Gujarat. From this we can imagine the association of Abhir people with those Alpine people whose remains have been found from the cemetery H from Harappa[7].

The scholars are of the view that originally the word Abhira did not mean a cow herder but it was the name of a caste. Amarkosh and the later lexicographers have described the meaning of the word 'Ghosha' as Abhirpalli or the place where Abhiras used to live. On the basis of the above proofs we can conclude that the clear meaning of the word 'Sudra Abhira' mentioned by Prof. Ram Sharan Sharma is Abhir Sudra. Here the writer has called the Abhira people as Sudras. Even then in order to remove the doubts of the writer about the racial affinity of Abhirs we give some proofs of anthropology which clearly show that Abhiras were in fact Sudras.

Table XIII Cephalic & nasal index of castes

S.No.	Caste	Cephalic index	Nasal index	Facial index
1.	Brahman	72.89	72.16	87.74
2.	Agari	73.31	72.81	87.89
3.	Kshattriya	72.12	68.81	89.72
4.	Ahir	73.76	73.35	86.88
5.	Kurmi	72.97	73.90	87.99
6.	Chamar	72.92	75.41	86.80
7.	Dom	73.69	75.98	90.76

(Races and Culture of India, p 85, D.N. Majumdar)

From the above table we would discuss the nasal index only. It is quite clear from the table that among the higher castes the nasal index of Brahmans and Kshattriyas is 72.16 and 68.61 respectively whereas that of the Ahir and Kurmi is 73.35 and 73.90 respectively which means the Ahir is nearer to the Kurmi caste as compared to the higher castes which is an agriculturist Sudra caste. According to Prashar Smriti (11-24) the union of a Kshattriya man and Sudra woman, the offspring will be called Gopal or Ahir which means that Ahir is a Sudra.

Even today the Ahir caste is considered to be a backward caste or the Sudra caste. Therefore, it is clear that the Ahirs are not Aryans. As such, the Sudra tribe also cannot be Aryan. It has already been said in detail in the historical origin of the Sudra (Chapter See P-198) that the Sudras were definitely the cooks of Aryans. They must have been debarred from adopting the above profession by the Aryans due to some particular incident which may have been very fatal and later on they settled in the Indus valley where they have been described as living along with the Abhiras. Later at the time of invasion of Alexander the Great, they were there with the name of Sodroi. A generation earlier before the Araba invasion (712AD). They were in power in Sindh. From there they moved and settled in west north Rajasthan and then moved further and spread over the whole of Punjab. That is the reason why the Soods live only in the north-western part of Delhi and in no other region.

It has already been proved that the Dasas were not Aryans but they were non-Aryans living along with non-Aryan Dasyus in the Indus valley. Therefore, the establishment of the view of Dr. Sharma, that the Sudras were that part of the Aryans, which was poor or had lagged behind their other brothern for some specific reason, is proved baseless.

S.R. Rao

Mr Rao[8] has expressed the view in his book: "Lothal and the Indus Civilization" "that former Aryans and Rigvedic Aryans also lived in the Indus valley besides some other tribes. He has expressed the 1 first view that "the first wave of Aryans was consisting of Dasas which is mentioned in Rigveda". This view has already been refuted.

2- The second view has been given at page 159 of his book that one of the religious customs of Harappans which they adopted in Lothal outside the Indus valley, was fire worship and the second was animal sacrifice whereas Prof. Chattopadhyaya has given his view that the Rigvedic Aryans adopted the custom of fire worship from Angrisas whom they considered as their ancestors.

It has already been discussed in detail in chapter 2 PP-26-27 that it was an integral part of the society of the Dravidians to worship the village deity, Cobra (Naga), fire, Shiva and mother Goddess Shakti and also the practice of animal sacrifice. In the 10th chapter it has been said that the non-Aryan traders, the Panis of the Indus valley had a god Bal, who held a huge container for sacrifice in both of his hands. This container had fire always burning in it and they used to sacrifice children and men in it, in order to ward off any natural calamity confronting the nation. In addition to this, in second chapter it has been said that in the 'Bull grappling sports' tradition of Indus valley the bull was sacrificed in the end[9]. Similarly, it has been shown on P-65 that the Alpines, who had arrived and settled in Sindh and Gujarat (Lothal) before advent of Aryans, had the tradition of sacrificing white horse in their society[10]. Mr. Wheeler has informed that the present Brahmanism stands on the foundation of 'Dravidian Religion'. The Dravidian religion is an interesting thing on account of its intelligibility.

It is quite clear that the custom of fire worship and animal sacrifice was also prevalent amongst the people in Indus valley. It would not be proper to say that it was the civilization of the Aryan people or the Aryans lived there, on the only basis that proofs of fire worship and animal sacrifice have been found in Lothal.

3. In the third point that he has raised at page 173 of his book that, Mr Ghosh is of the view that amongst the people of Indus valley, the Harappan people were with some distinction some what similar to those of Punjab, the people of Mohenjo-daro were similar to the present day people of Sindhu, in Lothal they were similar to the present day people of Gujarat. It clearly shows that the Harappans were not of the same race. This civilization was the result of joint efforts of so many types of people.

Today, the Harappa and Mohenjo-daro regions are abundantly populated by Aryans and the Lothal region is populated by Scythian. It means that the writer wants to tell that Aryans lived in Punjab and Sind regions of Indus valley and the Scythians in Gujarat which is not proper.

It has already been proved on Chapter II, from the skeletal remains found from Harappa, Mohenjodaro, Chanhudaro and Lothal, that inhabitants of these towns were Mediterraneans and Australoids. Four Aryans were found from a Stratum of Lothal belonging to 1600 BC (later Harappan) while Aryans had already arrived in this region.

To remove the doubt of scholars on the subject, bones and teeths of Skeletal remains were examined by famous dental anthoropologist Kenneth AR Kennedy and others. (Skulls, Aryans and Flowing drains, the interface of Archaeology and Skeletal Biology in the study of the Harappan civilisation, Edited by Posschl L.Gregory 'Harappan civilisation' PP 289-294). He writes, "It has been my privilege to examine all of the human skeletal remains recovered from the Harappan sites of Mohenjodaro, Harappa Chanhudaro and Lothal in 1964......" He further quoting concluding remarks of his another colleague scholar Brace, writes "The longer the period of time a population has enjoyed the benefits of technology, particulary whose that concerns food prepartion, the smaller are its teeth. In charting the distribution of relative tooth size before the Age of discovery in South Asia the smallest teeth appear in the northern western sectors of the Subcontient................... These observations, confirmed by studies of ancient human dentitions from South Asia as attested by the emergence of the Harappan Culture by 3000 B.C." Further he quotes Cappieri. "There is no evidence of brachy cephalic population in the period covered by my study (the Harappan period) and there is no element proving migration of population from one region to another in the period mentioned.....Most differences-83.4 were not significant and such a high value proves the genetics and somatic homogeneity of all these (specimens) as a single population."

It is clear that brachy cephalic (Alpines) were not available in the population only the dolicho-cephalic Dravidians formed the part of Harappan civilisation, though Alpines settled in India atleast 500 years before the advent of nordic Aryans and druing mature Harappan age.

4. The next point he has mentioned at pages 165-166 and needs to be noted carefully is that it has repeatedly been mentioned in Satpath Brahman that the gods (Devtas) and Asurs developed from the same origin.

It has already been said on foregone pages that Assyrians had already arrived and settled in Indus Valley. They were ethnically different people from nordic Aryans, known as Alpine a round headed stock, having a different language (see PP 65-67) and of black colour, called slaves in Mahabharata.

Mr Rao has tried to distort the facts of history and to reverse its flow. But natural flow cannot be reversed. At last the current will come to its natural course and will flow in its right direction. This theoretical establishment of the Historical origin of caste system and Sudra" is symbolic of the same natural flow. Contradictory views of Mr R.S. Sharma and Rao have been proved to be baseless.

CONCLUSION (Varna and Caste System Colonial)

It is but natural to conclude from the foregoing chapter that the Indus Valley civilization was greater than the Mesopotamian and Egyptian civilizations. It is because the common man in the Indus Valley was a prosperous and happy and the amenities of life which are available today were available to him during that period, such as the pucca houses constructed under the town planning, underground sewerage system, bath rooms, latrines with English bond seats etc. It means the standard of living of common Harappan was very high, certainly the atmosphere there was very peaceful and there was neither caste-system nor slavery whereas in other both the civilizations the slaves were used like animals, the craftsment lived in ordinary cells or chambers and the slaves were kept in the barracks.

It has also been proved that the Founders of the Indus Valley Civilization were the Dravadians who were invaded by the Aryans between 1700-1500 B.C. and their civilization was destroyed. At that time the Aryans were in a savage and semi civilized stage and they had no knowledge of the urban civilization.

After the above mentioned Aryan invasion naturally the society came into being into two classes, the conquerors tall, healthy and fair complexioned Aryans and black coloured small sized, and the defeated non-Aryans. The defeated non-Aryans were suffering from inferiority complex and the victors, the Aryans, were proud of their victory and suffered with superiority complex. This feeling of defeat and victory or inferiority and superiority complex was the basic reason for the origin of Varna and the caste system. As the Arynas had three varnas in their other colony Persia i.e. the Priests, charioteers and the artisans and the farmers, similarly they had three Varnas in India also i.e. Brahman, Kshattriyas and Vaishyas. Thus there were four Varnas in the new society, three of the Aryans and the fourth of the non-Aryan aboriginals Dasyus and the Dasas, who were later called Sudras.

In order to explain the historical origin of the sudras, they have been divided into four parts: servile castes, artisans, traders, and the castes connected with agriculture. The castes falling in the first part were born of the widows and off spring of the Dasyus and Dasas who were massacred by the Aryan invaders or killed in the battlefield. These children and widows were enslaved and kept in the homes for doing domestic chores, such as cooks (soods), personal servants (Kayasthas) utensil cleaners and sweepers etc.

Similarly, it becomes quite clear from the archaeological evidences found from the excavations of the Indus Valley cities that all the artisan castes such as potter, carpenter, copper smith, gold smith etc. lived in the cities of the Indus Valley from where their workshops furnances, tools, raw material, finished and semi-finished goods have been found.

It has also been proved that after the period of the origin of the above mentioned system if we make a critical appreciation of the stringent laws of Varna and caste system given in the Sanskrit literature-Brahmans, Upnishads, Suttras, Arthshastra, Smritis and Puranas in chronological order, it becomes clear that the fourth apartment of Varna system, the Sudras, whose name first of all appeared in the Purusha Sukta of Rigveda, in which the great people of Indus Valley were pushed, went on becoming further stronger in due course, so much so that even the most powerful non-Aryans Sudra kings like Sisunagas, Nandas could not break it. Inspite of all powers into hands the king Pasenadi of Kosal could not marry the daughter of Shakya Kshattriyas, whose life and death was in his own hands. The Maurya kings pursued the policy of tolerance after hearing the stories of disrespect of their ancestors, the Nands, not only embraced Jain and Buddha religion, which was diametrically opposed to the Brahmanism, on finding an appropriate opportunity but also utilized their full might in preaching the same by making it a state religion. Similarly, when the real founder of Gupta monarchy, Chandra Gupta-1 in the very beginning of his life carrier had to face the opposition of the Brahmans of Magadha and their supporters for being a Sudra, inspite of being a powerful emperor, submitted to the Brahmans and embraced their religion and left no stone unturned in the upliftment of this religion and the Sanskrit literature in order to please them.

It has also been discussed that the laws which were made against the Sudras had become more stringent by the Gupta period not only this, this was the period when such stringent laws were inserted in the Puranas, Smritis, Epics and others religious books written earlier.

In this way, the change of caste or profession or marrying a woman of another caste, became impossible. As such in the guise of Varna-dharma, jobs of service, filthy work requiring hard labour, were entrusted to the great sons of Indus Valley country and slavery was perpetuated on them. Even today, most of them are living a life of slavery and doing the same professions of the service of Aryans, which were entrusted to them in the beginning. Even today, Dravidian blood is flowing in their veins, their physical characteristics are identical to the Dravidian tribes and castes. It has been proved with evidences that the high nasal index and 'B' blood group frequency is one of the land mark of the Dravidian Castes & Ttribes, As such higher the value of nasal index & frequency of B blood group of a caste, so much lower would be social status, so it is scientifically proved that the blood of the Dravidian and the Sudra castes is one and the same, it means the ancestors of the Sudras were Dravadians who were the Founders of the Indus Valley Civilization, who were conquered and enslaved by the Aryans and were called Sudras and included in their Varna system. Thus the varna and caste system, indisguise, is colonial in character.

References

1. Sharma, R.S.'Sudras in Ancient India'. P 23.
2. Rao, S.R.'Lothal and the Indus Civilization' PP 158-159.
3. C.H.I. P 59.
4. 'The Indo Aryan Races'.IC 105.
5. Parpola Asko. 'The Indus script decipherament'.P 11. Madras 1970.
6. After Rao. S.R. P 107.
7. Rao. S.R. P 157. and Stuart Piggott P 148. Chanda R.P. I.C. 25.33.
8. Ibid PP 158-159.
9. Shastri K.N. "New Light on the Indus Civilization", Vol. I (1957) PP 36-39.
10. Parpola Asko, "Front line", Feb. 7.22, 1987. P 99.
11. Wheeler, M. 'Indus civilization'. P 69 and Rao P.6.

SELECTED BIBLIOGRAPHY

(a) ORIGINAL TEXT BOOKS

Aitreya Brahman

Amar Kosha

Angutara Nikaya (Pali)

Apastamb Dharma Sutra

Arthsastra (By Kautalya)

Ashta-Addhyai (by Panini)

Atharva-Veda

Baudhayan Sraut Suttra

Bhagwat Purana

Brahadadharma Purana

Brahma Vaivart Purana

Brihadaranya Kopnishad

Chhandodya Upnishad

Dirgha Nikaya (edited by B.J. Kashyap Pali Pub. Board Bihar, 1958)

Divyavadanam (Pali)

Gautam Dharm Suttra

Gautam Samhita

Gautam Smriti

Gopath Brahman

Jatak Katha (Bodh) all volumes

Jemini Brahman

Katyayan Sraut Suttra

Kathaka Samhita

Kaushtiki Brahman

Kaumudi Mahotsava

Mahabharata (Gorkhpur and Calcutta ed.)

Majjhima Nikaya (Pali)

Mahabhashya (Patanjali)

Maittrayani Samhita

Malvikagini Mittra (By Kali Dass)

Manu Smriti

Markandeya Purana

Matsya Purana

Mudra Rakshasa (By Vishakha Dutta)

Narad Smriti

Panch Bimsa Brahman

Parashar Smriti

Ramayan (Balmiki)

Rigveda (Shripad damodar Satavalekar)

Samhitop Brahman

Satpath Brahman

Shankhyayan Brahman

Taitreya Brahman

Taitreya Samhita

Vedvyasa Smriti

Vishnu Purana (English Translation by Wilson)

Yagya Valikya smriti

Yajur Veda

(b) LIST OF JOURNALS

American Anthropologist 65 No. 4 (August, 1963) and 66 No. 2 (1964).

American Oriental Society 84 (1948).

Ancient India (Bulletin of Archaeological Survey of India) Vol. III Jan. 1947 and Vol. IV (1948).

Vol. VII (1951), Vol. X & XI (New Delhi).

Anthropological Survey of India, Calcutta, 1963.

Anthropology on the March, Madras 1963, edited by Bala Ratnam.

Antiquity XXXVI, 1962, XXXII, 1958, XXXIX 1965

Archaeology, 18 No.2 (1965).

Bulletin of the Deccan College Research Institute, Vol. II, No. 1 and 2 (Nov. 1940)

Bulletin of the National Institute of Science in India No. 1 (1952).

Epigraphia Indica XV

Frontline Feb. 7-12 (1987).

The Indian Antiquary, Vol. 30 (1901) 32 (1903)

The Indian Antiquary (Bombay), Vol. I.

Indian Contribution to World Thoughts and Culture (New Delhi)

(Vivekananda rock Memorial Committee).

Indian Archaeological Review.

Indian Historical Quarterly XXIV (1948).

Journal of the American Oriental Society, No.65 (1945) 76.

Journal of Bihar and Orissa Research Society, IV (1918).

Journal of the Royal Asiatic Society of Great Britain and Ireland, 1907 and 1908.

Journal of the Bombay Branch of the Royal Asiatic Society, Bombay, NS XXIII.

Journal of the Royal Asiatic Society, Bengal, Vol. XVI No. 1 (1950)

Journal of the Oriental Institute, Vol. XXII, No. 1 & 2 (1972)

Journal of the Royal Asiatic Society, Vol. II (1866)

'Man', Vol. 56 (1956)

Modern Review (Nov. 1929)

Puratatva No. 1.

Science Today, January, 1982.

(C) MODERN WORKS

Aggarwal V.S. — Vision in long darkness (1963).

Aggarwal V.S. — Panini Kalin Bharat (Hindi) Moti Lal Banarsi Dass Varanasi.

Ambedkar B.R. — Who were the Sudras? Bombay 1970

Alberuni — Albaruni ka Bharat (Hindi). 1967, Allahabad.

Apte V.M. — 'Dictionary'

Arjun Dev — Manav Samaj Ka Itihas (Hindi). Delhi

Asko Parpola — The Indus Script decipherament (1970), Madras

Asthana Shashi — History and archaeology of India's contacts with other countries. B.R. Publishing Corporation, Delhi (1947).

Bahadur K.P. — Caste and Tribe Culture of India, Vol. I to IV. Ess ess Publication, New Delhi 1976.

Belvakar and Ranade — History of Indian Philosophy IInd ed. Oriental Books. New Delhi, 1974.

Bhandarkar D.R. — Some aspects of Ancient Indian Culture Madras 1940.

Bhomik K.L. — Tribal India, World Publication Calcutta 1971.

Buddha Parkash — Rigveda and the Indus Valley Civilization Hoshiarpur 1966.

Blunt E.A.H. — The Caste system of North India, Chand & Co., Delhi 1969.

Bhupesh Chandra Saksena and Savita Dutta — Gupta Kalin Bharat (Hindi)

Bose Nirmal Kumar — Culture and Society in India. Asia Publishing House, New Delhi 1977.

Bridget and Allchin Raymond — The rise of civilization in India and Pakistan (Cambridge World Archaeology), 1983, select book service Syndicate, New Delhi.

Buhier G — Indian palaeography, Bombay 1904

Burnes Sir Alexander — Travells into Vokhara Vol. III Oxford University Press, London, 1973.

Chanda R.P. — The Indo Aryan Races. Indian Studies, past and present, Calcutta, 1969.

Chatterjee Sris Chandra — Magadha architecture and Culture. Calcutta University, 1942.

Chattopadhyaya S. — Racial affinities of early North Indian Tribes. Munshi Ram Manohar Lal. New Delhi, 1973.

Childe V. Gordon — New Light on the Most Ancient East, London, 1952-54.

Colebrooke H.T. — Miscellaneous Essay II ed. E.B. Cowell, London. 1873.

Crindle JWM — The Invasion of India, Cosmo Publications, New Delhi, 1983.

Cunningham Sir Alexander — Ancient Geography of India Indological Book House, Varanasi, 1963.

Dahia B.S. — Jats-The Ancient Rulers, Sterling Pub., New Delhi, 1980.

Das A.C. — Rigvedic Culture. R. Cambray & Co., Calcutta, 1925.

Das A.C. — Rigvedic India R. Cambray & Co., Calcutta, 1927.

Denzil Ibbetson — 'Punjab Caste' Language Deptt., Punjab, 1970.

Deshmukh P.S. — Religion in Vedic literature, Bombay 1933.

Dutt N.K. — Aryanization of India-Calcutta 1925.

Dutt N.K. — Origin and growth of caste in India, Calcutta, 1968.

Elphinstone M — An Account of the Kingdom of Cabul, Vol. II

Ghurye, G.S. — Caste and Races in India. Popular Prakashan Bombay 1969

Ghurye G.S. — Vedic India, Popular Prakashan Bombay 1979

Gokhley B.G. — Samudra Gupta, Asia Publishing House, Delhi 1962.

Goyal S.R. — A History of the Imperial Gupta, Central Book Depot, Allahabad 1967.

Grierson G.A. — Linguistic Survey of India Part I Vishweshwaranand Institute, Hoshiarpur, 1973.

Grierson G.A. — Linguistic Survey of India, Part IV Moti Lal Banarsi Dass, Delhi.

Guha B.S. — Racial elements in the population, London 1944.

Guha B.S. — Bharat Varsh Ka Jati Parichay (Hindi).

Gustab Oppert — The Original inhabitant of India. Oriental Publication, Delhi 1972.

Hall Dr. H.R. — Ancient History of the near east ,Methuen & Co. London 1920.

Hawkes Jacquetta — The first great civilization. Hutchinson London 1973.

Henry M. Elliot — Supplement glossary of Indian Terms Vol.I

Henry Maine — Village Community

Hewitt J.F. — The ruling races of Prehistoric time. Delhi Oriental Pub. 1972.

Hillebrandt — Vedic Mythology Vol. I.

Hira Dr. Rajbans Sahai — Sanskrit Sahitya Ka Itihas (Hindi) Chaukhamba Parkashan Banaras 1977.

Hopkins E.W. — The great epic of India-New haven.

Hrozmy C.F. (ed) — Encyclopaedia Britannica Vol. I

Hutton J.H. — Caste in India. Oxford University Press 1961.

Kane P.V. — History of Dharam Shastra II (1) Poona 1930-1946.

Keane A.H. — Man past and present. Cambridge University Press. 1899.

Keith A.B. — The Harvard Oriental series XVIII and XXV Harvard University Press London, 1895.

Knorozob y. — Proto Indika, Nauka Publishing House, Moscow 1981.

Kosambi D.D. — The culture and civilization of Ancient India in historical outline. Vikas Pub. House, New Delhi 1975.

Kosambi D.D. — Bhagwan Buddha (Hindi) Rajkamal Prakashan Delhi 1956-57.

Law B.C. — Ancient mid Indian Kshattriya tribes, Calcutta 1924.

Law B.C. — Historical Geography of Ancient India, Paris 1954.

Law B.C. — Tribes in ancient India Poona 1943.

Loui's Finkeltein — The jews their history culture and Religion Vol. I Harper New York 1960.

Louis. Renou — Vedic India (Translated by Philip Spratt) Sushil Gupta Pvt. Ltd., Calcutta 1957).

McCrindle J.W. — The invasion of India by Alexander the Great Westminster 1896.

Macdonell A.A. — India's Past-A survey of her literature etc. Oxford 1927.

Macdonell A.A. — Vedic Mythology. Oxford University Press, London 1954.

Macdonell A.A. and Keith A.B. — Vedic Index of names and subjects Vol. I Varanasi 1955.

Mackay E. — Further excavation at Mohenjo-daro. Vol.I., New Delhi, 1938.

Mackay E. — Early Indus Civilization-Indological Book Corp. New Delhi 1976.

Mackay E. — Chanhudaro-excavation, New hoven 1943.

Mahajan Vidyadhar — Prachin Bharat Ka Itihas, S. Chand, Delhi 1973.

Majumdar D.N. — Races and Culture of India. Asia Publishing House, New Delhi 1961.

Majumdar R.C. — The Vedic age. London 1957.

Marshall John — Mohenjo-daro and Indus Civilization. Indological Book House, Delhi.

Marshall John — The Thousand Syllabled Speech Vol.I.

Mookerjee R.K. — Chander Gupta Maurya and his time III, Edition Moti Lal Banarsi Dass Delhi 1966.

Mookerjee R.K. — The Gupta Empire. Moti Lal Banarsi Dass Delhi 1969.

Mookerjee R.K. — Hindu civilization

Muir J. — Original Sanskrit texts. Oriental Pub., Delhi 1972.

Muller Fredrich max — Ancient Sanskrit Literature. Chowkhamba Varanasi 1968.

Muller F. Max — The home of Aryan.

Muller F. Max — Lecture on the Science of language.

Muller F. Max — Sacred books of the east Vol I & IV. Moti Lal Banarsi Dass Delhi 1965.

Nanavati J.M. — 'Som Nath' Dept. of Archaeology Ahmedabad 1956.

Nesfield — Caste in India.

Nesfield — Caste system of the N.W. Province and Oudh

Oldham — The Sun and Serpant.

Pargitor F.E. — Ancient India Historical Tradition and dynasties of Kali age, Oxford 1913, London.

Possehl L. Gregory — Ancient cities of the Indus. Vikas Pub New Delhi 1979.

Possehl L. Gregory — Harappan civilization; a contemporary perspective, Oxford and IBH publishing Co Delhi-1982.

Penka — Origines Aricae-1883.

Pennell Dr. T.L. — Among the Wild Tribes of the Afgan Frontier. Seelay & Co., London 1908.

Piggott stuart — Prehistoric India. Penguin Books, Harmondsworth 1952.

Ray Choudhuri H.C. — Political History of Ancient India. Calcutta 1938-1953.

Ram Prasad Saraf (Pub). — Aggarwal Itihas Chintnika Aggrsen Smriti Bhavan, Calcutta.

Rao S.R. — Lothal and the Indus civilization. Asia Publishing House, New Delhi 1973.

Rechard Fick — The social organisation in north east India in Budha's time, Translated by MaittraS. Calcutta 1920.

Reo Vishweshar Nath — Rigved par EK Etihasik Drashti, Moti Lal Banarsi Dass, Delhi 1967.

Rapson E.J. — The Cambridge History of India, Vol. I.Chand & Co., Delhi 1955 and 1922.

Risley H.H. — The People of India. Oriental Book reprint Corp. Delhi 1969.

Risley H.H. — Census report of India 1901, vol. I

Roy S.C. — The Mundas and their country. Bombay Asia 1970

Saran A.B. — Tribal studies (Ranchi 1978).

Sarkar Jadu Nath — Shivaji and his time. Calcutta 1961.

Sarkar S.S. — The Aboriginal Races of India, Vol. IV Book land Ltd., Calcutta 1954.

Sastri Kedar Nath — Sindhu Sabhyata Ka Adi Kendra 'Harappa' Atma Ram and Sons, Delhi.

Sastri Neelkant — Age of the Nandas and Mauryas, Moti Lal Banarsi Dass, Delhi 1967.

Sastri Neelkant — Nand-Maurya Yugin itihas, Moti Lal Banarsi Dass Delhi 1969.

Sankalia H.D. and others — Excavation at Ahar (Tambavati) Poona 1969.

Sankalia H.D. — Prehistory and Protohistory of India and Pakistan, Deccan College (1974).

Sénart Emile — Caste in India, Ess Ess Pub Delhi 1975.

Sen Sukumar — Old Persian inscription University of Calcutta 1941.

Sharma R.S. — Sudras in ancient India, Moti Lal Banarsi Dass 1958.

Sherring Rev M.A. — Hindu Tribes and Castes. Tribuner and Co. London 1972.

Slotter Gilbert — The Dravidian element in Indian Culture. Ess Ess Pub. Delhi 1976.

Smith V.A. — The early history of India IV ed. Oxford University Press London

Smith V.A. — Ashoka IInd ed. S. Chand & Co. Delhi 1959

Sood Ram Rattan — Origin of Soods, New Delhi 1979

Stephen fuchs — The Aboriginal Tribes of India-Macmillon India New Delhi 1973

Strange G.Le — The Lands of the eastern Caliphate-Royal Asiatic Society, London 1912

Strabo — Geography, Hamilton and Falconer XIV

Taylor Isaac — The Origin of the Aryan Bahari Pub., New Delhi 1980

Thakur V. Kumar — Urbanisation in Ancient India, Abhinav Pub., New Delhi 1981

Tilak B.G. — The Arctic home of the Aryans in Rigveda (Poona)

Toyanbee Arnald J. — A study of History Vol. VII, India Vol. 14

Tripathi Vibha — The Painted Grey ware, an Iron age culture of N. India, Delhi 1976

Trived Dr. Dev Sahai — Prag-Maurya Bihar, Bihar Rastra Bhasha Parishad Patna 1954

Upadhyaya Dr. Bhagwat Saran — 'Bhartiya Samaj ka Etihasik Visleshan'

Vishwa Nathan S.V. — Racial Synthesis in Hindu Culture. Oriental Book Corp., New Delhi 1978

Waddell L.A. — Report on excavation at Pataliputtra. Sankaran Prakashan Delhi 1975

Weber Albrecht	Indische Studien II
Wheeler Martimer	The Indus civilization, Cambridge 1968
William M. Monier	Sanskrit English Dictionery Oxford 1961
Wilson John	Indian Caste Vol. I, Bombay 1887
Woolley Leonard & J. Hawkes	History of man kind Vol. I Prehistory and beginning of civilization. London 1963
Wright Daniel ed.	History of Nepal, Calcutta 1966

INDEX